D1286868

COOL PLANTS FOR HOT GARDENS

COOL

PLANTS FOR

HOT

GARDENS

200 Water-Smart Choices
for the Southwest

GREG STARR

RIO NUEVO PUBLISHERS
TUCSON, ARIZONA

To Carol, the rock and guiding light in my life—without her love, support, and dedication, this never would have become a reality. To Warren Jones, a mentor and inspiration, who opened my eyes to the world of plants. He is with me every time I test a plant for its landscape potential. I will miss him.

Rio Nuevo Publishers®
P.O. Box 5250, Tucson, Arizona 85703-0250
(520) 623-9558, www.rionuevo.com

Text and photographs copyright © 2009 by Greg Starr, except: photos on front cover bottom left, back cover top, and pages 2–3 by Scott Calhoun; photo on page 321 by Brian Starr.

Shown on the front cover (clockwise from top left): *Agave ovatifolia* (whale's tongue agave), *Pedilanthus macrocarpus* (slipper flower), *Sphaeralcea ambigua* (globe mallow) and *Opuntia phaeacantha* (prickly pear). On the spine: *Buddleja marrubiifolia* (wooly butterfly bush). On the back cover: the author photographing an as-yet unnamed agave on the Mesa de Oso. On page 1: *Pedilanthus macrocarpus* (slipper flower;) pages 2–3: *Sphaeralcea ambigua* (globe mallow) and *Opuntia phaeacantha* (prickly pear); page 5: *Anisacanthus thurberi* (desert honeysuckle); pages 6 and 316: *Nolina nelsonii* (blue leaf nolina); page 321: *Carnegiea gigantea* (saguaro)

All rights reserved. No part of this book may be reproduced, stored, introduced into a retrieval system, or otherwise copied in any form without the prior written permission of the publisher, except for brief quotations in reviews or citations.

Library of Congress Cataloging-in-Publication Data

Starr, Greg, 1957-
Cool plants for hot gardens : 200 water-smart choices for the Southwest / Greg Starr.
    p. cm.
Includes index.
ISBN-13: 978-1-933855-34-9 (pbk. : alk. paper)
ISBN-10: 1-933855-34-7 (pbk. : alk. paper) 1. Drought-tolerant plants--Southwest, New. 2.
Landscape gardening--Water conservation--Southwest, New. 3. Xeriscaping--Southwest, New. I. Title.
  SB439.8.S74 2009
  635.9'525--dc22

                                2008051679

Design: Karen Schober, Seattle, Washington

Printed in Korea.

10 9 8 7 6 5 4 3 2 1

CONTENTS

INTRODUCTION

THE PLANT ENCYCLOPEDIA

This book will help the property owner, gardener, and landscape professional understand, select, install, and maintain landscape plants that thrive in the southwestern United States and adjacent areas of Mexico. Most are native to this part of the continent, while some come from dry places in other parts of the world, and all have been selected based on their availability at nurseries and their adaptability to the Southwest. I have helped tame some of these plants for the landscape trade and I've interjected some of my personal experiences with many of these in their natural habitat. Some have been around for a number of years, while others are nursery-industry newcomers. With a few exceptions, these plants will grow happily in this region without huge amounts of extra water. There are a handful of beauties listed here that need frequent hot-season watering. Your graywater or water-harvesting system can clear your conscience if you choose to plant something thirsty but stunning. Every one of these "cool plants" is at home in gardens throughout the southwestern United States. Plants are listed alphabetically by botanical name.

Frequently, landscape plants are put into artificial categories based on size and form. While some plants fit neatly into these categories, there are many that straddle two or more. In this book, you will find plants categorized by size and form, and also by usage (pollinator attractors, plants that go great in containers, and plants for pool areas).

Ground cover is a loose category that is generally used for plants that are wider than they are tall. Usually, they have low-growing, prostrate stems, but some plants can be massed together. They can be used to prevent erosion, cover bare ground, or eat up a lot of space.

I use flowering perennials to encompass those plants that have herbaceous stems and are used primarily for their seasonal flower display and generally die back either in the winter or the heat of summer, or look their best when cut back severely during their non-peak season.

Typically, shrubs have many woody stems arising from near ground level with only the new growth being herbaceous. Shrub sizes are designated as small, those less than 3 feet tall; medium, those 3-6 feet tall; and large, those over 6 feet tall. You will find that shrubs do not understand our arbitrary size limits and will often straddle two categories because of climate and varying growing conditions.

Trees can have either a single trunk or multiple trunks but generally grow tall enough for people to walk under them. There are three designations for tree sizes: small trees are less than 20 feet tall; medium trees are 20–30 feet tall; and large trees are more than 30 feet tall. Some trees will also straddle two categories depending on climate and growing conditions.

Cacti are succulent plants, usually with spines and a very cool appearance, while the definition of a succulent plant is not always clear. Remember the adage, "all cacti are succulents, but not all succulents are cacti." With that said, these two are grouped together because they are both succulent, they are often used as focal points in a landscape, and their cultural needs are similar.

Palms and cycads are not related but do have a similar look; therefore they are grouped together. The grasses are larger ornamental plants with seasonally colorful flowers and are not turf grasses. **Bulbs** are seasonal plants with showy flowers and narrow, grass-like leaves that usually die back in the off season.

Plants that attract butterflies, plants that attract hummingbirds, plants that can be used in containers, and plants for pool areas are drawn from other categories and are provided to assist you in selecting plants for these specific niches. These plant uses are designated by the following symbols:

Plants that attract butterflies

Plants that attract hummingbirds

Plants for containers

Plants for pool areas

FIELD NOTES

With the exception of a few horticultural creations, the plants described in this book started out in natural habitats, mostly in arid North America. I offer some information about native distribution, **soil** type, exposure, and elevation to give you an idea about optimal conditions for plants and where you might see them in habitat. To plant nerds like me or natural history buffs, these details are inherently interesting. Knowing these things may also help you select plants that are compatible with each other or plants that will give a consistent look or feel to your landscape. Remember that temperatures associated with elevation change with latitude; it is colder at 8,000 feet in southeastern Arizona than in central Mexico.

DESCRIPTION

A full description of the plant is included and describes the height and width, the leaves, **flowers**, flowering season, and any significant **fruit** characteristics. The focus is on striking features of the plant, which might be the overall form, the leaves, or the flowers. Pay attention to the size data, because most plants refuse to stay at that one-gallon nursery standard.

CULTURE/MAINTENANCE

Hardiness Some plants are inherently more frost-tolerant than others. Plants that have evolved in cold climates are capable of tolerating lower temperatures than those from tropical areas. Plants from cold climates undergo winter acclimation or shutting down in preparation for winter. This physiological hardening process can begin as early as late summer. Winter acclimation might be triggered by decreasing day length, in which case the plant will begin to shut down regardless of temperature and will be dormant even if fall temperatures are abnormally high. Decreasing temperature could also trigger the process. Plants that start going dormant based on temperature are more susceptible to frost damage if fall temperatures stay abnormally high.

FROST DAMAGE FACTORS

The severity of damage to frost-sensitive plants is influenced by several factors:

Overnight low. The lower the temperature the more likely that damage will occur.

Hours of low temperature exposure. The longer a plant is exposed to sub-freezing temperatures, the more likely it is to be damaged.

Daytime temperatures after cold nights. Again, the colder the next day, the more likely the plant will be damaged.

Consecutive nights below freezing. Some plants are able to withstand one night of extreme cold but not a second night.

Winter precipitation. Plants that can normally tolerate subfreezing temperatures when they are dry generally are not as cold-hardy when subject to both cold and wet conditions. But perennials grown in an area that receives snow might actually benefit from the insulation provided by that snow layer.

Drinking Habits Water needs will vary depending on soil type, sun exposure, type of plant, size of leaves, time of year, the age of the plant, and watering demands after planting:

SOIL TYPE	WATER USE
Coarse texture, sandy soil type drains faster	Water more frequently
Fine texture, heavy, clay soil drains slowly	Water less frequently

SUN EXPOSURE	WATER USE
Full sun, reflected heat, south or west exposure	Water more frequently
Part shade, filtered light, north exposure, under a tree	Water less frequently

TIME OF YEAR	WATER USE
Winter: summer-growing plants are dormant	Water infrequently
Spring: temperature warms and plant becomes active	Increase frequency and duration
Summer: temperature is maximum	Increase frequency and duration
Fall: temperature cools, plant starts to go dormant	Decrease frequency to about the same as spring

AGE OF PLANT	WATER USE
Young, newly installed plant	Water every day for short duration
As the plant grows and gets larger	Decrease the frequency you water, and increase the duration or length of time you water

Growth Rates Are Relative In general, the terms "fast," "moderate," and "slow" are used to describe the growth rate of a plant relative to its form (i.e., ground cover, shrub, tree, succulent) and its eventual size. What I call a fast-growing cactus or succulent is generally slower than a fast-growing "leafy" plant like a tree, shrub, or perennial. A fast-growing shrub will reach its mature size more quickly than a fast-growing tree.

You will notice in this book that I couldn't fit some plants into "fast" or "slow," so I used fuzzy, overlapping terms "moderately fast" or "moderately slow."

PLANT NAME	GROWTH RATE	YEARS TO FULL SIZE	SIZE
Salvia greggii (shrub)	Fast	2–3 years	2' x 2'
Agave schidigera (succulent)	Fast	5–8 years	2' x 2'
Parkinsonia x 'Desert Museum' (tree)	Fast	10–15 years	20' x 20'
Vauquelinia californica (shrub)	Slow	10–12 years	15' x 12'
Agave victoriae-reginae (succulent)	Slow	15–20 years	1' x 1'
Ebenopsis ebano (tree)	Slow	20+ years	20' x 15'

Exposure Every plant looks and grows best when planted in the proper exposure. Some require full sun, while others require some shade. Many plants that need some afternoon shade in desert cities like Tucson and Phoenix will grow fine in full sun in the more moderate climate of cities like San Diego and Austin. Remember that there is a distinction between partial shade and filtered light. Partial shade means the plant can be in full shade for part of the day, such as when planted on the east or west side of a building. Filtered light means that the plant can be placed under a tree or shrub that provides some shade and some sun all day long. Many desert and desert-adapted plants will require less maintenance and look more natural if they are "grown hard." This refers to placing the plant in as much sun as it will tolerate and applying as little water as it will tolerate. You don't want to stress the plant to the point of no return, but you should be able to cut back just a bit on the frequency of watering so the plant does not put out abnormally long flushes of growth.

Avoiding Pruning Atrocities Too often we see plants in public and private landscapes that have been forced to become globes, boxes, or other unnatural shapes, then we watch those plants struggle to grow and flower. I believe in minimal pruning, but because we are pampering plants in our landscapes, they may grow faster than in the wild. Therefore, occasional pruning is sometimes necessary. It will usually work best to prune unnaturally large or leggy plants once at the beginning of the growing season. For plants needing a second clipping, the middle of the growing season is about the right time. Some plants will flower repeatedly if they are "deadheaded." No, that is not a reference to the Grateful Dead but a pruning technique where the fading flowers are sheared off before they can develop seeds. This allows the energy that would normally go into seed production to be used for growth and subsequently more flower production.

Unnecessary pruning can be eliminated if we can get past the notion that our landscapes look better if the shrubs are pruned into round balls or square boxes every couple of weeks. We just need to select the right plant for the right spot. Plants allowed to attain their natural shapes show us their natural beauty and also create habitats for birds, butterflies, and other wildlife.

Avoid pruning plants into boxes, like this *Leucophyllum* shrub.

PRECAUTIONS

I've picked plants for this book that can succeed in the Southwest. But every gardener runs into challenges, and I've tried to give you a heads-up on some of the more common ones. Sometimes it may be that rabbits will munch on your new plantings or shoots as the plant bursts forth with the first growth of the season. I mention likely insect pests and other diseases that affect the plants. By no means do I cover every problem encountered in every situation. If you and your plants are struggling, you should contact your local agricultural extension service (or therapist) for more specialized help. Their agents are trained to diagnose plant problems in your area.

There are two simple criteria to consider when choosing plants for your landscape. First, make sure you don't put a plant that gets too large in a space that is too small. Second, make sure the plant will grow in the sun exposure offered by the particular spot. A plant that is adapted to full sun will get larger when planted in full sun than when planted in deep shade, and a plant that needs shade will burn if planted in full sun.

GEOGRAPHIC SCOPE AND CLIMATE ZONES

Geography is one key to a good fit between your landscape and what thrives in it. The geographic range covered here generally includes the arid areas in the southwestern United States extending from southern California east through southern Nevada, Arizona, New Mexico, and into central Texas. Plants described in this book will also be comfortable in much of northern Mexico excluding the high mountains. The area encompasses Chihuahuan, Mojave, and Sonoran Desert climates plus parts of coastal southern California that receive similar amounts of annual rainfall as some places in the Sonoran Desert. Each plant described in this book is suitable for cultivation in some of the following metropolitan areas: Los Angeles, San Diego, and Palm Springs in California; Las Vegas, Nevada; Phoenix, Sierra Vista, Green Valley, Tucson, and Yuma in Arizona; Albuquerque, Lordsburg, and Las Cruces in New Mexico; El Paso, Austin, and San Antonio in Texas; and Guyamas, Puerto Peñasco, Hermosillo, Agua Prieta, Chihuahua, Juarez, Nogales, Torreón, Saltillo, and Monterrey in Mexico.

If you live in between these places, use the one most similar to your neighborhood to guide your selections. Austin and San Antonio, which may not be your idea of the desert Southwest, show up in this book because a lot of these water-thrifty plants do just fine in those cities. You will also see those cities as not recommended for plants that really need to dry out now and then.

In the charts on pages 14–15, each city is assigned to a low, mid or high-elevation zone. I have further divided the low-elevation zone into four subcategories.

High-Elevation Zone: over 3,500 feet
Mid-Elevation Zone: 2,000 to 3,500 feet
Low-Elevation Zone: under 2,000 feet
CC = cool coastal, HC = hot coastal, DI = hot, dry interior, WI = wet interior

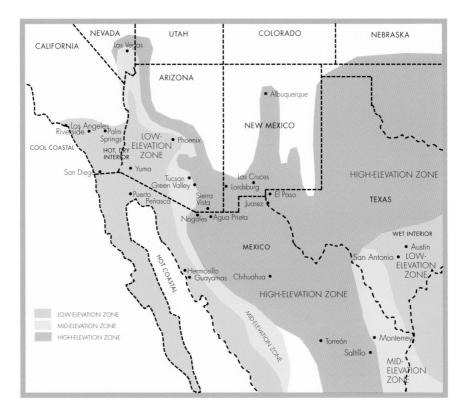

These designations are slightly arbitrary, but the "best" planting season is consistent within the zones and subzones, therefore making a more or less natural grouping for the section in each plant account called "Suitable Cities." Treat these zones simply as loose recommendations. If you are an adventurous soul or just a plant geek as I am, I urge you to test the boundaries and try out all types of plants in your landscape. Who knows what gems are waiting to be added to your local landscape palette? There are obsessed growers around the country who frequently experiment with new plants. One of my favorite sayings comes from Tony Avent at Plant Delights Nursery in Raleigh, North Carolina. He says, "I consider every plant hardy until I've killed it myself at least three times." Sometimes it might take even more than three trials to find the right spot for that special plant, so don't give up. Try it again.

Cold-hardiness is a hugely important climatic factor to consider when choosing plants for the landscape. However, it is not the only climatic factor that affects the health of your plants. Summer highs and rainfall ought to figure into the selection of plants that can thrive in your region. So take time to become familiar with the winter lows plus summer highs and annual rainfall in your area.

CLIMATE ZONES

City	Zone	Elevation (feet)	Average annual rainfall (inches)	Record low
Los Angeles CA	Low CC	360	14.8	28 (Jan 1971)
San Diego CA	Low CC	580	12.4	26 (Jan 1971)
Palm Springs CA	Low DI	420	5.5	19 (Jan 1937)
Riverside CA	Low DI	900	9.3	19 (Jan 1950)
Las Vegas NV	Mid	2,170	4.2	8 (Jan 1963)
Phoenix AZ	Low DI	1,110	7.5	17 (Jan 1971)
Tucson AZ	Mid	2,400	11.1	6 (Jan 1913)
Green Valley AZ	Mid	2,980	15.2	21 (Dec 2003)
Yuma AZ	Low DI	210	3.0	5 (Feb 1995)
Sierra Vista AZ	High	4,600	14.5	11 (Feb 1985)
Albuquerque NM	High	5,130	8.5	-10 (Feb 1950)
Lordsburg NM	High	4,250	10.9	-14 (Dec 1970)
Las Cruces/Jornada NM	High	4,270	12.1	-19 (Jan 1962)
Mesilla NM (Las Cruces)	High	3,910	9.5	-10 (Jan 1962)
Austin TX	Low WI	600	33.7	-2 (Jan 1949)
El Paso TX	High	3,940	8.7	-8 (Jan 1962)
San Antonio TX	Low WI	650	30.2	0 (Jan 1949)

CC = cool coastal • HC = hot coastal • DI = hot, dry interior • WI= wet interior

CLIMATE ZONES FOR NORTHERN MEXICO		
City	State	Zone
Guaymas	Sonora	Low HC
Puerto Peñasco	Sonora	Low HC
Hermosillo	Sonora	Low DI
Monterrey	Nuevo León	Mid
Agua Prieta	Sonora	High
Chihuahua	Chihuahua	High
Juarez	Chihuahua	High
Nogales	Sonora	High
Saltillo	Coahuila	High
Torreón	Coahuila	High

Best planting season for natives	Average rainfall by quarter (inches)				Average January low (° F)	Average July high (° F)
	Jan–Mar	Apr–Jun	Jul–Sep	Oct–Dec		
Fall	9.0	1.4	.3	4.1	48	83
Fall	7.2	1.4	.3	3.5	45	83
Mid Oct–Nov	2.7	.3	.8	1.7	42	108
Fall	6.0	1.1	.4	2.8	40	94
Late winter–early spring	1.6	.4	1.2	1.0	34	105
Oct	2.4	.5	2.5	2.1	42	105
Fall, early spring	2.5	.8	5.3	2.5	38	100
Fall, early spring	2.8	1.2	8.0	3.2	38	99
Late fall	.9	.2	1.0	.9	44	107
Spring through fall	2.2	1.3	8.5	2.5	34	92
Late spring	1.1	2.1	3.8	1.5	23	93
Late spring	2.2	1.0	5.2	2.5	25	97
Late spring	1.2	1.2	5.5	2.2	21	96
Late spring	1.1	1.2	5.1	2.1	26	94
Spring	6.0	11.4	7.2	9.1	40	95
Spring	1.1	1.3	4.6	1.7	32	95
Late Spring	5.2	10.4	7.6	7.0	39	95

LANDSCAPING AND GARDEN DESIGN IN THE WEST

This book is a plant encyclopedia, not a design manual. But a few tips on design can help you choose the right plants. Find healthy gardens you like in your area and shamelessly copy favorite elements. Dream up ideas as you peruse beautiful books. Check plantings in the street medians and along sidewalks for really tough plants that do well in your area.

You'll probably agree that many commercial landscapes throughout the western United States lack flair. You can avoid this uninspiring effect in your space. You can grow a wonderful garden if you unlock your imagination, lose your inhibitions, and especially let go of your need to control. Key building blocks are permanent plants like trees and accents and built features like patios and walkways. These elements provide structure, yet they allow the flexibility of adding new plants and not fretting over dead ones.

You don't have to feel like the landscape is finished after the plants are installed. Some of the plants might be naturally short-lived and will need replacing, or you might find a new plant that you want to experiment with. Whether you're working with a professional landscape designer, an installer, or gardening on your own, try to think of your landscape garden as a living, dynamic project that is always growing and changing.

DESIGN FIRST STEPS

- Route paths between areas
- Deal with any slopes or grade changes
- Decide how you want to grow or build shade
- Select trees, considering:
  Evergreen versus deciduous
  How close thorns might come to people
  How much you care about cleaning up leaf or seed drop

You should be having fun by now and ready to get creative as you choose and place the rest of the permanent plants like shrubs and long-lived succulents, bold and beautiful *Agave, Aloe, Dasylirion, Hesperaloe,* and *Yucca* species, and members of the cactus family. Along with your trees, these accents will make up the backbone of your garden and allow you to play around with other perennials, bulbs, and seasonal flowers. Treat objects of art as you would plants, with some permanent fixtures and others rotating through the landscape "gallery."

Ferocactus pilosus (fire barrel)

If you're fearful about landscape design, consult a professional. A licensed landscape architect or certified designer should have the experience and creativity to look at your situation from a fresh perspective. Gather more ideas as you ask these pros to take you to see their past successes.

DIGGING IN THE DIRT

Admit it. You've only skimmed the "soils" section of those other gardening books on your shelf. You've gone straight to the pretty pictures of plants. You're forgiven if you do that with this book, but there are some things it won't hurt you to know about the primary source of nutrients, water, and oxygen for all land plants. In this section I offer the basics about soil composition, texture, depth, and chemistry.

SOILS 101

Think of soil as a mixture of organic and inorganic ingredients. Many of the large cities in the southwestern United States are located in dry climates where there is very little opportunity for organic matter to accumulate in the soil. Therefore, the native plants are adapted to these soils and don't need large amounts of organic material to grow.

Salvia leucantha (Mexican bush sage)

Inorganic materials can be **sand, silt,** and/or **clay,** and these materials affect the rate of water movement in the soil, its availability to plants, and the subsequent watering schedule for the plants. Sand particles are relatively large, allowing for fast penetration and good drainage. Sandy soils generally mean more frequent watering. Clay particles are the smallest, which translates into slow water penetration and poor drainage, greater water holding, and less frequent watering. For example, you might need to thoroughly soak the root zone of an established low-water-use plant in a sandy soil 1–2 times a week during the summer, while that same plant in a clay soil might need soakings only 2–3 times a month.

Soil depth and consistency can make or break root growth. In general, the deeper the soil, the deeper the roots can go, giving the plant a larger base from which to draw nutrients and water. Keep in mind that feeder roots are generally in the top 2 feet of soil and can spread 2–3 times, or more, the width of the plant. Soil consistency is important because water does not move easily from one type of soil to another.

Hardpan and caliche are two distinct soil conditions that hamper water movement and plant growth. **Hardpan** is a general term for a dense layer of fused soil that is impervious to water. Try working some sand and compost into the soil to improve drainage. **Caliche** is composed of calcium carbonate and acts like a layer of cement. At

Zauschneria californica (hummingbird trumpet bush)

times you may feel that your landscape sits on the largest caliche deposit ever discovered, but it is found widely across arid and semi-arid parts of the world.

There are 17 elements that all plants require to make it through life. Plants need macronutrients in relatively large quantities and micronutrients in relatively small quantities. You take vitamins when you suspect you're not getting what you need from your food, and you fertilize plants when you suspect the soil isn't providing adequate nutrition. A complete fertilizer contains the "big three" macronutrients, nitrogen (N), phosphorous (P), and potassium (K). All fertilizers will list the N-P-K as percentages and always in that order. A fertilizer labeled as 20-20-20 contains 20% nitrogen, 20% phosphate (P_2O_5) and 20% potash (K_2O). The remainder of the fertilizer might consist of secondary nutrients, micronutrients, or inert material.

Iron chlorosis results from a common micronutrient deficiency in plants that are adapted to an acidic soil but are grown in alkaline soil. The classic symptom is the yellowing between the veins of the new leaves while the veins themselves remain green. The long-term solution is to make the soil more acidic by adding organic matter or sulfur.

A quick fix is to apply chelated iron either directly on the new leaves as a foliar spray or in the soil. As always, follow the instructions on the label—more really may not be better.

If you suspect a nutrient deficiency, consult the literature, ask your neighbors, or track down your local extension agent. One of the purposes of this book is to help you avoid such problems by offering a palette of plants adapted to your area—natives and plants from regions with similar climates and soils.

PLANTING

The currently accepted method for planting desert plants is to dig a hole the depth of the container. If you value your time or are lazy as I am, the following advice will pay for this book repeatedly. Loosen the soil to about three times the diameter of the root ball. This preparation will help with even water penetration, encouraging roots to grow out away from the root ball. Fill the hole with water and check the drainage. If the water drains out at the rate of about 1 inch per hour, the soil is fine. If the water remains, it might be necessary to dig deeper and check for an underlying layer of caliche. There are several ways to cope with caliche.

- Layer is deeper than 3 feet—shouldn't be a problem growing most plants since their feeder roots are usually not that deep.
- Layer is shallow and extent minimal—try moving the hole to avoid the caliche.
- Layer is shallow and wide and you want to plant a tree—try punching two or three holes through the caliche to allow the water to drain.
- Layer is shallow and you want to plant shallowly rooted plants—you could try creating a raised planting bed using soil of a similar texture.

Claypan can be broken up physically and amended with sand and composted organic matter to help increase water penetration and root growth. Desert natives don't demand you add organic amendments unless the soil is extremely sandy or heavy with clay. In either case, adding about 25% compost bark mulch to the backfill will make it easier for your plants to tolerate those soil types. For plants that are not native to a desert region, it might be necessary to dig a large hole and add about 25% organic matter to help with water and nutrient retention. Planting an oak in Tucson or something special in an oasis zone, for example, might be worth this trouble.

After you dig the hole, remove the plant from the pot and make two vertical cuts on opposite sides of the root ball to encourage root branching. If the plant is not too root-bound, simply roughen and loosen the root ball. Root-bound plants may require some additional slicing along the sides as well as the standard untangling. This promotes vigorous rooting that gives the plant a much larger nutrient and water base to draw from, resulting in a healthy plant. Place the plant at the proper level, then backfill with the native soil that was removed when digging the hole. It is important for the top of the root ball to be placed slightly above existing grade. If planted too deep, water could collect around the trunk (if you plant a tree) or stems (if you plant a shrub), possibly causing collar rot, stem rot, or root problems.

Sit back and watch your plants grow!

Echinocactus grunsonii (golden barrel)

Abutilon palmeri | Pelatazo

MEDIUM SHRUB

SIZE (height x width)	3–5 feet x 3–5 feet
FLOWER COLOR	Orange-yellow
FLOWER SEASON	Spring–summer
EXPOSURE	Full sun, filtered sun
WATER	Low–moderate
GROWTH RATE	Fast
PRUNING	None or prune frozen growth in spring
HARDINESS	Hardy to low 20s
NATURAL ELEVATION RANGE	1,000–3,000 feet
SUITABLE CITIES	All low-elevation-zone cities except San Antonio and Austin; Tucson in a warm spot

FIELD NOTES: *Abutilon palmeri* is a hot-country native that inhabits desert washes and rocky hillsides in southwestern Arizona, southeastern California, Sonora, and Baja California. Plants are found between 1,000 and 3,000 feet elevation.

DESCRIPTION: Large (4 inches long and 3 inches wide), fuzzy, gray-green leaves create a soft yet eye-catching effect that adds appeal to any enclosed landscape. This medium-size rounded shrub usually grows to about 3–5 feet tall. Rich orange-yellow, 1½-inch-wide flowers appear in the spring and continue blooming through the summer. Sculpted tan seed capsules follow the flowers.

CULTURE/MAINTENANCE: *A. palmeri* is half-hardy, showing some damage at temperatures in the mid-20s F. Once established, it asks for minimal supplemental water but will grow and flower more enthusiastically if watered every 7–10 days during the dry months of spring and summer. It grows fast and will bounce back from most frost damage very quickly as the weather warms enough in the spring. Place the plant

in full sun or filtered sun, as it rebels with too much shade and puts out weak, leggy growth. It may need to be pruned occasionally, especially if it freezes over the winter.

IDENTIFICATION: Orange-yellow flowers and large, fuzzy, gray-green leaves easily identify *A. palmeri.*

LANDSCAPE APPLICATION: Take advantage of the soft, velvety leaves with their luxuriant appearance, and place front and center. Combine the gray-green foliage with plants of contrasting leaf color such as *Ageratum corymbosum*, *Poliomintha maderensis*, and *Salvia greggii*. Try matching blooms with other yellow or yellowish-orange flowers; good prospects include *Caesalpinia mexicana*, *Chrysactinia mexicana*, *Encelia farinosa*, and *Wedelia acapulcensis* var. *hispida. A. palmeri* also looks great at the base of big, tall *Nolinas* and *Yuccas*. Use it around pools, streets, and medians, and to attract both butterflies and hummingbirds.

PRECAUTIONS: Whiteflies find refuge in the hairy leaves. Rabbits sometimes lop off stems but generally do not destroy plants. Remember the frost sensitivity and the need to trim off winter-killed stems.

Acacia aneura | Mulga

SMALL TREE	
SIZE (height x width)	15–20 feet x 12–16 feet
FLOWER COLOR	Yellow
FLOWER SEASON	Spring
EXPOSURE	Full sun
WATER	Low
GROWTH RATE	Moderately slow
PRUNING	Train as single-trunk tree
HARDINESS	Hardy to the low 20s F
NATURAL ELEVATION RANGE	Near sea level–1,000 feet
SUITABLE CITIES	All low and mid-elevation-zone cities except Austin and San Antonio

FIELD NOTES: *Acacia aneura* is native to many different habitats throughout much of the central part of Australia from near sea level to 1,000 feet. It grows as a shrub in areas with low rainfall and thin soil, but put it somewhere with ample rainfall and deep soil and suddenly it's a tree. *A. aneura* is one of the dominant species in Australian shrub woodlands with familiar features: 10–20 inches of annual rainfall, hot summers, and light frost in winter at elevations.

DESCRIPTION: The thin, silvery **phyllodes** (**petioles** modified to perform the function of leaves) and knack for repeated flowering make mulga a distinctive import for the plant palette in the desert Southwest. Its striking form somewhat resembles *Pinus halepensis* (Aleppo pine), with an upright main trunk and side branches that spread up and out. Mulga is generally grown as a small tree to 15–20 feet tall by about

12–16 feet across. The silvery gray phyllodes are about 2½–3 inches long and narrowly to broadly linear. Yellow flowers form rod-like clusters, appearing primarily in the spring but occasionally popping out other times following rains. Flat pods, 1–2 inches long, follow the flowers.

CULTURE/MAINTENANCE: *A. aneura* is hardy, tolerating temperatures into the low 20s or high teens F without damage. It grows moderately slowly, taking 10–15 years to reach 10 feet tall. The plant tolerates drought, but it will grow a little faster when given extra water from spring through summer. Place it in full sun and a soil with good drainage. Minimal maintenance is required. Select one main trunk and keep others pruned off for a conventional look, or try three trunks and nurture for a generous, spreading crown.

IDENTIFICATION: *A. aneura* can be identified by the combination of its shape, leaves, and flowers.

LANDSCAPE APPLICATION: Use mulga as an evergreen, single-trunked tree in a desert or low-water-use landscape. Go for a Down-Under theme and mix it with other Australian plants such as *Acacia redolens, Eremophila maculate, Senna artemisioides,* and *Senna nemophila.* Create a grove with mass plantings, insert along streets and medians, or give it room in wide-open spaces, public or private.

PRECAUTIONS: Allow the soil to dry out between water applications.

Acacia berlandieri | Guajillo

LARGE SHRUB, SMALL TREE

SIZE (height x width)	12–15 feet x 10–15 feet
FLOWER COLOR	Creamy white
FLOWER SEASON	Spring
EXPOSURE	Full sun, reflected sun
WATER	Low–moderate
GROWTH RATE	Moderate
PRUNING	Shape to tree form, thinning afterwards
HARDINESS	Hardy to about 15° F
NATURAL ELEVATION RANGE	1,000–3,000 feet
SUITABLE CITIES	All low- and mid-elevation-zone cities

FIELD NOTES: *Acacia berlandieri* prefers limestone soil in western and southern Texas and occurs south to central and east-central Mexico. It appears on ridges and roadsides from 1,000 to 3,000 feet elevation. You might see a few along the drive to Big Bend National Park in west Texas. In its natural habitat, *A. berlandieri* is a large shrub, usually about 6–7 feet tall with several main stems arising from the ground.

DESCRIPTION: Lush-looking guajillo has delicate, fern-like foliage with endless **leaflets**. Deep green leaves measure about 4 inches and are "semievergreen." These leaves mostly hang on through mild winters and drop as new leaves emerge in the spring, but they can give up and fall if the winter gets too cold. Small, straight prickles along the stems are hardly noticeable with bare hands and no challenge to a good pair of gloves. In addition to jungle-ready foliage, guajillo produces creamy white, puffball-like flower clusters in the spring that are loved by bees and sometimes butterflies. Although it tends to grow as a large bush, it is easily pruned into a small, lacy patio tree. You may even find the pods are the perfect accessory to this plant.

CULTURE/MAINTENANCE: Once cultivated, guajillo can be grown as a dense tree reaching 12–15 feet tall and 10–15 feet across. The species is hardy to 15° F. It survives on low amounts of rainfall in nature but will benefit from regular watering in spring and summer. This water boost may vary from once a week to once a month depending on the soil type. The plant has a moderate growth rate and may take a few years to achieve small-tree stature. A native to nutrient-poor, limestone soils, it grows extremely well in desert soils with adequate drainage. Full or reflected sun allows for the best development. No pruning is required to grow the plant as a shrub; however, you should agonize a little bit in selecting the best trunks to make it a small tree. The suckering branches that sprout from near ground level will call to your loppers on a regular basis.

IDENTIFICATION: Ferny foliage and a tropical look are reminiscent of both *Acacia abyssinica* and *Lysiloma watsonii* ssp. *thornberi*. However, small thorns, which the other two plants lack, and distinct striations along young growth easily distinguish *A. berlandieri*.

LANDSCAPE APPLICATION: When forced to become a tree, guajillo fits nicely into a small, sunny patio or near entryways to give that lush, subtropical effect. It offers filtered light to other plants that need light shade, such as perennials and shrubs like *Ageratum corymbosum, Bulbine frutescens, Conoclinium dissectum, Hibiscus mar-*

tianus, Justicia spicigera, and *Salvia greggii.* Guajillo mixes beautifully with a variety of succulent and semisucculent plants such as *Agave ocahui, Agave schidigera, Dasylirion acrotrichum, Dasylirion wheeleri, Hesperaloe funifera, Hesperaloe parviflora,* and many *Yucca* species. If left in shrub form, guajillo can be massed to form a soft screen, or planted singly behind smaller shrubs and ground covers.

PRECAUTIONS: Young plants will probably need to be screened from wildlife damage for the first several years, at least until the trunks are large enough to be ignored by rabbits. Shade is not the place for this plant. Soil with good drainage is required. Guajillo produces quite a few seedpods, but they are large and easy to pick up.

Acacia constricta | White Thorn Acacia

LARGE SHRUB, SMALL TREE

SIZE (height x width)	12–15 feet x 12–15 feet
FLOWER COLOR	Yellow
FLOWER SEASON	Late spring, occasionally fall
EXPOSURE	Full or reflected sun
WATER	Drought-tolerant–low
GROWTH RATE	Moderate
PRUNING	Select main trunks to grow as a tree
HARDINESS	Hardy to 5° F
NATURAL ELEVATION RANGE	1,500–6,500 feet
SUITABLE CITIES	All cities in all zones

FIELD NOTES: You don't have to be an intrepid explorer to see *Acacia constricta* in the wild. It's everywhere—on dry slopes, mesas, washes, plains, hillsides in southern Arizona across to western Texas, and in similar terrain south into central Mexico. It occurs between 1,500 and 6,500 feet elevation, and it can gang up to form thick stands that inflict scratches on unsuspecting hikers in places such as the Tucson Mountains.

DESCRIPTION: This native is naturally a spreading shrub that grows to about 12–15 feet tall and 12–15 feet across. It features twice-**compound leaves**, yellow puffball flowers, and slender brown seedpods. Sur-

prise—it has white thorns. White thorn acacia can be pruned into a small tree with multiple trunks. The small, fine-textured, rich green leaves make an attractive canopy in summer and fall. When pruned as a tree, the trunks will have interesting angles that give character. Fragrant flowers are visited by both bees and butter-flies and bloom from late spring into summer and occasionally fall. The species name *constricta* is a reference to the pods being constricted between the seeds.

CULTURE/MAINTENANCE: *A. constricta* is cold-hardy to at least 5° F. Leaves drop off in winter, revealing a dense branching pattern with noticeable reddish-brown bark on the younger growth. Plants tolerate an incredible amount of abuse, growing quite well in full or reflected sun and, once established, exist on 10 inches of annual rainfall. However, they will grow a little faster and flower longer and more profusely if given extra water once a month from late spring through summer. *A. constricta* can tolerate a variety of soil types from shallow, caliche-rich soil to a deep, sandy loam. It requires some pruning to develop as a walk-under tree.

IDENTIFICATION: *A. constricta* superficially resembles *Acacia minuta* but can be distinguished by its smaller size; smaller, more plentiful yellow flowers that bloom later; and slender, readily **dehiscent** seedpods.

LANDSCAPE APPLICATION: As a large shrub or pruned as a small tree, white thorn acacia fits into the transition and outer zones of any xeriscape. Combine with drought-tolerant shrubs, ground covers, and accent plants. Some pleasing companions include *Agave* species, *Chrysactinia mexicana, Dalea capitata, Dalea frutescens, Ericameria laricifolia*, all *Hesperaloe* species, all *Leucophyllum* species, *Poliomintha maderensis,* and *Yucca* species.

PRECAUTIONS: Make sure to place white thorn acacia with plants that remain evergreen through the winter to compensate for its deciduous nature. Beware of the paired, 1-inch-long white thorns that give the plant its name. If seed drop offends you, plant where it can be overlooked or cleanup is easy.

Acacia craspedocarpa | Leatherleaf Acacia

LARGE SHRUB, SMALL TREE

SIZE (height x width)	10–15 feet x 10–15 feet
FLOWER COLOR	Golden yellow
FLOWER SEASON	Late winter, early spring
EXPOSURE	Full or reflected sun
WATER	Low–moderately drought-tolerant
GROWTH RATE	Moderately slow
PRUNING	To shape as a dense, rounded, small tree
HARDINESS	Hardy to 15° F
NATURAL ELEVATION RANGE	1,500–2,000 feet
SUITABLE CITIES	All low- and mid-elevation-zone cities except Austin and San Antonio

FIELD NOTES: *Acacia craspedocarpa* grows on loamy or clay soils in the south-central part of the state of Western Australia. In the journal *Desert Plants*, Matt Johnson noted that *A. craspedocarpa* can be found "to the west of Leinster [1,600 feet elevation] on arid plains and occasionally rocky outcrops." It also enjoys life on watercourses.

DESCRIPTION: This dense, rounded, evergreen shrub can be transformed by pruning into a small tree with a lollipop form growing to 10–15 feet tall and across. The small, rounded leaves are thick and somewhat leathery. Golden yellow flower **spikes** appear in the late winter or early spring, then flat, rounded pods with a thick edge form. For those who like to speak Latin, *craspedo* refers to the thick edge, and *carpa* means fruit. The plant gets extra points for being neat and clean and makes a great evergreen multipurpose shrub.

CULTURE/MAINTENANCE: Leatherleaf acacia is hardy to about 15° F. Risk-taking gardeners may find that "hardened" plants can briefly withstand slightly lower temperatures. Leatherleaf acacia has a moderately slow growth rate, is moderately drought-tolerant, and grows best in a soil with good drainage. When grown as a large shrub, it is virtually maintenance-free. However, with minimum fuss, it can be pruned into a small single-trunked or multi-trunked tree.

IDENTIFICATION: Small, round, leathery leaves are easily identifiable.

LANDSCAPE APPLICATION: *A. craspedocarpa* can be used singly as a large specimen shrub, or massed to create an informal screen or hedge. It's pretty marginal as a shade tree. The dense, compact shape and showy flowers make a good recipe for an appealing ornamental plant. When pruned, it can turn into a small specimen tree with a dense, rounded crown; it will not develop the broader, open canopy of mesquites. In the Down Under corner of your landscape, mix with other Australians like *Eremophila maculata*, *Senna artemisioides*, and *Senna nemophila*.

PRECAUTIONS: There don't seem to be any drawbacks, unless you're a purist and want only local native plants.

Acacia farnesiana | Western Sweet Acacia

MEDIUM TREE

SIZE (height x width)	20–25 (rarely 30–35) feet x 20–25 (rarely 25–50) feet
FLOWER COLOR	Golden yellow
FLOWER SEASON	Late winter–spring
EXPOSURE	Full or reflected sun
WATER	Moderate–ample
GROWTH RATE	Moderate–fast
PRUNING	Prune to shape as a tree, cut off suckers, thin crown
HARDINESS	Desert form hardy to 12° F, tropical form hardy to low 20s F
NATURAL ELEVATION RANGE	0–4,500 feet
SUITABLE CITIES	All low- and mid-elevation-zone cities

FIELD NOTES: In nature, *Acacia farnesiana* finds areas where water collects. It grows along roadsides, minor washes, and depressions, growing in wet, clay loam soils in southern Texas and adjacent northern Mexico from near sea level to 4,500 feet. The largest wild sweet acacia I've seen was in southern Texas. I was a student traveling with my advisor, Warren Jones, when we stopped to photograph a monster specimen that was easily 35 feet tall with a spread of about 50 feet and a trunk diameter of at least 18 inches. This exceptional tree grew in a depression along the roadside that collected more than enough water to meet its needs.

DESCRIPTION: *A. farnesiana* is a small to medium-size evergreen or partly deciduous tree. With no special treatment it grows to 20–25 feet tall and will develop a 20–25-foot canopy. Under ideal conditions with deep soil and ample water, the occasional tree can reach 30–35 feet tall by 25–50 feet across. The plant will sucker freely from the base. Twice-compound leaves are

about 3 inches long and divided into many small leaflets, which give the tree a fine texture. Fragrant, golden yellow, puffball-like flowers appear in late winter and through the spring and buzz with bee activity and the infrequent butterfly. Short, dark brown, woody pods follow flowers, and abundant seeds sprout readily with extra moisture. With sufficient water, it has a lush, almost tropical appearance.

CULTURE/MAINTENANCE: This form is hardy to 12° F, though that temperature will kill flower buds and cause some twig damage. To look its best, the tree requires consistent, thorough irrigation from spring through the end of summer. Even an established plant wants its root zone thoroughly soaked twice a month in the summer. The growth rate is moderate to fast depending on amount of water available. Place *A. farnesiana* in full sun and in a soil that has good drainage. As with other desert plants, it does not demand rich soil but is much happier without impenetrable caliche lurking nearby. It does require a good deal of maintenance—pruning to keep its shape as a tree, sweeping up seedpods, and yanking volunteers.

IDENTIFICATION: Western sweet acacia is part of a complex classification problem that has plagued botanists and nurserymen for years. It is the hardy form of a plant that has gone by a variety of botanical names. The hardy form has been variously called *A. minuta* and *A. smallii* while the more tender, tropical form has been called *A. farnesiana*. The only species that resembles *A. farnesiana* is *A. schaffneri* and that species differs by being firmly deciduous, with lighter yellow flowers and closely set leaves so the branches look like bottlebrushes.

LANDSCAPE APPLICATION: Place this tree only in full or reflected sun and allow ample room for proper development. It is highly prized for the blast of seasonal color and sweet fragrance produced by its little round flowers, and for its adaptability to harsh environments. It thrives in medians, roadway plantings, retention basins, parks, and golf courses. Grow it as a large shrubby barrier plant or pruned as a single- or multiple-trunked tree or mix with either subtropical-looking plants or desert plants. Because of its pod drop and thorny branches, it should be used away from patios, pools, and high-traffic areas.

PRECAUTIONS: If grown without periodic deep soaking in the summer, plants can die back and lose twigs and stems. A young plant should be protected from rabbits. Branches have 1-inch-long white thorns that can bite when pruning. Seeds will germinate in areas with a rock or mulch covering and can become a nuisance.

Acacia greggii | Catclaw Acacia

LARGE SHRUB, SMALL TREE

SIZE (height x width)	15–20 feet x 15–20 feet
FLOWER COLOR	Creamy yellow
FLOWER SEASON	Spring–summer
EXPOSURE	Full sun
WATER	Drought-tolerant–low
GROWTH RATE	Moderate
PRUNING	Shape as a tree
HARDINESS	Hardy to 0° F
NATURAL ELEVATION RANGE	0–6,000
SUITABLE CITIES	All cities in all zones

FIELD NOTES: *Acacia greggii* is found on shallow caliche soils on rocky hillsides and in deep sandy soils of desert washes throughout the southwestern United States and northern Mexico, with an elevation range from sea level to nearly 6,000 feet. Hiking around Tucson, if I'm not paying attention, my clothes and skin occasionally get snagged by the recurved claws of this *Acacia*. I'm thinking this plant gives cats a bad name.

DESCRIPTION: In nature *A. greggii* is a large shrub. You can take advantage of the decorative trunk and picturesque form and grow it as a small tree that reaches about 15–20 feet tall with a spread of 15–20 feet. Grayish-green, winter deciduous leaves are twice **pinnate**, lightly **pubescent**, and about 3 inches long. Branches are clothed with vicious, short, recurved spines. Cylindrical spikes of lightly fragrant, pale yellow flowers are 2–3 inches long and appear in spring and summer, attracting both bees and butterflies. Striking 6-inch long, reddish-brown, slightly twisted seedpods follow the flowers.

CULTURE/MAINTENANCE: *A. greggii* is hardy to 0° F and drought-tolerant with a moderately slow growth rate. However, the plant will get larger, grow faster, and flower better if given supplemental water from spring through summer. Place it in a spot where it gets full sun all day, and in a soil with good drainage. With some careful pruning, the plant can be grown with a twisting, curving main trunk. Don't wear your favorite shirt when you go out to prune.

IDENTIFICATION: Sharp, recurved thorns that resemble a cat's claw easily identify *A. greggii.*

LANDSCAPE APPLICATION: Use *A. greggii* as a small, decorative tree in a low-water-use landscape. With supplemental water, it will have a lush appearance and will blend smoothly into any type of landscape. Place in an open area to show off the late spring to summer flower display. For a colorful desert look, mix with other low- to moderate-water-use plants. Some suggestions include: *Agave* species, *Ageratum corymbosum, Anisacanthus quadrifidus* var. *wrightii, Buddleja marrubiifolia, Calliandra eriophylla, Dasylirion* species, *Fouquieria splendens, Hesperaloe* species, *Poliomintha maderensis, Simmondsia chinensis,* and *Yucca* species.

PRECAUTIONS: Because of the recurved thorns, keep *A. greggii* away from high-traffic areas, unless, of course, you are trying to reduce that traffic.

Acacia redolens | Prostrate Acacia

MEDIUM SHRUB, GROUND COVER ('DESERT CARPET')	
SIZE (height x width)	1–6 feet x 6–15 feet
FLOWER COLOR	Yellow
FLOWER SEASON	Late winter–spring
EXPOSURE	Full sun
WATER	Low
GROWTH RATE	Slow–moderate
PRUNING	Early summer
HARDINESS	Hardy to about 20° F
NATURAL ELEVATION RANGE	Unknown
SUITABLE CITIES	All low- and mid-elevation-zone cities except Austin and San Antonio

FIELD NOTES: *Acacia redolens* occurs naturally in the southwestern part of Western Australia, usually putting up with slightly salty or alkaline soil.

DESCRIPTION: The profusion of puffball-like clusters of yellow flowers produced in late winter to spring add a colorful bonus to a plant that can break up a large expanse of bare ground. *A. redolens* is a variable specimen, ranging 1–6 feet tall by 6–15 feet across. 'Desert Carpet' and 'Low Boy' are two cultivars that are grown from cuttings. Keep in mind that they are supposed to stop growing up at about 1 foot tall but spread as much as 15 feet across. The phyllodes (modified petioles) are dark, olive green and remain on the plant through cold or drought. *A. redolens* gets very dense and actually keeps the soil moist and cool even in the summer.

CULTURE/MAINTENANCE: Plants are hardy to at least 20° F and possibly lower if kept dry through the winter. In Las Vegas, *A. redolens* 'Desert Carpet' froze out at 5° F. It demands very little supplemental water after the first 2–3 years in the ground. In fact, too much water can be lethal. Soil should be very well drained to cut losses due to root rot. Place plants only in full sun, as they get rangy when planted in shade. Prostrate acacia has a slow to moderate growth rate, taking a couple of years to get established, but it takes off after getting roots out. It can fill a 4-foot-diameter niche in two or three growing seasons.

IDENTIFICATION: *A. redolens* is easily distinguished from New World *Acacia* species by the phyllodes, and from other Australian *Acacia* species by its wide-spreading growth habit.

LANDSCAPE APPLICATION: Use either 'Desert Carpet' or 'Low Boy' as an evergreen ground cover in the transition or outer zones of a xeriscape. *A. redolens* can do actual work in the fields of erosion control and slope stabilization; call on it when you need to cover a large expanse of bare ground or a bank. It prefers full sun or very light shade and will grow fine if planted at the edge of the canopy of a native mesquite. A landscape with *A. redolens* and a variety of other Australian natives can look quite stunning in large open spaces.

PRECAUTIONS: Plant only in full sun and keep dry. There have been no reports of damage by any insects, rabbits, or javelinas. Remember that these plants are slowpokes, so give them more than a year or two to fill up a large space.

Acacia rigidula | Blackbrush Acacia

LARGE SHRUB, SMALL TREE

SIZE (height x width)	10–15 (20) feet tall x 10–15 (25) feet across
FLOWER COLOR	Creamy yellow
FLOWER SEASON	Late spring–early summer
EXPOSURE	Full or reflected sun
WATER	Low–moderately drought-tolerant
GROWTH RATE	Moderately slow
PRUNING	Shape to desired tree form
HARDINESS	Hardy to at least the high teens F
NATURAL ELEVATION RANGE	1,100–1,800 feet
SUITABLE CITIES	All low- and mid-elevation-zone cities

FIELD NOTES: When out driving the back roads near Langtry, Texas, along the Rio Grande, watch for the dark green leaves and zigzag growth of *Acacia rigidula*. Its long, stout spines can run right through a tire or the sole of a hiking boot, if you're traipsing around rocky limestone areas from the Trans-Pecos region to southern Texas and northeastern Mexico. This plant is relatively common and can generally be found between 1,100 and 1,800 feet elevation.

DESCRIPTION: In habitat, *A. rigidula* is a large shrub reaching about 10 feet tall and across. Under cultivation, the plant can grow another 2–5 feet and qualify as a small tree. If grown in deep soil, it is possible to get a specimen 20 feet tall by 25 feet across. Winter deciduous leaves are **bipinnate** and measure about 1 inch long. The dark green foliage contrasts nicely with the light gray bark. A pair of rigid, white, needlelike thorns subtends each leaf. Two- to three-inch-long spikes of lightly fragrant, creamy yellow flowers appear in spring and early summer and are cause to find a spot for this plant in any desert landscape. As with many other

Acacia species, bees and occasionally butterflies will visit the flowers. Narrow, woody pods follow the flowers in the summer.

CULTURE/MAINTENANCE: *A. rigidula* is hardy to at least the high teens F. The plant is moderately drought-tolerant but will grow a little faster and pump out more flowers if given supplemental water on a regular basis. It grows fine in native soil with adequate drainage, but it will get larger in a deep soil. For best appearance, place it in full or reflected sun. Select main trunks early and prune to grow as a tree. The plant will launch shoots near ground level, and these suckers will need to be removed to maintain it as a tree.

IDENTIFICATION: The combination of dark green foliage, long, white, needlelike thorns, and spectacular spikes of yellow flowers easily identify this plant.

LANDSCAPE APPLICATION: *A. rigidula* can be grown as a large shrub and used as a physical barrier or screen. It can serve as a colorful accent or specimen tree. Mix that rich, dark foliage with drought-tolerant shrubs and perennials such as *Buddleja marrubiifolia, Dalea frutescens, Encelia farinosa,* all *Leucophyllum* species, *Melampodium leucanthum, Poliomintha maderensis, Salvia greggii, Simmondsia chinensis,* and *Zinnia acerosa.*

PRECAUTIONS: The sharp thorns can pose a hazard near high-traffic areas. Prune the branches to be above head height.

Acacia salicina | Willow Acacia

MEDIUM–LARGE TREE	
SIZE (height x width)	20–25 (40) feet x 15–18 (20) feet
FLOWER COLOR	Creamy white
FLOWER SEASON	Fall–late winter or early spring
EXPOSURE	Full or reflected sun
WATER	Low–moderate
GROWTH RATE	Moderately fast
PRUNING	Thin to prevent it from becoming top-heavy
HARDINESS	Hardy to 20° F or a little below
NATURAL ELEVATION RANGE	150–1,000 feet
SUITABLE CITIES	Tucson and all low-elevation-zone cities except Austin and San Antonio

FIELD NOTES: *Acacia salicina* can be found growing along river courses in drier parts throughout Australia, which is an awful lot of that continent, usually occurring from

150 to 1,000 feet elevation. Trek along creeks or bandy about in woodlands in the upper Hunter Valley and Tamworth District in New South Wales in order to spot these willowy trees.

DESCRIPTION: An upright main trunk and drooping branches makes this a beautiful specimen tree. This fast-growing evergreen tree has gray-green foliage and pendulous branches that create an interesting, weeping form. It can get tall by desert standards—maxing out around 40 feet tall by 20 feet wide. Normal specimens hit 20–25 feet tall by 15–18 feet wide. Round, ½-inch-diameter clusters of creamy white flowers can appear as early as late fall, and continue through winter and into early spring. Flowers lure in bees and butterflies then turn into slender seedpods.

CULTURE/MAINTENANCE: *A. salicina* tolerates temperatures to about 20° F without damage. It likes a little water and grows best when the root zone is thoroughly soaked every 2–3 weeks in the summer and every 4-5 weeks in the winter. Too much water results in a top-heavy tree that needs constant thinning. Kept on the dry side, the growth rate moderates and thinning requirements lessen to once or twice a year. For the best growth, place plants in full or reflected sun.

IDENTIFICATION: *A. salicina* is easily identified by its willowy appearance and cream-colored flowers.

LANDSCAPE APPLICATION: Use *A. salicina* as a specimen tree or to shade the side of a building. It willingly does duty in parking lots and street medians as well as mass planted in parks and recreational areas. It is striking as a silhouette plant and in transition areas from mini-oasis to desert zones in a xeriscape. It plays nicely with other Australian natives such as *Eremophila maculata* 'Valentine' and *Senna artemisioides.* Or plant with colorful, low-water-use shrubs from this side of the globe, such as *Lantana* x 'New Gold,' *Leucophyllum* species, *Salvia greggii,* and *Tecoma stans.*

PRECAUTIONS: Be sure to apply water deeply and allow the soil to dry between water applications to encourage a deep, well-established root system. Thin the tops to prevent them from getting too heavy and becoming one of those trees you see on the ground after a fierce storm.

Acacia schaffneri | Twisted Acacia

SMALL–MEDIUM TREE	
SIZE (height x width)	15–25 feet tall x 15–30 feet across
FLOWER COLOR	Light yellow
FLOWER SEASON	Spring–early summer
EXPOSURE	Full or reflected sun
WATER	Low–moderate
GROWTH RATE	Moderate
PRUNING	Shape to desired tree form
HARDINESS	Hardy to at least 15° F
NATURAL ELEVATION RANGE	5,000–7,500 feet
SUITABLE CITIES	All low- and mid-elevation-zone cities

FIELD NOTES: *Acacia schaffneri* is a densely crowned small tree dotting the rolling open hills in the central plateau of Mexico from the state of Durango south to Guanajuato and Querétaro. It grows between about 5,000 and 7,500 feet elevation. This tree is a prominent feature in the natural landscape near the picturesque and magical town of Mineral de Pozos in Guanajuato, where apparitions are sometimes seen emerging from the nearby ruins.

DESCRIPTION: Depending on the soil and amount of water applied, *A. schaffneri* is a small to medium-size tree, growing to 15–25 feet tall with a thick crown to 15–30 feet across that is full of twisting, snaky branches. Finely divided, bipinnate leaves are closely set to the branches, giving the stems the appearance of a bottlebrush. Dark green foliage contrasts nicely with light gray bark. The brilliant display of light yellow flowers can start in the spring while the tree is still leafless and continue until new leaves emerge. Small, round, puffball-like flower clusters create quite a buzz of bee activity, with the occasional butterfly testing the nectar also. Narrow, woody pods replace the flowers in the summer.

CULTURE/MAINTENANCE: This native of central Mexico is hardy to at least 15° F. The plant is a low- to moderate-water-user with a moderate growth rate. The plant will grow a little faster and get bigger if treated with extra water on a regular basis from spring through summer. It is not particular about soil as long as the drainage is adequate. Its best form develops in full sun with ample room to spread. Careful pruning is required to shape an attractive form and avoid a crown that is too dense.

IDENTIFICATION: Twisting stems and tightly set leaves with a bottlebrush-like appearance readily distinguish *A. schaffneri* from other *Acacia* species.

LANDSCAPE APPLICATION: *A. schaffneri* has a desert look and can be used as a colorful specimen or shade tree. Full grown, it makes a wonderful street tree and can be planted in retention basins. Try mass planting for an interesting grove effect and to avoid the stress of picking companion plants. It mixes reassuringly with drought-tolerant shrubs and perennials such as *Buddleja marrubiifolia*, *Dalea frutescens*, *Encelia farinosa*, all *Leucophyllum* species, *Melampodium leucanthum*, *Poliomintha maderensis*, *Salvia greggii*, *Simmondsia chinensis*, and *Zinnia acerosa*.

PRECAUTIONS: Allow sufficient space for full development of the intriguing crown and prune the branches to be above head height.

Acacia stenophylla | Shoestring Acacia

MEDIUM TREE	
SIZE (height x width)	20–30 (40) feet x 15–20 (30) feet
FLOWER COLOR	Creamy white
FLOWER SEASON	Fall–spring
EXPOSURE	Full or reflected sun
WATER	Moderate when young, low when established
GROWTH RATE	Moderate
PRUNING	Minimal, only to shape
HARDINESS	Hardy to at least 15° F
NATURAL ELEVATION RANGE	380–500 feet
SUITABLE CITIES	All low- and mid-elevation-zone cities except Austin and San Antonio

FIELD NOTES: *Acacia stenophylla* occurs in open woodlands and grasslands primarily in eastern and southeastern Australia, with a few localities in northern and northwestern Australia. It is content along rivers, creeks, and swampy areas in heavy clay soils. If you ever get to Australia be sure to check out the creeks and rivers in New South Wales

west of Inverell to spy these attractive trees, around 380–500 feet elevation.

DESCRIPTION: This medium-size tree has an upright main trunk and spreads to weeping branches. Typically it grows to about 20–30 feet tall with a spread of 15–20 feet. It can expand to 40 feet tall by 30 feet wide, although it may take a decade or two. Long, narrow, dark green "leaves" are actually phyllodes and look like shoestrings hanging down from the branches. Creamy white flowers occur in rod-like clusters, appear anytime from fall through spring, and attract bees and sometimes butterflies. Thin, woody seedpods may develop after flowering but do not create an unreasonable amount of litter.

CULTURE/MAINTENANCE: *A. stenophylla* is considered hardy, tolerating 15° F. It has a moderate growth rate and does best in full or reflected sun. It puts up with many soil types and will accept heavy clay soil and periodic flooding. Young plants require moderate amounts of water, but they can withstand some drought with age. Water deeply once every 3–4 weeks in spring and summer. If you're looking for neatness, remember it asks for a little "leaf" cleanup and minimal seedpod removal. You may want to prune young trees to develop a desirable form.

IDENTIFICATION: The weeping form and shoestring-like leaves identify *A. stenophylla*.

LANDSCAPE APPLICATION: Shoestring acacia makes it as a specimen tree or mass planted for a grove effect. It creates an interesting silhouette against large, blank walls. This tree is often used in skinny planting areas between tall buildings. Its weeping form and clean aspect make it a popular choice for planting around water features. The open silhouette provides an opportunity to use many **understory** plants. Some great plant combinations include many other Australian natives that have similar cultural requirements such as *Acacia craspedocarpa, A. redolens, Eremophila* species, *Senna artemisioides, Senna nemophila,* and *Senna phyllodinea.* Shoestring acacia also blends right into landscapes dominated by regional natives.

PRECAUTIONS: There are no known pest problems. You might not want to push the envelope on frost tolerance; when temperatures dropped to 10° F in Las Vegas, trees froze to the ground.

Acacia willardiana | Palo Blanco

SMALL TREE

SIZE (height x width)	15–20 feet x 10–15 feet
FLOWER COLOR	Creamy white-yellow
FLOWER SEASON	Spring
EXPOSURE	Full or reflected sun, or partial shade
WATER	Drought-tolerant–moderate
GROWTH RATE	Moderately slow
PRUNING	Prune dead stems in early spring
HARDINESS	Hardy to the high 20s F, twig damage at mid-20s F, substantial damage below 20° F
NATURAL ELEVATION RANGE	Sea level–2,500 feet
SUITABLE CITIES	All low-elevation-zone cities except Austin and San Antonio; warm spots in Tucson in mid-elevation zone

FIELD NOTES: Enchanting palo blanco caught my eye on my very first trip to Mexico with University of Arizona professor Warren Jones. We were scouting sites around Hermosillo, Sonora, for an institution similar to the Arizona-Sonora Desert Museum. On the outskirts, Warren introduced me to this fine, willowy tree with attractive white bark growing on the bouldery hills. It grows from near sea level to 2,500 feet elevation on rocky hillsides and flat land from Hermosillo south to Guaymas in Sonora, Mexico.

DESCRIPTION: The wispy, delicate appearance and open form provides light shade for understory plants. Palo blanco can grow to 15–20 feet tall and spread to 10–15 feet across. One main trunk grows crookedly upright, while smaller branches grow out and droop down, giving a weeping appearance. Leaves are reduced down to the elongated petioles with small leaflets at the tips. Spikes of creamy white-yellow flowers appear in late spring, drawing in the occasional bee. Attractive, peeling outer bark reveals beautiful white trunks, providing up-close interest.

CULTURE/MAINTENANCE: Young plants and new growth are considered half-hardy, sustaining frost damage in the mid-20s F, with major damage and even total kill occurring in the mid-teens F. In marginal locations, *A. willardiana* should be planted in warm microclimates, such as hugging the south side of a building or tucked in a protected south-facing entryway. It will tolerate full sun, reflected sun, or even some shade for part of the day. The growth rate is moderate–slow, taking a few years to develop into a nice specimen. This tree is quite drought-tolerant once established, but it will grow faster if given supplemental water in the summer. Soil that has good drainage is best. Maintenance is relatively trivial, with some leaf cleanup in the spring. Wait until early spring to prune out any dead wood.

IDENTIFICATION: *A. willardiana* is easily recognized by its graceful, weeping form and delicate, white, peeling bark.

LANDSCAPE APPLICATION: Use this beautiful small tree in entryways, small courtyards, or other high-traffic areas to show off its peeling bark up close. Plant it against a large, blank wall, where the silhouette can be enjoyed. Although an individual tree can provide impact in a small space, consider planting a grove in larger areas. Wispy foliage provides light shade preferred by showy plants such as *Agave bovicornuta, Agave geminiflora, Ageratum corymbosum, Conoclinium dissectum, Dioon edule, Gaura lindheimeri, Justicia spicigera, Poliomintha maderensis,* and *Salvia greggii.*

PRECAUTIONS: The main concern is frost sensitivity. In areas where temperatures drop below 20° F, young plants should be protected until the trunk diameter reaches a hefty 1–2 inches. Larger trees can sustain some damage and not lose their beautiful form and appealing bark. Wildlife chewing is deterred by planting close to buildings where rabbits are usually not brave enough to venture.

Agave bovicornuta | Cow's Horn Agave

CACTUS/SUCCULENT	
SIZE (height x width)	2–3 feet x 3–4 feet
FLOWER COLOR	Yellow
FLOWER SEASON	Spring (blooms once, then dies)
EXPOSURE	Part shade, filtered light

WATER	Low
GROWTH RATE	Fast
PRUNING	None
HARDINESS	Hardy to about the mid-20s F, leaf burn at low 20s, but recovers quickly
NATURAL ELEVATION RANGE	3,000–6,000 feet
SUITABLE CITIES	All low-elevation-zone cities, warm spots in Tucson

FIELD NOTES: When driving on Mexico Highway 16 from Hermosillo to Yecora in east-central Sonora, you will come across a noteworthy band of *Agave bovicornuta* that lasts for only about 4 kilometers. The plant also shows up on rocky slopes in the oak woodland and pine-oak forests in eastern and southern Sonora, southwestern Chihuahua, and northern Sinaloa in the Sierra Madre Occidental between 3,000 and 6,000 feet elevation.

DESCRIPTION: The broad, dark green leaves and highly decorative dental work along the margin make *A. bovicornuta* a rather showy specimen. This medium-size, non-**offsetting** plant grows 2–3 feet tall and 3–4 feet wide. Leaves are lance-shaped, nearly 2 feet long, and 6 inches wide, narrowing to a sharp terminal point. Dark brown teeth along the leaves curve both away from and back towards the center of the plant. The 15–22-foot-tall flower stalks have short side branches with bright yellow and green flowers clustered at the ends. As with all *Agave* species, the flower stalk signals the end of the line.

CULTURE/MAINTENANCE: While plants can tolerate full sun in the mid-elevation desert and the coastal regions, they prefer filtered sun or morning sun and

afternoon shade in the hot deserts. Plants are considered half-hardy, suffering damage when winter lows hit the middle or low 20s F for an extended period. *A. bovicornuta* grows quickly in spring, and damaged foliage is usually covered up by the end of the growing season. Although thrifty about water use, plants will grow more quickly with supplemental water in summer, and plants in full sun will need consistent summer irrigation. Soil with good drainage is best. This *Agave* does not offset, so no maintenance is required, but no free babies, either.

IDENTIFICATION: The combination of leaf color and marginal teeth set *A. bovicornuta* apart from any other cultivated *Agave* species. The com-

mon name is a literal translation; *bovi* is Latin for "cow" and *corn* means "horned." The larger teeth along the leaf edge are sometimes paired and curved towards each other, thus resembling cow's horns.

LANDSCAPE APPLICATION: Use cow's horn agave in the mini-oasis, away from high-traffic areas because of the stout terminal spine and sharp teeth. Filtered light or partial shade produces the finest form, and plants do just fine under the protection of an overhang. Mass them under the canopy of a shade tree or show one off in a large decorative container. A variety of plant styles look stylish next to this *Agave: Acacia willardiana, Conoclinium dissectum, Dioon edule, Dalea capitata, Justicia spicigera, Penstemon baccharifolius,* and *Salvia greggii.* Bulbs such as *Cooperia drummondii, Zephyranthes citrina,* and *Zephyranthes grandiflora* also combine well.

PRECAUTIONS: It's best to keep *A. bovicornuta* out of full or reflected sun to prevent sunburning of the leaves. An overhanging patio roof or tree canopy reduces the chances of frost damage. So far rabbits or javelinas have not eaten this agave, but my plants are close to the house, where they are less likely to be bothered. Precautionary measures against agave snout weevil might be a good idea, especially if there are other *Agave* species around.

Agave bracteosa | Green Spider Agave, Squid Agave

CACTUS/SUCCULENT	
SIZE (height x width)	2 feet x 3 feet
FLOWER COLOR	White
FLOWER SEASON	Summer (blooms once, then dies)
EXPOSURE	Filtered sun
WATER	Drought-tolerant (< 20 inches per year when established)
GROWTH RATE	Moderately slow
PRUNING	None

HARDINESS	Hardy to at least 10° F
NATURAL ELEVATION RANGE	3,000–5,500 feet
SUITABLE CITIES	All low- and mid-elevation-zone cities; Sierra Vista in high-elevation zone

FIELD NOTES: During a photographic journey into Mexico, I spotted this incredible plant clinging to sheer, vertical, limestone cliffs. The plants looked like big, green spiders plastered against a wall. Individual **rosettes** produced a few offsets around the base to form 3-foot-wide masses. *Agave bracteosa* is restricted to a couple of spots in northeastern Mexico and can be found on limestone at elevations from 3,000 to 5,500 feet in the Sierra Madre Oriental.

DESCRIPTION: In the garden, this medium-size, clumping species grows to 2 feet tall and clumps out to 3 feet across. The narrow, upright, recurved leaves measure about 1 foot long and 1–2 inches wide near the base and taper to the tip, creating a graceful urn-like appearance. Unarmed both along the edge and at the tip, the leaves are soft and pliable. This agave offsets freely, which can detract from the beauty of individual specimens. On the other hand, why not remove the pups and repot or plant elsewhere. Leave a few in place to take over when the main plant dies after sending up its spectacular spike of white flowers. You may wait 25 years to see the flowers—I got lucky and saw them once at Huntington Gardens outside Los Angeles. Growing the plant for its interesting, architectural form is plenty rewarding.

CULTURE/MAINTENANCE: Place *A. bracteosa* in filtered sun; it is quite at home under the shade of small trees. The plant is hardy to at least 10° F. It is drought-tolerant but responds to supplemental water. Growth rate varies from slow to moderate-slow depending on the amount of supplemental water. As with other succulent or semisucculent plants, *A. bracteosa* grows best in a soil with good drainage. Aside from pulling the offsets very little maintenance is required.

IDENTIFICATION: Look for the narrow, recurved leaves.

LANDSCAPE APPLICATION: *A. bracteosa* in a decorative pot is an instant focal point on a patio. In the ground, it is suitable for all zones of a xeriscape. It thrives when placed under the shade of small trees like *Acacia willardiana, Eysenhardtia orthocarpa,* or *Leucaena retusa,* and will also handle the shade under larger, denser trees such as *Prosopis* species. It fits in nicely with cacti and other succulent and semisucculent plants and looks smart among large boulders. There's not much point mixing *A. bracteosa* with shrubs that would eventually grow up to hide it.

PRECAUTIONS: Javelina might uproot the plants and rabbits or javelinas could eat the leaves. Critters are less likely to pester a plant that is grown hard, but there are no guarantees. As with other *Agave* species, the main plant will die after flowering, but offsets will survive.

Agave colorata | Mescal Ceniza

CACTUS/SUCCULENT	
SIZE (height x width)	2–4 feet x 2–4 feet
FLOWER COLOR	Golden yellow
FLOWER SEASON	Late spring–summer (blooms once, then dies)
EXPOSURE	Full, reflected, or filtered sun
WATER	Low–moderate
GROWTH RATE	Slow–moderate
PRUNING	None
HARDINESS	Hardy to low 20s F if kept dry
NATURAL ELEVATION RANGE	Near sea level to > 3,000 feet
SUITABLE CITIES	All low-elevation-zone cities; warm spots in mid-elevation-zone cities

FIELD NOTES: I've encountered *Agave colorata* growing in rocky outcrops and ledges while hiking in Nacapuli Canyon and scaling the microwave hill near San Carlos, Sonora, in northwestern Mexico. Its natural habitat is primarily rocky hills and canyons along the coast, but botanists also know it from a couple of localities in thorn forest and pine-oak forest in southern Sonora and northern Sinaloa.

DESCRIPTION: This medium-size plant grows to 2–4 feet tall and wide, depending on the model. One form is smaller with short, broad, almost spoon-shaped leaves and gets to only about 2 feet by 2 feet, while the other might become a 4 by 4, with long, sword-shaped leaves and a more open form. Powdery blue-gray leaves record interesting imprints made by the teeth of surrounding leaves while tightly wrapped in the bud stage. Leaf edges are armed with dark brown teeth and a 2-inch-long terminal spine. Some year, a 10-foot-tall, branched flower stalk will appear in late spring or early summer. The stalk signals the end of that plant's life cycle—time to nurture an offset, install a replacement, or dedicate the spot to something else.

CULTURE/MAINTENANCE: *A. colorata* is hardy to the low 20s F as long as it is

not wet. Plants are very drought-tolerant, surviving and flowering on only 11 inches of annual rainfall. They have a slow to moderate growth rate depending on whether supplemental water is applied. Place in full or reflected sun, or the lightest filtered sun, and well-drained soil. Leaves color up best with blasting by the sun. Plants require virtually no maintenance once they are established, but it's a bit of a chore to remove dying parent plants post-flowering. Offsets keep the line alive.

IDENTIFICATION: *A. colorata* is readily distinguished from other *Agave* species in cultivation by a combination of its size and powder blue-gray leaves.

LANDSCAPE APPLICATION: Tough, sun-loving *A. colorata* is easily grown in most landscapes. Use as a bold accent plant, mix with low-water-use shrubs and perennials for seasonal color, mass for an impressive display, or even show it off in a large, decorative container. Try surrounding it with *Berlandiera lyrata, Chrysactinia mexicana, Ericameria laricifolia, Justicia candicans, Menodora longiflora, Penstemon* species, *Salvia greggii, Scutellaria suffrutescens,* and *Tetraneuris acaulis* for splashes of color throughout the year.

PRECAUTIONS: Control for a new juice-sucking insect, as well as the snout beetle that has shown up on most species of *Agave,* with a contact insecticide. Give the pokey leaf edges and tips plenty of room.

Agave geminiflora | Twin-flowered Agave

CACTUS/SUCCULENT

SIZE (height x width)	2–3 feet x 2–3 feet
FLOWER COLOR	Greenish with reddish-purple
FLOWER SEASON	Spring–summer (blooms once, then dies)
EXPOSURE	Full, reflected, or filtered sun, or part shade
WATER	Low–moderate
GROWTH RATE	Moderately fast
PRUNING	None
HARDINESS	Hardy to at least 20° F

NATURAL ELEVATION RANGE	3,000–4,500 feet
SUITABLE CITIES	All low-elevation-zone cities; warm spots in mid-elevation-zone cities

FIELD NOTES: *Agave geminiflora* is known only from a small area in Nayarit, Mexico. Plants are found in oak woodland at 3,000–4,500 feet elevation in an area that receives about 40 inches of annual rainfall.

DESCRIPTION: *A. geminiflora* is a non-offsetting plant that forms a dense, symmetrical rosette of hundreds of long, thin, flexible leaves. These rosettes look beautifully sculptured on a mature plant, and they might reach 2–3 feet tall by 2–3 feet across. User-friendly leaves are toothless along the margin and have a small terminal spine. The flower stalk is a narrow spike without side branches, 15–18 feet tall. The name *geminiflora* is derived from the twin flowers at each **bract** along the spike. The flowers are greenish near the base, flushed with red or purple above. As with all *Agave* species these plants bloom once, then die. As a solitary type, it leaves no relatives behind.

CULTURE/MAINTENANCE: Plants are hardy to at least the low 20s or high teens F. They are low- to moderate-water-using, growing faster when given supplemental water when the weather is warm. The growth rate is moderately fast, and plants can make nice-size specimens in a short time. Grow in full sun, reflected sun, filtered sun, or partial shade. A plant grown in full sun will be more dense and compact than one grown in some shade.

IDENTIFICATION: Very narrow, dark green leaves that are smooth and flexible make this an easily identifiable species. *A. striata* and *A. stricta,* both narrow-leafed species, have stiff, light green leaves with no marginal threads. *A. parviflora* and *A. toumeyana* both have dark green leaves with white markings and white marginal threads, but they are much smaller than *A. geminiflora.*

LANDSCAPE APPLICATION: *A. geminiflora* performs well as an accent plant or mixed into a cactus and succulent garden in mild-winter areas. Install it as a container plant in places where it gets cold like Albuquerque, Las Vegas, and El Paso, and it can enjoy the shelter of a covered patio. It will grow in full sun or under *Acacia* species, *Olneya tesota,* or *Prosopis* species that provide light shade and a buffer from cold night skies. *A. geminiflora* is adaptable to the north side of a house where it slows down in the winter shade and perks up in the summer sun. Try planting in with a grouping of low-growing plants like *Conoclinium dissectum, Dalea capitata,* or *Scutellaria suffrutescens,* or mix with perennials like *Ageratum corymbosum, Baileya multiradiata, Berlandiera lyrata, Menodora longiflora, Penstemon* species, *Thymophylla pentachaeta,* or *Zinnia grandiflora.*

PRECAUTIONS: Protect plants from rabbits; they find the leaves quite tasty and can destroy a plant in short order. Preventative treatments for the agave snout weevil may be helpful. Take care with sharp leaf tips.

Agave multifilifera | Shaggy Head Agave

CACTUS/SUCCULENT

SIZE (height x width)	2–3 feet x 2–4 feet
FLOWER COLOR	Pale green tinged with pink
FLOWER SEASON	Late spring–early summer (blooms once, then dies)
EXPOSURE	Full or filtered sun
WATER	Low–moderate
GROWTH RATE	Slow–moderate
PRUNING	None
HARDINESS	Hardy to at least 15° F
NATURAL ELEVATION RANGE	4,500–7,000 feet
SUITABLE CITIES	All low- and mid-elevation-zone cities; Sierra Vista in high-elevation zone

FIELD NOTES: My experience with *Agave multifilifera* in the wild came with help of a local guide who led Ron Gass and me up Sierra de Alamos in Sonora. We found a few plants on a ridge near the top of the mountain. The next glimpses were pretty thrilling, coming at Cascada de Basaseachi (Basaseachic Falls) in Chihuahua, the second-highest waterfall in Mexico. These beautiful plants dot the slopes along the walk to the waterfall. *A. multifilifera* generally occurs at high elevations on pine- and oak-covered mountains and on shaded slopes of canyons in Chihuahua, Sonora, Sinaloa, and Durango, Mexico. These plants like cliffs and rocky slopes between 4,500 and 7,000 feet elevation.

DESCRIPTION: The common name says it all. The dense cluster of leaves packed with numerous, curly fibers evokes the image of a thick, lustrous head of hair. This medium-size, generally non-offsetting plant grows to about 2–3 feet tall by 2–4 feet across. The numerous, linear-lanceolate leaves are medium green, about 1½–2 feet long by ¾ inch wide, and adorned with beautiful white markings and many long, thin fibers along the margin. Pink-tinged, pale green flowers sprout from a 12–15-foot-tall spike in late spring to early summer. As with all other *Agave* species, flowering is a terminal disease.

CULTURE/MAINTENANCE: *A. multifilifera* is hardy to at least 15° F. Plants grow moderately slowly, attaining appreciable size within 5 or 10 years from seed. Plants are low- to moderate-water-use and attain their pretty, compact form when grown in full sun or very light shade in the hot, low desert areas. When planted in the ground, give occasional supplemental water during the heat of late spring and summer. As a container plant, *A. multifilifera* asks to be watered only once or twice weekly even during the heat of summer. The plants are tolerant of most soil types as long as drainage is good.

IDENTIFICATION: *A. multifilifera* is easily identified by its numerous, very narrow leaves and generally solitary nature. It is closely related to *A. filifera* and *A. schidigera*. *A. schidigera* leaves are wider and shorter, while *A. filifera* is a clumping species. The hybrid *Agave* x *leopoldii* is similar but is a much smaller plant that produces offsets.

LANDSCAPE APPLICATION: *A. multifilifera* stands out as a specimen in a cactus and succulent garden, a perennial garden, or even in raised planters. It also makes a splash in a pot. In a perennial flower garden, mix with low-growing plants such as *Berlandiera lyrata, Calylophus hartwegii, Hibiscus martianus,* any *Penstemon* species, *Thymophylla pentachaeta,* or *Zinnia grandiflora.* Try it under the light shade cast by plants such as *Acacia willardiana* and *Eysenhardtia orthocarpa.*

PRECAUTIONS: Protect young plants from the ravages of rabbits and javelina. Treat a couple times in spring and summer for agave snout weevil.

Agave ocahui | Ocahui

CACTUS/SUCCULENT

SIZE (height x width)	24–30 inches x 30–36 inches
FLOWER COLOR	Golden yellow
FLOWER SEASON	Summer (blooms once, then dies)
EXPOSURE	Full or filtered sun
WATER	Drought-tolerant–low
GROWTH RATE	Moderately slow
PRUNING	None

HARDINESS	Hardy to at least 15° F
NATURAL ELEVATION RANGE	1,500–4,500 feet
SUITABLE CITIES	All low- and mid-elevation-zone cities; Sierra Vista in high-elevation zone

FIELD NOTES: I've encountered *Agave ocahui* growing on open, exposed rock near an interesting palm canyon southeast of Magdalena in north central Sonora, Mexico. The population is not large, but on my last visit it was reassuring to see seedlings and small plants. Plants cling to cliffs and volcanic outcrops in central and eastern Sonora, between 1,500 and 4,500 feet elevation.

DESCRIPTION: Elegant *A. ocahui* forms a tight, dense ball of narrow, dark green leaves with a thin, reddish brown edge and no marginal teeth. It is a lazy, non-offsetting type and reaches a mature size of about 24–30 inches tall and 30–36 inches wide. Its dark green leaves are 12–15 inches long and nearly 1 inch wide, with toothless margins and a short, yet sharp terminal spine. When the plant is mature and ready to flower, a 10–15-foot-tall spike begins to emerge in late winter or early spring and continues growing until late spring or early summer when the flowers will begin to open. This unbranched stalk is densely crowded with golden yellow flowers, signaling the end of the plant's life.

CULTURE/MAINTENANCE: *A. ocahui* is easy to grow. It is hardy to at least 15° F, and it develops its best shape when grown in full sun or very light shade with supplemental water kept to a minimum. This soil generalist grows well under varied, tough conditions. In the summer, saturate the root zone, and then leave alone to dry out before approaching again with the hose. Winter watering should be held to no more than once a month. The growth rate is moderate to slow, depending on the amount of water applied.

IDENTIFICATION: *A. ocahui* is quite distinctive and cannot be confused with any other *Agave* except maybe *A. pelona*. *A. pelona* is a little smaller with the slightly curved leaves having a larger, white margin.

LANDSCAPE APPLICATION: *A. ocahui* is an excellent plant to use with either subtropical or desert companions. Plant singly or mass and combine with herds of large boulders. It works well with plants that will not overshadow it all the time. Perennials that complement attractively include *Baileya multiradiata, Chrysactinia mexicana, Dalea capitata, Hibiscus martianus, Penstemon baccharifolius, Salvia greggii, Sphaeralcea* *ambigua, Tetraneuris acaulis*, and *Zephyranthes* species. *A. ocahui* also looks handsome when planted near the base of larger accents like *Brahea armata, Nolina nelsonii, Sabal uresana* and *Yucca rigida*. In the hot, interior low and mid-elevation regions, plants breathe easier in the shade of small trees such *Acacia constricta, Eysenhardtia orthocarpa*, and *Parkinsonia microphylla*.

PRECAUTIONS: Grow the plants slowly to develop the most compact form. They are not bothered by rabbits or javelinas and can be planted in an open desert landscape. Preventive treatments with a systemic insecticide for the agave snout weevil help avert tragic loss of favorite specimens. Also, remember that plants bloom only once, then die.

Agave ovatifolia │ Whale's Tongue Agave

CACTUS/SUCCULENT	
SIZE (height x width)	3–5 feet x 4–6 feet
FLOWER COLOR	Greenish-yellow
FLOWER SEASON	Summer (blooms once, then dies)
EXPOSURE	Full or filtered sun
WATER	Drought-tolerant–low
GROWTH RATE	Slow–moderate
PRUNING	None
HARDINESS	Hardy to 5° F with no damage if kept dry
NATURAL ELEVATION RANGE	3,700–7,000 feet
SUITABLE CITIES	All low- and mid-elevation-zone cities; Sierra Vista in high-elevation zone

FIELD NOTES: In the year 2000, I heard about a mysterious *Agave* growing on a large ranch in northeastern Mexico. Access was through a locked gate, so I contacted Jose Angel Villarreal, a botanist in Mexico, who helped Ron Gass and me find the owner and obtain permission to pursue this plant. After much study, this unusual species became known as *A. ovatifolia*. Currently it is known only from the mountains in northeastern Mexico at elevations from 3,700 to 7,000 feet.

DESCRIPTION: My friend Pat took one look at the large, wide, distinctly concave, silvery blue leaves and blurted out, "The leaf looks like a whale's tongue." Thus the common name was born. *A. ovatifolia* is solitary (non-offsetting) with a hemispherical rosette reaching anywhere from 3–5 feet tall by 4–6 feet across, making a spectacular specimen in any desert landscape. When grown hard, the plant will stay smaller, while ample moisture will encourage maximum size. Marginal teeth are small, and the dark

grayish-black terminal spine is about 1 inch long. The **paniculate**, kiss-of-death **inflorescence** is 10–14 feet tall and consists of several side branches, each densely clustered with greenish-yellow flowers.

CULTURE/MAINTENANCE: *A. ovatifolia* is hardy, having withstood winter lows of about 4–5° F in Dallas without sustaining damage. It will be most compact when planted in full sun and given infrequent, yet thorough irrigation only in the summer. In the low, interior desert of the southwestern U.S. (Phoenix and Palm Springs), the plants would benefit from very light, afternoon shade. The growth rate is moderate to slow, taking 15 years or more to achieve flowering size. Plants are tolerant of most soil types with good drainage.

IDENTIFICATION: The leaves of *A. ovatifolia* are quite distinctive and separate it from any other species.

LANDSCAPE APPLICATION: Use this agave as a focal point in a desert landscape. It thrives under the shade of small trees like *Acacia willardiana, Eysenhardtia orthocarpa,* or *Leucaena retusa.* It fits in nicely with cacti and other succulent and semisucculent plants and is striking when planted near large boulders. Try mixing in some flowering perennials or small shrubs to give seasonal color. Some suggestions include *Berlandiera lyrata, Chrysactinia mexicana, Penstemon* species, *Poliomintha maderensis, Salvia greggii,* and *Zinnia grandiflora.* It's a perfect specimen plant for wide-open street medians and can even be mass planted in king-size spaces.

PRECAUTIONS: As with most *Agave* species, this one should be pre-treated for the agave snout weevil.

Agave parrasana | Cabbage Head Agave

CACTUS/SUCCULENT	
SIZE (height x width)	18–24 inches x 24–30 inches
FLOWER COLOR	Yellow, flushed with red or purple
FLOWER SEASON	Summer (blooms once, then dies)
EXPOSURE	Full sun or light afternoon shade
WATER	Drought-tolerant–low
GROWTH RATE	Slow–moderate

PRUNING	None
HARDINESS	Hardy to at least 10° F
NATURAL ELEVATION RANGE	4,500–8,000 feet
SUITABLE CITIES	All low- and mid-elevation-zone cities; Sierra Vista in high- elevation zone

FIELD NOTES: In the summer of 2006, I traveled to northeastern Mexico on a quest to see *Agave parrasana* in habitat. We drove for what seemed like forever on a rough, dirt road that finally crested a high ridge where we could pull off. We could see the flowering stalks on plants still higher up the slope, so we hopped out and hiked until we encountered some of the most beautiful plants I have ever seen. At this particular spot, *A. parrasana* was growing on treeless, mostly north-facing slopes. It also inhabits chaparral scrub and pine-oak forests on limestone in a few mountains in southeastern Coahuila, Mexico, from 4,500 to 8,000 feet elevation.

DESCRIPTION: The short, wide, waxy, bluish leaves deeply marked with decorative bud imprints, will take your breath away. This is a medium-small species, growing to about 18–24 inches tall and 24–30 inches across. The closely overlapping, blue-gray to deep blue-green leaves measure about 8–12 inches long and 4–6 inches wide. The teeth are largest near the leaf tip, getting smaller towards the base. The branched flower stalk is 10–15 feet tall with large, distinctive, reddish to purplish bracts that subtend the clusters of flowers. In bud, the flowers are flushed with red or purple and open yellow. It sounds like a fairy tale, but even this stunning plant will flower once and then die.

CULTURE/MAINTENANCE: This cold-hardy species tolerates temperatures down to at least 10° F. The plants are low-water-using to drought-tolerant, requiring supplemental water once every 2 or 3 weeks in the summer. They take several years to achieve a mature size and are best grown in full sun or light afternoon shade in the low, interior desert regions. *A. parrasana* is native to limestone soil and should be planted in a soil with good drainage. Offsets may remain when you take away the mother plant after flowering.

IDENTIFICATION: *A. parrasana* is easily recognized by its short, broad, closely **imbricate** leaves with the marginal teeth larger at the tip of the leaf and nearly absent towards the base.

LANDSCAPE APPLICATION: The size makes this just right for mass planting, tucking up against large boulders in a cactus and succulent garden, or comingling with bulbs, perennials, and small shrubs. Mix with *Berlandiera lyrata, Chrysactinia mexicana, Cooperia pedunculata, Ericameria laricifolia, Habranthus robustus, Penstemon* species, *Poliomintha maderensis, Salvia greggii, Scutellaria suffrutescens, Tetraneuris acaulis, Zephyranthes* species, and *Zinnia grandiflora.* Try them in large decorative pots where they can attract a lot of attention. In the hot, interior low- and mid-elevation cities of Phoenix, Palm Springs, Tucson, and Las Vegas, the plants do great under the light shade of small trees like *Acacia berlandieri, Acacia constricta, Eysenhardtia orthocarpa,* and *Parkinsonia microphylla.*

PRECAUTIONS: Treat for the agave snout weevil. In the past couple of years, a small sucking insect has also been infesting several species of *Agave.* This insect will cause spotting on the leaves. A systemic insecticide applied preventatively once or twice each in the spring and summer should take care of both critters.

Agave parryi | Artichoke Agave

Variety *truncata*

CACTUS/SUCCULENT	
SIZE (height x width)	2–3 feet x 2–3 feet
FLOWER COLOR	Golden yellow
FLOWER SEASON	Summer (blooms once, then dies)
EXPOSURE	Full or filtered sun
WATER	Drought-tolerant–moderate
GROWTH RATE	Slow–moderate
PRUNING	None
HARDINESS	Var. *parryi* and var. *huachucensis* are hardy to <10° F, while var. *truncata* is hardy to about 15° F
NATURAL ELEVATION RANGE	5,000–8,000 feet
SUITABLE CITIES	*A. parryi* var. *truncata* in low-elevation-zone cities and Tucson; other varieties in all zones

FIELD NOTES: *Agave parryi* has a wide distribution and is typically divided into four or five varieties, with three in the landscape trade. Plants can be found in oak wood-

Variety *huachucensis*

land, oak-juniper grassland, and pine forests at 5,000–8,000 feet elevation in southeastern Arizona, northeastern Sonora, and adjacent northwestern Chihuahua. I see variety *huachucensis* in the Huachuca Mountains of southern Arizona and variety *parryi* on the drive up the Cumbres de Majalca, a national park in Chihuahua, Mexico. Variety *truncata* is found only in a couple of small, out-of-the-way areas in west-central Mexico.

DESCRIPTION: This pretty, dense, medium-size, offsetting plant has individual rosettes resembling an artichoke. Individuals vary in size from 18–24 inches tall by 24–36 inches across, with clusters reaching 5–6 feet across, due in part to the natural variation within the species and in part to the culture. Leaves are blue-gray or light gray and 8–15 inches long by 3–5 inches across. Leaf margins have dark brown teeth that are usually curved back towards the base of the plant. The terminal spine is about 1 inch long, dark brown, and very stout. Tall, branched flower stalks grow to 15–20 feet high. Flowers are pink or red in bud, opening to golden yellow. The flowering plant will die after blooming, but the thinned-out clump will carry on.

CULTURE/MAINTENANCE: Plants emerge unscathed from exposure to winter lows of about 15° F and, judging by native habitats, they should be able to tolerate even lower temperatures. Plants are considered drought-tolerant but will stay gorgeous if treated with consistent supplemental water during the summer. Place in native soil with good drainage. They have a moderately slow growth rate and will take several years to reach maturity and begin offsetting. Grow in full sun, or in the low, hot, interior desert regions, filter that sun for a little relief.

IDENTIFICATION: The leaves and pleasing shape easily identify *A. parryi*.

LANDSCAPE APPLICATION: It takes a few years, but these self-mass planters can take up quite a large area by the spreading underground runners. Try planting them on the east side of small trees that give light shade. They have been mixed successfully with *Acacia berlandieri, Acacia constricta, Eysenhardtia orthocarpa,* and *Havardia pallens.*

PRECAUTIONS: Watch out for the agave snout weevil. Also, keep plants out of deep shade; that artichoke effect happens best in full sun. Avoid overwatering. Young plants may need protection from rabbits and/or javelinas, but older, more established plants do not.

Agave schidigera | Durango Delight

CACTUS/SUCCULENT

SIZE (height x width)	18–30 inches x 36–40 inches
FLOWER COLOR	Reddish-purple
FLOWER SEASON	Spring–summer (blooms once, then dies)
EXPOSURE	Full or filtered sun
WATER	Low–moderate
GROWTH RATE	Moderately fast
PRUNING	None
HARDINESS	Hardy to at least 17° F
NATURAL ELEVATION RANGE	3,000–8,000 feet
SUITABLE CITIES	All low- and mid-elevation-zone cities; Sierra Vista in high-elevation zone

FIELD NOTES: My first encounter with these plants was during a trip in 1983 when we spotted them growing on sheer vertical cuts through the botanically rich area along Mexico Highway 40. We noticed the silhouette of the plants in flower, screeched to a stop, and scrambled up a steep slope to get at the plants growing on the very top of the road cuts. *A. schidigera* is found on steep walled cliffs and open, exposed sites in oak woodlands from 3,000 to 8,000 feet elevation. The form called Durango Delight originally came from a population of very symmetrical plants found on Highway 40.

DESCRIPTION: The symmetry is quite beautiful and lends itself to use as a close-up specimen. The densely leafy, medium-size plant reaches about 18–30 inches tall and 36–40 inches across. Dark green leaves are 12–18 inches long by 1 inch wide and decorated with white markings and thin white marginal fibers. The flower stalk is 10–12 feet tall and densely loaded with dark reddish-purple flowers.

CULTURE/MAINTENANCE: *A. schidigera* is hardy and has been known to weather winter lows of 17° without suffering any damage. Place in full sun or very light shade in the low, hot, interior desert region. Plants are tolerant of most Southwestern soils with adequate drainage. Plants have a moderate to fast growth rate, responding to supplemental water during the growing season (spring through early fall) but should be kept on the dry side during the winter.

IDENTIFICATION: *A. schidigera* is typically a solitary (non-offsetting) species, which distinguishes it from *A. filifera* (the only *Agave* it could be mistaken for), an off-setting type.

LANDSCAPE APPLICATION: Use this agave singly or grouped near boulders in a cactus and succulent garden. It mixes with perennials and small shrubs such as *Ageratum corymbosum, Conoclinium dissectum, Dalea capitata, Penstemon baccharifolius, Salvia greggii, Tetraneuris acaulis, Thymophylla pentachaeta*, and *Zephyranthes citrina*. Candidates for **overstory** shade include *Acacia willardiana, Bauhinia lunarioides, Parkinsonia* x 'Desert Museum,' *Eysenhardtia orthocarpa, Havardia mexicana, Leucaena retusa*, and *Parkinsonia microphylla. A. schidigera* also attracts attention when grown in large, decorative pots.

PRECAUTIONS: As with all other *Agave* species, treat two or three times a year for the agave snout weevil that tunnels into the stem. A systemic insecticide can take care of a type of sucking insect that may cause leaf spotting. Resist the urge to sprinkle from overhead early in the morning in the winter as the water may freeze on the leaves and cause spotting.

Agave striata | Needle Leaf Agave, Espadin

CACTUS/SUCCULENT

SIZE (height x width)	20–36 inches x 24–40 inches (clumps to 8 feet across)
FLOWER COLOR	Reddish or purplish (blooms once, then dies)
FLOWER SEASON	Summer
EXPOSURE	Full sun
WATER	Drought-tolerant–moderate
GROWTH RATE	Moderately fast
PRUNING	None or remove old flowering stalks
HARDINESS	Hardy to at least the mid-teens F
NATURAL ELEVATION RANGE	3,200–6,400 feet
SUITABLE CITIES	All low- and mid-elevation-zone cities, Sierra Vista in high-elevation zone

FIELD NOTES: Take a drive through the Chihuahuan Desert of northern Mexico and you are almost assured of seeing some beautiful stands of *A. striata*. There are some nice stands between Saltillo and Monterrey, and south on the highway to Matehuala. I've

seen plants with silvery blue leaves near Doctor Arroyo in Nuevo León, some with purplish-red leaves in the state of Hidalgo, and still others with green leaves throughout much of the rest of the desert. It can be found in dry valleys, and on slopes and plains from 3,200 to 6,400 feet elevation with annual average rainfall ranging from 8 to 20 inches.

DESCRIPTION: A single plant forms a beautiful ball of leaves, while a cluster of them looks a bit like a bunch of porcupines huddled together. Individual rosettes are compact, grow to 20–36 inches tall and 24–40 inches wide, and form large, dense clusters 5–8 feet across. Leaves can be silver-blue or pale to deep green, sometimes tinged red, or even purple up to three-fourths their length. They are linear, ½-inch wide by 12–24 inches long, and very rigid. Leaves have no marginal teeth, but they are equipped with a sharp, stiff, terminal spine. Greenish-yellow or red-to-purple flowers bloom on unbranched spikes that reach 5–8 feet tall and appear primarily in summer.

CULTURE/MAINTENANCE: This species is cold-hardy to at least the mid-teens F and survives the hot summers of southern Arizona with minimal supplemental irrigation once established. It tolerates native soil without any additional organic matter, and has a moderately fast growth rate, depending on amount and frequency of supplemental water during summer. Remember that when an *Agave* flowers, that plant will die. However, *A. striata* forms large clumps, so the loss of a few plants in a mature clump is not disastrous.

IDENTIFICATION: *A. stricta* is a similar-looking species from Tehuacán, Mexico. It is tender, more evenly symmetrical, and typically grown as a container plant.

LANDSCAPE APPLICATION: Use *A. striata* in full sun in the outer, dry zone of a xeriscape, allowing ample room for the plant to clump out. Match it with drought-tolerant ground covers and low-rider shrubs and perennials. Some plants that stay short enough to not overshadow it are *Ageratum corymbosum, Asclepias linaria, Conoclinium dissectum, Dalea capitata, Hibiscus martianus, Penstemon* species, *Salvia farinacea, Salvia greggii,* and *Zauschneria californica.* For some height, but not too much bulk, use small trees such as *Acacia willardiana, Bauhinia lunarioides,* and *Eysenhardtia orthocarpa.*

PRECAUTIONS: As with other species of *Agave,* flowering is the kiss of death. However, abundant offsets will keep the clump intact. Also, watch for signs of the agave snout weevil and pretreat with a systemic insecticide as a preventive measure.

Agave victoriae-reginae | Queen Victoria Agave

CACTUS/SUCCULENT	
SIZE (height x width)	8–18 inches x 12–24 inches
FLOWER COLOR	Reddish or purplish
FLOWER SEASON	Summer (blooms once, then dies)
EXPOSURE	Full or filtered sun
WATER	Low
GROWTH RATE	Very slow
PRUNING	None
HARDINESS	Hardy to at least 10° F
NATURAL ELEVATION RANGE	4,000–5,000 feet
SUITABLE CITIES	All low- and mid-elevation-zone cities, Sierra Vista in high-elevation zone

FIELD NOTES: The most easily accessible, wild population of *Agave victoriae-reginae* is found in Huasteca Canyon outside Monterrey, Nuevo León, in northeastern Mexico. More of a challenge are patches in rugged isolated areas of Coahuila, Durango, and Nuevo León in north-central Mexico. This species generally grows on rocky limestone slopes and steep walled canyons from 4,000 to 5,000 feet elevation. I've been fortunate enough to visit four populations, each consisting of a mildly distinct form.

DESCRIPTION: The dense, compact habit and elegant white markings make this one of the most striking species in cultivation. This small, compact plant grows to 12–18 inches tall and 12–24 inches across. Short, stout leaves are dark green with white markings, no teeth along the edges, but with a very sharp terminal spine. Flowers are reddish or purplish and are densely packed on an unbranched spike that can reach 15 feet high. The species is quite variable, with solitary forms and forms that offset profusely. According to Gentry's *Agaves of Continental North America*, there are at least 7 horticultural forms of *A. victoriae-reginae*. One of the more prominent of these has long been called *A. ferdinandi-regis* and has longer, dark green leaves and a more open rosette.

CULTURE/MAINTENANCE: The species is hardy to at least 10° and possibly lower if kept dry through the winter. Plants are low-water-using but need some supplemental water during summer in the low, hot, interior desert region. They can be planted in full sun in cooler or coastal regions but grow best with some shade in the hot, interior areas. They grow fine in native, desert soil with adequate drainage. Plants are slow-growing, taking 20 or more years to reach flowering size. The non-offsetting forms do not require any maintenance. Thin forms offset profusely, and your neighbors will be grateful for the pups.

IDENTIFICATION: *A. victoriae-reginae* is easily recognized by its size and leaves. It does not resemble Queen Victoria.

LANDSCAPE APPLICATION: Mix and mass in a cactus and succulent garden, with perennials and small shrubs, among large boulders, in raised planters, or even in decorative pots. Try combining with perennials and small shrubs with striking flowers: *Ageratum corymbosum, Asclepias linaria, Conoclinium dissectum, Dalea capitata, Hibiscus martianus, Penstemon* species, *Salvia farinacea, Salvia greggii,* and *Zauschneria californica.* For light shade, place under small trees such as *Acacia willardiana, Bauhinia lunarioides, Eysenhardtia orthocarpa,* and *Parkinsonia praecox.*

PRECAUTIONS: Succulent leaves and roots are likely to be uprooted by javelinas, so you'll want to protect them. Make sure the plant gets the sunlight it needs and is in soil with good drainage. Do not overwater. *A. victoriae-reginae* does not need to be watered in the winter. Remember that, as with other *Agave* species, when the plant flowers it will die and leave a gap in your garden unless you have a freely offsetting form.

Agave vilmoriniana | Octopus Agave

CACTUS/SUCCULENT	
SIZE (height x width)	4 feet x 6 feet
FLOWER COLOR	Golden yellow
FLOWER SEASON	Late spring–summer (blooms once, then dies)
EXPOSURE	Full or filtered sun, or part shade
WATER	Drought-tolerant–low
GROWTH RATE	Fast
PRUNING	None
HARDINESS	Hardy to the low 20s F if kept dry in winter
NATURAL ELEVATION RANGE	2,000–5,500
SUITABLE CITIES	All low-elevation cities and Tucson in mid-elevation zone; it's a bit tender in Las Vegas

FIELD NOTES: Whenever I head east from Hermosillo, Sonora, into the mountains, I'm always delighted to spot *Agave vilmoriniana* with its long, droopy leaves growing on slopes and steep road cuts. It can also be found growing on steep barranca cliffs from central Sonora south to Jalisco and Aquascalientes in Mexico between 2,000 and 5,500 feet elevation.

DESCRIPTION: This medium to large plant grows to 4 feet high by 6 feet wide. The medium-green, undulating, twisting, unarmed leaves are long, narrow, and deeply channeled. The common name is not a stretch. A 10–20-foot-tall spike of bright golden yellow flowers will sprout from a mature plant in the spring, signaling the end of that plant's life. Both seed capsules and small plantlets appear along the spike after flowering is finished. These plantlets can be collected and cultivated to replace the dead mother plant.

CULTURE/MAINTENANCE: *A. vilmoriniana* will suffer some leaf damage when winter lows drop into the high teens F, but it recovers quickly when the weather warms in the spring and early summer. Locate plants in full sun, light shade, or even partial shade and native soil with adequate drainage. The species is drought-tolerant once established yet opportunistically uses any water applied to grow faster and bloom sooner. *A. vilmoriniana* is fast-growing, sometimes flowering in as little as 4 years after planting. Very little maintenance is required until the plant flowers and sets miniature plants called **bulbils**.

IDENTIFICATION: No other *Agave* species looks like an octopus.

LANDSCAPE APPLICATION: Use *A. vilmoriniana* as an accent plant in the landscape. The arching and twisting leaves are a little unusual in the desert plant world and look especially daring with mass planting. Plants perform well in street medians or hot planters but are just as happy under the shade of desert trees. Because it is completely unarmed, *A. vilmoriniana* is safe where people might lightly brush against it. Do remember to consider its eventual size when picking the perfect spot in the garden. Try classic companion trees and shrubs: *Acacia constricta, Bauhinia lunarioides, Larrea divaricata, Leucophyllum* species, *Parkinsonia florida, Parkinsonia microphylla, Salvia greggii, Simmondsia chinensis,* and *Vauquelinia californica.*

PRECAUTIONS: As with all other *Agave* species, this one will die after flowering. However, it produces countless bulbils on the flower spike that are ready to become the next generation. Rabbits do not readily munch an established plant, but sometimes javelinas will uproot young plants.

Ageratum corymbosum | Blue Mist Flower

FLOWERING PERENNIAL	
SIZE (height x width)	3 feet x 3 feet
FLOWER COLOR	Powder blue-lavender
FLOWER SEASON	Summer–fall
EXPOSURE	Full or filtered sun, or partial shade
WATER	Moderate
GROWTH RATE	Fast
PRUNING	Occasional in spring & summer
HARDINESS	Root-hardy to at least 15° F
NATURAL ELEVATION RANGE	Approximately 1,000–8,000 feet
SUITABLE CITIES	All low- and mid-elevation-zone cities

FIELD NOTES: *Ageratum corymbosum* is found in southwestern New Mexico, then throughout much of the Mexican highlands south into Central America at elevations between 1,000 and 8,000 feet. I've also spotted plants decorating the roadside in northeastern Mexico while cruising from Laredo, Texas, south to Monterrey, Nuevo León.

DESCRIPTION: This perennial beauty has soft, powder blue-lavender flowers set against rich green foliage. Highly branched stems are upright to partially **decumbent**, depending on amount of sun or shade they receive, and the plant can fill out to 3 feet

tall by 3 feet wide. Bright green leaves are ovate in outline, about 2 inches long and 1 inch wide, with **crenate** margins. Flowers occur in "misty" 1–2-inch-wide clusters at the ends of branches and are famous for attracting queen butterflies. Blooms can appear from late May or early June and continue until frost.

CULTURE/MAINTENANCE: The plants are root-hardy to at least 15° F. The tops handle the high teens or low 20s F. They require regular supplemental water in the summer but will perk right up with watering if allowed to wilt. The tops can stretch to 2 feet or more in a single season. This species tolerates many soils, from those with high clay content to those that are rocky with fast drainage; just remember to adjust the watering frequency accordingly. Maintain by shearing nearly to ground level in winter and cutting hard in summer if it gets too leggy.

IDENTIFICATION: Other species of *Ageratum* have blue or lavender flowers; however, *A. corymbosum* is perennial while the others give up after a year. Flowers resemble those of *Conoclinium dissectum*, which has pinnately divided leaves while *A.corymbosum* does not.

LANDSCAPE APPLICATION: *A. corymbosum* is an attractive complement to accents such as *Agave* and *Yucca* species. Try planting it in a large container as a perennial bedding plant or using it to soften a cactus or rock garden. Plants serve agreeably as summer and fall flowering perennials in a perennial garden. Blue mist flower should be placed in full sun in mild summer climate areas and filtered light or partial shade in low, hot, interior desert regions. This perennial blends well with other mini-oasis specimens and looks great in the filtered light of a mesquite tree. Mass plant to attract bevies of queen butterflies. Mix with *Aquilegia chrysantha, Chrysactinia mexicana, Justicia spicigera, Muhlenbergia dumosa, Poliomintha maderensis, Salvia greggii,* and *Stachys coccinea.*

PRECAUTIONS: *A. corymbosum* can be grown in full sun but requires more water than when grown in filtered sun. Also, protect it from rabbits for at least the first couple of years. Whiteflies seem to like the leaves. Prune hard only in late winter or early spring, then ignore it for the rest of the year.

Aloe cryptopoda | Hidden Foot Aloe

CACTUS/SUCCULENT	
SIZE (height x width)	2 feet x 2–3 feet
FLOWER COLOR	Red, yellow
FLOWER SEASON	Late fall or winter
EXPOSURE	Full or filtered sun, or part shade
WATER	Moderate
GROWTH RATE	Moderate
PRUNING	None
HARDINESS	Hardy to at least high teens F
NATURAL ELEVATION RANGE	200–5,000 feet
SUITABLE CITIES	All low-elevation-zone cities; Tucson in mid-elevation zone

FIELD NOTES: *Aloe cryptopoda* is easy to find in the northeastern part of South Africa and has been recorded in Malawi, Mozambique, Zambia and Zimbabwe from 200 to 5,000 feet elevation. It grows in flat, open places or on rocky slopes where annual rainfall is 18–25 inches and summer temperatures reach over 100° F.

DESCRIPTION: This striking, stemless *Aloe* is usually solitary with a dense rosette of deep green to blue-green leaves. It makes it to about 2 feet tall, spreading to 2–3 feet across. The leaves are narrow, triangular, and 12–18 inches long and have small teeth along the edges. In the fall or late winter a 3–6-foot-tall inflorescence appears and is covered with 1½-inch-long flowers. *A. cryptopoda* comes in three color schemes, one

with red buds and open flowers, one with yellow buds and open flowers, and one with red buds and yellow open flowers.

CULTURE/MAINTENANCE: *A. cryptopoda* is hardy to at least the high teens F, although early season flowers are sometimes damaged by late frost. Plants take several years to reach full size and survive on low to moderate watering. Supplemental water applied every 10–14 days in the summer and every 14–21 days in the winter—depending on soil type and planting location—will perk them up quite a bit. Plants flourish when placed in filtered light, or in morning sun and afternoon shade.

IDENTIFICATION: The single, stemless rosette of leaves and the flowers that are red in bud and yellow when open let you know you're dealing with *A. cryptopoda*.

LANDSCAPE APPLICATION: *A. cryptopoda* fits well in a rock garden or a cactus and succulent garden and really pulls in the hummingbirds. Mass plant them for a spectacular flush of flowers in winter. Mix in some low-growing, small shrubs or cool season perennials to expand the color palette. The plant blends nicely with *Baileya multiradiata, Melampodium leucanthum, Menodora longiflora, Penstemon* species, *Thymophylla pentachaeta,* and *Zinnia grandiflora*. Place at the base of small trees such as *Acacia willardiana, Bauhinia lunarioides, Leucaena retusa,* and *Havardia pallens*. Keep dry in the winter in the wet, low-elevation-zone cities of Austin and San Antonio.

PRECAUTIONS: As with all *Aloe* species, watch for aloe mites, which cause deformed growth of leaves and flower stalks.

Aloe ferox | Fierce Aloe

CACTUS/SUCCULENT	
SIZE (height x width)	6–10 feet x 4 feet
FLOWER COLOR	Yellow-orange, orange-red, scarlet
FLOWER SEASON	Mid- to late winter–early spring
EXPOSURE	Full or reflected sun, or light shade
WATER	Low–moderate
GROWTH RATE	Moderately slow
HARDINESS	Hardy to mid-20s F, protect flower stalks below mid-20s F
PRUNING	Remove old flower stalks in spring
NATURAL ELEVATION RANGE	3,000–4,500 feet
SUITABLE CITIES	All low-elevation cities; warm microclimates in Tucson

FIELD NOTES: The natural distribution ranges throughout south-central and south-eastern South Africa, and because of its height, *Aloe ferox* is easy to spot. I saw it at elevations between 3,000 and 4,500 feet in the Groot-Swartberge mountain range in the Little Karoo in South Africa. At times, the plants were common in the open or among bushes on flat, rocky areas or rocky slopes along river valleys and canyons.

DESCRIPTION: A tall trunk and large leaves make this a striking plant even when not in flower. It can grow to 6–10 feet tall with a leaf crown spreading to 4 feet across. Leaves are thick, succulent, nearly 2 feet long. They are a dull green color and may or may not have wicked spines on both the top and bottom surfaces. Old leaves dry and hang down, covering the trunk and giving a shaggy appearance. The flower stalk is a branched **panicle** with 5–8 upright **racemes** giving a candelabra appearance. Flowers are tubular, about 2 inches long, and vary in color from yellow-orange to orange-red or brilliant scarlet. Flowering usually occurs in late winter and early spring, attracting hummingbirds.

CULTURE/MAINTENANCE: *A. ferox* is hardy to the mid-20s, but flowers suffer when exposed to prolonged cold temperatures. This slow- to moderate-growing plant will take several years to develop a sizable trunk. It survives with moderate to little water; consistent watering during the growing season will give the growth rate a boost. *A. ferox* can be grown in nearly any soil type as long as watering frequency is adjusted accordingly. Place plants under a shade tree, in full sun, or even reflected sun. No maintenance is required.

IDENTIFICATION: *A. marlothii*, *A. spectabilis*, and *A. candelabrum* also develop trunks. It's tricky to identify these aloes by looking at their leaves, but the flower stalks provide clues for separating species. To further confuse the distinctions, hybridization creates a variety of forms.

LANDSCAPE APPLICATION: *A. ferox* can be used singly or grouped to create an eye-catching display. Place it against the south or west side of a building or under the canopy of a *Parkinsonia* or *Prosopis* for winter protection. Try mixing with other *Aloe* species, or new world succulents like *Agaves, Dasylirions, Nolinas,* or *Yuccas.* Use low-growing shrubs or perennials to surround *A. ferox* with color throughout the year. Some suggestions include *Baileya multiradiata, Calylophus hartwegii, Encelia farinosa, Penstemon* species, *Salvia greggii, Scutellaria suffrutescens, Tagetes lemmonii, Tetraneuris acaulis,* and *Zauschneria californica.* It makes a spectacular container specimen.

PRECAUTIONS: Flower stalks appear in midwinter and are susceptible to frost damage. Covering with paper sacks or frost cloth is usually sufficient to protect the flower stalks and creates intrigue in your garden.

Aloe marlothii | Mountain Aloe

CACTUS/SUCCULENT	
SIZE (height x width)	6–10 feet x 4–5 feet
FLOWER COLOR	Orange-red, red, yellow, bicolor (orange and red, red and white)
FLOWER SEASON	Midwinter
EXPOSURE	Full sun or light shade
WATER	Drought-tolerant–low
GROWTH RATE	Moderately slow
PRUNING	Remove old flower stalks in spring
HARDINESS	Hardy to low 20s F; protect flower stalks below mid-20s F
NATURAL ELEVATION RANGE	> 3,000 feet
SUITABLE CITIES	All low-elevation cities; warm microclimates in Tucson

FIELD NOTES: *Aloe marlothii* lives above 3,000 feet throughout much of eastern South Africa and north up into East Africa. It grows out in the open or among bushes on flat,

rocky areas or rocky slopes and hillsides. Rainfall over its range averages 15–40 inches per year.

DESCRIPTION: With its tall trunk and bold leaves, *A. marlothii* can grow to 6–10 feet tall and occasionally taller, with a leaf crown spreading to 4–5 feet across. Dull green to grayish-green leaves are thick and juicy and measure nearly 2 feet long. Leaves may or may not have wicked spines along the edges and top and bottom surfaces. Old leaves dry and hang down, covering the trunk and creating a shaggy look. The emergence of the flower stalk is a spectacular sight in winter or spring. The 10–30 side branches are held horizontally or slanted and are covered with tubular, 2-inch-long flowers that are usually bright orange-red but can also be red, yellow, and sometimes even bicolored.

CULTURE/MAINTENANCE: *A. marlothii* is hardy to the low 20s, although flowers are damaged when exposed to prolonged cold temperatures. Moderately slow-growing, it takes several years to develop a sizable trunk. It is drought-tolerant but grows faster with some regular watering during the growing season. Grow *A. marlothii* in nearly any soil type, as long as watering frequency is adjusted accordingly. Place plants in full sun or under a shade tree to resist frost.

IDENTIFICATION: *A. marlothii* and *A. ferox* have similar leaves and trunk but different flower arrangements. *A. marlothii* has the horizontal to slanted branches while those of *A. ferox* are more vertical. Occasionally plants called *A. spectabilis* and *A. candelabrum* show up for sale. Some now consider *A. spectabilis* to be a form of *A. marlothii* and *A. candelabrum* to be a form of *A. ferox*. To further confuse the sorting into species, these plants will hybridize, creating unpredictable offspring.

LANDSCAPE APPLICATION: *A. marlothii* can be used singly or grouped to create an eye-catching display. Place it against the south or west side of a building or under the canopy of a *Parkinsonia* or *Prosopis* for winter protection. Try mixing with other *Aloe* species and succulents with similar habits: *Agave, Dasylirion, Nolina,* or *Yucca* species. Use with *Baileya multiradiata, Calylophus hartwegii, Penstemon* species, *Salvia* species, *Tagetes lemmonii, Tetraneuris acaulis,* and *Zauschneria californica.* Keep dry in the winter in the wet, low-elevation-zone cities of Austin and San Antonio.

PRECAUTIONS: Flower stalks are produced in midwinter and susceptible to frost damage. Covering with attractive paper sacks or frost cloth is usually sufficient to protect the flower stalks.

Aloe striata | Coral Aloe

CACTUS/SUCCULENT

SIZE (height x width)	18–36 inches (with flower stalk) x 24–30 inches
FLOWER COLOR	Coral orange
FLOWER SEASON	Spring
EXPOSURE	Full, filtered, or reflected sun, or part shade
WATER	Low–moderate
GROWTH RATE	Moderately fast
PRUNING	None
HARDINESS	Hardy to low 20s F; protect flowers
NATURAL ELEVATION RANGE	3,000–4,500 feet
SUITABLE CITIES	All low-elevation-zone cities; Tucson in mid-elevation zone

FIELD NOTES: I saw the typical form of *Aloe striata* perched on rocky hillsides on my trip to South Africa in September of 2002. The plants were not very common, but we found a few at an elevation of about 3,000–4,500 feet while driving through the Witberge Mountains from Laingsburg to Oudtshoorn.

DESCRIPTION: With its compact size, typically solitary nature, and clusters of coral-orange flowers, *A. striata* attracts attention anywhere you put it. Plants reach about 18–24 inches tall and stretch to about 36 inches with the flower stalk. Leaf spread runs about 24–30 inches across, although some clumping forms can be as broad as 4 feet across. Leaves are thick, succulent, and triangular—broad at the base and narrow at the tip. Branched inflorescences appear in late spring.

CULTURE/MAINTENANCE: Coral aloe is hardy to the low 20s F, although early season flowers are sometimes damaged by late frost. This species grows moderately fast, reaching flowering size after a few years in the ground. Plants are low- to moderate-

water-using, thriving with supplemental water applied every 10–14 days in the summer and every 14–21 days in the winter. Fine-tune watering frequency depending on soil type and planting location. Plants flourish when placed in filtered light, or morning sun and afternoon shade. Coral aloe will tolerate most soil types with good drainage.

IDENTIFICATION: *A. striata* can be identified by its smooth, broad, finely lined leaves.

LANDSCAPE APPLICATION: Use coral aloe for its glorious late spring flower display, and mix it with a variety of plant forms. It blends particularly well with cacti and other succulents. Combine with spring-flowering shrubs that have a contrasting flower color such as *Chrysactinia mexicana, Encelia farinosa, Larrea divaricata,* and *Ruellia peninsularis.* Place at the base of small trees such as *Acacia willardiana, Bauhinia lunarioides, Leucaena retusa,* and *Havardia mexicana.* Keep dry in the winter in the wet, low-elevation-zone cities of Austin and San Antonio.

PRECAUTIONS: As with all *Aloe* species, watch for aloe mites, which cause deformed growth of leaves and flower stalks.

Aloe variegata | Partridge Breast Aloe

CACTUS/SUCCULENT	
SIZE (height x width)	12–18 inches (with flower stalk) x 15–24 inches
FLOWER COLOR	Deep pinkish-red or orange-red
FLOWER SEASON	Late winter–spring
EXPOSURE	Light shade–full sun
WATER	Low–moderate
GROWTH RATE	Moderate
PRUNING	None
HARDINESS	Hardy to at least 15° F
NATURAL ELEVATION RANGE	< 3,000 feet
SUITABLE CITIES	All low-elevation-zone cities; Tucson in mid-elevation zone

FIELD NOTES: On a trip to South Africa, we found *Aloe variegata* growing in hard, stony soil in the arid region known as the Little Karoo. We spotted it as we traveled from Laingsberg to Oudtshorn in the Western Cape below 3,000 feet elevation. Flower stalks poking up among small shrubs announced the presence of the otherwise hidden succulent.

DESCRIPTION: *A. variegata* is stemless, growing to 6–8 inches tall and spreading to 12–24 inches across. Deeply folded, tiger-striped, triangular leaves are stacked in 3 vertical rows. Deep pinkish-red to orange-red flowers on 12–15-inch-long inflorescences appear in late winter and early spring. Large capsules bearing a squadron of winged seeds follow the flowers.

CULTURE/MAINTENANCE: If kept on the dry side in the winter, *A. variegata* is cold-hardy, withstanding overnight lows in the middle to high teens F. While plants can tolerate full sun, they should be grown in light shade where summer temperatures routinely top 100° F. Plants are low-water-using with a moderate growth rate but will grow a little faster and look a little healthier with extra water in the summer. The plants will tolerate most soil types as long as watering frequency is adjusted accordingly. No maintenance is required.

IDENTIFICATION: With its three-ranked, deeply **keeled**, triangular leaves, *A. variegata* is a very distinctive species.

LANDSCAPE APPLICATION: Use *A. variegata* for its late winter–spring flowering in a cactus and succulent garden. Mix it with sculptural plants like *Aloe ferox*, *Aloe striata*, *Euphorbia antisyphilitica*, *Euphorbia resinifera*, and *Pedilanthus macrocarpus*. Try it with perennials and small shrubs like *Ageratum corymbosum*, *Chrysactina mexicana*, *Conoclinium dissectum*, *Ericameria laricifolia*, *Poliomintha maderensis*, *Salvia greggii*, *Zinnia acerosa*, and *Zinnia grandiflora*. *A. variegata* also makes a smart statement alone in an artistic pot.

PRECAUTIONS: Keep the soil slightly dry through the winter to prevent the roots from rotting, especially in the wet, low-elevation-zone cities of Austin and San Antonio.

Aloysia gratissima | Whitebrush, Bee Brush

MEDIUM–LARGE SHRUB	
SIZE (height x width)	6–10 feet x 6–8 feet
FLOWER COLOR	White
FLOWER SEASON	Spring–fall
EXPOSURE	Full, reflected, or filtered sun, or part shade
WATER	Low–moderate
GROWTH RATE	Moderately fast
PRUNING	None, or shear in late winter or early spring every 2–3 years
HARDINESS	Hardy to at least the high teens F
NATURAL ELEVATION RANGE	1,100–5,000 feet
SUITABLE CITIES	All cities in all zones

FIELD NOTES: Home for *Aloysia gratissima* is a swath across southern Arizona and New Mexico, much of Texas, parts of Mexico, and even South America. It grows between 1,100 and 5,000 feet along creek beds, rocky slopes, arroyos, and canyons, and sometimes on limestone soil.

DESCRIPTION: This large, deciduous, upright to spreading shrub can get 6–10 feet tall and 6–8 feet wide. Small, rich green, lightly fragrant leaves are simple and **opposite** on the stem, and measure about ¾ inch long by ¼ inch wide, giving the plant a fine texture. Six-inch-long spikes of tiny, white, vanilla-scented flowers attract bees and butterflies from spring through fall.

CULTURE/MAINTENANCE: *A. gratissima* withstands overnight lows down into the teens F without damage. Plants handle most light situations—part shade, filtered light, full sun—plus reflected heat. They do well in a rocky, fast-draining soil, or one with some organic matter worked into the top layer, but will also grow in a heavy, clay/rocky soil or a loam/sandy soil. Offer some supplemental water in summer. Thoroughly saturate soil in the root zone, then allow to dry before watering again. In winter, a thorough soaking once a month is ample. The only pruning you might need is shearing once every few years.

IDENTIFICATION: Vanilla-scented flowers and elliptical leaves separate *A. gratissima* from *A. wrightii*, which has rounded leaves with scalloped edges.

LANDSCAPE APPLICATION: Use *A. gratissima* as a background plant and for summer and fall butterfly-attracting flowers. This tough plant can tolerate the harsh conditions of street medians and other areas where neglect is the norm. Leaves drop in winter so consider combining with something that shows off at that time of year. Try it with bold accents like *Agave*, *Dasylirion*, *Nolina*, and *Yucca* species. It fits right in with small trees like *Acacia willardiana*, *Bauhinia lunarioides*, *Eysenhardtia orthocarpa*, *Leucaena retusa*, and *Sophora secundiflora*. Plants have been used for honey production.

PRECAUTIONS: *A. gratissima* is an excellent choice for attracting wildlife but is reportedly toxic to horses, mules, and burros. If it is toxic to rabbits, there is a time delay because they chow down on stem growth to about pencil thickness if nothing else is available.

Anisacanthus quadrifidus var. *wrightii* | Flame Anisacanthus

MEDIUM SHRUB	
SIZE (height x width)	3–5 feet x 3–5 feet
FLOWER COLOR	Red-orange
FLOWER SEASON	Summer–fall
EXPOSURE	Full or filtered sun
WATER	Low–moderate
GROWTH RATE	Moderately fast
PRUNING	Early spring
HARDINESS	Hardy to at least 15° F
NATURAL ELEVATION RANGE	1,000–3,000 feet
SUITABLE CITIES	All low- and mid-elevation-zone cities; warm spots in high-elevation-zone cities

FIELD NOTES: *Anisacanthus quadrifidus* var. *wrightii* is found in southern Texas and northeastern Mexico between 1,000 and 3,000 feet elevation. Drive through the mountains south from Saltillo in Coahuila to Matehuala in summer or fall and watch for the brilliant orange-red flowers covering the shrubs.

DESCRIPTION: Spikes of flaming orange-red flowers light this shrub on fire, midsummer to fall. This irregularly rounded to wide-spreading, medium-size, deciduous shrub grows 3–5 feet high and 3–5 feet wide. Rich green leaves measure about 2 inches by 1 inch. Bright red-orange, hummingbird-luring, 2-inch-long flowers occur in 6–8-inch-long spikes at the ends of branches. This marathon bloomer can start flowering as early as June and continue through summer and into fall, bringing in hummingbirds and occasionally butterflies. The last blossoms might fade out in late October or November.

CULTURE/MAINTENANCE: Flame anisacanthus will perform in full sun or filtered light. Plants will grow fine in a heavy, clay/rocky soil or a loam/sandy soil and do especially well in soils that retain some moisture. Once established, these shrubs are very drought-tolerant, requiring supplemental water every three or four weeks in summer. In winter, plants should receive a thorough watering once a month. Cut them back by one-half or two-thirds in winter to encourage dense growth and increased flowering the following fall. Stem growth to about pencil thickness is susceptible to rabbit damage if nothing else is available. This shrub is hardy to below 15° F.

IDENTIFICATION: Flame anisacanthus is not easily confused with any other species. *Anisacanthus puberulus* sticks primarily to spring blooming, as does *A. thurberi,* though the latter is more likely to spill over into summer and fall. *A. linearis* blooms in summer and fall but has very narrow leaves and longer curly petals. *A. andersonii* blooms primarily in winter and spring.

LANDSCAPE APPLICATION: Use this species in a summer- and fall-flowering hummingbird or butterfly garden. It drops leaves in winter and needs neighbors that will provide interest at that time of year. Some accent plants that combine handsomely include *Agave, Dasylirion, Nolina,* and *Yucca* species. *A. quadrifidus* var. *wrightii* sets off small trees like *Acacia willardiana, Bauhinia lunarioides* (syn. *B. congesta*), *Eysenhardtia orthocarpa, Leucaena retusa,* and *Sophora secundiflora.* It also spices up the foreground for large, evergreen shrubs such as *Leucophyllum frutescens, Sophora secundiflora,* and *Vauquelinia californica.*

PRECAUTIONS: Flame anisacanthus is an excellent choice for attracting wildlife, but that category unfortunately includes voracious jackrabbits and possibly cottontails. Try screening it for the first couple of years.

Anisacanthus thurberi | Desert Honeysuckle

MEDIUM SHRUB

SIZE (height x width)	4–6 feet x 3–5 feet
FLOWER COLOR	Brick red, pale orange
FLOWER SEASON	Spring, occasionally summer and fall
EXPOSURE	Full, filtered, or reflected sun, or part shade
WATER	Drought-tolerant–moderate
GROWTH RATE	Moderate
PRUNING	Shear in winter or every other winter
HARDINESS	Hardy to at least 10° F
NATURAL ELEVATION RANGE	2,500–5,500 feet
SUITABLE CITIES	All low- and mid-elevation-zone cities; Sierra Vista in high-elevation zone

FIELD NOTES: An early May hike through Fort Bowie National Historic Site in Arizona's Dos Cabezas Mountains should reveal *Anisacanthus thurberi* growing in the dry washes. *A. thurberi* ranges through central and southern Arizona, southwestern New Mexico, and northern Mexico, growing in rocky soils in canyons and along sandy washes from 2,500 to 5,500 feet elevation.

DESCRIPTION: This tough hummingbird favorite is a striking addition to any Southwestern desert landscape. *A. thurberi* is a deciduous shrub that has an upright to spreading form, reaching a size of 4–6 feet tall by 3–5 feet wide. The 1–2-inch-long, medium green leaves are deciduous in winter or during prolonged drought. Clusters of brick-red or pale orange, tubular, 1½-inch-long flowers appear primarily in spring either before or just as the leaves begin to appear. Sporadic blooming during summer and fall is a possibility.

CULTURE/MAINTENANCE: Desert honeysuckle is hardy to at least 10° F and possibly lower. Plants are low- to moderate-water-using, even drought-tolerant once established, but will grow faster and look lusher if watered a bit in spring and summer. Plant in full sun or reflected sun to see its beautiful potential. The plant requires very little care but will be fuller and deliver more flowers if pruned once a year in winter.

IDENTIFICATION: *A. thurberi* is readily distinguished from other species of *Anisacanthus* and species of *Justicia* by its elegant, earth-tone flowers. The brick-red or pale orange blossoms are narrowly tubular, with the four petals rolled back over the tube.

LANDSCAPE APPLICATION: Plants will tolerate filtered sun, or even part shade, but grow best in full sun. Because they are deciduous, cozy them up with bold accent plants such as *Agave, Dasylirion, Nolina,* and *Yucca* species. *A. thurberi* steals the show when planted among large boulders and in simulated washes. Mass plant to attract hummingbirds, mix with other bird-attracting plants, or use along streets and in medians. Try combining with spring and early summer flowers such as *Baileya multiradiata, Penstemon* species, *Sphaeralcea ambigua, Thymophylla pentachaeta,* and *Verbena gooddingii.*

PRECAUTIONS: *A. thurberi* is susceptible to browsing by wildlife. Deer and rabbits will nibble even established plants if other vegetation is scarce.

Antigonon leptopus | Queen's Wreath

VINE

SIZE (height x width)	20–25 feet long
FLOWER COLOR	White, pink, or red
FLOWER SEASON	Summer–fall
EXPOSURE	Full, reflected, or filtered sun
WATER	Drought-tolerant–moderate
GROWTH RATE	Slow to establish, fast when established
PRUNING	Winter cleanup
HARDINESS	Root-hardy to at least 20° F
NATURAL ELEVATION RANGE	Near sea level–about 2,000 feet
SUITABLE CITIES	All low-elevation-zone cities; freezes back but recovers in mid-elevation-zone cities

FIELD NOTES: Drive through Baja California or east of Hermosillo in Sonora in the summer and you are bound to spot the pink to red flowers of *Antigonon leptopus* as the vine climbs up through shrubs and trees. It is widespread in Mexico and can be found along roadsides and in washes in Baja California and Sonora, south to Oaxaca from near sea level to nearly 2,000 feet elevation.

DESCRIPTION: Queen's wreath is celebrated for its 4–8-inch-long sprays of showy pink to red, rarely white flowers that appear when the weather heats up in summer. The vine grows herbaceous stems to 20–25 feet or more long, which die back to an enlarged root in winter. Stems climb by tendrils, which wrap around anything that stands still long enough. Heart-shaped, lush green leaves can be as large as 4 inches long and 3 inches wide. The cultivar 'Baja Red' is a selection with the deepest red color, and comes from seeds collected in southern Baja California.

CULTURE/MAINTENANCE: Queen's wreath thrives in the sun and heat, so an ideal planting location would be against a south or west-facing wall. When temperatures dip into the mid to high 20s F, the leaves and stems will die back to the root, but a little cleanup is a small price to pay for the glorious flower display. As the root becomes older and more established, it will produce longer and more abundant stems each successive year. Queen's wreath tolerates a variety of soil types, ranging from amended garden soil to dry, rocky, desert soil. Although drought-tolerant, the opportunistic vine will grow faster if given regular supplemental water in the sum-

mer. It may grow so fast that you need to rein it in with some pruning and training.

IDENTIFICATION: Heart-shaped leaves and long sprays of very distinctive flowers easily identify queen's wreath.

LANDSCAPE APPLICA-TION: *A. leptopus* relishes the heat and is a great plant for the desert regions of the Southwest as long as it is given sufficient water. It provides bold summer color whether on trellises or chain-link fences, on overhead supports to provide summer shade, or up the trunks of desert trees. Plant at the base of *Parkinsonia* or *Prosopis* trees and let the vines climb to provide a splash of unexpected pink or red. When grown on an overhead frame, it provides summer shade, while allowing sunshine through in the winter. It also makes an effective summer ground cover.

PRECAUTIONS: The enlarged root will need some frost protection and should be covered with a thick layer of mulch for the winter. The dead leaves and stems become winter cleanup chores. While the flowers attract butterflies, they can also draw in bees. In wetter climates (like Hawaii's), queen's wreath can become invasive.

Aquilegia chrysantha | Golden Columbine

FLOWERING PERENNIAL

SIZE (height x width)	2–4 feet x 2–3 feet
FLOWER COLOR	Golden yellow
FLOWER SEASON	Spring–fall
EXPOSURE	Part shade or filtered sun
WATER	Moderate–ample
GROWTH RATE	Fast
PRUNING	Minimal
HARDINESS	Hardy to at least 0° F
NATURAL ELEVATION RANGE	3,000–11,000 feet
SUITABLE CITIES	Cool coastal low-elevation-zone cities; all mid- and high-elevation-zone cities

FIELD NOTES: *Aquilegia chrysantha* is found in rich, moist soil in the pine belt but also along streams at lower elevations. It is native to Arizona, New Mexico, southern Colorado, and northern Mexico from 3,000 to 11,000 feet, and its large, canary-yellow, long-spurred flowers make it the most easily recognizable species. Get out in higher canyon habitats in late spring, summer, or fall, and this yellow-flowered beauty will make your day.

DESCRIPTION: Large, golden yellow flowers with long, showy spurs make this perennial one of the most attractive species of *Aquilegia*. Rich green, divided, delicate foliage is a perfect backdrop for the showy display of bright flowers. Hummingbirds are attracted to the nectar-rich flowers.

CULTURE/MAINTENANCE: *A. chrysantha* is hardy to at least 0° F, and probably lower. A higher-elevation form is better at withstanding cold, and the lower-elevation form is more tolerant of the summer heat. This plant requires moderate to ample supplemental water, depending on the planting location. It performs best in partial shade or filtered sun, and in a soil that has been amended with some organic matter. It grows fast and needs little maintenance except for plucking spent flowers to encourage it to keep blooming. In the cities where winters are mild and summers are very hot, fall is the optimum planting season, and in areas with harsh winters, spring is the best planting season.

IDENTIFICATION: Large, golden yellow flowers easily identify golden columbine.

LANDSCAPE APPLICATION: Keep golden columbine in part shade or filtered sun with plants that require similar conditions. Use it as a color accent with other "green" plants that give a lush look to small spaces. Companion plants could range anywhere from traditional landscape plants to those that are more xeriphytic. Try companions as diverse as *Agave bovicornuta, Agave ocahui, Cycas revoluta, Dioon edule, Justicia spicigera, Heuchera sanguinea, Ruellia peninsularis,* and *Salvia greggii.*

PRECAUTIONS: Out in the open, a young, newly planted columbine is likely to be eaten by rabbits. Put it in your bustling mini-oasis or other enclosed space.

Asclepias linaria | Pine Leaf Milkweed

SMALL–MEDIUM SHRUB

SIZE (height x width)	2–3 feet x 2–3 feet
FLOWER COLOR	White

FLOWER SEASON	Spring–fall
EXPOSURE	Full or filtered sun, or part shade
WATER	Low–moderate
GROWTH RATE	Moderately fast
PRUNING	None
HARDINESS	Hardy to at least 15° F
NATURAL ELEVATION RANGE	1,500–9,000 feet
SUITABLE CITIES	All low- and mid-elevation-zone cities

FIELD NOTES: *Asclepias linaria* is found on dry, rocky slopes in southern Arizona south into the mountains of Mexico from 1,500 to 9,000 feet elevation. On a trip through the mountains of northwestern Mexico from Hermosillo to Basaseachic Falls we spotted a few of these shrubs growing along the side of the road. You can find them easily at mid-elevation in the Sky Island region in southeastern Arizona.

DESCRIPTION: This compact shrub has a rounded form and 3-foot-long herbaceous stems that are woody at the base. Its intriguing, 1-inch needlelike leaves set it apart from most shrubs of the region. It offers a bonus feature—clusters of white, butterfly-attracting flowers that appear from February through October. Individual blossoms are only about ¼ inch across, but clusters mass to 2 inches across. Flowering is followed by the deployment of inflated fruits that turn brown and papery upon maturity. These distinctive fruits are about 2 inches long, 1 inch wide, and they taper to a narrow tip.

CULTURE/MAINTENANCE: Pine leaf milkweed is hardy to at least 15° F, and low- to moderate-water-using. It stays happy if the root zone is thoroughly soaked every 7–14 days in the summer. Make sure the soil has good drainage; otherwise the roots have a tendency to rot. In warmer climates, plants installed on the north side of low walls will receive winter shade and some summer sun. The individual stems are moderately fast-growing, but the shrub is slow to fill in. Plants don't require pruning to shape them or keep them petite. If you can't resist pruning, be sure to cut the stem near the base, as only the buds near the cut will grow.

IDENTIFICATION: Its rounded shape, needlelike leaves, and clusters of pure white flowers easily distinguish *A. linaria*. *A. curassavica* has larger leaves and clusters of orange and red flowers. *A. subulata* has long, upright, nearly leafless stems with yellowish-white flowers.

LANDSCAPE APPLICATION: Use *A. linaria* as a minimalist shrub against a plain wall or out in the open and mixed with a variety of desert plants. It responds positively to life under small trees that give light shade, such as *Acacia willardiana, Bauhinia lunarioides* (syn. *B. congesta*), *Caesalpinia mexicana, Eysenhardtia orthocarpa,* and *Leucaena retusa*. It also mixes effectively with many accent plants, including all *Agave,* all *Dasylirion,* and all *Yucca* species. Group with other friendly small shrubs like *Dalea frutescens* and *Salvia greggii*. Queen and monarch butterflies feed on its leaves and flowers, while many other types of butterflies also use the flowers as a nectar source.

PRECAUTIONS: Although the plants are hardy to below 15° F, the tips may turn white when exposed to winter lows of 20° or less. This response may occur only on plants that are actively growing. Pine-leaf milkweed is just lush enough to work in small backyards, but take care not to place plants where stems may get broken as the milky sap will seep out and may be a nuisance.

Asclepias subulata | Desert Milkweed

MEDIUM SHRUB

SIZE (height x width)	3–5 feet x 3–4 feet
FLOWER COLOR	Creamy yellow
FLOWER SEASON	Spring–fall
EXPOSURE	Full or reflected sun
WATER	Drought-tolerant–low
GROWTH RATE	Moderate
HARDINESS	Hardy to at least low 20s F
PRUNING	None
NATURAL ELEVATION RANGE	< 3,000 feet
SUITABLE CITIES	All low- and mid-elevation-zone cities

FIELD NOTES: *Asclepias subulata* prefers dry washes and rocky slopes, plains, and mesas below 3,000 feet in southern Nevada, western Arizona, southeastern California, and northwestern Mexico.

DESCRIPTION: An abundance of 3–5-foot-tall, upright, wand-like, herbaceous stems creates visual appeal in any desert landscape. Linear-lanceolate leaves about 2 inches long by ⅛ inch wide appear on new growth but drop soon after. Clusters of attractive creamy yellow flowers appear at the tips of branches intermittently from spring until fall and are beloved by butterflies. Pairs of ornamental, horn-shaped seedpods that measure about 3 inches long by ¾ inch wide follow flowers. At maturity the

pods split to launch fluffy seeds into the wind.

CULTURE/MAINTENANCE: Desert milkweed loves summer heat and will tolerate winter temperatures down into the low 20s F for short periods. Watch for stem damage when those low-20s nighttime temperatures persist. The plant requires a fast-draining soil and is admirably tolerant of drought once established. It responds to supplemental summer water with new growth, but the soil should be allowed to dry out between doses. Place it only in full or reflected sun. It will take its time to achieve a full mature form—at least a few growing seasons.

IDENTIFICATION: *A. subulata* is easily recognized by its tall, wand-like, usually leafless stems, the distinctive pastel yellow flower clusters at the stem tips, and the unusual seedpods. Superficially it resembles *Euphorbia antisyphilitica*, which forms dense clusters of shorter, stiffer stems, small pale pink flowers scattered individually along the waxy stem, and small round seedpods.

LANDSCAPE APPLICATION: Desert milkweed's strong vertical lines qualify it as an eye-catching accent in any desert landscape. It mingles well with a broad range of heat-loving succulents, perennials, and small shrubs. Use singly or group plants in a simulated wash or among large boulders to naturalize the rockscape. Compatible succulents include *Agave, Dasylirion, Ferocactus, Opuntia,* and *Yucca* species and *Echinocactus grusonii.* It also complements other butterfly-attracting plants such as *Ageratum corymbosum, Aloysia gratissima, Asclepias linaria, Calliandra eriophylla, Conoclinium dissectum, Dalea frutescens, Lantana montevidensis, Lantana* x 'New Gold,' and *Verbena gooddingii.*

PRECAUTIONS: The plant oozes a rubber containing latex when wounded. Overwatering may result in death from root rot. Milkweed aphids are common and can look ugly but do little harm to the plant.

Baileya multiradiata | Desert Marigold

FLOWERING PERENNIAL

SIZE (height x width)	6–18 inches x 10–12 inches
FLOWER COLOR	Yellow
FLOWER SEASON	Spring–fall
EXPOSURE	Full sun
WATER	Drought-tolerant–low
GROWTH RATE	Fast
PRUNING	Shear off spent flower heads
HARDINESS	Hardy to at least 10° F
NATURAL ELEVATION RANGE	< 5,000 feet
SUITABLE CITIES	All low- and mid-elevation-zone cities; biennial to short-lived in high-elevation-zone cities

FIELD NOTES: Take a hike just about any place in the desert Southwest in the spring and *Baileya multiradiata* will surely be one of the most prevalent wildflowers you encounter. It grows as high as 5,000 feet and occurs on both sides of the Mexican border.

DESCRIPTION: This friendly but short-lived perennial has a cluster of leaves about 6–8 inches high. It can expand to 12–18 inches tall and 10–12 inches wide when in flower. Desert marigold spreads readily by seed and naturalizes. Bright yellow, daisy-like flowers top the tuft of fuzzy gray leaves primarily in spring and summer and bring in a plethora of butterflies as well as bees. Cheat a little on the moisture and flowering can occur nearly year-round, except during extreme drought or cold.

CULTURE/MAINTENANCE: Desert marigold is hardy to at least 10° F and quite drought-tolerant, surviving on as little as 4 inches of annual rainfall. However, it will flower longer if given a little supplemental water during spring and fall. It zooms to blooming size in only one year from seed. It should be planted in full sun and in native soil without organic amendments. Virtually no maintenance is required. Plant container-grown plants any time of the year, but sow your seeds in the fall.

IDENTIFICATION: *B. multiradiata* is too cute to be easily confused with any other plant.

LANDSCAPE APPLICATION: Desert marigold does fine as a spring- and summer-flowering perennial in the outer zone of a xeriscape, and even a small planting of this can provide a splash of color. It is happy with full sun and reflected heat exposures. You might scatter plants in a simulated wash or a cactus and succulent garden. In a natural landscape it mixes beautifully with other low-water-use plants such as *Agave* species, *Calliandra eriophylla*, *Dasylirion* species, *Ericameria laricifolia*, *Larrea divaricata*, *Melampodium leucanthum*, *Nolina* species, *Penstemon* species, *Psilostrophe cooperi*, *Sphaeralcea ambigua*, *Verbena gooddingii*, and *Yucca* species.

PRECAUTIONS: Rabbits and pack rats will probably eat young plants, so it may be necessary to cage individuals or a large planting area. Naturalized plants seem to be less susceptible to getting eaten. Go easy with the water as this plant rots out easily.

Bauhinia lunarioides | synonym: *Bauhinia congesta* | Chihuahuan Orchid Tree

LARGE SHRUB, SMALL TREE

SIZE (height x width)	15–18 feet x 10–15 feet
FLOWER COLOR	White, pink
FLOWER SEASON	Late spring–early summer
EXPOSURE	Full or reflected sun, or part shade
WATER	Drought-tolerant–moderate
GROWTH RATE	Slow–moderate
PRUNING	Spring, summer
HARDINESS	Hardy to at least 5° F
NATURAL ELEVATION RANGE	1,500–6,000 feet
SUITABLE CITIES	All low- and mid-elevation-zone cities

FIELD NOTES: While traipsing around in northeastern Mexico and taking photos of some attractive specimens of *Yucca rostrata*, I was delighted to come across the butterfly-like leaves of *Bauhinia lunarioides*. Seeing *Bauhinia lunarioides* in habitat and its rugged companion plants, I realized this tree is one tough customer. It is found mainly on rocky hills in **calcareous** soils in the states of Coahuila and Nuevo León, growing among desert scrub vegetation from about 1,500 to 6,000 feet elevation.

DESCRIPTION: This large shrub or small tree grows 15–18 feet tall and 10–15 feet wide. Deciduous leaves are **alternate** on the branches and composed of two 1-inch by 1-inch leaflets that look like butterfly wings. The crown is dense, with showy clusters of white or occasionally pink flowers appearing in spring, usually mid-March through May. Clusters are composed of 6–10 flowers with each butterfly-attracting flower measuring about 1 inch across. A 2-inch-long, woody pod forms after flowering.

CULTURE/MAINTENANCE: Chihuahuan orchid tree is hardy to at least 5° F provided you let the plant shut down in the fall. While it tolerates being planted on the east side of a building where it gets afternoon shade, for best results try full or reflected sun. Plants get by on 12 inches of annual rainfall once they have been fully established. However, they will grow faster and pump out more flowers if given supplemental water in spring and summer. Their growth rate is moderate, taking several years to reach 10 feet tall. Requiring very little maintenance, they can be left alone to grow as large shrubs or pruned to tree form.

IDENTIFICATION: Correctly called *Bauhinia lunarioides,* this plant is more widely known as *B. congesta* in the nursery trade. It is easily separated from its more famous cousins *B. variegata* and *B. forficata* by the smaller leaves and flowers. Also, if you grow *B. lunarioides* next to the other two and it gets a little too cold, it'll be the only one that comes back to life in the spring.

LANDSCAPE APPLICATION: This small, thornless patio tree is excellent in the mini-oasis. Sweeping leaf litter from hard surfaces such as brick or flagstone is an easy job for your kids. The trees mix gracefully with other mini-oasis favorites as well as hard-core desert plants. They share habitat in Mexico with *Fraxinus greggii, Leucophyllum frutescens, Vaquelinia* species and *Yucca rostrata.* A good mix of companion plants would include these natural neighbors as well as *Agave geminiflora, Agave ocahui, Agave schidigera, Ageratum corymbosum, Asclepias linaria, Asclepias subulata, Buddleja marrubiifolia, Conoclinium dissectum, Leucophyllum candidum, Salvia greggii, Salvia leucantha, Wedelia acapulcensis var. hispida,* and *Zephyranthes* species.

PRECAUTIONS: Young growth is susceptible to rabbit damage, so screen plants until the main trunks are past nibbling size. Although plants tolerate serious cold, they should still be weaned from supplemental water in fall and winter to harden off growth. Also, plants tend to be brittle and may split where trunks fork. Keep the tops of trees thinned to minimize the stress on the trunk.

Beaucarnea recurvata | Ponytail Palm

CACTUS/SUCCULENT

SIZE (height x width)	4–10 (or more) feet x 1–6 (or more) feet
FLOWER COLOR	Creamy white
FLOWER SEASON	Summer
EXPOSURE	Full or filtered sun, or part shade
WATER	Low–moderate
GROWTH RATE	Slow
PRUNING	None
HARDINESS	Hardy to the high 20s
NATURAL ELEVATION RANGE	1,000–1,500 feet
SUITABLE CITIES	In the ground in all low-elevation cities; warm microclimates in Tucson; potted plants in any zone with adequate winter protection

FIELD NOTES: Drive south out of Brownsville, Texas, through Ciudad Victoria, Tamaulipas, then on to Ciudad Mante on Mexico Highway 85, and your reward is a

view of king-size *Beaucarnea recurvata* poking out through the densely forested hillsides along the road. They are easiest to spot when in flower during the summer. Ponytail palm is native to densely forested habitats in Tamaulipas and Veracruz in eastern Mexico at low elevations, generally between 1,000 and 1,500 feet.

DESCRIPTION: A swollen base and long, drooping leaves make this a great in-ground accent plant in mild winter climates. The base of a young plant is rounded to slightly oblong, is exposed above the soil, and tapers sharply to a narrow trunk. The topknot fountain of rich green leaves that droop to the ground is right out of Dr. Seuss. Large, old specimens in mild coastal areas of southern California are 15–20 feet tall with a spread of about 10–12 feet. In the interior desert regions, where the winter nights can get colder, it reaches 8–10 feet tall, while large potted specimens that can be moved to avoid frost top out at 5–8 feet tall. Leaves range 1–3 feet long by ¾ inch wide. Minute teeth along the leaf edges make them razor sharp. Very old specimens may produce clusters of small white flowers. Plants are **dioecious**, meaning only female plants will produce seeds.

CULTURE/MAINTENANCE: Ponytail palm is generally considered half-hardy in the mid-elevation inland areas and hardy in the low, hot, interior desert regions and along coastal southern California. However, large, potted plants have survived winter temperatures of high 20s without damage. A potted plant takes its time growing a base about 1 foot across and trunk 4–5 feet tall. Grow it in a large, decorative container with a rich, fast-draining soil mix. Water and fertilize consistently to speed the growth rate some. Decrease watering and fertilizing frequency in the fall to induce dormancy for the winter. No pruning is required, but trim off old, dead leaves to expose the trunk. Young plants need light shade in the summer, while older plants can tolerate full sun. Plants accept full shade as long as watering frequency is reduced accordingly.

IDENTIFICATION: *B. recurvata* is sometimes placed in the genus *Nolina*. It is easily distinguished from other *Beaucarnea* species and *Nolina* species by its cartoony look—the combination of the smooth, oversize, swollen base and rich green, drooping leaves.

LANDSCAPE APPLICATION: *B. recurvata* needs to be the center of attention, so use it as a potted plant on a patio, near the front entry, or any other place it can be admired. In mild winter areas, plant as the focal point. The versatile plant can be mixed with either subtropicals or desert stalwarts. Try placing groupings of *Agave* species, *Echinocactus grusonii, Echinocereus,* or *Ferocactus* species with *B. recurvata.* Mix in some colorful perennials or small shrubs to give seasonal interest. Some striking combinations include *Chrysactinia mexicana, Justicia spicigera, Penstemon* species, *Poliomintha maderensis,* and *Salvia greggii.*

PRECAUTIONS: Although the plants will tolerate winter lows of low-20s F, they appreciate a blanket if the temperatures reach the low 20s two or three nights in a row or if they drop into the teens.

Berlandiera lyrata | Chocolate Flower

FLOWERING PERENNIAL

SIZE (height x width)   6–8 inches (14–18 inches with flowers) x 12–18 inches
FLOWER COLOR   Yellow-and-maroon

FLOWER SEASON	Spring–fall
EXPOSURE	Full, filtered, or reflected sun
WATER	Low–moderate
GROWTH RATE	Fast
PRUNING	Spring; deadheading as seed heads develop
HARDINESS	Hardy to at least 5° F
NATURAL ELEVATION RANGE	4,000–8,000 feet (unknown elevation in Kansas and Colorado)
SUITABLE CITIES	All cities in all zones

FIELD NOTES: One of the first field trips my wife and I took with our son was to the grasslands around Sonoita, Arizona, where we encountered *Berlandiera lyrata* in bloom along the roadside. We all smelled the delicious fragrance of the chocolate and decided right then and there that was one of our favorite plants. It occurs in Kansas, Colorado, Texas, New Mexico, and Arizona south into central Mexico on dry, rocky, limestone soils and roadsides in the grasslands. It is found at around 4,000–5,000 feet elevation in Arizona and Texas, up to 6,000 feet in New Mexico, and up to 8,000 feet in northern Mexico.

DESCRIPTION: The common name refers to the delicious fragrance of chocolate that emanates from the flowers. This low-growing perennial has medium green fiddle-shaped leaves that grow in a basal rosette 6–8 inches high by 12–18 inches across. Masses of yellow-and-maroon, daisy-like flowers appear in summer and fall, adding another 8–10 inches to the height. After the flowers have faded, brown seed heads develop from late summer through late fall.

CULTURE/MAINTENANCE: Chocolate flower is hardy to at least 5° and probably lower. The plant is low- to moderate-water-using, growing well with supplemental irrigation every 7–10 days. It grows best in full sun or reflected sun and will also tolerate filtered sun. Plants grow easily in just about any type of soil with adequate drainage. It is fast-growing and should be cut back in winter to develop a fuller plant. "Deadhead" flowers to encourage more blooms, but leave them to go to seed as a means of growing more plants.

IDENTIFICATION: The distinctive lobed, lyre-shaped, **basal** rosette of leaves, and the unusual chocolate-like fragrance of the flowers make this plant easy to identify.

LANDSCAPE APPLICATION: Place chocolate flower in full sun or filtered light in the mini-oasis or transition zone. It is effective up close because of the fragrance of the flowers, and it blends well with other transition zone plants. Install near a breakfast nook or patio where people will be eating outside in the early morning. What a perfect choice for a sensory garden! Chocolate flower is also at home in the outer zone with other drought-tolerant plants. Mass for the seasonal color and fragrance or to attract butterflies. Because of its size, it fits in well with large accent plants such as *Agave, Dasylirion, Hesperaloe, Nolina,* and *Yucca* species; and in the hot, interior low elevation, it likes a little shade from trees such as *Acacia constricta, Chilopsis linearis,* or *Eysenhardtia orthocarpa.* Use with other flowering perennials to create visual overload, like *Ageratum corymbosum, Conoclinium dissectum, Salvia farinacea, Thymophylla pentachaeta, Verbena gooddingii* and *Zinnia grandiflora.*

PRECAUTIONS: Initially, the plant may be munched on by rabbits and might need some protection. Take care not to water too much as the plants become leggy and top-heavy. In nutrient-poor soils and with minimal water, dense mounds can form.

Brahea armata | Mexican Blue Palm

PALM/CYCAD	
SIZE (height x width)	20–25 (rarely 40) feet x 8–12 feet
FLOWER COLOR	Creamy white
FLOWER SEASON	Spring–summer
EXPOSURE	Full or reflected sun, or part shade
WATER	Low–moderate
GROWTH RATE	Slow
PRUNING	Remove leaves, and flower and fruit stalks
HARDINESS	Hardy to at least high teens F
NATURAL ELEVATION RANGE	Near sea level to about 1,200 feet
SUITABLE CITIES	All low- and mid-elevation-zone cities

FIELD NOTES: *Brahea armata* hides out in desert and semidesert canyons in Baja California from near sea level to about 1,200 feet elevation. I've come across this blue beauty near Cataviñá, which is about halfway down the state of Baja California Norte.

DESCRIPTION: Full-grown *Brahea armata* creates a breathtaking sight with its robust size and striking color. This large, thick-trunked species that grows to 20–25 feet (rarely 40 feet) tall, with the crown spreading to 8–12 feet in diameter. The fan-

shaped, **glaucous**, bluish leaves are up to 6–9 feet long and 3–6 feet wide, and they hang persistently to form a protective skirt around the trunk for many years before eventually falling off. The 3–4-foot-long petioles are armed with vicious, hooked spines. In spring or summer, clusters of lightly fragrant, creamy yellow flowers weigh down spreading, 12–15-foot-long stalks.

CULTURE/MAINTENANCE: Known to be hardy to at least 18° F, Mexican blue palm is low- to moderate-water-using when established but grows best with supplemental water applied at regular but infrequent intervals. It needs many years to attain a substantial height but grows well in a variety of fast-draining soil types. There is no need to prune off old leaves—they protect the more tender growing tip of the palm from excessive heat and cold then drop naturally.

IDENTIFICATION: *B. armata* is one of only a few blue-leaf specials in cultivation. *Sabal uresana* stands apart with its long, curving leaf **midrib**. Other species of *Brahea* are harder to distinguish. *B. brandegeei* has a slimmer trunk, *B. edulis* has light green leaves, and *B. elegans* is smaller, slower growing, with gray-green leaves.

LANDSCAPE APPLICATION: Place plants in full sun, reflected sun, or on the west side of buildings where they will receive morning shade and get blasted in the afternoon. *B. armata* stands out as a single specimen, or groups nicely in a grove. It is a fitting plant for large open spaces such as parks and street medians. Its striking bluish foliage contrasts handsomely with either lush green plants or gray-toned desert vegetation. It can also sustain a subtropical mood, especially combined with ferny-looking characters like *Acacia berlandieri, Caesalpinia gilliesii,* and *Lysiloma watsonii* spp. *thornberi.*

PRECAUTIONS: Plant palms from containers in the spring or summer to give ample time for pre-frost establishment. Resist the urge to transplant from one spot to another. They need lots of sun and warmth in a soil with good drainage.

Buddleja marrubiifolia | Woolly Butterfly Bush

MEDIUM–LARGE SHRUB	
SIZE (height x width)	4–6 feet x 4–6 feet
FLOWER COLOR	Yellow, orange
FLOWER SEASON	Spring–fall
EXPOSURE	Full or reflected sun
WATER	Drought-tolerant–low
GROWTH RATE	Moderate
HARDINESS	Hardy to at least 5° F
PRUNING	None
NATURAL ELEVATION RANGE	1,800–3,800 feet
SUITABLE CITIES	All low- and mid-elevation-zone cities; Sierra Vista, Lordsburg, Las Cruces, El Paso. Rainfall is too high farther east in Texas.

FIELD NOTES: *Buddleja marrubiifolia* occurs on limestone ledges and slopes in canyons and arroyos, and along roadsides in New Mexico and western Texas south to central Mexico from 1,800 to 3,800 feet elevation. Find plants near Shafter, Texas, along the drive from Marfa, south towards the Rio Grande. It also shows up southeast of Redford, Texas, along State Route 170, which parallels the Rio Grande; and in Black Gap Refuge in the Big Bend region of western Texas.

DESCRIPTION: This medium-size shrub has an irregularly rounded form. Small, soft, gray leaves measure about 1 inch long and ½ inch wide. One-inch-diameter clusters of small flowers, debuting yellow then turning orange, appear from spring through fall and attract several species of butterflies.

CULTURE/MAINTENANCE: *B. marrubiifolia* is hardy to at least 5° F and can survive on 12 inches or less of annual rainfall. The moderate growth rate accelerates if plants are given occasional drinks in the summer. Plant it in full or reflected sun and in

a soil with excellent drainage. Roots rebel and rot if they are exposed to standing water. Virtually no maintenance or pruning is required.

IDENTIFICATION: *B. marrubiifolia* is very easily distinguished from *B. davidii* by its clusters of tiny orange flowers as opposed to elongated spikes of purple, blue, pink, or white flowers. *B. alternifolia* is a large shrub or small tree. Also, both *B. alternifolia* and *B. davidii* are deciduous while *B. marrubiifolia* holds on to its leaves.

LANDSCAPE APPLICATION: Gentle slopes or raised areas are ideal for keeping roots drier. Mass plant and use as an informal hedge or group with bold accent plants such as *Dasylirion, Hesperaloe, Nolina* and *Yucca* species. Because of its drought tolerance, *B. marrubiifolia* is compatible with a variety of cacti and catches attention when mixed with *Echinocactus grusonii, Ferocactus* species and *Opuntia* species. It shines when mixed with tough, beautiful native shrubs such as *Calliandra californica, Dalea frutescens, Leucophyllum* species, *Salvia greggii, Sophora secundiflora,* and *Vauquelinia californica.*

PRECAUTIONS: Plants go dormant in the winter and need to be kept dry in order to prevent the roots from rotting. Plant in a fast-draining soil to reduce the potential for root rot and avoid low areas or depressions unless the soil is sandy or very well drained.

Bulbine frutescens | Shrubby Bulbine

SMALL SHRUB,
CACTI & SUCCULENTS

SIZE (height x width)	2 feet x 3–4 feet ('Hallmark' and 'Tiny Tangerine' are smaller)
FLOWER COLOR	Yellow, Yellow-and-orange ('Hallmark' and 'Tiny Tangerine')
FLOWER SEASON	Winter–spring
EXPOSURE	Full or reflected sun
WATER	Low–moderate
GROWTH RATE	Fast
PRUNING	Occasional thinning
HARDINESS	Hardy to low teens F
NATURAL ELEVATION RANGE	Near sea level–3,000 feet
SUITABLE CITIES	All low- and mid-elevation-zone cities; Sierra Vista in high-elevation zone

FIELD NOTES: Once upon a time in the Groot Swartberg Mountains in South Africa, while photographing an intriguing bulb called *Boophone disticha* on a dry, rocky slope, we happened upon a lonely, flowering *Bulbine frutescens.* The species is native to dry areas throughout South Africa from near sea level to 3,000 feet elevation.

DESCRIPTION: This low, wide-spreading, shrubby plant has thick fleshy leaves. The mass of leaves and stems forms clumps to about 2 feet tall and 3–4 feet across. In late winter and spring 12–18-inch-long flower spikes decorate the plants. Yellow flowers top the most common type, while the cultivars, 'Hallmark' and 'Tiny Tangerine,' sport two-tone orange-and-yellow flowers.

CULTURE/MAINTENANCE: Plants are hardy to about the low teens F although there may be some leaf damage in an extended hard frost. New leaves quickly replace damaged foliage in the spring. Succulent leaves equip *B. frutescens* to withstand long periods of drought. They are fast-growing and fill out quickly, especially in soil with good drainage. Prune only occasionally when stems get top-heavy.

IDENTIFICATION: The common form has solid yellow flowers. More compact cultivars 'Hallmark' and 'Tiny Tangerine' have orange petals instead of the usual yellow.

LANDSCAPE APPLICATION: Use shrubby bulbine for the seasonal color in full or reflected sun. It combines naturally with other succulents in a cactus garden or a rock garden. It dresses up pool areas, raised planters, or tight planting spaces along sidewalks or entryways, as well as open slopes. Southwestern native trees such as *Acacia, Parkinsonia,* and *Prosopis* species are comfortable mixing with this South African bulb, as are perennials and shrublets from the region such as *Conoclinium dissectum, Dalea capitata, Justicia candicans, Hibiscus coulteri, Wedelia acapulcensis* var. *hispida,* and *Zauschneria californica.*

PRECAUTIONS: Be careful not to overwater, especially in fall and winter.

Caesalpinia gilliesii | Yellow Bird of Paradise

MEDIUM–LARGE SHRUB	
SIZE (height x width)	6–10 feet x 6–8 feet
FLOWER COLOR	Yellow petals, red stamens
FLOWER SEASON	Spring–fall
EXPOSURE	Full sun
WATER	Drought-tolerant–low
GROWTH RATE	Moderate–fast
PRUNING	To grow as a tree
HARDINESS	Hardy to at least 0° F

NATURAL ELEVATION RANGE   Near sea level–6,000 feet (nearing 9,000 feet closer to the
                            equator in Bolivia)

SUITABLE CITIES   All low- and mid-elevation-zone cities; Sierra Vista in high-
                            elevation zone

FIELD NOTES: *Caesalpinia gilliesii* is native to Argentina, but has naturalized in parts of Mexico and the southwestern United States. The occasional escaped plant is spotted while driving through the grasslands of southeastern Arizona from Benson south towards the border with Mexico.

DESCRIPTION: This striking shrub has a graceful, fern-like appearance. It produces a glorious display of yellow flowers with long, red **stamens** from spring until fall. Explosively dehiscent seedpods replace the flowers. The plant has few main stems; this eases training it as a very small tree that is great for growing cacti and succulents underneath, though it does not get large enough to utilize as a shade tree for people or vehicles. Twice pinnate, "ferny" leaves are composed of up to 14 pairs of **pinna**, and each of these is divided into about 10 pairs of leaflets.

CULTURE/MAINTENANCE: *C. gilliesii* is hardy to at least 0° F and possibly lower as plants have been found naturalizing in cold spots with adequate moisture in southeastern Arizona. The growth rate is considered fast, although the plant is slow to fill out completely. Though drought-tolerant, it grows faster and flowers more profusely when given supplemental water once every 7–10 days. This plant is comfortable as a shrub or pruned as a small tree. Self-scattering seeds will naturalize with sufficient moisture.

IDENTIFICATION: *C. gilliesii* is distinguished from all other *Caesalpinia* species by the combination of large yellow flowers and long, red stamens.

LANDSCAPE APPLICATION: Plant singly as a color accent or massed for an extremely colorful display from spring through fall. Plant it with bold accents such as *Agave* and *Dasylirion* species, *Fouquieria splendens*, and *Hesperaloe*, *Nolina*, and *Yucca* species. Mix with other drought-tolerant characters with contrasting flower colors

such as *Calliandra*, *Dalea*, and *Leucophyllum* species, and *Salvia greggii*, *Sophora secundiflora*, and *Vauquelinia californica*.

PRECAUTIONS: Many seeds germinate readily with the right moisture and temperature conditions. Pods could be removed to reduce the seeding potential. Mix with plants that look good through the winter, since *C. gilliesii* foliage becomes sparse in cold. It is known to have naturalized in parts of Texas and southeastern Arizona where rainfall is higher than in the desert proper. It also occasionally pops up in desert landscapes, but the threat of it taking over is minimal.

Caesalpinia mexicana | Mexican Bird of Paradise

LARGE SHRUB, SMALL TREE	
SIZE (height x width)	15 feet x 10 feet
FLOWER COLOR	Yellow
FLOWER SEASON	Spring–fall
EXPOSURE	Full or reflected sun
WATER	Drought-tolerant–moderate
GROWTH RATE	Moderate–fast
PRUNING	Prune to shape as a tree
HARDINESS	Hardy to at least the high teens F
NATURAL ELEVATION RANGE	20–6,500 feet
SUITABLE CITIES	All low- and mid-elevation-zone cities

FIELD NOTES: *Caesalpinia mexicana* can be found at low elevations in subtropical short-tree forests in the western Mexican states of Sinaloa, Nayarit, and Jalisco, and at low to high elevations in the eastern Mexican states from Nuevo León and Tamaulipas, south to Querétaro and Hidalgo. When driving through the mountains from Ciudad Victoria in Tamaulipas south to the famed cactus area near Jaumave, one might spot these beautiful plants with their sprays of bright yellow flowers.

DESCRIPTION: This *Caesalpinia* grows as a large shrub or small tree in its native Mexico. Under cultivation, it strives to be a 15–foot tree with a canopy spread of about 10 feet across. You'll want to pick one main trunk with two or three runners up to give the tree its shape. Twice-pinnate leaves are evergreen and divided into rounded leaflets. Long racemes of small, yellow flowers occur at the ends of stems and draw attention from spring through fall. The plant will be covered with blossoms, then sit sadly flowerless while pods develop. The yellowish-tan pods mature and dehisce, vegetative growth occurs, and then flowers again appear. The process repeats several times throughout the year.

CULTURE/MAINTENANCE: Although of subtropical origin, *C. mexicana* has pulled through winter lows of high teens without damage. The plant should be hardened off in the fall to reduce the effects of severe frost. The plant survives on little water but will grow faster and flower more profusely when given regular, supplemental drinks from spring until fall. Water every 1–2 weeks encourages it to keep pumping out the flowers. Plant it in full sun or reflected heat on the south or west side of a building. If you lose your loppers, the plant will stay shrubby longer but eventually grow into a small tree.

IDENTIFICATION: *C. mexicana* is distinguished from *C. gilliesii* and *C. pulcherrima* by growth habit and flowers. You can coax *C. mexicana* into being a small tree more easily. Also, it has smaller flowers that resemble those of palo verde more than they do the flowers of its two cousins.

LANDSCAPE APPLICATION: Use *C. mexicana* as a shrub or small tree with other drought-tolerant landscape plants in the transition and outer zones of a xeriscape. Mix with bold succulents such as any *Agave, Dasylirion, Hesperaloe, Nolina,* and *Yucca* species or *Fouquieria splendens.* Make it the big shot and plant with smaller shrubs such as *Chrysactinia mexicana, Dalea* species, *Justicia spicigera, Leucophyllum candidum, Poliomintha maderensis, Salvia greggii,* and *Salvia leucantha.*

PRECAUTIONS: Beware of the explosively dehiscent seedpods and keep plants away from high-traffic areas.

Caesalpinia pulcherrima | Red Bird of Paradise

MEDIUM–LARGE SHRUB

SIZE (height x width)	4–6 feet (or more) x 4–6 feet (or more)
FLOWER COLOR	Orange-red, yellow (cv. 'Phoenix')
FLOWER SEASON	Summer–fall
EXPOSURE	Full or reflected sun
WATER	Drought-tolerant–moderate
GROWTH RATE	Fast
PRUNING	Shear to 6–12 inches above ground level in late winter or early spring to make dense and bushy.
HARDINESS	Hardy to about 30° F, stem damage at the high 20s F, freezes to ground at high teens
NATURAL ELEVATION RANGE	Near sea level in the Caribbean
SUITABLE CITIES	Top-hardy in low-elevation-zone cities and root-hardy in mid-elevation-zone cities

FIELD NOTES: *Caesalpinia pulcherrima* comes from the tropical West Indies in the Caribbean. It has escaped in parts of Mexico but so far does not appear to pose a threat to the southwestern United States. Occasionally plants show up along the roadside scattered throughout the thorn forest along Mexico Highway 16 from Hermosillo, Sonora, east to the Basaseachic Falls in Chihuahua.

DESCRIPTION: Fern-like foliage gives a wonderful, subtropical feel, and clusters of brilliant orange-red flowers build on that effect. In frost-free areas, this shrub grows quickly to 6–8 feet tall and 6–12 feet across. 6–8-inch-long clusters of the butterfly- and hummingbird-attracting flowers top the plant from summer until frost. A pure yellow flowered form is being sold as cultivar 'Phoenix.' Its flowers are smaller than the 1½-inch-wide blossoms on the typical orange-red flowered form but occur in an irresistible profusion. Showy flowers morph into dark pods that explode when ripe, catapulting seeds 20 feet away.

CULTURE/MAINTENANCE: This shrub experiences major stem damage below 30° F. However, it has a fast growth rate, attaining its mature size quickly in one growing season. It is drought-tolerant but will bloom more profusely if given weekly supplemental water in summer. It is easy to grow in the landscape, tolerating nearly all soil types and a wide range of watering schedules. For maximum flower production, place it in full sun and provide summer irrigation. In areas that occasionally receive frost, the plant should be cut back to about 6–12 inches above the ground in late winter or early spring.

IDENTIFICATION: The orange-red flowers are quite distinctive. *C. gilliesii* has yellow flowers with long red stamens which distinguish it from the yellow-flowered form of *C. pulcherrima*. *C. mexicana* has elongated racemes of small yellow flowers. *C. cacalaco* has thorny branches and trunks.

LANDSCAPE APPLICATION: *C. pulcherrima* is right at home in the mini-oasis with lush, subtropical-looking plants. It works in an outer zone with more xeric plants as long as adequate water is applied in summer. It looks great in combination with accent plants including various large cacti such as *Carnegiea gigantea*. It contrasts beautifully with *Agave, Dasylirion, Fouquieria, Nolina,* and *Yucca* species. For maximum flower production, place it in full or reflected sun. Massing or combining the yellow-flowered cultivar 'Phoenix' with the standard red-flowered form creates an incredible display of flowers in summer and fall.

PRECAUTIONS: Aside from freezing back in the winter, this shrub does not seem to have any real disadvantages. After it freezes back, it should be cut back nearly to ground level in late winter or early spring. Very young plants can experience some rabbit damage, but more mature plants are not bothered.

Callaeum macropterum | synonym: *Mascagnia macroptera* | Yellow Orchid Vine, Butterfly Vine

VINE

SIZE (height x width)	Stems grow longer than 20 feet
FLOWER COLOR	Yellow
FLOWER SEASON	Spring–summer, occasionally fall
EXPOSURE	Full or reflected sun, or partial shade
WATER	Thorough soaking twice a month in summer
GROWTH RATE	Fast
PRUNING	Cut out frozen stems in spring
HARDINESS	Half-hardy (mid-20s F)
NATURAL ELEVATION RANGE	50–5,000 feet
SUITABLE CITIES	All low-elevation cities; Tucson in mid-elevation zone

FIELD NOTES: *Callaeum macropterum* grows mixed in with tropical and subtropical vegetation along washes and on hillsides and sandy flats from central Sonora and Baja California, east and south throughout much of Mexico from near sea level to about 5,000 feet elevation. On a recent trip into the Sierra Madre Occidental in central Sonora, I saw plants growing along the roadside, trailing along the ground, and scrambling up other plants. Flowering was just about finished at the end of May, and the winged seedpods were still green and translucent.

DESCRIPTION: Plants climb by twining stems and, with support, can reach as much as 20 feet long. Without support, plants tend to become more shrub-like, reaching 4–6 feet tall and 6 feet or more across. The medium green leaves are about 2 inches long and ½ inch wide. Blossoms resemble orchids, and clusters of these flowers appear in the spring (if plants were not frozen the previous winter), summer, and sometimes fall. Butterfly-attracting flowers are followed by 3-inch-wide, 3-winged seedpods that look like butterfly wings.

CULTURE/MAINTENANCE: Plants are hardy to the mid-20s F, suffering twig damage in the low 20s or high teens F. They will recover very quickly from any frost damage. They need little water but respond to watering in spring and summer, and grow happily in full sun, reflected sun, or partial shade, although flower production cranks up with more sun. Not particular about soil type, they grow fine in native, unamended soil. Cleaning up the winged fruit and cutting out dead parts in winter take care of maintenance chores.

IDENTIFICATION: *C. macropterum* used to be known as *Mascagnia macroptera* and is still sometimes sold under that name. *Mascagnia lilacina* is similar, but it has blue-purple flowers and has been allowed to keep its name. The five-petaled flowers and large, three-winged fruits are quite distinctive from other vines.

LANDSCAPE APPLICATION: Let it sprawl over a trellis or similar support to shade southern and western exposures. Try it in both the mini-oasis or transition zones. Because of its fast growth and twining habit, *C. macropterum* can be used to cover a chain-link fence, abandoned car, or other unsightly feature. An unsupported plant will twine upon itself and form a large, scrambling shrub that blends well in simulated washes or natural, Sonoran Desert landscapes. If planted near a tree, this vine will find it, climb it, and possibly overtake it.

PRECAUTIONS: Tender new shoots might get eaten by rabbits, but older, woodier stems wrap themselves tightly around a support and become too much trouble for wildlife. Aside from occasional frost damage, there do not seem to be any major disadvantages.

Calliandra californica | Baja Fairy Duster

MEDIUM–LARGE SHRUB	
SIZE (height x width)	5–7 feet x 5–7 feet
FLOWER COLOR	Red
FLOWER SEASON	All year
EXPOSURE	Filtered, reflected, or full sun
WATER	Drought-tolerant–moderate
GROWTH RATE	Moderate–fast
PRUNING	Prune hard after frost, pinch seedpods as they develop.
HARDINESS	Hardy to the low 20s F, stem damage at the high teens F

NATURAL ELEVATION RANGE   Near sea level–4,600 feet

SUITABLE CITIES   All low-elevation-zone cities; warm spots in mid-elevation-zone cities

FIELD NOTES: My first encounter with *Calliandra californica* came in October 1983. We were botanizing in Baja California and made a stop about a third of the way down the peninsula. I was scrambling around on large boulders looking at everything in sight, and I stumbled upon the 2–3-foot-tall shrubs in full blooming glory. Plants are found in dry washes and gravelly flats as well as rocky, bouldery hills throughout much of Baja California from near sea level to 4,600 feet elevation. It is interesting to note that in habitat, these plants rarely get as large as 3 feet tall, while in cultivation they can easily reach 5–7 feet.

DESCRIPTION: This shrub's dark green, twice-divided leaves are about 2 inches long and give it a lush, almost tropical feel. Long, bright red stamens are the showy part of the flower. Flowering season varies with the winter temperatures. If plants are frozen, flowering is delayed until late spring through fall. If not frozen, they will flower through winter and spring, slow down for summer (unless watered regularly), then resume massive blooming in the fall. When in full bloom, the brilliant red stamens attract both butterflies and hummingbirds.

CULTURE/MAINTENANCE: Plant Baja fairy duster in full, filtered, or reflected sun. Though drought-tolerant, it will grow and flower more if given supplemental water in summer, and it can be tempted to bloom nearly throughout the year if watered from spring through fall. Taper off watering later in the fall and winter to harden off growth. You'll be sacrificing flowering for surviving temperatures into the mid or low 20s F. Ample supplemental water encourages fast growth. If plants are frozen, they should be cut back prior to putting out new growth in the spring. They go through cycles of blooming, then seed production. To increase flower production, try snipping off the young seedpods.

IDENTIFICATION: Three species of *Calliandra* are currently in cultivation. Baja fairy duster is easily distinguished from our native *Calliandra eriophylla* by its brilliant red stamens compared to the white to pink stamens of our native species. *C. peninsularis* is harder to distinguish. *C. californica* leaves have fewer primary divisions and fewer leaflets per primary division than *C. peninsularis*, which appears more lush.

LANDSCAPE APPLICATION: This can be used as a medium-size shrub in all zones of a xeriscape. It will survive winters more happily if given a warm, protected location. It does extremely well in the mini-oasis. The moderate to thick density can create a low, informal screening. It blends well with cactus and other semisucculent plants such as *Agave, Dasylirion,* and *Yucca* species. It also makes ground covers, low or upright shrubs, and small trees look good. Some suggested companions include *Dalea capitata, Dalea frutescens, Eysenhardtia orthocarpa,* and *Leucaena retusa.* Baja fairy duster attracts hummingbirds and butterflies. According to butterfly expert Jim Brock, the Marine and Ceranus Blue butterflies lay their eggs near a budding inflorescence, and the caterpillars eat the flowers. Ants tend the small slug-like caterpillars.

PRECAUTIONS: Young, newly planted shrubs may be susceptible to rabbit damage. Older, more established plants are not.

Calliandra eriophylla | Fairy Duster

SMALL–MEDIUM SHRUB	
SIZE (height x width)	2–3 feet x 2–4 feet
FLOWER COLOR	White to shades of pink
FLOWER SEASON	Heaviest in spring, occasionally in summer or fall
EXPOSURE	Full or reflected sun
WATER	Drought-tolerant–moderate
GROWTH RATE	Moderate
PRUNING	None, or shear once in summer to make more compact
HARDINESS	Hardy to at least 10° F
NATURAL ELEVATION RANGE	Below 5,000 feet
SUITABLE CITIES	All low- and mid-elevation-zone cities; Sierra Vista in high-elevation zone

FIELD NOTES: When covered with the flowers that give it its common name, *Calliandra eriophylla* is one of the more easily recognizable plants seen on late winter hikes in the desert around Tucson. Plants are found on dry, gravelly slopes and mesas from southeastern California to western Texas and northern Mexico below 5,000 feet.

DESCRIPTION: This deciduous shrub has finely divided leaves measuring about 1½ inch long and wide, which are composed of 1–7 pairs of pinnae, with 5–15 pairs of leaflets per pinnae. This arrangement gives the plant a fern-like appearance. Fairy duster can be quite spectacular when in full bloom. Clusters of white or pink, hummingbird- and butterfly-attracting flowers appear in the spring and sometimes again in the summer or fall. Deep pink flowers seem to be the most desirable, and growers continue to select plants with more intense flower color.

CULTURE/MAINTENANCE: Fairy duster is hardy to at least 10° F and probably lower. It is extremely drought-tolerant, surviving and growing on less than 11 inches of annual rainfall. However, it will have a more lush appearance, bloom better, and grow faster with supplemental water in the spring and summer. Place it in full sun for the best appearance, as it tends to get a little leggy in the shade. It may require occasional pruning to encourage a full, dense form, especially if given supplemental water.

IDENTIFICATION: Currently, *C. eriophylla* can be separated from *C. californica* and *C. peninsularis* by the white or pink flowers of the former and the red flowers of the latter two. However, plant breeders working overtime to develop hybrids with red flowers and greater cold-hardiness may someday make it difficult to separate these three species.

LANDSCAPE APPLICATION: Rely on fairy duster for spring color. It is very effective when massed and can be used as an informal low border. It is very tolerant of reflected heat and has a great reputation as a median and roadway planting. It complements other seriously drought-tolerant species because of appearance and water com-

patibility. Good companions include *Dalea frutescens, Dasylirion* species, *Encelia farinosa, Hesperaloe funifera, Leucophyllum laevigatum, Salvia greggii, Scutellaria suffrutescens,* and *Yucca* species.

PRECAUTIONS: Soft, lush foliage may be attractive to rabbits and deer. Older, established plants that are not irrigated and fertilized heavily are less likely to be browsed.

Calliandra x 'Sierra Starr' | Sierra Starr Fairy Duster

MEDIUM SHRUB	
SIZE (height x width)	4–5 feet x 4–5 feet
FLOWER COLOR	Bright red
FLOWER SEASON	Nearly year-round
EXPOSURE	Full or reflected sun

WATER	Low–moderate
GROWTH RATE	Moderately fast
PRUNING	Shear once in spring if frozen or to make more compact
HARDINESS	Hardy to at least low 20s F
NATURAL ELEVATION RANGE	Not applicable
SUITABLE CITIES	All low- and mid-elevation-zone cities

FIELD NOTES: This is a manmade cross between *Calliandra californica* and *Calliandra eriophylla,* combining the best traits of both parents.

DESCRIPTION: This medium-size, semievergreen shrub has a dense, uniform growth habit. Bright red, butterfly- and hummingbird-attracting flowers can appear nearly year-round. Finely divided, dark green leaves give a fern-like look and texture.

CULTURE/MAINTENANCE: Stems can incur frost damage when temperatures hit the high teens F, while the plant will grow back from roots if frozen to the ground. This hybrid uses little water and grows moderately fast, but it will flower more profusely with extra water in the spring and summer. Place it in full sun for the best appearance, as it tends to get leggy in the shade. Shearing once a year can keep it thriving, especially if it suffers some frost damage.

IDENTIFICATION: *Calliandra* x 'Sierra Starr' is very similar to *Calliandra californica* but has denser branching.

LANDSCAPE APPLICATION: Use 'Sierra Starr' for a splash of color and its knack for bringing in hummingbirds in any low-water-use landscape in the low- and mid-elevation zones. It is very effective when massed and can be used as an informal low border. Tolerant of reflected heat, it serves willingly as a median and roadway plant. It blends well with other smart plants, like *Dalea frutescens, Dasylirion* species, *Encelia farinosa, Hesperaloe funifera, Leucophyllum laevigatum, Salvia greggii,* and *Yucca* species.

PRECAUTIONS: Soft, lush foliage may be attractive to rabbits and deer. Older, established plants that are not irrigated and fertilized heavily are less likely to be browsed.

Calylophus hartwegii | Sundrops

GROUND COVER,
FLOWERING PERENNIAL

SIZE (height x width)	2 feet x 3 feet
FLOWER COLOR	Lemon yellow
FLOWER SEASON	Spring (best)–fall
EXPOSURE	Full or filtered sun
WATER	Low–moderate
GROWTH RATE	Fast
PRUNING	Shear in late winter
HARDINESS	Root-hardy to at least 0° F
NATURAL ELEVATION RANGE	4,500–7,500 feet
SUITABLE CITIES	All cities in all zones

FIELD NOTES: Home for *Calylophus hartwegii* is grasslands from Kansas and Oklahoma, west to southeastern Arizona, and south to the highlands of central Mexico generally from about 4,500 to 7,500 feet. See these beauties along Arizona state highway 82 from Sonoita east towards Tombstone.

DESCRIPTION: This low-growing, sprawling subshrub forms a mound to nearly 2 feet tall by 3 feet wide. Stems are woody at the base and herbaceous above. Bright green, linear leaves measure up to 2 inches long and ½ inch wide. Large, lemon-yellow flowers up to 2 inches across are freely produced throughout spring, blanketing the plant with color. *C. hartwegii* cranks out flowers through summer but produces smaller blossoms during the peak of the heat.

CULTURE/MAINTENANCE: *C. hartwegii* is hardy to 0° F. Cut back to nearly ground level in winter to rejuvenate plants and keep them dense. This plant grows fast and hits full size each year even after seasonal shearing. Plants are low- to moderate-water-using and thrive in a soil with excellent drainage. They will grow and flower best if given consistent irrigation in spring and summer. Plants tolerate different soil types,

but monitor watering carefully in a heavy soil. Grow them in full sun or very light filtered sun for most bountiful blooming.

IDENTIFICATION: Narrow leaves and semishrubby growth habit separate *Calylophus* from its cultivated cousins *Oenothera*.

LANDSCAPE APPLICATION: Use *C. hartwegii* in a cactus and succulent garden in combination with various *Agave* species, *Echinocactus grusonii, Ferocactus* species, and *Hesperaloe funifera.* Its cheerful yellow flowers add interest at the base of tall succulent or semisucculent plants such as *Yucca elata, Y. rigida,* and *Y. rostrata.* It is also compatible with evergreen shrubs like *Dalea pulchra, Penstemon baccharifolius,* and *Salvia greggii.* It tucks nicely into small spaces such as planter boxes or narrow entryways.

PRECAUTIONS: A young plant may be susceptible to rabbit damage, but it becomes less tasty as it matures. Try it in the mini-oasis where rabbit traffic and damage are not as common. A member of the evening primrose family, it may be susceptible to aphids and possibly flea beetles.

Carnegiea gigantea | Saguaro

CACTUS/SUCCULENT

SIZE (height x width)	40 feet x 15 feet
FLOWER COLOR	White
FLOWER SEASON	May–June
EXPOSURE	Light shade when young, full sun when older
WATER	Drought-tolerant–low
GROWTH RATE	Slow
HARDINESS	Hardy
PRUNING	None
NATURAL ELEVATION RANGE	0–4,500 feet
SUITABLE CITIES	Hot, interior low-elevation-zone cities; Tucson in mid-elevation zone

FIELD NOTES: Take a hike anywhere in the Sonoran Desert and you are likely to encounter a majestic saguaro cactus, an easily recognized icon that frequents rocky hillsides and outwash slopes below 3,500 feet. Its late-spring bloom is Arizona's state flower. Gila woodpeckers and gilded flickers will peck holes into a plant and use them as homes for their babies. If you're lucky, you might see an elf owl later using the same holes.

DESCRIPTION: This tall, stately columnar species grows slowly to a height of 40 feet or more. Branches that remind us of arms emerge 6 feet or more above the ground on older, mature specimens. The main stem can reach 18 inches in diameter and has vertical ribs that allow for expansion and contraction as determined by available water. Large, white, funnel-shaped flowers are 2–3 inches across and appear in May and June. These are followed by 3–4-inch-long fruits that, upon ripening, turn red or purplish and split open, revealing the bright red, edible fleshy portion. Human desert dwellers have harvested these fruits for centuries.

CULTURE/MAINTENANCE: This warm desert species' hardiness varies with age. Temperatures in the low 20s F can wipe out seedlings, while older plants can withstand the high teens F. Plants grow best in full sun or light shade and a soil with good drainage. When planting a saguaro, mark the south side, and preserve the original orientation to prevent sunburn on the more tender side. Please note that it is illegal to dig up and move a native plant without the proper authorization and corresponding plant tag purchased from Arizona Department of Agriculture. However, some nurseries raise plants from seed, and you can buy and plant these saguaros without tags. Although wild plants are drought-tolerant (growing on less than 12 inches annual rainfall), young transplants will benefit from receiving supplemental water once a month from late spring until the end of summer. Do not provide supplemental water in fall and winter. Older, well-established plants will survive on rainfall alone. *C. gigantea* grows very slowly, averaging 1⁄16 inch per year as a seedling, then up to 4–6 inches per year when it reaches about 10–12 feet tall. It takes 30–35 years to reach flowering size, with branches starting to form after that. No maintenance is required except clearing a path for your walker in later years so you can get close enough to admire it.

IDENTIFICATION: *C. gigantea* is a famous symbol of the Sonoran Desert. Only *Trichocereus terscheckii* from Argentina might be confused with it. *Pachycereus pringlei* and *Pachycereus pectin-aboriginum* are Sonoran Desert natives that, as young plants, resemble *C. gigantea*. Neither *Pachycereus* species is very common in horticulture.

LANDSCAPE APPLICATION: Use saguaro as a focal point in a low-water-use or desert landscape. It looks beautiful with all *Agave, Dasylirion, Hesperaloe, Nolina,* and *Yucca* species. Some compatible "leafy" plants include various *Caesalpinia, Dalea,* and

Leucophyllum species, and *Prosopis velutina, Sophora secundiflora,* and *Verbena gooddingii.*

PRECAUTIONS: Beware of overwatering. Plants, especially older ones, are susceptible to bacterial rot. By the time the black, ill-smelling liquid registers, it is generally too late to save the plant. Several nurseries are field-growing this cactus, so the need for transplanting from the wild is greatly diminished. Current thought is that young plants (spears of 6–8 feet or less) transplant more easily than larger, more mature specimens (especially those with arms). Transplants have been known to fake it for 2–3 years before they finally use all their reserves and die.

Chilopsis linearis | Desert Willow

SMALL–MEDIUM TREE	
SIZE (height x width)	20–30 feet x 20–30 feet
FLOWER COLOR	Light pink to deep purple, sometimes white
FLOWER SEASON	Late spring–fall
EXPOSURE	Full sun
WATER	Low–moderate, best with extra water in summer
GROWTH RATE	Moderate
PRUNING	Train to tree form, remove seedpods
HARDINESS	Hardy to at least -10° F
NATURAL ELEVATION RANGE	2,000–6,000 feet
SUITABLE CITIES	All cities in all zones

FIELD NOTES: *Chilopsis linearis* is native throughout the southwestern United States and northern Mexico including Baja California. Plants are generally found along arroyos, washes, and roadsides from 2,000 to 6,000 feet elevation. In habitat, they are usually seen as large shrubs. They are easily spotted along the roadside around Tucson. In fact, the first test of my identification skills after a plant materials class at the University of Arizona was on a desert willow sprig brought to me by a coworker at the drugstore where I worked to pay my way through college.

DESCRIPTION: Under cultivation, desert willow is easily grown as a medium-size, deciduous tree reaching 12–25 feet tall and nearly as wide. The common name is derived from the long, thin leaves that hang down and resemble a true willow. There is something miraculous about the blossoms that begin to appear at the driest time of year. The bloom can continue through late spring, summer, and even early fall. Flower color varies from white to pale pinkish-lavender to even deep, rich purple. Although attractive, the darker flower color seems to get lost in the mass of green leaves. Long, slender, tan-colored seedpods follow the flowers and can remain on the plant throughout the winter while the leaves drop. Large, funnel-shaped flowers are quite showy when the plant is in full flower, while the crooked, angular main trunk gives the tree a sculptural quality in any landscape.

CULTURE/MAINTENANCE: Desert willow is hardy to at least -10° F. In nature, it is generally restricted to dry washes, roadsides, and other areas where excess moisture

collects; thus in your yard it will benefit from regular dousing from spring until early fall. New growth is susceptible to frost damage, so it is best to stop watering in early fall. It prefers a soil with good drainage. It will look its best and flower most profusely when grown in full sun or reflected sun, although the plant will tolerate some afternoon shade and can survive along the east side of a building. The growth rate is moderate to fast depending upon the amount of water it receives. In a manicured landscape, this is a high-maintenance tree. It produces suckers that need to be pruned, and its countless pods and seeds produce a glut of seedlings wherever there is enough moisture.

IDENTIFICATION: Flowers and seedpods readily identify *C. linearis*. There are several cultivars being grown; 'Barranco' (pink flowers), 'Burgundy' (deep purplish-red flowers), 'Dark Storm' (wine-red lower lip with lavender upper lips, slower-growing), 'Hope' (white flowers with a pale yellow throat), 'Lois Adams' (pale lavender-and-magenta two-tone flowers, few to no seedpods), 'Lucretia Hamilton' (slower-growing, dark purplish-red flowers, max. size of 18 feet x 18 feet), 'Marfa Late' (double, pink flowers), 'Regal' (lavender and wine-red flowers), 'Rio Salado' (vigorous grower, large, ruffled deep burgundy flowers), and 'Warren Jones' (fast-growing, clusters of large, light pink flowers, retains leaves longer in winter).

LANDSCAPE APPLICATION: This tree is perfect for the south and west sides of a house, providing summer shade and allowing winter sun. Flowers serve as warm-season color. Use it with plants that will remain evergreen through the winter and draw attention away from its bare branches. It is great for attracting both butterflies and hummingbirds, and it can be planted along streets, and in medians and retention basins.

PRECAUTIONS: Be sure the tree is not a focal point through the winter as seedpods hang on while the tree is leafless, giving it a somewhat scraggly look.

Chrysactinia mexicana | Damianita

SMALL SHRUB	
SIZE (height x width)	1–2 feet x 1–2 feet
FLOWER COLOR	Yellow
FLOWER SEASON	Spring–fall
EXPOSURE	Full sun
WATER	Low–moderate
GROWTH RATE	Moderately fast
PRUNING	Spring, summer after flowers fade
HARDINESS	Hardy to at least 0° F
NATURAL ELEVATION RANGE	1,800–3,000 feet
SUITABLE CITIES	All cities in all zones

FIELD NOTES: *Chrysactinia mexicana* is found on limestone soil in western Texas and south into northeastern Mexico from about 1,800 to 3,000 feet elevation. You should be able to spot it on one of the many hiking trails in Big Bend National Park.

DESCRIPTION: Dark green leaves and showy yellow flowers combine to create a highly ornamental shrub that fits into any desert landscape. One of its most attractive features is the sheer number of flowers that can be produced at one time, literally covering the shrub with yellow. Daisy-like butterfly-attracting flowers occur in small clusters at the tips of long stalks from March through October or November, although excessive summer heat in the low, hot, interior desert slows down the flowering. The ½-inch-long, needlelike leaves are fragrant when crushed.

CULTURE/MAINTENANCE: Damianita is hardy to about 0° F. It tolerates most soils, but good drainage is always a plus. In full sun it stays round and tight, while it can get leggy and open in shade. Once established, it survives on very little supplemental water. Plants have a moderate growth rate, taking two or three seasons to reach full size. They respond with more flowers when given extra water in the heat of summer and when the old flower heads are pruned off.

IDENTIFICATION: *C. mexicana* could be confused with turpentine bush (*Ericameria laricifolia*). *C. mexicana* usually has a longer flowering season and has about 12 **ray flowers**, while *E. laricifolia* blooms only in the fall and has fewer than 6 ray flowers and sometimes none.

LANDSCAPE APPLICATION: Use *C. mexicana* as a low, flowering shrub, or mass plant for a dynamic effect in all zones in the desert Southwest. Its compactness works well in small or narrow spaces such as street or parking lot medians or small courtyards. In patio areas or a sensory garden, people can enjoy the wonderful fragrance. Because of its long flowering season, it is well suited for dressing up succulent accents: *Agave geminiflora, Agave parryi* var. *truncata, Dasylirion acrotrichum, Dasylirion quadrangulatum, Nolina matapensis, Nolina nelsonii, Yucca elata, Yucca rigida,* and *Yucca rostrata.*

PRECAUTIONS: *C. mexicana* demands full sun, and established plants can't stand overwatering, especially if you are blessed with caliche. If drainage is poor, keep plants dry during cold weather.

Conoclinium dissectum | Synonym: *Eupatorium greggii* (incorrectly sold as *Conoclinium greggii)* | Mist Flower

FLOWERING PERENNIAL, SMALL SHRUB	
SIZE (height x width)	1 ½–2½ feet x 2–3 feet
FLOWER COLOR	Lavender-blue, blue-purple
FLOWER SEASON	Spring–fall
EXPOSURE	Full or filtered sun
WATER	Moderate
GROWTH RATE	Fast
PRUNING	Shear in late winter
HARDINESS	Hardy (perennial; stems die back, but roots are hardy to 0° F.)
NATURAL ELEVATION RANGE	3,500–6,000 feet
SUITABLE CITIES	All cities in all zones

FIELD NOTES: *Conoclinium dissectum* is found along streambeds and on mesas and flats from western Texas to southeastern Arizona, south into northern Mexico. Plants are frequently found on sandy soil, loam or limestone-derived soil between 3,500 and 6,000 feet elevation.

DESCRIPTION: This small herbaceous perennial can be upright and bushy or have stems sprawling along the ground and then turning up near the ends. Its light green, pinnately lobed leaves give it a fine texture.

Lavender-blue to blue-purple blossoms are arranged in tight clusters at the ends of branches and attract butterflies, especially the queen butterfly. Flowering may begin as early as March and can continue until October or November.

CULTURE/MAINTENANCE: Plants are root-hardy to at least 0° F, with the tops freezing back when nighttime temperatures drop into the low 20s F. They will appreciate midday filtered light in the hot, interior desert regions but will grow fine in full sun all day if given supplemental water regularly in the summer. Plants are low- to moderate-water-using and grow fine in loose, rocky, native soil, reaching 2 feet tall and 2 feet wide in a couple of years. Cut back any dead stems in late winter, and if the plants overwinter without dying back, cut them to ground level, as they will resprout from underground stems called **rhizomes.**

IDENTIFICATION: *C. dissectum* is very easily distinguished from any other *Eupatorium* species by its combination of highly divided leaves and lavender-blue flowers. The flowers are very similar to those of *Ageratum corymbosum,* but the divided leaves of *Conoclinium* or *Eupatorium* readily separate the two plants.

LANDSCAPE APPLICATION: This plant is the perfect size to use in a cactus and succulent garden or to plant near large boulders. Match it up with *Agave* species, *Dasylirion* species, *Echinocactus grusonii, Ferocactus pilosus, Hesperaloe funifera, Nolina nelsonii,* and with tall accents like *Yucca rigida* and *Yucca rostrata.* Get it into the butterfly garden with *Ageratum corymbosum, Lantana* 'New Gold,' and *Salvia greggii.*

PRECAUTIONS: Rabbits will likely eat the stems if there is nothing else around. Best flower production takes full sun, which takes more watering at the hottest time of year.

Cooperia drummondii | Cooper's Rain Lily

BULB	
SIZE (height x width)	6–12 inches x 4–6 inches
FLOWER COLOR	White
FLOWER SEASON	Summer–fall
EXPOSURE	Full or filtered sun
WATER	Low–moderate
GROWTH RATE	Moderate
PRUNING	None

HARDINESS	Hardy
NATURAL ELEVATION RANGE	2,000–4,150 feet
SUITABLE CITIES	All cities in all zones

FIELD NOTES: *Cooperia drummondii* ranges from Kansas to Louisiana, Texas, and New Mexico, and south into northern Mexico. Plants show up on dry slopes and flats in alkaline soil types. In western Texas and northern Mexico, plants are part of the typical Chihuahuan Desert mix from 2,000 to 4,150 feet elevation.

DESCRIPTION: Large white flowers last 3–4 days. This ephemeral burst of beauty is complemented by small clumps of narrow, grass-like leaves that persist from spring through fall. Leaves are 6–12 inches long and appear as the soil warms in the spring. The showy, long-tubed flowers can appear as early as June but are most prevalent in the fall. Solitary lilies at the ends of 12-inch-long stalks open at night and stay open the following day. Three-lobed fruits contain thin, flat, black seeds.

CULTURE/MAINTENANCE: Bulbs are hardy across most of the Southwest if allowed to dry out during the winter. In areas dipping below 10° F, they may need to be dug for winter. Plants have a moderate growth rate and are drought-tolerant but benefit from supplemental water in the summer. Place plants in full or filtered sun in any soil. When planted in native soil and left on its own, Cooper's rain lily is almost maintenance-free.

IDENTIFICATION: Forget telling *C. drummondii* apart from other bulbs until flowers appear—then it is unmistakable. There are no other bulbs that produce the characteristic long, thin flower. *Zephyranthes candida* is another white-flowered bulb, but it has a short tube.

LANDSCAPE APPLICATION: This species is used more as a "bonus" plant and not as a focal point. Bulbs can be planted in the same hole as large accents like *Agave*, *Dasylirion*, and *Yucca* species. Install them in rock or cactus gardens, or place in raised planters or large clay pots. These lilies can stand alone for seasonal color or share space with various *Agaves* to add variety to the container.

PRECAUTIONS: Leaves and flowers will be eaten by a variety of wildlife, including rabbits and rodents. You can screen with 1-inch mesh chicken wire, but you might try inserting the bulbs at the base of stout-leafed *Agave* species. There are no known insect pests or diseases.

Cooperia pedunculata | Rain Lily

BULB

SIZE (height x width)	12 inches x 4 inches
FLOWER COLOR	White
FLOWER SEASON	Spring–summer
EXPOSURE	Full sun or partial shade
WATER	Low–moderate
GROWTH RATE	Moderate
PRUNING	None
HARDINESS	Hardy
NATURAL ELEVATION RANGE	850–6,500 feet
SUITABLE CITIES	All cities in all zones

FIELD NOTES: *Cooperia pedunculata* shows up along streams, in valleys, or on hillsides in Texas and adjacent northeastern Mexico. In May of 2001, Ron Gass and I trekked into northeastern Mexico in search of *Agave ovatifolia.* Success came after a private rancher who knew about the plant gave us permission to enter his land. While flitting ecstatically between agaves, I had the good fortune of spotting *C. pedunculata* in bloom.

DESCRIPTION: Small clumps of narrow, grass-like leaves arise from a small to medium bulb. Leaves grow to 12 inches long by ½ inch wide and emerge as the soil warms in the spring. White, long-tubed, 2-inch-wide flowers appear in the spring and summer. The showy flowers make solo appearances at the ends of 8–12-inch-long stalks. They open at night and stay that way only for the following day. Three-lobed fruits contain several thin, flat, black seeds.

CULTURE/MAINTENANCE: Bulbs are hardy to at least 10° F, and in most of the Southwest they can be left in the ground. Plants are drought-tolerant but lap up supplemental water in the summer. They have a moderate growth rate and multiply over time. When planted in native soil and left to their own devices, the bulbs are very easy to grow. They tolerate just about any soil type and do fine in full or filtered sun.

IDENTIFICATION: *C. pedunculata* is readily distinguished from other bulbs when in flower. *Zephyranthes candida* also has white flowers, but they have much shorter tubes.

LANDSCAPE APPLICATION: Rain lily is quite versatile and makes a great "bonus" plant rather than a focal point. Bulbs can be placed in the same hole as large accents like *Agave, Dasylirion, Hesperaloe, Nolina,* and *Yucca* species. Try them in rock or cactus gardens or planted in raised planters. Install them in large clay pots either alone for seasonal color, or grouped with various *Agaves* to add a little drama to the container.

PRECAUTIONS: Leaves and flowers are irresistible to a variety of wildlife, including rabbits and rodents. You can screen with 1-inch mesh chicken wire, or place bulbs at the base of armored *Agave* species. There are no known insect pests or diseases.

Cordia boissieri | Mexican Olive

LARGE SHRUB, SMALL TREE

SIZE (height x width)	10–15 (25) feet x 10–15 feet
FLOWER COLOR	White
FLOWER SEASON	Spring–fall
EXPOSURE	Full or reflected sun
WATER	Low–moderate
GROWTH RATE	Slow
PRUNING	Train to tree form if desired, prune out dead wood in spring
HARDINESS	Hardy to mid to high 20s, leaf burn and stem damage at low 20s, significant damage at mid-teens F
NATURAL ELEVATION RANGE	50–7,500 feet
SUITABLE CITIES	All low-elevation-zone cities and warm, protected spots in mid-elevation-zone cities

FIELD NOTES: *Cordia boissieri* occurs in thickets and chaparral, on gravelly slopes, and along fences, stream banks, and roadsides in extreme south Texas and northeastern Mexico. I've seen flowering plants in northeastern Mexico while driving from Laredo, Texas, to Monterrey. Some pretty trees, probably planted, appear on the drive to Falcon Dam in southern Texas. Their elevation range is wide, from 50 feet in hot, subtropical Tamaulipas to 7,500 feet in the arid region of the east-central state of Hidalgo, Mexico.

DESCRIPTION: This exceptionally decorative plant has dark green foliage and a hot-weather display of showy white flowers. It is a large evergreen shrub or small tree. In deep, rich soil, it might stretch as tall as 25 feet. The 2–4-inch-long, rough, oval, dark green leaves are the perfect backdrop for the huge clusters of 2-inch-wide, funnel-shaped, white flowers with yellow throats. Cycles of flowering and fruiting extend nearly year-round, but watch for the best flower displays in the spring and fall. Pale yellow, succulent, olive-like fruits turn dark purple when mature.

CULTURE/MAINTENANCE: While evergreen in its native range, *C. boissieri* will suffer foliage burn and stem damage when temperatures drop into the mid to low 20s F. Dead leaves persist until new growth begins to appear in the spring. It will suffer major damage when winter lows hit the middle teens, but it is rarely killed outright. Although drought-tolerant once established, plants require water on a regular basis when young, then later to boost growth and flowering.

IDENTIFICATION: *C. boissieri* is easily told apart from its shrubby cousin, *C. parvifolia,* by its overall bigger form, leaves, and flowers.

LANDSCAPE APPLICATION: *C. boissieri* can be grown as a large shrub or trained as a single- or multi-trunk tree. Locate it in full or reflected sun, and, in mid-elevation deserts, provide a warm microclimate if you're encouraging it to be a tree. Lush, dark green foliage fits right in with mini-oasis and transition zone plants. Try it with *Ageratum corymbosum, Anisacanthus quadrifidus, Buddleja marrubiifolia, Dalea* species, *Hesperaloe* species, *Lantana* species, *Leucophyllum* species, *Poliomintha maderensis, Salvia greggii, Yucca rigida,* and *Y. rostrata.* Blossoms attract hummingbirds.

PRECAUTIONS: *C. boissieri* needs to be planted in warm locations to minimize frost damage. Olive-like fruit may mess up your beautiful brick or flagstone patio.

Cordia parvifolia | Little Leaf Cordia

MEDIUM–LARGE SHRUB

SIZE (height x width)	4–6 feet x 4–8 feet
FLOWER COLOR	White
FLOWER SEASON	Spring–fall
EXPOSURE	Full or reflected sun
WATER	Low–moderate
GROWTH RATE	Moderately slow
HARDINESS	Hardy to high teens F

PRUNING	None or prune out frozen stems
NATURAL ELEVATION RANGE	100–2,300 feet
SUITABLE CITIES	All low-elevation-zone cities; warm, protected spots in Tucson and Las Vegas

FIELD NOTES: *Cordia parvifolia* is found along washes and **alluvial outwash** slopes in Baja California and northwestern and north-central Mexico from about 100 to 2,300 feet elevation. I've seen these shrubs in bloom in September on Mexico Highway 30 between Torreón and Cuatrocienagas. They were out in the wide-open desert with *Echinocactus horizonthalonius, Larrea divaricata,* and *Leucophyllum frutescens.* I've also encountered flowering specimens in washes near Guaymas, Sonora, looking like a picture out of a gardening magazine with *Antigonon leptopus* scrambling all over everything.

DESCRIPTION: When the weather is hot, look for pure white flowers looking like puffs of snow covering this shrub. This medium to large, rounded to spreading, evergreen shrub has dark, gray-green leaves and a stiff branching pattern that provide year-round interest. Leaves are about 1 inch long and ½ inch wide, and they paint a nice background for the brilliant, 3–4-inch clusters of bell-shaped, 1½-inch-wide flowers. Flowering is possible spring through fall, but it is frequent and dazzling under warm, humid, rainy conditions.

CULTURE/MAINTENANCE: Plants are hardy to the high teens F if allowed to go dormant in the fall and winter. They can survive on about 12–15 inches of annual rainfall but will grow faster and flower more if given supplemental water from late spring through summer. They grow moderately slowly, but consistent irrigation will coax them to speed up. Place them in full or reflected sun, in native soil with good drainage. Because of the naturally dense growth habit, very little to no pruning is needed.

IDENTIFICATION: *C. parvifolia* and *C. boissieri* are the only two species being cultivated. *C. parvifolia* is readily distinguished by its small leaves, smaller flowers, and more shrub-like growth habit.

LANDSCAPE APPLICATION: This is a perfect shrub for the low- and mid-elevation zones and is quite attractive when used either singly or massed. Ample room is needed in order to mass plant, because individuals fill a lot of space. The white flowers mix nicely with red, pink, blue, or violet flowers. Place with tall plants that will stand out above the shrub. Tasteful companions include *Dalea frutescens, Dalea pulchra,* all *Leucophyllum* species, *Nolina matapensis, Nolina nelsonii,* and a whole slew of *Yucca* species.

PRECAUTIONS: Rabbits seek out young *C. parvifolia,* but they do not usually bother established plants. In colder regions, prune out any frost-damaged foliage.

Cycas revoluta | Sago Palm

Male cone

PALM/CYCAD	
SIZE (height x width)	4–6 (rarely 10) feet x 4–6 feet
FLOWER COLOR	Not applicable
FLOWER SEASON	Cones produced in summer
EXPOSURE	Full or filtered sun, or full or partial shade
WATER	Low–moderate
GROWTH RATE	Slow
PRUNING	Remove old leaves prior to emergence of new leaves
HARDINESS	Hardy
NATURAL ELEVATION RANGE	To 1,000 feet
SUITABLE CITIES	All low- and mid-elevation-zone cities

FIELD NOTES: *Cycas revoluta* is usually found on open, exposed, steep, limestone cliffs and rocks near the coast in Japan. It is less common in the deep shade of low, dense forest from sea level to nearly 1,000 feet elevation. I have never had the good fortune to travel to Japan and see these beasts in habitat, but I paid attention in class and know they are primitive relatives of modern conifers.

DESCRIPTION: The dense crown of bright to dark green leaves and stout trunk make a bold statement in most any landscape. This plant is especially striking after the new flush of leaves is unveiled. The trunk reaches 4–6 (rarely 10) feet tall with one to several smaller side branches. Numerous pinnately divided leaves are straight, stiff, and palmlike, measuring 2–3 feet long. When plants are young, the leaves eke out one at a time. Older plants crank it up with two or more crops of leaves annually. Plants are dioecious with male and female **cones** on separate plants. Female cones are solitary, **ovoid** to somewhat dome-shaped, and measure 8–10 inches long by 5–7 inches across. Male cones are solitary, upright, and conical to ovoid-oblong, 16–24 inches long by 3–4 inches across. No comment.

Female cone

CULTURE/MAINTENANCE: *C. revoluta* is hardy, and rumor has it that it with-

stands temperatures as low as 15° F. The growth rate is interminable when compared to trees and shrubs but speedy compared with other cycads. Plants will grow in most any soil, but they seem to be healthiest in a rich soil. They will tolerate moderate amounts of drought but do best with consistent watering in the summer. Place in full sun, filtered sun, or full shade. Remove old leaves just prior to the emergence of new leaves in the spring.

IDENTIFICATION: *C. revoluta* is identified by its stiff, bright to dark green leaves, with leaflets held at a nearly 45-degree angle.

LANDSCAPE APPLICATION: *C. revoluta* makes a great accent or focal point in shaded entryways with other tropical- and subtropical-looking plants in low- and mid-elevation zones. Good companions include *Agave bovicornuta, Dioon edule, Lysiloma watsonii* ssp. *thornberi,* and even *Quercus emoryi* and *Sophora secundiflora.* Plant in a large container and use as a dramatic focal point anywhere.

PRECAUTIONS: Watch for scale insects and mealybugs, and treat the plants if they become infested.

Dalea bicolor | Indigo Bush

Variety *bicolor*

MEDIUM–LARGE SHRUB	
SIZE (height x width)	2–8 feet x 3–8 feet
FLOWER COLOR	Purple and white with yellow
FLOWER SEASON	Late summer–spring
EXPOSURE	Full or reflected sun
WATER	Drought-tolerant–moderate
GROWTH RATE	Moderately fast
PRUNING	Once every 2–3 years in spring or light shearing in summer also
HARDINESS	Hardy–half-hardy
NATURAL ELEVATION RANGE	2,000–9,000 feet
SUITABLE CITIES	Varieties argyrea and bicolor: all zones. Variety orcuttiana: all low-elevation-zone cities; protected microclimates in Tucson

FIELD NOTES: *Dalea bicolor* is a wide-ranging, exceedingly variable plant that spans an elevation range of 2,000–9,000 feet. It grows on stony hillsides and dry washes

Variety *bicolor*

among boulders in Baja California and on limestone hills and mountains in the Chihuahuan Desert region of western Texas, southern New Mexico, and eastern Mexico. In my spare time, I've collected and photographed the variety *argyrea* in the Guadalupe Mountains of southern New Mexico and western Texas, the variety *bicolor* in eastern Mexico, and the variety *orcuttiana* in northern Baja California. Each one of the shrubs is horticulturally distinct and drops into a different garden niche.

DESCRIPTION: The size of this rounded to spreading shrub varies depending on which variety you put in the ground. Variety *argyrea* reaches about 2–2½ feet by 3–3½ feet, variety *bicolor* is the largest, reaching 6–8 feet by 6–8 feet, and variety *orcuttiana* tops out at about 3–4 feet by 3–4 feet. Small, fragrant, **pinnately compound** leaves are green to silvery and can be evergreen to semievergreen. This fickle plant produces dense clusters of pealike, tricolored flowers that vary from purple, to rose-purple, to blue-purple and white with a spot of yellow. Look for it to bloom in late summer and fall, and in the case of variety *orcuttiana* the flowers will go right through the winter if the plants are not frozen.

CULTURE/MAINTENANCE: *D. bicolor* is hardy to half-hardy depending on the variety. Variety *argyrea* can tolerate winter lows of at least 5° F, variety *bicolor* has been subjected to winter lows of 17° F with no damage, while variety *orcuttiana* routinely suffers frost damage when winter lows drop into the low 20s F. All varieties will grow well in full sun or reflected sun and native soil with adequate drainage. Although drought-tolerant once established, plants will grow faster with supplemental summer irrigation. Prune out any frozen stems in the spring, and cut back ruthlessly once every couple of years to increase density and rejuvenate plants.

IDENTIFICATION: Compared with its shrub *Dalea* relatives, *D. bicolor* is the most variable. *D. pulchra* is a spring bloomer, while *D. bicolor* mostly blooms in the fall. *D. frutescens* also blooms in the fall, but it is smaller with green leaves.

Variety *argyrea*

LANDSCAPE APPLICATION: This beautiful shrub gets along nicely with many desert-adapted plants in sunny situations. The fine foliage sets off medium to large accents such as *Dasylirion*, *Nolina*, and *Yucca* species, and desert trees such as *Diospyros texana*, *Ebenopsis ebano*, *Eysenhardtia orthocarpa*,

Havardia pallens, and *Leucaena retusa. D. bicolor* variety *argyrea* and variety *bicolor* are at home in all elevation zones of the desert Southwest while variety *orcuttiana* works well in all low-elevation-zone cities and warm microclimates in Tucson.

PRECAUTIONS: *D. bicolor* may be susceptible to rabbit attack. It is not bothered by insect pests and does not seem to be susceptible to root rot or fungus problems, although good soil drainage is a must. Shaded plants get leggy and often languish without blooming fully.

Dalea capitata | Lemon Dalea

GROUND COVER, FLOWERING
PERENNIAL, SMALL SHRUB

SIZE (height x width)	12–15 inches x 2–4 feet
FLOWER COLOR	Yellow
FLOWER SEASON	Fall (sometimes spring)
EXPOSURE	Full sun
WATER	Low–moderate
GROWTH RATE	Fast
PRUNING	Shear in early spring
HARDINESS	Hardy to at least 5° F
NATURAL ELEVATION RANGE	5,000–8,000 feet
SUITABLE CITIES	All cities in all zones

FIELD NOTES: *Dalea capitata* grows in desert grassland, pine-oak, and pinyon vegetation in northeastern Mexico from about 5,000 to 8,000 feet elevation. Ron Gass and I were driving along Highway 54 south of Saltillo when Ron spotted a police car and decided to pull off to take some pictures. I ended up prone, trying to get a close-up shot of the yellow flowers of a scruffy-looking, unfamiliar *Dalea.* Ron snagged a couple of cuttings from the same plant, and it turned out to be *D. capitata.* We affectionately dubbed it "Policeman's *Dalea*" because had it not been for the police car, we probably would not have stopped where we did and stumbled across this incredible little gem.

DESCRIPTION: In the fall *D. capitata* is ablaze with yellow flowers topping a low mound of bright green foliage. This low-growing spreader tops out at about 12–15 inches tall and 2–4 feet across. New growth consists of thin, red-colored stems that grow close to the ground. Bright green, pinnate, fine-textured foliage is about 1 inch long and consists of 7–11 leaflets. Dense, 1-inch-long flower spikes hold 20–35 flowers. Light banana-yellow blossoms cover the plant in the fall.

CULTURE/MAINTENANCE: *D. capitata* is cold-hardy. Treat it as a perennial and shear to nearly ground level in late winter. Plants prefer full sun and soil that drains well. Thoroughly soak the root zone on a regular basis from spring through fall. Fast-growing plants should have no trouble reaching full size every year even after being cut back. In fact, they really shine when cut back to nearly ground level in the winter. This keeps them dense and compact and not growing into nearby plants.

IDENTIFICATION: *D. capitata* is readily distinguished from all other cultivated *Dalea* species by the combination of size and flower color. Currently there are no other low-growing, yellow-flowered species with rich green leaves.

LANDSCAPE APPLICATION Lemon dalea can be used in all elevation zones in the desert Southwest. Plant singly or mass together to cover large areas, or place at the base of tall accents like *Nolina nelsonii* or *Yucca rostrata*. It is also very attractive when used with large boulders in a rockscape, or mixed with cactus and other succulents. Try planting it alongside bold accents like *Agave, Dasylirion, Ferocactus,* or *Stenocereus* species plus *Echinocactus grusonii* or *Hesperaloe funifera*. This compact plant can fit into narrow planters along walkways and in street medians. It's a good choice for retention basins.

PRECAUTIONS: *D. capitata* will be a magnet for whiteflies in the summer and should be treated if infested. There are no reports of other insect pests. Flowers will attract some bees, but not a lot. I heard of one case where plants out in the open were not eaten, but I think the jury is still out on rabbit resistance.

Dalea frutescens | Black Dalea

SMALL–MEDIUM SHRUB

SIZE (height x width)	2–4 feet x 3–6 feet
FLOWER COLOR	Rose-purple
FLOWER SEASON	Fall
EXPOSURE	Full or reflected sun
WATER	Low–moderate
GROWTH RATE	Moderately fast
PRUNING	Shear in early spring

HARDINESS	Hardy to at least 0° F
NATURAL ELEVATION RANGE	5,000–7,500 feet
SUITABLE CITIES	All cities in all zones

FIELD NOTES: *Dalea frutescens* occurs on rocky hillsides, washes, and stony clay flats in scrub oak, juniper, or mesquite zones at about 5,000–7,500 feet elevation. The species is wide-ranging and found from Oklahoma to New Mexico, Texas, and northeastern Mexico. In the early 1980s, I collected seeds from plants growing in the rocky outcrops in the Davis Mountains of west Texas that led to the cultivar 'Sierra Negra.'

DESCRIPTION: The profusion of bright rose-purple flowers in fall makes for a brief but spectacular floral display. This attractive, rounded to spreading, medium-size shrub can sometimes get as large as 4 feet by 6 feet. Small compound leaves measure about 1 inch long and ½ inch wide and are composed of 4–9 pairs of leaflets. Main stem leaves are deciduous, while leaves of short shoots hang on through winter. Light-colored, nearly white branches keep the plant interesting over the winter. Short, rounded to slightly elongate, 1½-inch-long flower spikes nearly cover the bush in late September and October. Bright blossoms attract butterflies.

CULTURE/MAINTENANCE: *D. frutescens* is hardy to 0° F, although it drops leaves when lows hit the mid-20s, to reveal creamy white bark. Plants are low- to moderate-water-using, thriving when the root zone is thoroughly soaked every 7–14 days from spring until fall. They grow relatively quickly and hit full size in 2–3 growing seasons. Although hardy, plants fill out and have more flowers if pruned severely in late winter.

IDENTIFICATION: *D. frutescens* is easily distinguished from other fall-blooming *Dalea* species by its distinctive white bark, **subcapitate** inflorescence, and brilliant rose-purple floral display.

LANDSCAPE APPLICATION: This tough, smart plant has been used effectively in full sun along roadsides and in hot parking lots in Phoenix, Tucson, and Sierra Vista, so should be able to make it anyplace. Plant several in a desert landscape mixed with tall accent plants like *Nolina matapensis* and *Yucca rigida,* or in combination with other accents like *Agave* species, *Dasylirion* species, *Hesperaloe funifera,* or *Nolina nelsonii.* Compatible shrubs include *Ageratum corymbosum, Asclepias linaria, Conoclinium dissectum, Dalea capitata, Leucophyllum* species, *Poliomintha maderensis,* and *Salvia greggii.*

PRECAUTIONS: Rabbits will eat newly planted *D. frutescens*. Older, more established plants weaned from supplemental irrigation are less likely to be eaten. Flowers bring in the bees with the butterflies.

Dalea greggii | Trailing Indigo Bush

GROUND COVER	
SIZE (height x width)	18–24 inches x > 4–6 feet
FLOWER COLOR	Rose-purple
FLOWER SEASON	Summer
EXPOSURE	Full or reflected sun
WATER	Drought-tolerant–moderate
GROWTH RATE	Fast
PRUNING	Some to control spread
HARDINESS	Hardy to at least 15° F when established
NATURAL ELEVATION RANGE	0–7,500 feet
SUITABLE CITIES	All low, mid, and high-elevation-zone cities; Sierra Vista in high-elevation zone

FIELD NOTES: *Dalea greggii* is found in open desert habitat on stony hills and plains from western Texas south into eastern Mexico as far south as Puebla and Oaxaca. Plants do fine near sea level in Tamaulipas to as high as 7,500 feet in Zacatecas. The form most commonly found in cultivation was collected by Warren Jones near Alpine, Texas, on the side of state highway 90. I have seen *D. greggii* growing in a similar situation, about 30 miles northeast of Saltillo along Mexico highway 40 going to Monterrey.

DESCRIPTION: The soft, velvety appearance of this low-growing, wide-spreading plant softens a harsh desert landscape. Because the stems take root as they trail along the ground, this plant keeps on spreading. Ignore predictions of a 3–4-foot ultimate diameter; it is safer to figure at least 6–8 feet or more across for a single plant. Small, once pinnate, silvery gray leaves provide year-round color and interest. Dense, 1-inch-long clusters of small rose-purple flowers appear in the spring and summer.

CULTURE/MAINTENANCE: *D. greggii* is hardy to 0° F if allowed to harden off in fall. Place the plants in full sun or reflected sun, native soil with good drainage, and a big space. Although able to survive on only 11 inches of annual rainfall, plants will fill out better if given some supplemental water in the spring and summer. However, withholding water is one way to control the spread of this fast-growing ground cover.

It requires very little maintenance if given enough room to spread.

IDENTIFICATION: *D. greggii* could be confused with *D. pulchra* only when very young. The flowers of *D. greggii* are more purple than the pink flowers of *D. pulchra*.

LANDSCAPE APPLICATION: Use trailing indigo bush as a ground cover or stabilizer in a desert landscape. It works well with many other drought-tolerant, desert-adapted plants. Because it needs lots of room and full sun to develop properly, it is well suited for large street medians and large slopes where erosion control is needed. It is a good match for large *Yucca* species such as *Y. grandiflora*, *Y. rigida*, and *Y. rostrata*.

PRECAUTIONS: Allow ample space for full development. Don't plant it too close to low-growing cactus and succulents as it will eat up the slow-growing succulents. Rabbits may nibble on youngsters but should leave the plant alone after it starts to get big.

Dalea pulchra | Indigo Bush

MEDIUM SHRUB

SIZE (height x width)	4–5 feet x 4–5 feet
FLOWER COLOR	Pink-purple
FLOWER SEASON	Fall–spring
EXPOSURE	Full or reflected sun
WATER	Drought-tolerant–moderate
GROWTH RATE	Moderately fast
PRUNING	Shear in early summer
HARDINESS	Hardy to at least 15° F
NATURAL ELEVATION RANGE	3,000–4,500 feet
SUITABLE CITIES	All low- and mid-elevation-zone cities; Sierra Vista in the high-elevation zone

FIELD NOTES: *Dalea pulchra* grows on rocky mountain slopes and roadsides, in grasslands at the western edge of the Sonoran Desert in Arizona and Sonora, Mexico, from 3,000 to 4,500 feet elevation. It is common in the Catalina and Rincon mountains

around Tucson, Arizona, and a treat to see in bloom when hiking in the spring.

DESCRIPTION: The abundance of showy, pink-purple flowers produced from late winter through spring creates a cloud of color topping this medium-size, evergreen shrub. Small, silvery leaves are once pinnate with 5–9 leaflets, giving the plant a fine texture. Butterfly-attracting flowers occur in ovoid, 1-inch-long clusters, from November until April, depending on location. If the winter is too cold, the flowering shuts down until it gets warmer. Flower spikes are very hairy and give the plant a smoky appearance when it is in bloom.

CULTURE/MAINTENANCE: Plants are hardy to 15° F and probably lower as long as they are allowed to go dormant in the fall. Place them only in full or reflected sun and native soil with adequate drainage. They are drought-tolerant, surviving on 10–12 inches of annual rainfall. However, they will grow faster and larger and bloom more prolifically if watered from spring through fall. Plants have a moderate–fast growth rate and require very little maintenance but will tolerate shearing once or twice during the growing season.

IDENTIFICATION: *D. pulchra* is readily distinguished from other shrubby *Dalea* species, but can be confused with young *D. greggii*. *D. pulchra* is more woody and upright, and blooms from fall to spring.

LANDSCAPE APPLICATION: Place indigo bush in full or reflected sun in a desert landscape. It can be massed and used along street sides, in street medians, and even retention basins. Clean and thornless, it's harmless around pools. It accessorizes shrubs, trees, and large accent plants like *Anisacanthus quadrifidus* var. *wrightii*, *Buddleja marrubiifolia*, *Ebenopsis ebano*, *Eysenhardtia orthocarpa*, *Leucophyllum* species, *Salvia greggii*, *Sophora secundiflora*, and various species of *Agave*, *Dasylirion*, *Hesperaloe*, and *Yucca*.

PRECAUTIONS: Protect young plants from rabbits. When they mature and develop more woody growth, plants are a little more resistant to rabbit damage. *D. pulchra* grows and flowers poorly when placed in shade. Prune only in summer after it has flowered. Because it will attract bees when it is in bloom, keep it away from high-traffic areas.

Dalea versicolor var. *sessilis* | Mountain Dalea

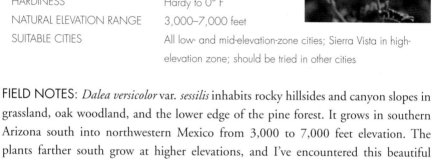

MEDIUM SHRUB

SIZE (height x width)	2–4 feet x 2–5 feet
FLOWER COLOR	Purple-and-white
FLOWER SEASON	Fall–spring
EXPOSURE	Full or filtered sun
WATER	Low–moderate
GROWTH RATE	Moderately fast
PRUNING	Summer
HARDINESS	Hardy to 0° F
NATURAL ELEVATION RANGE	3,000–7,000 feet
SUITABLE CITIES	All low- and mid-elevation-zone cities; Sierra Vista in high-elevation zone; should be tried in other cities

FIELD NOTES: *Dalea versicolor* var. *sessilis* inhabits rocky hillsides and canyon slopes in grassland, oak woodland, and the lower edge of the pine forest. It grows in southern Arizona south into northwestern Mexico from 3,000 to 7,000 feet elevation. The plants farther south grow at higher elevations, and I've encountered this beautiful shrub up in the pine forests along Mexico Highway 40 between Mazatlan, Sinaloa, and Ciudad Durango.

DESCRIPTION: In habitat, mountain dalea reaches 2 feet tall and 2–3 feet across. However, under cultivation it expands into a medium size, spreading to 3–4 feet high and 3–5 feet across. Small, dark green leaves are once pinnate, measure about 1 inch long, and are composed of 4–9 pairs of leaflets, giving the plant a fine texture. Dense, 1½-inch-long flower spikes, composed of butterfly-attracting, dark purple-and-white flowers appear from September or October into March or April. Winter cold can shut down the blooming, but it will resume when the weather warms enough.

CULTURE/MAINTENANCE: This tough plant is cold-hardy to 0° F and tolerant of nutrient-poor soils if the drainage is good. It is relatively drought-tolerant, requiring supplemental water once every 7–14 days during the warm season, and once every 3 or 4 weeks in winter. This shrub grows fast, reaching full size in just one or two seasons in the ground. It tends to get leggy, especially when planted in some shade, so trim it back once or twice during the summer and early fall.

IDENTIFICATION: *D. versicolor* is distinguishable by its thick, cylindrical flower spike and stand-out leaves. *D. frutescens* has somewhat similar leaves, but its overall aspect is more rounded, and the flower cluster is not long and cylindrical.

LANDSCAPE APPLICATION: This tough shrub performs reliably in a variety of situations. Place it in filtered sun or full sun in a desert landscape mixed with other plants from arid climates. It delivers some color during a season when not much else is in bloom. For the best display, mass it to spread winter color to large areas. Good companion shrubs include *Buddleja marrubiifolia, Leucophyllum* species, *Poliomintha maderensis,* and *Salvia greggii.* It also holds its own with cacti, succulents, and accent plants like *Hesperaloe funifera, Nolina nelsonii*, and *Agave, Dasylirion, Ferocactus,* and *Yucca* species.

PRECAUTIONS: Young plants attract rabbits, and flowers attract bees.

Dasylirion acrotrichum | Green Desert Spoon

CACTUS/SUCCULENT	
SIZE (height x width)	3–7 feet x 3–5 feet
FLOWER COLOR	Tan (male), greenish (female)
FLOWER SEASON	Late spring–summer
EXPOSURE	Full or reflected sun
WATER	Low–moderate
GROWTH RATE	Moderately fast
PRUNING	Remove old flower stalks
HARDINESS	Hardy to at least 15° F
NATURAL ELEVATION RANGE	6,000–8,500 feet
SUITABLE CITIES	All low- and mid-elevation-zone cities; Sierra Vista in the high-elevation zone

FIELD NOTES: *Dasylirion acrotrichum* grows on stony, rocky hills and slopes in east-central Mexico from about 6,000 to 8,500 feet elevation.

DESCRIPTION: This rich green plant has a beautiful, attention-grabbing symmetry to it. Generally you'll see a large, trunk-forming plant that gets about 3–4 feet tall with a spread of 4–5 feet in the landscape. Rare, elderly specimens have been known to reach an overall height of 7 feet (with a 4-foot-tall trunk) with a crown diameter of 5 feet across. The bright green leaves measure about 2–2½ feet long and ½ inch wide.

Leaf edges are adorned with small, prickly teeth that curve primarily towards the tip of the leaf, while the tips dry and fray to look like brushes. In late spring or early summer, the flower stalk begins to emerge from the middle of the plant. It grows rapidly to as tall as 15 feet, with male and female stalks on separate plants. Cultivated plants will set seed, but as you learned in school, you'll need both types of plants.

CULTURE/MAINTENANCE: *D. acrotrichum* is hardy to at least 15° F and probably lower. The growth rate is moderately fast, and plants can reach a reasonable size in 5–6 years. Low-water-using once established, it grows well if the root zone is thoroughly soaked once every 10–14 days in the summer. Plant it in full or reflected sun, and in a soil with good drainage. Maintenance is minimal, mainly removing the flower stalk once blooming is finished. The teeth detach from the leaf readily and can be a nuisance when weeding or handling the plant.

IDENTIFICATION: *D. acrotrichum* is easily separated from *D. wheeleri* by virtue of the bright green leaves. *D. texanum* is another green-leafed species, but it is darker green with fewer, stouter marginal teeth. *D. quadrangulatum* generally lacks marginal teeth on the leaves. However, I have seen a few *D. quadrangulatum* with occasional, weak, marginal teeth near the base of the leaf that may represent a juvenile characteristic or some possible hybridization in the wild.

LANDSCAPE APPLICATION: This is an ideal plant to use singly as a large, bold specimen, massed for a spectacular display, or cohabitating with *D. wheeleri* to set off its blue-gray color. Plant it with other desert accents such as *Nolina* and *Yucca* species. Smaller shrubs that make it look handsome include *Ageratum corymbosum*, *Asclepias linaria*, *Dalea capitata*, *Dalea frutescens*, *Gaura lindheimeri*, *Poliomintha maderensis*, *Salvia greggii*, *Scutellaria suffrutescens*, and *Wedelia acapulcensis* var. *hispida*.

PRECAUTIONS: Javelinas and jackrabbits will eat the leaves.

Dasylirion quadrangulatum | Toothless Desert Spoon

CACTUS/SUCCULENT

SIZE (height x width)	>4–8 feet x 5–9 feet
FLOWER COLOR	Insignificant
FLOWER SEASON	Summer
EXPOSURE	Full or filtered sun

WATER	Low–moderate
GROWTH RATE	Slow
HARDINESS	Hardy to at least 15° F
PRUNING	None
NATURAL ELEVATION RANGE	5,500–8,000 feet
SUITABLE CITIES	All low- and mid-elevation-zone cities; Sierra Vista in the high-elevation zone

FIELD NOTES: *Dasylirion quadrangulatum* grows on dry, rocky, limestone hills in southern Tamaulipas and southern Nuevo León in northeastern Mexico from about 5,500 to 8,000 feet elevation. It frequently associates with *Acacia, Agave,* and *Yucca* species, and *Larrea divaricata.* My first encounter with this plant was in the wet part of southern Tamaulipas where Ron Gass and I saw some massive individuals poking their heads above the impenetrable tangle of shrubs. I have since seen ancient ones ruling over the dry, less densely vegetated slopes closer to Doctor Arroyo in Nuevo León.

DESCRIPTION: This mammoth, dominating accent has the potential to grow to 8–10 feet tall (trunk and leaves) with a leaf crown of up to 9 feet across. A typical specimen is closer to 4–5 feet tall with a leaf spread of 5–9 feet. The thin, flexible leaves are ⅛ inch wide and can be as long as 4 feet. They are four-angled and toothless along the edge. With age, plants will develop dark, almost black trunks to 6 or more feet high. In spring, the 10–12-foot flower stalk shoots up, with male and female flowers on separate plants. The female stalk may produce seed if both sexes are planted together.

CULTURE/MAINTENANCE: This plant has withstood overnight lows of 15° without harm so long as it has been kept dry during the fall and winter. Place it in full sun and a soil with very good drainage. It uses little water once established but will respond to some supplemental water from spring to early fall. Plants are slow-growing and seem to take forever to develop the characteristic trunk. No pruning is necessary unless you want to remove the older, dried leaves.

IDENTIFICATION: The thin, flexible, toothless leaves set *D. quadrangulatum* apart from all other species of *Dasylirion.* For years, this plant had been grown and sold as *D. longissimum.* Recent fieldwork by botanist David Bogler has revealed that there are two species of *Dasylirion* with four-angled, smooth-edged leaves. *D. longissimum* occurs further south in Mexico.

LANDSCAPE APPLICATION: Only a handful of us will ever see a dramatic full-grown specimen. Here's the good news—it is a visual delight even when young. Toothless leaf edges allow for planting near high-traffic areas, although you should allow ample room since the leaf crown can fill out to 6–9 feet in diameter in a reasonable amount of time. Combine with shrubs for contrasting form and colorful blooms: *Anisacanthus quadrifidus* var. *wrightii*, *Cordia parvifolia*, *Dalea capitata*, *Dalea frutescens*, *Larrea divaricata*, *Leucophyllum candidum*, *Penstemon* species, *Poliomintha maderensis*, *Salvia greggii*, or with other accents such as *Agave* species and *Nolina nelsonii*. It works in either the outer zone of a xeriscape or in the mini-oasis. It is amenable to full or filtered sun and can tolerate a wide range of soil types.

PRECAUTIONS: Take care to protect these plants from wildlife, including rabbits and javelinas. In the past, plants were imported directly from wild populations in Mexico. Now, they are being grown from seed, hopefully resulting in less removal from the wild.

Dasylirion wheeleri | Desert Spoon

CACTUS/SUCCULENT

SIZE (height x width)	4–6 feet x 4–6 feet
FLOWER COLOR	Tan
FLOWER SEASON	Summer
EXPOSURE	Full or reflected sun
WATER	Low–moderate
GROWTH RATE	Moderate
PRUNING	Remove flower stalk if desired
HARDINESS	Hardy to at least 0° F
NATURAL ELEVATION RANGE	4,000–6,000 feet
SUITABLE CITIES	All cities in all zones

FIELD NOTES: *Dasylirion wheeleri* is native to gravelly and rocky hillsides and mesas in central and southern Arizona, southern New Mexico, western Texas, and Chihuahua and Sonora, Mexico, from about 4,000 to 6,000 feet elevation. Plants are readily spotted when driving up Mt. Lemmon in the Santa Catalina Mountains near Tucson and when hiking at mid-elevation throughout the borderlands. Desert spoon is famous for spreading fires in the Southwest. Lightning strikes a stalk, leaves burn off, a flaming plant top detaches, and a bowling ball of fire rolls down slopes, igniting the grasses in its path.

DESCRIPTION: This accent makes quite a statement in any desert landscape, growing to 4–6 feet or more tall with a spread of 4–6 feet. It's slow going to achieve this size, so the plants you see in landscapes are more like 3–4 feet across. The narrow, blue-green, 2–3-foot-long leaves radiate from the apex of the central trunk to form a nearly perfect hemisphere. Leaf edges are armed with teeth that curve back towards the trunk and can easily rip flesh. A 12–15-foot-tall flower spike appears in the summer. Male and female flowers occur on separate plants, and the spike of female flowers is larger in diameter than the spike of male flowers. Seeds will develop on the female spikes.

CULTURE/MAINTENANCE: *D. wheeleri* is hardy to 0° F. Plants are moderate to low-water-using, growing best when the root zone is thoroughly soaked once every 7–14 days in spring and summer. The growth rate is moderate, and plants will grow a little faster with supplemental summer irrigation. They grow naturally in rocky soils on slopes and should be cultivated in a soil with similarly good drainage. Place desert spoon in full or reflected sun. This easygoing accent requires almost no maintenance except to remove spent flower spikes if desired.

IDENTIFICATION: *D. wheeleri* is readily distinguished from its relatives by the leaves. It has blue-gray leaves, while *D. acrotrichum, D. miquihuanensis,* and *D. texanum* have rich green leaves, and *D. quadrangulatum* has leaves with no marginal teeth.

LANDSCAPE APPLICATION: Desert spoon looks good when used with other desert natives in all elevation zones in the Southwest. Plant it solo among perennials and shrubs or mass for a spectacular effect. Compatible ground covers and shrubs include: *Anisacanthus quadrifidus* var. *wrightii, Asclepias linaria, Chrysactinia mexicana, Conoclinium dissectum, Dalea capitata, Dalea frutescens, Ericameria laricifolia, Larrea divaricata, Poliomintha maderensis, Salvia greggii, Scutellaria suffrutescens* and *Wedelia acapulcensis* var. *hispida.* Put spring perennials in the same hole with desert spoon to give added color. Plants such as *Baileya multiradiata, Penstemon* species, *Thymophylla pentachaeta,* and even bulbs like *Cooperia* and *Zephyranthes* are compatible. Desert spoon is best grown in full sun to maintain a dense rosette. Allow plenty of room for this plant to develop fully. It can get cozy with other plants but should not occupy high-traffic areas or tight spaces.

PRECAUTIONS: Even mature leaves are sometimes eaten by javelinas. Posting a 24-hour watch may be all that can be done to deter these critters. The teeth on the leaf margins are small, but they mean business. Teeth curve back towards the trunk, allowing you to reach in, but tearing you on the way back out. Wear a long-sleeved-shirt and heavy gloves when weeding or working around this plant.

Dioon edule | Palmita

CACTUS/SUCCULENT, PALM/CYCAD	
SIZE (height x width)	2–3 feet (rarely 10 feet) x 3–4 feet
FLOWER COLOR	Cones are produced
FLOWER SEASON	Summer
EXPOSURE	Filtered sun, or full or partial shade
WATER	Moderate
GROWTH RATE	Slow
HARDINESS	Hardy to at least low 20s F
PRUNING	Remove old leaves prior to emergence of new leaves
NATURAL ELEVATION RANGE	1,600–4,900 feet
SUITABLE CITIES	All low- and mid-elevation-zone cities

FIELD NOTES: When cruising along Mexico Highway 31 between Galeana and Linares in Nuevo León, keep your eyes peeled for the distinctive leaves of *Dioon edule*. I have seen it on a shaded slope about 20 miles west of Linares. This plant prefers steep cliffs and rocky habitats and is hidden among the semitropical vegetation in eastern Mexico between 1,600 and 4,900 feet elevation.

DESCRIPTION: *D. edule* is a slow-growing cycad that eventually develops a trunk up to about 10 feet tall. Realistically we'll rarely see these primitive, palm-like plants taller than about 2–3 feet with a leaf spread of about 3–4 feet. The leaves are straight, stiff, green, and abundant, measuring 3–4 feet long and 7–8 inches wide. They are pinnate with numerous narrow, linear leaflets each measuring 3–4 inches long. Young plants manufacture leaves one at a time. Older plants will produce all their leaves for the season in one flush in spring, and this crown of foliage creates a tropical mood. This species is dioecious, with male and female cones prominently displayed on separate plants. Female cones are solitary, ovoid to somewhat dome-shaped, and measure about 10–11 inches long by 7–10 inches in diameter. The non-subtle, solitary male cones are upright, cylindrical, and distinctive, measuring 7–8 inches long by 3–4 inches across.

CULTURE/MAINTENANCE: Palmita is hardy to at least the low 20s F and possibly lower. Growth seems like an afterthought—it will take years and years to develop a noticeable trunk. Rainfall in the natural habitat averages 40–60 inches a year, but plants make it with moderate watering. Install in a soil with fast drainage, and give a good thorough soaking of the root zone once every 7–10 days in the summer. Place in filtered sun, part shade, or full shade. Early-morning summer sun is fine, but in the interior, low-elevation, and even mid-elevation areas, afternoon shade is a must. Even in coastal southern California, plants benefit from some summer shade. Remove old leaves just before the new leaves emerge in the spring.

IDENTIFICATION: The leaflets become smaller at the tip of the leaf and form an inverted V-shape versus the regular V-shape at the end of the leaves of the other cycad grown in our area, *Cycas revoluta*.

LANDSCAPE APPLICATION: Palmita is right at home in shaded entryways with other plants that give that subtropical feel. For contrasting textures try eclectic mixes with *Acacia willardiana, Agave bovicornuta, Aquilegia chrysantha, Justicia spicigera,* and *Muhlenbergia dumosa.* Palmita benefits from the shade of trees and lives peacefully under New World *Acacia, Prosopis,* and *Quercus* species. This is a perfect fit for those north sides of buildings and walls in the low- and mid-elevation zones.

PRECAUTIONS: There are no reported problems with *D. edule* as a landscape plant.

Diospyros texana | Texas Persimmon

LARGE SHRUB, SMALL TREE

SIZE (height x width)	10–15 feet x 10–15 feet (in ideal conditions 35 feet x 25 feet)
FLOWER COLOR	Yellowish-white
FLOWER SEASON	Spring
EXPOSURE	Full or reflected sun, or part shade
WATER	Low–moderate
GROWTH RATE	Slow
HARDINESS	Hardy to at least 10° F
PRUNING	None or shape to tree form
NATURAL ELEVATION RANGE	1,100–5,700 feet
SUITABLE CITIES	All low- and mid-elevation-zone cities; Sierra Vista in high-elevation zone

FIELD NOTES: *Diospyros texana* grows on limestone and igneous soil in western, central, and southern Texas and adjacent Mexico from 1,100 to 5,700 feet elevation. It shows up as the occasional shrub or tree along Texas State Highway 285 from Fort Stockton south to Del Rio. Nice specimens display themselves for visitors in Big Bend National Park.

DESCRIPTION: This large, deciduous or semievergreen shrub or small, multiple-trunked tree typically fills out to 10–15 feet tall and 10–15 feet wide, but under ideal conditions has been known to stretch to 35 feet tall with a 25-foot spread. Older plants have an attractive mottled surface as the thin, gray outer bark peels off in patches to reveal smooth white inner bark. The oval to oblong, dark green leaves are nearly 2 inches long and have a thick, leathery feel. Small, yellowish-white, bell-shaped flowers appear in the spring, with male and female flowers segregating on separate plants. Although blossoms often hide under the leaves, their presence is betrayed by a strong sweet fragrance. You'll know you have a female tree if flowers give way to 1-inch-diameter, dark purple, fleshy fruits. Although not as tasty as common persimmon, the fruits are edible and relished by birds and small mammals.

CULTURE/MAINTENANCE: *D. texana* is hardy to at least 10° F and likely lower temperatures. Plants grow best when placed in full or reflected sun but put up with half-days in the shade. The species is tolerant of a variety of soil types but does best in one that has good drainage. It uses moderate to low amounts of water once established but will benefit from a little more water when young. It will take several years to develop into a decorative, small tree. Large, multiple-stemmed shrubs take selective pruning to grow as a small tree. Pick three promising main trunks, and then prune periodically to maintain those main trunks and shape the crown. Those female plants can make a mess with their fruits.

IDENTIFICATION: Texas persimmon is easily identified by its leaves, flowers, and mottled bark.

LANDSCAPE APPLICATION: As a shrub, Texas persimmon works as an excellent screening or barrier plant. It also serves well in a wildlife garden in the low- and mid-elevation zones and Sierra Vista in the high-elevation zone. It gets along with many other native Chihuahuan Desert shrubs including *Ageratum corymbosum*,

Anisacanthus quadrifidus var. *wrightii, Buddleja marrubiifolia, Dalea capitata, Dalea frutescens, Leucophyllum candidum, Salvia greggii,* and *Wedelia acapulcensis* var. *hispida.* Try it with big, bold succulents such as *Agave, Dasylirion,* and *Yucca* species.

PRECAUTIONS: As cultivation becomes more common, we will learn more about potential problems. Hedge your bets and screen young plants in case the bark is palatable to rabbits. Let the soil dry out between waterings to avoid root rot.

Dodonaea viscosa | Hopbush, HopSeed Bush

MEDIUM–LARGE SHRUB

SIZE (height x width)	6–12 feet x 4–10 feet
FLOWER COLOR	Inconspicuous flowers
FLOWER SEASON	Spring
EXPOSURE	Full or reflected sun
WATER	Low–moderate
GROWTH RATE	Moderately fast
PRUNING	None or clip as a hedge
HARDINESS	Hardy to at least 15° F
NATURAL ELEVATION RANGE	2,000–5,000 feet in Arizona, up to 9,800 feet near the equator in Ecuador
SUITABLE CITIES	All low- and mid-elevation-zone cities, Sierra Vista in high-elevation zone

FIELD NOTES: *Dodonaea viscosa* inhabits tropical, subtropical, and warm temperate regions in the Americas, Africa, and Australia. Closer to home, *D. viscosa* var. *angustifolia* is found on rocky slopes and gravelly plains in southern Arizona at about 2,000–5,000 feet elevation, and south to Sinaloa, Mexico. Once upon a time a favorite sight when returning from Mexico was "Dodonaea Hill," dubbed so by Professor Warren Jones. The hill, just south of Nogales, Arizona, on Mexico Highway 15, used to be covered with *Dodonaea* and *Dasylirion* but now is dominated by grass with the occasional *Dodonaea*.

DESCRIPTION: This large, upright to spreading shrub is evergreen with long, narrow, medium green leaves measuring 2–5 inches long by ½–1 inch wide. Flowers are nothing to write home about, but the papery, pinkish, three-winged fruit is interesting at close range. Fruits display themselves in the summer, and "Hopbush" comes from their use by desperate people as a substitute for hops in the making of beer. *D. viscosa* var. *angustifolia* has much narrower leaves, is more drought-tolerant, and is slightly hardier to frost.

CULTURE/MAINTENANCE: The Arizona form, var. *angustifolia,* is hardy to

about 15° F, while the more tropical varieties are not as tough. Although plants are found at elevations as high as 8,000–9,000 feet, those plants tend to be found closer to the equator, and we here in the desert Southwest have more success with the variety found closer to home. The plant is moderate to low-water-using once established and can communicate about overwatering via iron chlorosis. The growth rate is moderately fast, depending on the amount and timing of supplemental water. It requires very little maintenance and is tolerant of extreme makeover pruning or no pruning at all. Two purple- or bronzy purple-leafed forms are available. By far the most popular variety is 'Purpurea' which is usually grown from seed so will vary greatly. Typically, it has bronzy green foliage that turns darker in the winter. The other form, variety 'Saratoga,' is grown from cuttings, thus has uniformly rich purple foliage. Both varieties are susceptible to root rot in soggy soil, and they both should be planted in full sun in order to keep the rich color.

IDENTIFICATION: *D. viscosa* is easily recognized by its bright green leaves, small 3-winged fruits, and classic screening-shrub form.

LANDSCAPE APPLICATION: Plant this shrub singly as a specimen or mass as a backdrop for plants with gray or silvery foliage or as a screen in the low- and mid-elevation zones, and even Sierra Vista in the high-elevation zone. When mass planted, the plants can either be left unclipped as an informal barrier or clipped to make a more formal statement. They blend smartly with bold accent plants such as *Dasylirion*, *Nolina*, and *Yucca* species. The bright green foliage gives a subtropical feel and looks inviting when used near patios and pools.

PRECAUTIONS: No wildlife or insect problems have been reported. Just remember to place the plant in full sun and a soil with good drainage. Let soil dry out some between water applications.

Ebenopsis ebano | Texas Ebony

LARGE SHRUB, SMALL–
MEDIUM TREE

SIZE (height x width)	15–20 (40) feet x 15–20 (40) feet
FLOWER COLOR	Creamy yellow

FLOWER SEASON	Spring–summer
EXPOSURE	Full or reflected sun
WATER	Low–moderate
GROWTH RATE	Slow
PRUNING	Select main trunks for tree form
HARDINESS	Established trees are hardy to mid-teens, while young plants are damaged at mid-20s F
NATURAL ELEVATION RANGE	600–2,300 feet
SUITABLE CITIES	All low-elevation cities; Tucson in mid-elevation zone

FIELD NOTES: *Ebenopsis ebano* grows in mesquite-blackbrush vegetation and live oak woodland between 600 and 2,300 feet elevation in southern Texas and the states of Tamaulipas, Nuevo León, Vera Cruz, and San Luis Potosí in Mexico. Spectacular trees show up in landscapes in south Texas towns along the Rio Grande and also south of the border along Mexico Highway 85 from Linares to Ciudad Victoria in Tamaulipas.

DESCRIPTION: Texas ebony is one of the most attractive trees in Southwestern horticulture. This slow-growing, evergreen tree will take years to reach 15–20 feet tall and 15–20 feet across. Given deep soil, ample rainfall, high humidity, and mild winter temperatures, the tree will grow to over 40 feet tall and 30–35 feet across. The trunk is dark silvery gray. Short, stout, angular branches are armed with stout spines at the base of dark green, once pinnate leaves. Dense spikes of yellow flowers accessorize in spring and summer. Thick, hard, woody pods measure about 6 inches long and nearly 1 inch wide.

CULTURE/MAINTENANCE: Texas ebony is hardy to at least 17° F and drought-tolerant, although it will benefit from supplemental water applied from spring through summer. It takes a long time to become a full-size tree. In habitat, the tree grows in a variety of soil types ranging from sandy to clay or thin, hard limestone, but good drainage doesn't hurt. It grows best in full or reflected sun. Some staking and pruning is required to develop as a tree form—start the pruning sooner rather than later.

IDENTIFICATION: *E. ebano* is distinguished from the other two ebonies, formerly known as *Pithecellobium (P. mexicanum* and *P. pallens)*, by its dark green color, very dense habit, and hard, woody pods. The other two have gray-green leaves, a more open habit, and pods that are easier to open.

LANDSCAPE APPLICATION: Texas ebony is used as a dense, evergreen shade tree or as a stand-alone specimen tree in the low-elevation zone and Tucson of the mid-elevation zone. Mass plant to create a thorny barrier or screen, then sit back and raise your kids. Its dark green foliage creates a lush subtropical effect in the mini-oasis. Mix with other plants that have bold, dark green or feathery foliage: *Agave bovicornuta, Cordia boissieri, Dalea versicolor* var. *sessilis,* and *Sophora secundiflora.* Combine with shrubs that have colorful flowers like *Ageratum corymbosum, Anisacanthus quadrifidus* var. *wrightii, Justicia spicigera, Lantana* 'New Gold,' *Salvia greggii, Salvia leucantha,* and *Tagetes lemmonii.*

PRECAUTIONS: Because of the stout thorns, don't plant in high-traffic areas. I'm not kidding about how slow Texas ebony is to develop its full size.

Echinocactus grusonii | Golden Barrel

CACTUS/SUCCULENT

SIZE (height x width)	12–24 inches x 12–24 inches
FLOWER COLOR	Yellow
FLOWER SEASON	Summer
EXPOSURE	Full sun or light shade
WATER	Drought-tolerant–low
GROWTH RATE	Moderately slow
PRUNING	None
HARDINESS	Hardy to at least 17° F
NATURAL ELEVATION RANGE	4,000–5,000 feet
SUITABLE CITIES	All low- and mid-elevation-zone cities; warm microclimates in Sierra Vista in high-elevation zone

FIELD NOTES: *Echinocactus grusonii* was once widespread in central Mexico but has been collected to near extinction and is no longer readily found in habitat. The occasional plant, when found, generally occurs around 4,000–5,000 feet elevation.

DESCRIPTION: As a youngster, this striking specimen is densely covered with brilliant golden yellow spines. As it matures, the ribs and spines grow farther apart, leaving the green body visible between the spines. Plants generally have a rounded form and get about 12–18 inches tall by 12–18 inches across; however, an extremely large specimen can get as big as 24 inches by 24 inches across. Yellow flowers are not highly visible among the more dominant golden yellow spines. A mass planting is a breathtaking sight.

CULTURE/MAINTENANCE: Golden barrel is hardy to at least 17° F and possibly lower. Allowing it to go dormant in the fall and winter will increase its hardiness. This species has a slow growth rate, taking several years to achieve maturity. It is drought-tolerant, surviving on 11 inches of annual rainfall, although supplemental water from spring until early fall will speed up growth. No maintenance is required. Mark the south side of the plant before moving it from the nursery and maintain the orientation when planting into its new home.

IDENTIFICATION: *E. grusonii* is easily identified by the mass of golden yellow spines.

LANDSCAPE APPLICATION: Golden barrel loves the low- and mid-elevation zones and will tolerate full sun or very light shade. Plants are reported to survive in Sierra Vista of the high-elevation zone, although they can get damaged in extreme cold. It is drought-tolerant enough to use with other cacti and succulents and will accept some supplemental water when planted with "leafy" plants. Some good companion accents include *Euphorbia antisyphilitica, Larrea divaricata, Simmondsia chinensis, Sophora secundiflora,* and all *Agave, Dasylirion, Ferocactus, Nolina,* and *Yucca* species. Mix it up with smaller shrubs and perennials like *Ageratum corymbosum, Baileya multiradiata, Chrysactinia mexicana, Ericameria laricifolia, Penstemon* species, *Poliomintha maderensis, Salvia greggii, Scutellaria suffrutescens, Verbena gooddingii,* and *Zinnia grandiflora.*

PRECAUTIONS: To reduce the risk of rot, do not supply supplemental water from mid-fall until early spring.

Echinocereus arizonicus | Scarlet Hedgehog

CACTUS/SUCCULENT	
SIZE (height x width)	8–16 inches x 10–18 inches
FLOWER COLOR	Red to orange-red
FLOWER SEASON	Late spring–early summer
EXPOSURE	Filtered sun
WATER	Drought-tolerant–low
GROWTH RATE	Slow
PRUNING	None

HARDINESS	Hardy to at least 0° F
NATURAL ELEVATION RANGE	3,000–6,200 feet
SUITABLE CITIES	All cities in all zones (although *E. triglochidiatus* is a bit better for high-elevation-zone cities)

FIELD NOTES: *Echinocereus arizonicus* was once included in *Echinocereus triglochidiatus,* but as so often happens in cactus taxonomy, it has been elevated to species rank. Regardless of the flip-flopping, it deserves a place in a desert garden. Find plants in the pine-oak vegetation of southeastern Arizona, southwestern New Mexico and adjacent Mexico from 3,000 to 6,200 feet elevation. Hike in the cool pines on Mt. Lemmon outside of Tucson, and plan on seeing *E. arizonicus* perched on large boulders on the steep slopes.

DESCRIPTION: This cactus produces few stems and forms low, clustering mounds. Dark green stems are adorned with many yellow to light brown or sometimes black spines. Splashy red to orange-red flowers appear in late spring or early summer. The blossoms have a narrow tube with wide-flaring tips, and they attract a flurry of hummingbirds. Spiny, 1-inch-long fruits follow in late summer.

CULTURE/MAINTENANCE: *E. arizonicus* is cold-hardy, tolerating winter lows of at least 0° F. The plant grows slowly and needs several years to achieve its full size. This little gem can survive on rainfall once established but will tolerate extra water in the summer as long as the soil drains quickly. No pruning is required.

IDENTIFICATION: *E. arizonicus* is difficult to distinguish from the closely related *E. triglochidiatus,* which tends to have more stems and fewer, dark brown to black spines.

LANDSCAPE APPLICATION: Put scarlet hedgehog in a slightly shady spot where it can grab the spotlight during its brief, yet showy flowering period in a natural landscape. Plant underneath small desert trees like *Acacia constricta, Acacia greggii, Bauhinia lunarioides, Eysenhardtia orthocarpa,* and *Parkinsonia microphylla;* or interplant with perennials and small shrubs like *Chrysactinia mexicana, Ericameria laricifolia, Hibiscus coulteri, Penstemon* species, *Salvia greggii, Scutellaria suffrutescens, Verbena gooddingii* and *Zinnia grandiflora.* It will hold its own with other bold accent plants such as *Agave, Dasylirion, Hesperaloe,* and *Yucca* species. It is ideal for the low- and mid-elevation zones, while *E. triglochidiatus* is very similar, can be used in virtually the same way, and is a bit hardier for the high-elevation zone.

PRECAUTIONS: This hedgehog grows slowly and does not like too much water.

Echinocereus engelmannii | Engelmann Hedgehog

CACTUS/SUCCULENT	
SIZE (height x width)	8–18 inches x 18–30 (rarely 36) inches
FLOWER COLOR	Magenta, purple, or lavender
FLOWER SEASON	Late winter–late spring
EXPOSURE	Full or filtered sun
WATER	Drought-tolerant
GROWTH RATE	Slow
PRUNING	None
HARDINESS	Hardy to at least mid-teens F
NATURAL ELEVATION RANGE	0–5,000 feet
SUITABLE CITIES	All low- and mid-elevation-zone cities; warm spots in high-elevation-zone cities

FIELD NOTES: This hedgehog is generally found on gravelly, sandy, or rocky soil of plains, washes, hillsides, and canyons in southern California, southern Nevada, southern Utah, Arizona, Baja California, and Sonora, Mexico, from near sea level to 5,000 feet elevation. I keep an eye on several plants during my early morning walks with my wife Carol and our rabbit chaser, Nikki. Year after year, we enjoy the spectacle of the flowering cycle for this cactus.

DESCRIPTION: *Echinocereus engelmannii* produces several stems and can form low, clustering mounds 8–18 inches tall by 18–30 (rarely 36) inches across. Numerous, multicolored spines mostly hide green, many-ribbed stems. The knockout punch comes in spring when 3-inch-wide, magenta, purple, or lavender flowers appear anytime from late winter until late spring. Spine-covered, 1-inch-long fruits follow in late spring or early summer.

CULTURE/MAINTENANCE: This hedgehog is cold-hardy, tolerating winter lows of at least the mid-teens F. It is no speed demon, taking several years to achieve its full size. This tough desert native can survive on rainfall once established—in fact, too much water can be hazardous to its health. It will tolerate most soil types as long as drainage is good. No pruning is required.

IDENTIFICATION: The combination of size, form, spines, and flower color easily distinguish *E. engelmannii* from other species.

LANDSCAPE APPLICATION: *E. engelmannii* relishes the heat of the low- and mid-elevation zones and would love to be in a natural landscape where it can be on display during its brief, yet showy flowering period. It blends well with other cacti, perennials, low shrubs, and small trees, such as *Acacia constricta, Acacia greggii, Bauhinia lunarioides, Eysenhardtia orthocarpa, Ferocactus* species, *Opuntia* species, *Parkinsonia microphylla, Penstemon* species, *Salvia greggii, Scutellaria suffrutescens, Simmondsia chinensis,* and *Verbena gooddingii.* Commingle with bold accents such as *Agave, Dasylirion, Hesperaloe,* and *Yucca* species.

PRECAUTIONS: It is slow-growing and does not like too much water.

Encelia farinosa | Brittlebush

FLOWERING PERENNIAL, MEDIUM SHRUB	
SIZE (height x width)	3–4 feet x 3–4 feet
FLOWER COLOR	Yellow
FLOWER SEASON	Winter–early summer
EXPOSURE	Full sun
WATER	Low
GROWTH RATE	Moderately fast
PRUNING	Minimal (prune frozen growth and remove old flower heads)
HARDINESS	Half-hardy (stem damage at mid 20s)
NATURAL ELEVATION RANGE	Near sea level–3,000 feet
SUITABLE CITIES	All low-elevation cities except Austin and San Antonio; Tucson in mid-elevation zone

FIELD NOTES: The Sonoran Desert hillsides explode with color every spring when *Encelia farinosa* shoots up its bright yellow flowers. I frequently find these cheerful

shrubs among large boulders with *Carnegiea gigantea, Fouquieria splendens, Lycium species,* and *Simmondsia chinensis* on rocky hills and along washes in the Tucson Mountains west of the city. The native range extends from southern Nevada south into southern California, Arizona, Sonora, Sinaloa, and Baja California up to about 3,000 feet elevation.

DESCRIPTION: This tough shrubby plant forms a silvery gray, hemispherical mound. Stems stay mostly herbaceous although they will get slightly woody near the base. Leaves hold on throughout the winter unless the temperature gets too cold. The leaves provide a great silvery gray background for the bright yellow, daisy-like flowers that blanket the top of the plant in the spring and early summer-attracting native butterflies. Cultivated plants get carried away and flower in the winter as seen along roadsides around Tucson. Birds love to eat the seeds produced after the flowers fade.

CULTURE/MAINTENANCE: Established plants are generally hardy to the high 20s F, although tender new growth is damaged at that temperature. The plant may freeze to the ground at the high teens F. Once established, it is drought-tolerant, although it will accept some supplemental water in the spring and summer. It will recover from any frost damage very quickly in the spring. Plant it in full or reflected sun and in a soil with good drainage. Prune out any frozen stems after frost, and knock off the old flower stalks in the summer.

IDENTIFICATION: The gray-green leaves, hemispherical shape, and bright yellow, daisy-like flowers distinguish *E. farinosa.*

LANDSCAPE APPLICATION: Brittlebush needs sun and a warm microclimate to achieve a dense, compact shape and to dodge frost damage. It makes a fine color accent in the transition and outer zones of a xeriscape and attracts butterflies when in bloom. It can be mass planted and brings seasonal color to streets and medians. Mix with bold accent species such as *Agave, Carnegiea gigantea, Dasylirion, Fouquieria, Nolina,* and *Yucca.*

PRECAUTIONS: Stop watering in the fall so the plant has a chance to harden off before winter hits. Black aphids will congregate on the new growth and flowering stems. Wash them off with a strong spray of soapy water or apply an insecticidal soap every four or five days.

Eremophila hygrophana | Purple Emu Bush

SMALL SHRUB	
SIZE (height x width)	2–3 feet x 2–3 feet
FLOWER COLOR	Blue-purple
FLOWER SEASON	Late winter–spring
EXPOSURE	Full or reflected sun
WATER	Drought-tolerant–low
GROWTH RATE	Moderate
PRUNING	Cut out any frozen growth
HARDINESS	Hardy to at least mid-20s F

NATURAL ELEVATION RANGE   Information not available
SUITABLE CITIES   All low-elevation-zone cities except Austin and San Antonio; warm microclimates in mid-elevation-zone cities

FIELD NOTES: *Eremophila hygrophana* has such a limited distribution in Western Australia that it was not officially named until 2000. It is found on clay flats in *Acacia* woodland, near the *Acacia* trees and other shrubs, and not out in the open. More recently, plants have been found in the extreme western part of South Australia.

DESCRIPTION: Once spring hits, *E. hygrophana* reveals its beautiful 1-inch-long, deep blue-purple flowers over the top of silvery white leaves. This dense, tidy, evergreen shrub gets 2–3 feet tall and 2–3 feet across. Silvery white leaves are about 1 inch long.

CULTURE/MAINTENANCE: Purple emu bush is hardy to about the mid-20s F, recovering quickly from any damage suffered at lower temperatures. Once established, it is quite drought-tolerant and gets along with infrequent supplemental irrigation. Keep it on the dry side going into winter to reduce frost damage. It has a moderate growth rate, attaining its full size after a few years. It retains the most dense and compact form when planted in full or reflected sun.

IDENTIFICATION: *E. hygrophana* looks a bit like *Leucophyllum candidum,* but the leaves are larger, and the flowers come earlier in the year.

LANDSCAPE APPLICATION: Use purple emu bush as a small, spring-flowering shrub in a low-water-use landscape. There may not be hummingbirds in Australia, but the flowers draw them in on this side of the world. Install in the company of shrubs that bloom in spring such as *Baileya multiradiata, Encelia farinosa, Eremophila maculata, Penstemon* species, *Salvia greggii* and *Verbena gooddingii,* or mix with summer- and fall-flowering shrubs for an extended season of color such as *Anisacanthus quadrifidus* var. *wrightii, Dalea frutescens, Leucophyllum laevigatum,* and *Poliomintha maderensis.* The silvery white foliage looks pretty against contrasting green plants. This plant is tough enough for streets and medians where it provides a splash of seasonal color.

PRECAUTIONS: As with many other Australian native plants, *E. hygrophana* does not like soggy soil around its roots. Plant in well-drained soil, water infrequently, and allow the soil to dry out before watering.

Eremophila maculata | Spotted Emu Bush

MEDIUM–LARGE SHRUB	
SIZE (height x width)	4–6 feet x 4–8 feet
FLOWER COLOR	Dark carmine-red, yellow
FLOWER SEASON	Late winter–spring
EXPOSURE	Full or reflected sun
WATER	Drought-tolerant–low
GROWTH RATE	Moderate
PRUNING	Shear after flowering
HARDINESS	Hardy to at least 15°–25° F
NATURAL ELEVATION RANGE	Recorded from 500 feet near Forrest in Western Australia
SUITABLE CITIES	Low-elevation-zone cities except Austin and San Antonio; all mid-elevation-zone cities

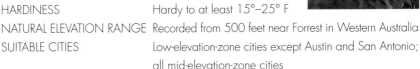

FIELD NOTES: *Eremophila maculata* is widespread throughout Australia at low elevations. It typically occurs with *Eucalyptus* and *Acacia* in low-lying areas—near rivers and drainages that experience periodic flooding. Breeders selected the cultivar 'Valentine' from offspring of the subspecies *brevifolia,* originally from Western Australia. The cultivar 'Winter Gold' is a yellow-flowered selection from the typical form. Other information is hard to find, so it looks like I need to make a trip Down Under to get a better handle on habitat information for almost all the Australian natives in cultivation.

DESCRIPTION: Come late winter, this dense, tidy, evergreen shrub launches an incredible display of 1½-inch-long flowers that stands out against a background of small, dark green leaves. **Leaf shape** varies from linear to oval, and leaves measure ½–1 inch long. Flowers come in gaudy shades from pinkish to dark carmine-red, yellow, or orange. The cultivar 'Valentine' grows to 4–5 feet tall and 5–8 feet across, with small, dark green leaves that develop a reddish tinge in the winter, and dark, carmine-red

flowers that will draw in the hummingbirds. 'Winter Gold' grows to 5–6 feet tall and 5–6 feet across, with light yellow flowers in spring.

CULTURE/MAINTENANCE: Depending on the cultivar, *E. maculata* can withstand winter lows to 15 or 25° F without suffering any damage. 'Valentine' is hardier than 'Winter Gold.' Once established, the plant is quite drought-tolerant, growing well on infrequent supplemental irrigation. It has a moderate growth rate, attaining its full size after a few years. It retains its most dense and compact form when planted in full or reflected sun, and it benefits from shearing after flowering, which boosts the following year's bloom.

IDENTIFICATION: Small, dark green, rounded leaves and deep red flowers that peak in mid-February readily distinguish 'Valentine,' while 'Winter Gold' can be identified by its light yellow flowers.

LANDSCAPE APPLICATION: Spotted emu bush is big enough to hold its own with other drought-tolerant plants in the transition and outer zones of a xeriscape. Mix with spring bloomers such as *Senna artemisioides, Encelia farinosa,* other *Eremophila* species, *Penstemon* species, and *Verbena gooddingii,* or throw it in with summer- and fall-flowering shrubs to extend the season of color. Handsome companion plants include *Dalea versicolor* var. *sessilis, Leucophyllum laevigatum,* and *Salvia greggii.* Its dark green foliage sets off gray and silvery species like *Buddleja marrubiifolia, Senna artemisioides, Encelia farinosa,* and *Leucophyllum candidum.* This smart plant attracts hummingbirds and works in heavy-duty street-side landscapes.

PRECAUTIONS: Soggy soil is no friend of *E. maculata.* Allow the soil to dry out before watering, then avoid watering too frequently.

Ericameria laricifolia | Turpentine Bush

SMALL–MEDIUM SHRUB	
SIZE (height x width)	2–3 feet x 2–3 feet
FLOWER COLOR	Yellow
FLOWER SEASON	Fall
EXPOSURE	Full or reflected sun
WATER	Low–moderate
GROWTH RATE	Moderate
PRUNING	Shear in spring, remove fading flower heads
HARDINESS	Hardy to -10° F
NATURAL ELEVATION RANGE	3,000–6,000 feet
SUITABLE CITIES	All cities in all zones

FIELD NOTES: *Ericameria laricifolia* grows on mesas and slopes in Arizona, across New Mexico, to western Texas, and south into northern Mexico from about 3,000 to 6,000 feet elevation. I've noted some nice plants near Camp Verde in central Arizona and in the Peloncillo Mountains of the bootheel of New Mexico.

DESCRIPTION: This grayish-green, long-lived, hemispherical shrub gets about 2–3 feet tall and 2–3 feet across. Plants have been reported to reach 3–4 feet tall and as much as 6 feet across. Although this could be a result of extraordinary conditions, it is always a good idea to keep the extreme cases in mind when rationing out space in your landscape. This fall showstopper livens up any Southwestern landscape. Plants have small, bright green, needlelike, aromatic leaves about ½ inch long, but it is the presence of resinous glands that really gives them their distinctive fragrance. Clusters of showy, bright yellow, daisy-like flowers decorate the tips of the stems from August to November and are frequented by butterflies.

CULTURE/MAINTENANCE: Plants are hardy to at least -10° F. Place in a sunny location for compact form and intense flowering. They seem to prefer a rocky soil with good drainage but will tolerate other types. Once established, they survive on 12 inches of annual rainfall. Plants take two or three seasons to reach full size and will reward you with more flowers when given some extra water in spring and summer. Shear in late winter or early spring to keep the shrub dense, and trim off the old flower heads as they start to fade.

IDENTIFICATION: *E. laricifolia* looks somewhat similar to *Chrysactinia mexicana*. *E. laricifolia* blooms only in the fall and tends to be lighter, grayish-green.

LANDSCAPE APPLICATION: Use turpentine bush where you need a low, flowering shrub, or mass plant for a dynamic effect. Because of its small size, it works well in small spaces or narrow areas such as street or parking lot medians, or small courtyards. It's great for patio areas or a sensory garden where people can enjoy the wonderful fragrance. Mix in with accent plants like *Agave* species, *Dasylirion* species, *Hesperaloe funifera*, *Nolina nelsonii*, and *Yucca* species. Perennials and shrubs that bloom in spring and summer will add a dash of color throughout the growing season. Try combining with other short guys with pretty flowers like *Ageratum corymbosum*, *Berlandiera lyrata*, *Calliandra eriophylla*, *Dalea frutescens*, *Penstemon* species, *Poliomintha maderensis*, *Salvia greggii*, and *Scutellaria suffrutescens*.

PRECAUTIONS: The flowers will attract bees.

Erythrina flabelliformis | Coral Bean

FLOWERING PERENNIAL	
SIZE (HEIGHT X WIDTH)	3–6 (20–25) feet x 3–6 (10–12) feet
FLOWER COLOR	Bright red
FLOWER SEASON	Late spring–summer
EXPOSURE	Full or reflected sun

WATER	Low–moderate
GROWTH RATE	Moderate
PRUNING	Trim out frozen stems
HARDINESS	Tender; frost damage at high 20s F
NATURAL ELEVATION RANGE	3,000–5,500
SUITABLE CITIES	All low- and mid-elevation-zone cities; treat as a perennial or potted plant in high-elevation-zone cities

FIELD NOTES: *Erythrina flabelliformis* is found in southeastern Arizona and southwestern New Mexico, northern Mexico, and the southern part of Baja California. Plants like dry, rocky, exposed slopes from about 3,000 to 5,500 feet elevation. In the colder parts of the range, plants are usually multi-sticked, shrub-like entities, while down south or in the lower, frost-free elevations, they attain treelike status. Take a drive up Mt. Lemmon near Tucson in the summer to catch the shrub types in flower. Treelike forms can be seen on Mexico Highway 16 about 80 miles east of Hermosillo, Sonora, as you drive towards Yecora in the Sierra Madre Occidental.

DESCRIPTION: As the weather fires up in the spring, so does the coral bean. In the low desert, beginning in March and continuing until May or June, leafless shrubs burst out with 6-inch-long clusters of narrow, 3-inch-long, brilliant red flowers that are a hummingbird magnet. In the mid-elevation desert, flowering starts a little later and might even coincide with leafing out. Where frost is a factor, the plant freezes repeatedly and might reach 3–6 feet tall by 3–6 feet across. In frost-free areas it can be trained as a tree, eventually reaching 20–25 feet tall and 10–12 feet across. Medium green leaves are composed of three triangular leaflets, each measuring 1–3 inches long by 2–4 inches across. Light brown, 6–8-inch-long pods contain bright red poisonous seeds that are frequently used in making jewelry.

CULTURE/MAINTENANCE: Coral bean may freeze back when temperatures drop into the 28–30° F range. The plant builds up large underground **tuberous** roots from which it regrows in the spring. Because the flowers emerge from the previous year's growth, protect the stems if you live in a colder area. Plants have a moderate growth rate, taking a couple of years to recover to full size if severely frozen. It's best to place the plants in a warm microclimate in full sun or reflected heat. They will easily tolerate our native soil as long as drainage is adequate. Trim any frozen stems after the plants have started to leaf out.

IDENTIFICATION: Brilliant red flowers on sticks and pretty green triangular leaflets in threes are features that help distinguish *E. flabelliformis.*

LANDSCAPE APPLICATION: Use coral bean for sculptural interest and its hummingbird-attracting flower display. Mix with steady, reliable accent plants, such as *Agave, Dasylirion, Hesperaloe,* or even *Yucca* species. Use low-growing, evergreen shrubs or cool-season perennials near the base to give some interest when coral bean is dormant. Plants like *Chrysactinia mexicana, Ericameria laricifolia, Melampodium leucanthum, Penstemon* species*, Poliomintha maderensis, Salvia greggii,* and *Scutellaria suffrutescens* are all great companions with contrasting forms and flowers. Show coral bean off in large, decorative containers on a patio, but be sure to surround it with other plants that look good all year.

PRECAUTIONS: All parts are poisonous, especially the red seeds.

Eucalyptus microtheca | Coolibah, Tiny Capsule Eucalyptus

LARGE TREE

SIZE (height x width)	30–40 (60) feet x 25–30 (50) feet
FLOWER COLOR	Creamy white
FLOWER SEASON	Summer
EXPOSURE	Full or reflected sun
WATER	Drought-tolerant–moderate
GROWTH RATE	Moderate–moderately fast
PRUNING	None
HARDINESS	Hardy to 5–10° F
NATURAL ELEVATION RANGE	Unknown
SUITABLE CITIES	All cities in all zones except Albuquerque

FIELD NOTES: *Eucalyptus microtheca* inhabits seasonally flooded flats, watercourse edges, and the margins of swamps and lakes throughout much of northern Australia.

DESCRIPTION: The crooked, leaning form and rough bark create a picturesque tree for Southwestern landscapes. This tough guy survives heat, cold, drought, and poor soil better than most of the other *Eucalyptus* species. It typically gets to 30 feet tall with a spread of 25 feet in the desert Southwest, with the possibility of 40 feet tall and 30 feet across in extra-benign conditions. The crown is upright when young, then spreads with age. Narrow, blue-green leaves are 5–8 inches long and ½ inch wide. Young trees have smooth, white or gray bark while older trees have cracked, wrinkled bark. Tiny seed capsules try to make up for insignificant, creamy white flowers.

CULTURE/MAINTENANCE: Although foliage may burn, established plants will survive winter lows of 5–10° F. The growth rate is moderate to fast depending on the soil, climate, and extra water. This tree accepts soil types ranging from heavy with poor drainage to a fast-draining soil as long as watering gets adjusted accordingly. It is considered drought-tolerant but will grow better with a few deep, thorough soakings in the summer. It should be placed in full sun or reflected sun on the west side of a building to provide shade. Very little pruning is called for, although the tree will shed leaves and small twigs in high winds.

IDENTIFICATION: The crooked trunk and irregular crown identify *E. microtheca.*

LANDSCAPE APPLICATION: *E. microtheca* can be used effectively in public landscapes—around condos and townhouses or in street medians or parking lots—where neglect is a possibility. This is a great tree to mix with all kinds of low- and medium-water-use landscape plants. Or stick to Australian mates like selected *Acacia* species, *Eremophila maculata,* other *Eucalyptus* species, and *Senna artemisioides.*

PRECAUTIONS: In Australia, *E. microtheca* has been found to be a host for one species of psyllid, a tiny insect sometimes called jumping plant louse, that likes to suck the juices out of plants. There are some psyllid infestations affecting *Eucalyptus* species in California and Arizona. Minor infestations can be controlled biologically with a parasitic wasp.

Eucalyptus papuana | (In Australia it is now called *Corymbia aparrerinja)* | Ghost Gum

MEDIUM–LARGE TREE

SIZE (height x width)	20–40 (50) feet x 15–30 (40) feet
FLOWER COLOR	White
FLOWER SEASON	Summer
EXPOSURE	Full or reflected sun
WATER	Drought-tolerant–moderate
GROWTH RATE	Moderate
PRUNING	None
HARDINESS	Hardy to low 20s F
NATURAL ELEVATION RANGE	1,800–1,900 feet
SUITABLE CITIES	All low- and mid-elevation-zone cities

FIELD NOTES: *Eucalyptus papuana* is found on rocky slopes, red sand flats, and dry creek beds in arid parts of central and northern Australia. Aboriginals used parts of the tree to treat colds. Some nice specimens can be seen growing in open areas near Alice Springs in the southern part of Northern Territory at about 1,800–1,900 feet elevation.

DESCRIPTION: Powdery white bark and light green to gray-green leaves combine for visual interest and make *E. papuana* a striking species for landscape use. It grows as a medium to large, upright tree with a single trunk and an open canopy. Mature plants reach anywhere from 20 to 40 feet tall and 15–30 feet across, with 50 feet by 40 feet possible in mild southern California. Light green, lance-shaped leaves are 3–5 inches long by 1 inch wide. Small white flowers that appear during the summer later morph into inconspicuous seed capsules.

CULTURE/MAINTENANCE: Ghost gum is hardy to at least the low 20s F. With its moderate growth rate it will take several years to attain a size close to maturity. It seems to grow well in most desert soils as long as drainage is adequate, and it is drought-tolerant but will grow faster when given periodic, thorough soakings in the root zone. Plenty of space helps, too. Put plants to work in full sun or on the west side of a building to provide shade. Very little pruning is required to maintain ghost gum as a tree.

IDENTIFICATION: The smooth powdery white bark readily identifies *E. papuana.*

LANDSCAPE APPLICATION: Ghost gum can be used effectively around two- to three-story buildings like condos and townhouses, or in street medians and parking lots. Plant this tree with a variety of other Australian natives to create a wholly "Down Under" feel. Some excellent companion plants include many of the Australian *Acacia* species, *Eremophila maculata,* other *Eucalyptus* species, and *Senna artemisioides.*

PRECAUTIONS: *E. papuana* is one of the cleanest species available for landscaping. So far I haven't heard that *papuana* is susceptible to any of the many psyllid species that have been infesting other *Eucalyptus* species.

Eucalyptus spathulata | Narrow Leafed Gimlet, Swamp Mallet

MEDIUM TREE

SIZE (height x width)	20–30 feet x 18–25 feet
FLOWER COLOR	Cream
FLOWER SEASON	Summer
EXPOSURE	Full or reflected sun
WATER	Low–moderate
GROWTH RATE	Moderate–moderately fast
PRUNING	None
HARDINESS	Hardy to 15–20° F
NATURAL ELEVATION RANGE	2,500–5,000 feet
SUITABLE CITIES	All low-elevation-zone cities except Austin and San Antonio; all mid-elevation-zone cities

FIELD NOTES: *Eucalyptus spathulata* is native to sandy clay and saline soils on valley floors and depressions in southwestern Australia. These areas, at 2,500–5,000 feet elevation, experience periodic flooding.

DESCRIPTION: This upright, multi-trunk tree reaches 20–30 feet tall and 18–25 feet across. Narrow, dark blue-gray leaves measure 2–3 inches long by ¼ inch wide. The smooth bark that ranges in color from salmon-pink and cinnamon-red to satiny gray, is an appealing feature even from a distance. Clusters of small, cream-colored flowers appear during the summer and are followed by small, bell-shaped seed capsules.

CULTURE/MAINTENANCE: Narrow leafed gimlet is hardy to at least 15–20° F and will tolerate a variety of soil types ranging from heavy with poor drainage to a fast-draining soil. It is tolerant of wet or dry conditions, even surviving periodic flooding, as long as the amount and frequency of watering is adjusted according to soil type. The growth rate is moderate, varying some with amount of supplemental water applied. It should be placed in full sun or on the west side of a building as a shade provider. It requires very little pruning to maintain as a small tree.

IDENTIFICATION: Smooth cinnamon-red bark and narrow, dark blue-gray leaves readily identify *E. spathulata*.

LANDSCAPE APPLICATION: Narrow leafed gimlet is useful as a small shade tree in the low- and mid-elevation zones except in Austin and San Antonio, where the higher annual rainfall can be detrimental. It can be used effectively around houses, condos, and townhouses, or as a street or parking lot tree. This is a great tree to mix with a variety of low- and medium-water-use landscape plants, such as *Anisacanthus quadrifidus, Dalea frutescens, Dasylirion quadrangulatum, Hesperaloe* species, *Leucophyllum* species, *Salvia greggii, Senna artemisioides,* and *Yucca* species.

PRECAUTIONS: There are no known problems. This is one of the cleanest *Eucalyptus* species available for landscaping.

Euphorbia antisyphilitica | Candelilla

SMALL SHRUB, CACTUS/SUCCULENT	
SIZE (height x width)	2–3 feet x 2–4 feet
FLOWER COLOR	Pink-and-white
FLOWER SEASON	Late spring–fall
EXPOSURE	Full or reflected sun
WATER	Drought-tolerant–low
GROWTH RATE	Fast, slow to fill in
PRUNING	None
HARDINESS	Hardy to at least 10° F
NATURAL ELEVATION RANGE	3,000–8,000 feet
SUITABLE CITIES	All low and mid-elevation zone cities; Sierra Vista in high-elevation zone; warm microclimates elsewhere in high-elevation-zone cities

FIELD NOTES: I've had the good fortune to discover *Euphorbia antisyphilitica* in several spots in the Chihuahuan Desert of northeastern Mexico. It mingles with cacti and low shrubs on limestone soil out in flat, open desert or tucks itself among large rocks on hills. Find it from western Texas south through the Chihuahuan Desert and into central Mexico from 3,000 to 8,000 feet elevation.

DESCRIPTION: *E. antisyphilitica* starts as a bunch of juicy sticks and transforms into an intriguing succulent as it matures. Slender, upright, grayish-green stems arise from below ground, reaching about 2–3 feet tall. Stems spread by rhizomes, resulting in large clumps up to 3–4 feet across with time. The leafless stems are coated with high-grade wax that causes this plant to be extensively harvested. Small pink-and-

white flowers grace the length of the stems from late spring through summer and even into fall.

CULTURE/MAINTENANCE: Plants are hardy to at least the mid-teens F and probably lower. They require very little water once established, surviving on 12 inches or less of annual rainfall, although they will grow faster if given a little extra in the summer. Individual stems grow quickly, but clumps take several years to reach 2–3 feet across. Use them in full or reflected sun and in soil with good drainage. Virtually no maintenance is needed.

IDENTIFICATION: The numerous, thin, upright stems readily identify *E. antisyphilitica*. You're not dreaming that the name implies a medicinal use.

LANDSCAPE APPLICATION: Candelilla was made to tuck among large boulders or rock gardens, and it combines strikingly with other desert plants both succulent and shrubby. On the succulent side, try it with *Agave, Dasylirion, Echinocereus, Ferocactus, Hesperaloe,* and *Nolina* species plus *Echinocactus grusonii.* Bring it together with perennials and small shrubs such as *Calliandra eriophylla, Chrysactinia mexicana, Dalea frutescens, Hibiscus coulteri, Penstemon* species, *Salvia greggii,* and *Scutellaria suffrutescens.*

PRECAUTIONS: Avoid getting the irritating, milky sap on your hands, and wash thoroughly if you do.

Euphorbia rigida | Gopher Plant

FLOWERING PERENNIAL, SMALL SHRUB	
SIZE (height x width)	2–3 feet x 3–4 feet
FLOWER COLOR	Chartreuse yellow
FLOWER SEASON	Late winter–early spring
EXPOSURE	Full or reflected sun, or light shade
WATER	Low–moderate
GROWTH RATE	Fast
PRUNING	Cut off old flowering stems in the summer
HARDINESS	Hardy to at least 20° F
NATURAL ELEVATION RANGE	Unknown
SUITABLE CITIES	All cities in all zones

FIELD NOTES: *Euphorbia rigida* is native to Asia Minor around the Mediterranean.

DESCRIPTION: This evergreen perennial or subshrub has a most unusual form and appearance. Its semisucculent, gray-green leaves are 2 inches long and ½ inch wide, with stems angling up and out. Broad clusters of chartreuse-yellow flowers at the stem tips create an impressive splash of late winter to early spring color. Flowers are followed by small brown seedpods that explode upon ripening. The stems die back after flowering and fruiting, leaving a small clump of gray-green foliage.

CULTURE/MAINTENANCE: Gopher plant is cold-hardy to at least 20° F. Although it is drought-tolerant, it will be showier with supplemental water while it is growing and flowering. It can attain full size in only two or three growing seasons. It handles full or reflected sun or light shade and prefers a soil that has good drainage. After the seeds ripen, the stems die back and should be removed.

IDENTIFICATION: *E. rigida* resembles *E. myrsinites* but can be distinguished by its larger size, bigger leaves, and more upright growth form.

LANDSCAPE APPLICATION: *E. rigida* provides early seasonal color and mixes well with cacti and other succulents. Plant it among boulders or tough accents for a softening effect. It works well in entryways and around pools if the developing seedpods are cut off before they ripen and explode. It can be massed and used along streets and medians and even holds its own as a container plant.

PRECAUTIONS: Be careful not to get the milky sap on your skin because it can be an irritant. It prefers not-too-moist, not-too-dry soil conditions.

Eysenhardtia orthocarpa | Kidneywood

SMALL TREE	
SIZE (height x width)	15–20 feet x 12–16 feet
FLOWER COLOR	White (vanilla-scented)
FLOWER SEASON	Spring–fall
EXPOSURE	Full or reflected sun
WATER	Low–moderate
GROWTH RATE	Moderately fast

PRUNING	Spring; shape to tree form
HARDINESS	Hardy to at least mid-teens F
NATURAL ELEVATION RANGE	Near sea level–6,500 feet
SUITABLE CITIES	All low- and mid-elevation-zone cities

FIELD NOTES: *Eysenhardtia orthocarpa* lives on slopes and in canyons in desert scrub, thorn scrub, tropical deciduous forest, grassland, and oak woodland from near sea level to 6,500 feet elevation. It occurs from southern Arizona and southwestern New Mexico south through Sonora, Chihuahua, and Sinaloa, Mexico. You can see some nice examples cruising along Mexico Highway 16 between Hermosillo and Yecora in Sonora.

DESCRIPTION: In late spring and early summer, clusters of small, white, vanilla-scented flowers cover this small tree just as it begins to leaf out. The flowers are a great source of nectar for many types of butterflies, including Hairstreaks and Blues. It has strongly upright, multiple trunks and upright to spreading branches. The overall look reminds me of a vase, and peeling bark adds intrigue. Leaves are 4–6 inches long and composed of 10–20 pairs of leaflets, each measuring about ½ inch long. The fruit is a small, one-seeded legume that does not split open.

CULTURE/MAINTENANCE: Plants are cold-hardy to at least the mid teens F and probably will tolerate lower temperatures than that. Typically, the trees are deciduous, but in mild climates, some leaves may hang on through the winter. Place them in full or reflected sun. They tolerate heat, drought, and poor soils, although they will grow faster if the root zone is thoroughly soaked 2–3 times per month from spring until fall. Trees grow fast at first but will slow some with age. Spend some quality time with your loppers for a few years to shape the plant into a multiple-trunked tree, but it is virtually maintenance-free after it reaches 8–10 feet tall. Seedpods are extremely small, and leaf debris is minimal.

IDENTIFICATION: *E. orthocarpa* is easily identified by the vanilla-scented leaves and flowers, and the small, one-seeded pods.

LANDSCAPE APPLICATION: Use kidneywood as a small tree in patios and court-yards, in narrow areas where you want some height, or even on the west side of a house for summer shade and winter sun. It casts the perfect light shade for cacti and succulents, and the open canopy and small size make a suitable umbrella for flowering perennials. Try surrounding it with small shrubs and perennials like *Ageratum corymbosum,*

Anisacanthus quadrifidus var. *wrightii, Asclepias linaria, Conoclinium dissectum, Dalea capitata, Salvia greggii, Wedelia acapulcensis* var. *hispida,* and *Zauschneria californica.*

PRECAUTIONS: It may take a couple of years for the trunks to get too large to be rabbit food. The pretty flowers that attract butterflies also attract bees.

Ferocactus glaucescens | Blue Barrel

CACTUS/SUCCULENT	
SIZE (height x width)	8–16 inches x 8–15 inches, clusters 20–30 inches across
FLOWER COLOR	Yellow
FLOWER SEASON	Spring
EXPOSURE	Full or filtered sun
WATER	Low–moderately drought-tolerant
GROWTH RATE	Slow
PRUNING	None
HARDINESS	Hardy to at least 15° F
NATURAL ELEVATION RANGE	3,600–5,000 feet
SUITABLE CITIES	All low- and mid-elevation-zone cities; Sierra Vista in high-elevation zone

FIELD NOTES: *Ferocactus glaucescens* is found growing on cliffs and slopes either in the open or hidden in shrubby vegetation in east-central Mexico from 3,600 to 5,000 feet elevation. On one of my first trips into central Mexico in August of 1983, my friend Russ Buhrow and I were driving along a dirt road in central San Luis Potosí and happened upon a perfect, solitary specimen growing out of a vertical, limestone outcrop.

DESCRIPTION: A waxy blue body and contrasting bright yellow spines make this barrel one of the most attractive available. This charming beauty gets only 8–16 inches tall and 8–15 inches in diameter, sometimes producing offsets to form clusters to about 20–30 inches across. Yellow, cup-shaped, 1-inch-diameter flowers appear in a ring near the top of the plant in spring. Small, yellow, tasty fruits ripen in late spring and early summer.

CULTURE/MAINTENANCE: This hardy plant tolerates winter lows of at least 15° F. Allow several years for plants to reach a substantial size. Water use is low to moderate, and established plants require only monthly

irrigation from late spring through summer. Potted plants will need watering about once or twice weekly in summer. Blue barrel needs its sunlight filtered in the hot, interior, low-elevation zones. It will tolerate more direct sun in coastal San Diego and Los Angeles and in mid-elevation Tucson. Put it in soil that has good drainage. No maintenance is required.

IDENTIFICATION: With its waxy blue body and yellow spines, *F. glaucescens* is not easily confused with any other species.

LANDSCAPE APPLICATION: Use blue barrel in a cactus and succulent garden, under the shade of a nurse tree in the hot interior zone. Mix with short perennials such as *Berlandiera lyrata, Calylophus hartwegii, Hibiscus martianus,* any *Penstemon* species, *Thymophylla pentachaeta,* or *Zinnia grandiflora.* Also tuck it around small shade trees such as *Acacia willardiana, Eysenhardtia orthocarpa, Havardia mexicana,* and *Leucaena retusa.*

PRECAUTIONS: Protect young plants from damage by rabbits and javelinas.

Ferocactus pilosus | Fire Barrel

CACTUS/SUCCULENT	
SIZE (height x width)	2–3 feet x 1–2 feet, old clusters up to 10 feet x 6 feet
FLOWER COLOR	Orange-yellow
FLOWER SEASON	Summer–fall
EXPOSURE	Full or filtered sun
WATER	Drought-tolerant–low
GROWTH RATE	Slow
PRUNING	None
HARDINESS	Hardy to at least 15° F
NATURAL ELEVATION RANGE	4,000–8,600 feet
SUITABLE CITIES	All cities in all zones except Albuquerque, where hardiness is unknown

FIELD NOTES: One of the most impressive sights in the Chihuahuan Desert is a full-grown *Ferocactus pilosus* with its central, bright red spines. It was a misty morning in southern Tamaulipas when Ron Gass and I spotted a massive specimen that was over 7 feet tall. It was in the company of numerous offshoots and formed a cluster about 6 feet across. This widespread species lives in open Chihuahuan Desert scrub and short-tree or thorn-forest vegetation of eastern Mexico. Elevation ranges from 4,000 to 8,600 feet and annual average rainfall ranges from 10 to 26 inches. Some of the nicest specimens I have seen, with prominent, white, bristly radial spines surrounding the

red ones, were at about 7,200 feet elevation on the Sierra Patagalana to the east of Parras in Coahuila, Mexico.

DESCRIPTION: In its natural habitat, *F. pilosus* can attain massive proportions—nearly 10 feet tall and up to 6 feet across. When backlit by early morning or late afternoon sun, the bright red spines seem to glow, creating the illusion of a plant on fire. Orangish or orange-yellow flowers emerge near the apex of the plant during summer. Typical yellow fruits, which taste like lime, form in late summer and fall.

CULTURE/MAINTENANCE: This hardy plant tolerates winter lows of at least 15° F. It took a lifetime for the cactus Ron and I saw to attain its size. This barrel grows about 1–1½ inches per year, reaching a realistic size of 2–3 feet tall in 20 years with 1 or 2 offshoots. Established plants use little water; monthly irrigation from late spring through summer is plenty. Potted plants will take more frequent irrigation, usually once a week in summer. Fire barrel grows best in a soil with good drainage and full sun but will tolerate filtered sunlight. Mark the south side of the plant before taking it out of the nursery and maintain the orientation when planting it in its new location.

IDENTIFICATION: With its bright red spines, *F. pilosus* is not easily confused with other species.

LANDSCAPE APPLICATION: Try placing this barrel where the spines will catch the early morning or late afternoon sunlight. Surround it with low-lying perennials such as *Berlandiera lyrata, Calylophus hartwegii, Hibiscus martianus,* any *Penstemon* species, *Thymophylla pentachaeta,* or *Zinnia grandiflora.* Install it with small shade trees such as *Acacia willardiana, Eysenhardtia orthocarpa,* and *Leucaena retusa,* or palms *Brahea armata* and *Sabal uresana.*

PRECAUTIONS: Protect young plants from damage by rabbits and javelinas. I'm guessing the monster specimens don't have this problem.

Ferocactus wislizenii | Fishhook Barrel

CACTUS/SUCCULENT

SIZE (height x width)	2–3 (6) feet x 1–2 feet stem diameter
FLOWER COLOR	Red, orange, yellow
FLOWER SEASON	Summer (July–September)
EXPOSURE	Full sun

WATER	Drought-tolerant
GROWTH RATE	Slow
PRUNING	None
HARDINESS	Hardy to at least 5° F
NATURAL ELEVATION RANGE	0–4,500 feet
SUITABLE CITIES	All cities in all zones except Albuquerque

FIELD NOTES: When hiking around in the desert of the southwestern U.S., don't get caught on the large hooked spines of *Ferocactus wislizenii*. This barrel cactus can be found from western Texas, across southern New Mexico, to southern Arizona, and south into adjoining northern Mexico, at elevations below 4,500 feet elevation.

DESCRIPTION: Although ancient specimens can grow as tall as 6–10 feet, nursery-grown plants take many years to reach 2–3 feet tall. The stem can reach nearly 2 feet in diameter. The central spines come in brown or gray with vicious, stout hooks. Bristlelike spines ring the edge of the **areole**. Red, orange, or yellow two-inch-wide flowers appear from July through September and form a brilliant crown around the growing point. This crown is resurrected when fruit turn yellow in the fall.

CULTURE/MAINTENANCE: Fishhook barrel is hardy to at least 5° F. It grows slowly, taking 15–20 years to reach a height of 20–24 inches. For best growth install plants in full sun and in a soil with good drainage. This cactus is extremely drought-tolerant once established, surviving on 10–12 inches of annual rainfall. Give young, newly planted plants some supplemental water during the growing season to help speed the growth rate, but overwatering does this plant no favors. Mature salvaged plants are sometimes available and can be reestablished in a landscape. Whether nursery-grown or salvaged, make sure to mark the south side of the plant and maintain the orientation when planting.

IDENTIFICATION: *F. wislizenii* is identified by the combination of hooked spines and bristles around the edge of the areole.

LANDSCAPE APPLICATION: Use this barrel in a xeriscape or cactus garden. Display its form artistically with other cacti such as *Carnegiea gigantea*, other *Ferocactus* species, and *Opuntia* species. Also combine it with Southwestern natives of all sizes, including *Chrysactinia mexicana, Encelia farinosa, Parkinsonia microphylla, Penstemon parryi, Penstemon superbus, Poliomintha maderensis* 'Lavender Spice,' *Salvia greggii, Simmondsia chinensis, Tetraneuris acaulis,* and *Verbena gooddingii.*

PRECAUTIONS: Go easy on the water.

Fouquieria columnaris | Boojum, Cirio

CACTUS/SUCCULENT

SIZE (height x width)	Realistically, 3–4 feet tall in 7–10 years
FLOWER COLOR	Creamy white
FLOWER SEASON	Late summer
EXPOSURE	Full sun or light shade
WATER	Low; water mature plants in winter
GROWTH RATE	Slow
PRUNING	None
HARDINESS	Hardy to at least 25° F
NATURAL ELEVATION RANGE	0–4,600 feet
SUITABLE CITIES	All low-elevation-zone cities; warmer spots in Tucson

FIELD NOTES: *Fouquieria columnaris* is native to central Baja California and one locality along the coast of Sonora, Mexico, near Puerto Libertad. Plants are found on rocky hillsides and alluvial plains on granitic or volcanic soil. There are some amazing plants in the Parque Nacional del Desierto Central de Baja California, which is situated along Mexico Highway 1. Get off the main highway and back into less heavily visited areas, and you will see some very unusual specimens. In 1981, my fellow explorers showed me the "Octopus Boojum," named for the eight arms radiating from a central point, all arching towards the ground, and then turning up at the ends.

DESCRIPTION: This bizarre plant typically has a single trunk resembling an upside-down carrot that, in habitat, can reach 50–60 feet tall. Most of us would confine a boojum to a pot as a novelty; however, if you follow the rules, you might get a 3–4-foot-tall plant after 7–15 years in the ground. I have seen a couple of cultivated ones in Tucson and Phoenix that are 20–25 feet tall, with side branches about 3 feet long, giving the plant a maximum diameter of about 6 feet. Small (less than 1 inch long) leaves appear from fall until spring. Cream-colored flowers first appear in late July or August and continue into September. Seeds develop in the fall and are ripe in time to germinate with winter rainfall.

CULTURE/MAINTENANCE: Young plants are susceptible to frost damage when temperatures fall into the mid-20s F. Older, more established plants can withstand winter temperatures down to the high teens F if not prolonged, or to the low 20s F if exposed for an extended period. In low desert areas, young plants need filtered light, while older plants can take full sun. In areas with milder summer temperatures, plants can be grown in full sun regardless of age. Place the plants in soil with good drainage.

One of the most critical aspects in growing boojum plants is to keep the roots from sitting in wet soil for extended periods during the heat of summer. Established plants will survive without any supplemental water from May to September.

IDENTIFICATION: "Ho, ho, a boojum, definitely a boojum!" With those words, Godfrey Sykes labeled this plant forever, and it cannot be confused with any other.

LANDSCAPE APPLICATION: Plants are best grown in containers; however, if placed in the right spot and treated properly, they can be used singly as a focal point or grouped to create an interesting effect when they get large and you get old. Mix boojums with colorful, low-water-use shrubs, perennials, and other accent plants, especially those that are winter-growing. Some suggestions: *Aloe ferox, Aloe striata, Cassia artemisioides, Dalea bicolor* var. *orcuttiana, Encelia farinosa, Eremophila maculata, Penstemon* species, and *Verbena gooddingii*.

PRECAUTIONS: Plants come from an area of winter rainfall and should be treated accordingly. Water when plants are in leaf, and keep dry when there are no leaves.

Fouquieria macdougalii | Tree Ocotillo

MEDIUM–LARGE SHRUB, CACTUS/SUCCULENT	
SIZE (height x width)	Realistically 4–10 (30) feet x 3–8 (20) feet
FLOWER COLOR	Red
FLOWER SEASON	Primarily spring, occasionally summer
EXPOSURE	Full or reflected sun
WATER	Drought-tolerant–low
GROWTH RATE	Slow
PRUNING	Generally none
HARDINESS	Hardy to mid-20s F
NATURAL ELEVATION RANGE	Near sea level–3,000 feet
SUITABLE CITIES	Low-elevation-zone cities; potted plant in mid-elevation-zone cities

FIELD NOTES: I've seen this very cool tree in several places in Sonora, Mexico. Some really nice ones can be found on Mexico Highway 15 from Hermosillo to Guaymas, also on Mexico Highway 16 from Hermosillo to Yecora, and some spectacular ones occur along Sonora Highway 117 between Santa Rosa and Moctezuma. *Fouquieria macdougalii* grows on slopes and plains in desert scrub and tropical deciduous forest from near sea level to 3,000 feet elevation.

DESCRIPTION: In habitat and with time in frost-free climates, this upright, shrub-like tree grows 10–30 feet tall and spreads 10–20 feet. It typically is smaller in cultivation, topping out at 4–10 feet tall by 3–8 feet. One or more thickened trunks have yellowish brown or greenish-brown peeling bark. Spiny stems are clothed with 1–2-inch-long leaves when there is sufficient water available. In times of cold and drought, the ephemeral leaves fall, off revealing the intricate bark patterns on the stems. Bright red, tubular, 1½-inch-long flowers adorn the stalk tips in the spring and summer following rains.

CULTURE/MAINTENANCE: This tree suffers frost damage when temperatures hit the mid-20s F, and it can be grown in the ground in the hot, low-elevation zone while making an excellent container patio plant in the mid-elevation zone. Established plants in the ground are drought-tolerant but will grow a bit faster if given a thorough soaking periodically in the summer. Grow them in full sun or reflected sun and in a soil that has good drainage. This slow-growing tree takes several years to reach full size. This maintenance-free plant needs no pruning.

IDENTIFICATION: *F. macdougalii* is easily identified by its short, thick trunk with peeling bark.

LANDSCAPE APPLICATION: Use this tree as a focal point in the low-elevation zone and as a potted patio plant in the mid-elevation zone. In a landscape, mix it with colorful, desert-adapted plants such as *Buddleja marrubiifolia, Chrysactinia mexicana, Dalea pulchra, Leucophyllum* species, *Poliomintha maderensis,* and *Salvia greggii;* or with a variety of other Southwestern natives, including: *Larrea divaricata, Opuntia* species, and *Simmondsia chinensis.*

PRECAUTIONS: Protect from frost.

Fouquieria splendens | Ocotillo

CACTUS/SUCCULENT	
SIZE (height x width)	10–12 feet x 8–10 feet
FLOWER COLOR	Red
FLOWER SEASON	Spring, occasionally late summer and fall
EXPOSURE	Full or reflected sun
WATER	Drought-tolerant–low

GROWTH RATE	Slow
PRUNING	Generally none (if you prune a cane, cut all the way back to the base)
HARDINESS	Hardy to at least 10° F
NATURAL ELEVATION RANGE	Near sea level–6,000 feet
SUITABLE CITIES	All cities in all zones

FIELD NOTES: *Fouquieria splendens* is one of the most distinctive plants seen from southern California to western Texas and south into northern Mexico. Plants frequently grow on limestone soil at the upper elevations, on fine or coarse soil, and sometimes on loose sandy soil. Spiky **monocultures** pop up in patches in southeastern Arizona's Mule, Swisshelm, and Whetstone Mountains. The elevation range is from near sea level to about 6,000 feet.

DESCRIPTION: A bouquet of slender, thorny branches arises from a central base, growing up and out and creating distinctive V-shapes. The plant typically grows to about 10–12 feet tall spreading to 8–10 feet, but on rare occasions it might reach nearly 20 feet tall with a spread of about 15 feet. Stems measure about ½–¾ inch in diameter, have light gray to nearly black bark, and are armed with stiff spines about 1 inch long. One-inch-long leaves appear within a couple of days after a generous rainstorm. In times of cold and drought, the ephemeral leaves fall off, leaving the slender, wand-like stems bare and dead-looking. Bright red, tubular, 1-inch-long flowers adorn the stalk tips in the spring and summer following rains.

CULTURE/MAINTENANCE: *F. splendens* is considered hardy to at least 10° F. Once established, a mature plant does not need supplemental water in areas with more than 7 inches of annual rainfall. It grows best in full sun or reflected sun and in a soil that has good drainage. In habitat, plants are seen in sandy or rocky slopes and areas

with abundant limestone. The plant grows slowly, taking several years to reach full size. No maintenance or pruning is needed.

IDENTIFICATION: *F. splendens* is not easily confused with any other landscape plant. Show you're a plant nerd by not calling it a cactus.

LANDSCAPE APPLICATION: Use ocotillo as a bold focal point in a desert landscape or in the transition or outer zones of a xeriscape. Mix with colorful, desert-adapted plants such as *Buddleja marrubiifolia, Chrysactinia mexicana, Dalea pulchra, Lantana* x 'New Gold,' *Leucophyllum* species,

Poliomintha maderensis, and *Salvia greggii.* Sturdy Southwestern natives, including *Larrea divaricata, Opuntia* species, and *Simmondsia chinensis,* set off its dramatic form.

PRECAUTIONS: Many ocotillos are sold as bare-root specimens that can be difficult to re-root. With the proper care, these plants can be grown successfully. Seed-grown plants are being offered in containers and would be a better choice than the bare-root specimens.

Fraxinus greggii | Little Leaf Ash

SMALL–MEDIUM TREE

SIZE (height x width)	18–20 feet x 15–18 feet
FLOWER COLOR	Inconspicuous flowers
FLOWER SEASON	March–April
EXPOSURE	Full or reflected sun
WATER	Low–moderate
GROWTH RATE	Moderate
PRUNING	Shape to tree form, remove lower branches
HARDINESS	Hardy to at least 10° F
NATURAL ELEVATION RANGE	1,000–7,000 feet (the more southern populations occur at higher elevation)
SUITABLE CITIES	All cities in all zones except Albuquerque

FIELD NOTES: *Fraxinus greggii* lives primarily on limestone-derived soil on bluffs, slopes, rocky hills, and in canyons and arroyos from western Texas to southeastern Arizona and northern Mexico from 1,000 to 7,000 feet elevation. It can be found in western Texas on the road from Ozona to Langtry and in Big Bend National Park. Although there is a broad elevation range for this species, the University of Arizona's Warren Jones probably collected this little gem at about 4,000–5,000 feet on one of his forays to western Texas.

DESCRIPTION: There never seem to be enough small patio trees to choose from, especially evergreen ones. *Fraxinus greggii* plays this role beautifully. Its smooth, light gray bark contrasts handsomely with the fine-textured bright green foliage. The nearly evergreen leaves are pinnately compound with 5–7 leaflets, and measure about 3 inches long and 1 inch wide. Small, insignificant flowers appear in March or April and are followed by single-winged, tan-colored seeds.

CULTURE/MAINTENANCE: *F. greggii* is hardy to at least 10° F, and probably down to 0°. The tree is solidly drought-tolerant once established but will benefit from supplemental irrigation during the spring and summer. It has a moderate growth rate, reaching a size of 10 feet tall and 6 feet wide in 5 years from a 15-gallon container. Place it in full or even reflected sun. It grows naturally in soils with good drainage and demands the same in your landscape. Multiple trunks and a naturally shrubby aspect require pruning to achieve a tree shape. When left unpruned, you can call it a large, low-maintenance, screening shrub.

IDENTIFICATION: The small stature, small leaves, and nearly evergreen habit help distinguish *F. greggii* from other Southwestern ash species.

LANDSCAPE APPLICATION: Little leaf ash thrives in the sun in any zone of a xeriscape. It is shapely, lush, and the right size to fit neatly into patios, courtyards, or entryways or draw attention elsewhere. It is also tough enough to be used in the transition and outer zones with other drought-tolerant species and can be pressed into service as shade for small understory plants such as *Ageratum corymbosum, Bulbine frutescens, Conoclinium dissectum,* and *Gaura lindheimeri.* Its bright green color contrasts pleasingly with the gray tones of plants like *Agave parryi* var. *truncata, Dalea greggii, Dasylirion wheeleri,* and *Leucophyllum candidum,* or try the all-lush look and go with brighter green combinations: *Agave geminiflora, Asclepias linaria, Dalea capitata, Dasylirion acrotrichum, Hesperaloe funifera, Justicia candicans, Salvia farinacea, Salvia greggii, Yucca grandiflora,* and *Wedelia acapulcensis* var. *hispida.*

PRECAUTIONS: This plant seems miraculously trouble-free. Neither rabbits nor javelinas show interest, and it shrugs off an erratic watering schedule with no added fertilizer. It also tolerates a wide range of soil types—just give it good drainage.

Gaura lindheimeri | Bee Blossom

FLOWERING PERENNIAL	
SIZE (height x width)	3 feet x 4 feet
FLOWER COLOR	White, various shades of pink
FLOWER SEASON	Spring–fall
EXPOSURE	Full or filtered sun
WATER	Moderate–ample
GROWTH RATE	Fast
PRUNING	Shear in late winter

HARDINESS	Root-hardy (tops may freeze), short-lived perennial
NATURAL ELEVATION RANGE	100–750 feet
SUITABLE CITIES	All cities in all zones

FIELD NOTES: *Gaura lindheimeri* is commonly found in rich, black-soil prairie in south-central and southeast Texas and southern Louisiana from about 100 to 750 feet elevation.

DESCRIPTION: This many-branched, short-lived perennial has herbaceous stems that arise from a woody base. An extremely showy flower display can start as early as March and continue into the fall. The softly pubescent, light grayish-green leaves are about 2 inches long and ½ inch wide. Pure white to deep pinkish-red, 1-inch-wide flowers occur on 12–20-inch-long flower stalks extending from the tips of the branches. White flowers blush light pink before opening.

CULTURE/MAINTENANCE: Bee blossom is a root-hardy perennial, meaning that although the top growth may freeze back, the plant will resprout from the rootstock. In most winters, the tops freeze back about halfway. You'll want to do some pruning in late winter or early spring, but don't be hesitant to cut this plant back severely each year. It grows very rapidly and will reach its mature size in a season. Although it can survive with moderate supplemental irrigation, it will guzzle all you give it. For best results, dig a large hole and amend the soil with organic matter to create a deep, rich loam. In mid-elevation desert areas, it grows well in full or filtered sun. In the low desert areas, give it some shade during the hottest time of the day.

IDENTIFICATION: *G. lindheimeri*'s larger flowers easily distinguish it from *G. coccinea.*

LANDSCAPE APPLICATION: This beautiful, short-lived perennial is best used for quick, temporary color. Use at the base of small trees such as *Bauhinia lunarioides, Eysenhardtia orthocarpa, Leucaena retusa,* and *Sophora secundiflora.* Mix with other understory specialists such as *Conoclinium dissectum, Salvia greggii,* and *Salvia leucantha.* Its delicate, airy form contrasts well with bolder accent plants such as *Dasylirion, Nolina,* and *Yucca* species. Bee blossom is well adapted for use in simulated washes or water harvesting channels. Its rich green color and outstanding flowers put it at ease in the mini-oasis. Despite its affinity for water, it is tough enough to be used in the transition and outer zones of a xeriscape.

PRECAUTIONS: *G. lindheimeri* can reseed if conditions are ideal. It will attract aphids and is susceptible to flea beetles. It may be on the menu for rabbits, at least when plants are young and grown soft. It lives fast and dies young so will probably need replacing after 2–4 years.

Gelsemium sempervirens | Carolina Jessamine

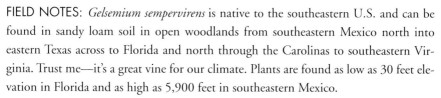

VINE	
SIZE (height x width)	Stems to 10–20 feet long
FLOWER COLOR	Yellow
FLOWER SEASON	Late winter–spring
EXPOSURE	Full or partial shade, or full sun
WATER	Moderate–ample
GROWTH RATE	Fast
PRUNING	Shearing at long intervals to rejuvenate
HARDINESS	Hardy to at least 15° F
NATURAL ELEVATION RANGE	Near sea level–5,900 feet
SUITABLE CITIES	All low- and mid-elevation-zone cities

FIELD NOTES: *Gelsemium sempervirens* is native to the southeastern U.S. and can be found in sandy loam soil in open woodlands from southeastern Mexico north into eastern Texas across to Florida and north through the Carolinas to southeastern Virginia. Trust me—it's a great vine for our climate. Plants are found as low as 30 feet elevation in Florida and as high as 5,900 feet in southeastern Mexico.

DESCRIPTION: Without support, this unusual plant's vine-like stems will twine around each other, creating a large mound of vegetation. The 10–20-foot-long stems seem to be searching for some type of thin support structure—try a trellis or chain-link fence. Glossy, dark to bright green, 2–3-inch-long, pointed leaves cover the stems year-round and turn bronze in the winter. Short clusters of lightly fragrant, funnel-shaped, 1½–2-inch-long, bright yellow flowers bloom profusely all up and down the plant from late winter to spring.

CULTURE/MAINTENANCE: *G. sempervirens* is hardy to about 15° F, maybe lower, and will quickly get over frost damage. Plants need moderate amounts of supplemental water from late spring until fall depending on the planting location. They love the heat and will tolerate full sun all day long. They will also grow in filtered sun and partial shade but will postpone flowering in too much shade. They grow fast and require little maintenance beyond making sure the stems are supported.

IDENTIFICATION: Pointed, glossy leaves and yellow, funnel-shaped flowers in late winter to spring set this vine apart. The cultivar 'Pride of Augusta' has double flowers, and you can actually find it in western U.S. nurseries.

LANDSCAPE APPLICATION: Carolina jessamine has a variety of uses, from a ground cover to vine. Stems are self-twining around a support that is thin, but they will need to be tied if the support is too fat. Plant this vine with other "green," mildly thirsty plants for late-winter to spring color in the mini-oasis, or stick it in any spot where you can enjoy all those yellow flowers. Let it spill over a wall or become a screen for privacy. It is a relatively tidy plant for pool areas and entryways. If you need a break from the desert and have enough guilt-free water at your disposal, try planting with *Quercus* species, *Fraxinus* species, and grasses like *Muhlenbergia* species for a woodsy feel.

PRECAUTIONS: All parts are poisonous. Old plants can get top-heavy and need to be sheared to rejuvenate them. Plants are likely to show iron chlorosis in high pH soil, so work compost into the top 3–4 inches of soil every year. Treat with iron chelate if symptoms are severe.

Guaiacum coulteri | Guayacan

MEDIUM–LARGE SHRUB, SMALL TREE

SIZE (height x width)	3–5 (10–20) feet x 3–5 (10–20) feet
FLOWER COLOR	Deep indigo blue
FLOWER SEASON	Summer
EXPOSURE	Full or reflected sun
WATER	Low
GROWTH RATE	Slow
PRUNING	Trim out any frozen growth or shape to grow as a tree
HARDINESS	Half-hardy
NATURAL ELEVATION RANGE	0–2,000 feet
SUITABLE CITIES	All low-elevation-zone cities; warm microclimates in Tucson

FIELD NOTES: *Guaiacum coulteri* is found on gravelly plains and gentle slopes from north-central Sonora south to Oaxaca from near sea level to 2,000 feet elevation. The plants reach their northern limit in Sonora with some nice, small, treelike specimens

occurring along Mexico Highway 15 from Hermosillo to San Carlos. Watch for them in full flower in May or June prior to the monsoon season.

DESCRIPTION: While *G. coulteri* is a beautiful large shrub or small tree in its native habitat, in areas that regularly experience frost, plants will generally grow slowly, reaching about 3–5 feet tall by 3–5 feet across. In frost-free areas, given sufficient time, plants can eventually reach 10–20 feet by 10–20 feet and be pruned as small trees. The extremely hard, dense, heavy wood is strikingly beautiful. Small, pinnate, dark green leaves give the plant a rich, almost tropical feel. Flowers are brilliant, indigo-blue, 5-petalled, and about 1 inch across; they appear in masses as the weather gets hot prior to the monsoon season. Fruits are intriguing—small, orange, and semifleshy with 1 or 2 black seeds surrounded by a bright red **aril**.

CULTURE/MAINTENANCE: Guayacan sustains damage when winter lows hit the high 20s F. Plants are low-water-using and will tolerate most soil types, as long as the drainage is adequate. Plants are best used in full sun or even reflected heat to minimize frost damage. Prune out any frost-damaged growth, or shape to grow as a tree in frost-free zones.

IDENTIFICATION: *G. coulteri* is related to *Larrea divaricata,* and it is easily distinguished by the leaf structure and the indigo-blue flowers as compared to the yellow flowers of *L. divaricata.*

LANDSCAPE APPLICATION: The extremely slow growth rate warrants finding as large a plant as possible and promotes the use of guayacan as a prized specialty plant where the flowers can be the focal point.

PRECAUTIONS: Slow growth, frost sensitivity, and lack of availability are what keep this plant rare in cultivated landscapes. But trust me, it's worth the effort.

Habranthus robustus | Robust Pink Rain Lily

BULB	
SIZE (height x width)	8–12 inches x 4–6 inches
FLOWER COLOR	Pink
FLOWER SEASON	Late spring–summer
EXPOSURE	Full or filtered sun

WATER	Low–moderate
GROWTH RATE	Moderate
PRUNING	None
HARDINESS	Hardy
NATURAL ELEVATION RANGE	500–6,000 feet
SUITABLE CITIES	All cities in all zones

FIELD NOTES: *Habranthus robustus* is native to Argentina and Brazil from about 500 to 6,000 feet elevation. It grows in an area with year-round rainfall except for a brief dry period in late summer.

DESCRIPTION: As the weather starts to heat up in late spring and early summer, *H. robustus* lets loose with an incredible show of large, pink, cup-shaped flowers from the underground bulb. Long, narrow, grass-like leaves form clumps reaching 8–12 inches tall by 4–6 inches wide. The 3-inch-long flowers go it alone at the ends of 8–12-inch-long stalks. Flowers begin to open first thing in the morning and peak a few hours later. Three-lobed fruits, containing several thin, flat, black seeds follow the flowers.

CULTURE/MAINTENANCE: Bulbs are hardy to at least 10° F, and in most of the Southwest they can be left in the ground. In extremely cold areas, consider digging bulbs for the winter. They are drought-tolerant but benefit from supplemental water in the summer. Induce blooming by enforcing a dry spell, then thoroughly soaking. The bulb will take several years to multiply and form large clumps. It will grow well in just about any soil type and in full sun or filtered sun.

IDENTIFICATION: Large cup-shaped flowers with no tube distinguish *H. robustus* from *Zephyranthes grandiflora* with flowers that taper to a long, narrow tube.

LANDSCAPE APPLICATION: Robust pink rain lily can be used in a variety of ways in Southwestern landscapes. Toss bulbs in the same hole when you plant large accents like *Agave*, *Dasylirion*, and *Yucca* species. They perk up rock or cactus gardens and do well in raised planters. Use robust pink rain lily as a container plant, a "bonus" plant around permanent residents, or for its temporary splash of color. Plant by itself for seasonal color or grouped with various *Agaves* to add variety to the container.

PRECAUTIONS: The leaves and flowers are on the menu for a variety of wildlife, including rabbits and rodents. Screen with 1-inch mesh chicken wire, or possibly place the bulbs at the base of intimidating, stout-leafed *Agave* species.

Havardia mexicana | Synonym: *Pithecellobium mexicanum* | Mexican Ebony

SMALL–MEDIUM TREE	
SIZE (height x width)	20–30 feet x 15–20 feet
FLOWER COLOR	Creamy yellow
FLOWER SEASON	Spring
EXPOSURE	Full or reflected sun
WATER	Moderate
GROWTH RATE	Slow–moderate
PRUNING	Select main trunks for tree form
HARDINESS	Hardy
NATURAL ELEVATION RANGE	200–3,300 feet
SUITABLE CITIES	All low- and mid-elevation-zone cities

FIELD NOTES: *Havardia mexicana* grows in the deep soils of desert washes and river floodplains throughout much of Sonora, Mexico, south into Sinaloa, and even in the Cape region of Baja California. It lives between 200 and 3,300 feet elevation, and the northernmost trees are native to the floodplain of the Rio Magdalena about 25 miles south of the Arizona border. The plants currently in cultivation are grown from seed collected off trees in the northern part of the range.

DESCRIPTION: This gorgeous, multiple-trunked tree has a high, narrowly spreading canopy. It grows slowly to 20–30 feet tall by 15–20 feet across. Fine, bipinnate, gray-green leaves provide a handsome backdrop for the creamy yellowish flowers. Small, paired spines sit at the base of each leaf. Butterflies will flit around the puffball-like flowers that cover the tree in late spring. Hummingbirds visit the flowers, but it is not known whether they are actually getting nectar or feeding on insects attracted to the flowers. Flowers give way to flat, narrow, 2–3-inch-long, papery pods. The hard, reddish wood is strikingly beautiful and prized for furniture, structural beams, and craftwork.

CULTURE/MAINTENANCE: Mexican ebony has survived winter lows into the mid-teens F without damage. Sufficient supplemental water in spring and summer can coax this slow grower to speed up a little. When planted in shallow, desert soil, it stays smaller and takes longer to achieve tree status. When planted in deep, sandy soil and watered regularly, it will get larger more quickly. To grow as a multiple-trunked shade tree, select the main trunks early and prune off side shoots after a couple of years in the ground. It will produce suckers and side shoots from near ground level and will need occasional pruning to maintain the tree form.

IDENTIFICATION: *H. mexicana* is easily distinguished from *H. pallens* by its fewer leaflets.

LANDSCAPE APPLICATION: Use Mexican ebony as a deciduous shade tree in any landscape. It's a good choice for the south or west side of a building to provide summer shade and winter sun. Keep it away from high-traffic areas because of the spines, and allow enough room for the sucker development. It works as an elegant screening or tall background plant. Use shrubs such as *Anisacanthus quadrifidus, Buddleja marrubiifolia, Calliandra californica, Larrea divaricata, Leucophyllum* species, *Ruellia peninsularis, Salvia* species, *Simmondsia chinensis,* and *Vauquelinia californica* as companion plants. If you have enough space, try planting several of these stately trees for a bosque or grove effect.

PRECAUTIONS: Spines are small yet sharp so handle trimming chores with good gloves.

Havardia pallens | Synonym: *Pithecellobium pallens* | Tenaza

SMALL–MEDIUM TREE	
SIZE (height x width)	20 feet x 15–18 feet
FLOWER COLOR	Creamy yellow
FLOWER SEASON	Spring–fall
EXPOSURE	Full or reflected sun
WATER	Low–moderate
GROWTH RATE	Fast
PRUNING	Select main trunks for tree form
HARDINESS	Hardy (some damage at high teens F)
NATURAL ELEVATION RANGE	30–1,800 feet
SUITABLE CITIES	All low-elevation-zone cities; Tucson in mid-elevation zone

FIELD NOTES: *Havardia pallens* occurs along the low-lying coastal part of the Rio Grande Plains in south Texas and adjacent Mexico from about 30 to 1,800 feet elevation. Your best bet for finding it in habitat is to head south from Brownsville to Ciudad Victoria, Tamaulipas, and check along the roadside in low-lying areas.

DESCRIPTION: *H. pallens* has a naturally shrubby form but is easily grown as a multiple-trunked tree. The species name *pallens* is Latin for "pale," which refers to the beautiful, light silvery gray bark. Medium green, bipinnate leaves are relatively small and finely textured. Small yet vicious, paired spines occur at the base of each leaf. Creamy yellow, puffball-like flowers appear in flushes repeatedly from late spring through summer and into the fall. Both butterflies and hummingbirds have been observed visiting the flowers. As with *H. mexicana,* it is unclear whether the hummingbirds are actually getting nectar or feeding on small insects visiting the flowers. Flat, narrow, 2–3-inch-long, papery pods add interest post-flowering.

CULTURE/MAINTENANCE: Mature plants are hardy to at least the low 20s F. Temperatures in the low 20s or high teens may nip young plants and the newest growth. The tree will recover quickly from any frost damage in the spring. It is drought-tolerant once established but will reward you with its flushes of flowers if given periodic supplemental water during the growing season. It will stay healthy in just about any type of soil without special amendments. To grow it as a multiple-trunked shade tree, select the main trunks early and prune off side shoots after a couple of years in the ground. Abundant side shoots and suckers appear from near ground level and will need occasional pruning to retain the tree form.

IDENTIFICATION: *H. pallens* is easily distinguished from *H. mexicana* by more numerous leaflets.

LANDSCAPE APPLICATION: Use *H. pallens* as an evergreen shade tree in any landscape. It is small enough to use in residential landscapes as well as a street tree. Keep it away from high-traffic areas because of the spines, and allow enough room for sucker development. It works as a non-drab screening or tall background plant and looks good planted with *Anisacanthus quadrifidus, Buddleja marrubiifolia, Calliandra californica, Larrea divaricata, Leucophyllum* species, *Ruellia peninsularis, Salvia* species, and *Simmondsia chinensis.*

PRECAUTIONS: Spines mean business, and trimmed branches should be handled with gloves. When grown as a tree, basal shoots will need to be pruned off a couple of times per year.

Hesperaloe campanulata | Bell Flower Hesperaloe

CACTUS/SUCCULENT	
SIZE (height x width)	3 feet x 3 feet
FLOWER COLOR	Pink-and-white
FLOWER SEASON	Summer
EXPOSURE	Full sun
WATER	Drought-tolerant–low
GROWTH RATE	Moderate
PRUNING	Remove old flower stalks in late summer
HARDINESS	Hardy to low teens F
NATURAL ELEVATION RANGE	1,500–1,700 feet
SUITABLE CITIES	All cities in all zones except Albuquerque

FIELD NOTES: In 1986, Ron Gass and I were botanizing on a rocky hillside in northeastern Mexico when he showed me what he thought was a *Hesperaloe parviflora* with a different leaf form. We figured out that it was an undescribed species, and after a lot of work it was dubbed *Hesperaloe campanulata*. Plants inhabit flat ground and rocky hills on limestone soil in Chihuahuan Desert scrub with *Acacia* species, *Bauhinia lunarioides, Cordia boissieri,* and *Leucophyllum frutescens* at about 1,500–1,700 feet elevation.

DESCRIPTION: This stemless, clumping accent plant grows to 3 feet tall and 3–4 feet wide. The bright green leaves are 2–3 feet long and ½ inch wide. They are channeled, stiff, and upright with a little bit of spread and fine threads along the margins. The 10-foot-tall flower spike puts out 2–5 branches on its upper half, where dainty 1-inch-long pink-and-white, bell-shaped flowers appear. Flowering can start as early as April and continue into October or November. Seeds are packaged in woody capsules that are 1 inch wide with a short, sharp beak.

CULTURE/MAINTENANCE: This easy-to-grow plant requires very little care. It prefers full sun and soil with good drainage. Quite drought-tolerant once established, it survives on 10–11 inches of annual rainfall. The growth rate is moderate and responds some to consistent, thorough watering in summer. You can try this plant on a stingy drip system with other drought-tolerant succulent and semisucculent plants. The only maintenance needed is to remove the flower spike after the blooming period. Plants are cold-hardy to at least the low teens F.

IDENTIFICATION: When not in bloom, bell flower hesperaloe looks like a small version of *H. funifera.* Flowers make them easy to separate; bell flower hesperaloe has pink-and-white ones, and *H. funifera's* are greenish-white. *H. parviflora* has a more open **flower shape**, and its leaves are lighter green and less channeled.

LANDSCAPE APPLICATION: Mass plant *H. campanulata* or display as a stand-alone accent plant in the transition or outer zone of a xeriscape. Try it next to a fine-textured tree like *Eysenhardtia orthocarpa,* or group with drought-tolerant shrubs like *Ageratum corymbosum, Calliandra eriophylla, Dalea capitata, Dalea versicolor* var. *sessilis, Leucophyllum candidum, Penstemon baccharifolius, Salvia greggii,* and *Wedelia acapulcensis* var. *hispida.* Flowers are wide open in the evening and attract nighttime pollinators, then close down the next day and can pull in a few hummingbirds.

PRECAUTIONS: Wildlife may snack on young plants, but they should be less appealing once they are established and growing without supplemental irrigation.

Hesperaloe funifera | Giant Hesperaloe

CACTUS/SUCCULENT	
SIZE (height x width)	4–6 feet x 4–6 feet
FLOWER COLOR	Greenish-white and purplish
FLOWER SEASON	Summer–fall
EXPOSURE	Full sun
WATER	Drought-tolerant–low
GROWTH RATE	Moderately slow
PRUNING	Remove old flower stalks
HARDINESS	Hardy to at least 5° F
NATURAL ELEVATION RANGE	1,500–3,000 feet
SUITABLE CITIES	All cities in all zones except Albuquerque

FIELD NOTES: *Hesperaloe funifera* grows on flats and plains in northeastern Mexico from 1,500 to 3,000 feet elevation. It inhabits Chihuahuan Desert scrub with *Acacia, Agave, Cordia boissieri, Larrea divaricata, Leucophyllum frutescens,* and *Prosopis glandulosa.* Annual rainfall in its native habitat ranges from 8 to 20 inches.

DESCRIPTION: This striking, stemless succulent grows to 4–6 feet tall and forms clumps to 6 feet in diameter. Stiff, upright, bright green leaves are about 2½ inches wide at the base and taper to the tip. Leaf margins have coarse, white fibers that peel back as the plant ages. A 12-foot-tall flower spike shoots from the center of the plant to announce the arrival of summer weather. Stalks have 3–8 side branches that hold

the 1-inch-long, greenish-white and purplish flowers. Flowers open in the evening in time for pollination by bats. Woody capsules are 1–2 inches long and house numerous flat, black seeds.

CULTURE/MAINTENANCE: Giant hesperaloe is hardy to at least 5° F. Established plants can go for 2 months or more without supplemental water in the Tucson area. The growth rate is moderately slow, which may warrant buying a plant in a larger-size container. You can nudge it along with thorough irrigation once every 7–10 days during the growing season. It performs best in full or reflected sun and a fast-draining soil. Rocky soil will allow the thick, succulent roots room to grow. Aside from removing old flowering stalks, no pruning is necessary.

IDENTIFICATION: Stiff, 4–6-foot-long leaves make this species easily identifiable at maturity. Seedlings and young plants are difficult to distinguish from *H. parviflora,* although *H. funifera* has a greener color and wider, stiffer leaves. The leaves of *H. funifera* and *H. campanulata* are similar, but flowers give away identity. *H. campanulata* has pink-and-white flowers, while *H. funifera* has greenish-white and purplish flowers and also gets larger.

LANDSCAPE APPLICATION: The bold form stands out next to short desert shrubs and perennials such as *Ageratum corymbosum, Asclepias linaria, Dalea capitata, Dalea frutescens, Justicia candicans* (syn. *J. ovata*), *Justicia spicigera, Penstemon* species, *Salvia greggii,* and *Wedelia acapulcensis* var. *hispida.* It can be used in all zones of a xeriscape, all the way from the mini-oasis to the dry zone. The essence of neatness, it can be massed or planted singly in street medians and even in pool areas. Show it off in a large, decorative pot.

PRECAUTIONS: Both rabbits and javelinas might eat leaves of young plants. Growing "hard," that is, not overwatering or overfertilizing, should make *H. funifera* much less appetizing.

Hesperaloe nocturna | Night-blooming Hesperaloe

CACTUS/SUCCULENT

SIZE (height x width)	5 feet x 6 feet
FLOWER COLOR	Greenish-lavender
FLOWER SEASON	Spring–early summer

EXPOSURE	Full sun or light shade
WATER	Drought-tolerant–moderate
GROWTH RATE	Moderate
PRUNING	None or remove old flower stalk
HARDINESS	Hardy to at least 10° F
NATURAL ELEVATION RANGE	3,200–3,500 feet
SUITABLE CITIES	All cities in all zones

FIELD NOTES: In spring and early summer, drive east from Magdalena, Sonora, Mexico, towards the town of Cucurpe, and look for the tall flower stalks of *Hesperaloe nocturna* along the roadside. *H. nocturna* grows only in central Sonora on slopes at 3,200–3,500 feet elevation in oak-grassland vegetation.

DESCRIPTION: Clusters of dense, stemless rosettes mature at 3–5 feet tall by 4–6 feet across. Narrow, strap-like leaves measure up to 4 feet long and ¾ inch wide at the base. They are deeply channeled, with fine white threads along the margins. This plant blooms from May through July, sending up a 12-foot-tall flower stalk. One-inch-long, greenish-lavender flowers open up all the way at night. Flowers are followed by woody capsules nearly 1½ inches long, which contain many flat, black seeds.

CULTURE/MAINTENANCE: Give this plant filtered light or full sun and a soil with good drainage. It is drought-tolerant once established but perks up with thorough watering every 2–3 weeks during the growing season. It will take a few years to form large clumps. It's hardy to at least 10° F. Maintenance is a breeze—removal of the old flower stalks.

IDENTIFICATION: Long, narrow leaves and night-blooming habit easily pin down this *Hesperaloe*. On first glance, it could be confused with *Nolina microcarpa*. However, the flowers and fruits are quite different.

LANDSCAPE APPLICATION: As with other species of *Hesperaloe*, this one makes a grand specimen plant for large, open spaces. The tall flower stalk with its horizontal side branches provides a nice perch for birds. It combines comfortably with annual wildflowers, perennials, and low-growing shrubs in a desert landscape, like *Chrysactinia mexicana, Dalea capitata, Dalea frutescens, Encelia farinosa, Penstemon* species, *Poliomintha maderensis, Salvia greggii,* and *Zinnia* *grandiflora*. A single plant makes a statement in pool areas or in a large decorative container. It is also impressive massed along streets and in medians.

PRECAUTIONS: Jackrabbits or javelinas might eat leaves of a young plant, but the lure should diminish as the plant matures and is hardened off.

Hesperaloe parviflora | Red Hesperaloe

CACTUS/SUCCULENT	
SIZE (height x width)	2½–3 feet x 3–4 feet
FLOWER COLOR	Red, pink, coral, sometimes yellow
FLOWER SEASON	Late spring–fall
EXPOSURE	Full or reflected sun
WATER	Drought-tolerant–moderate
GROWTH RATE	Moderate
PRUNING	None
HARDINESS	Hardy to at least 0° F
NATURAL ELEVATION RANGE	1,900–6,550 feet
SUITABLE CITIES	All cities in all zones

FIELD NOTES: *Hesperaloe parviflora* was once widespread in the creosote-dominated Chihuahuan Desert and oak vegetation from central Texas south into adjacent Mexico between 1,900 and 6,550 feet elevation. In the early 1900s, it was highly sought after in Europe and collected indiscriminately. It is now somewhat restricted to small colonies that are generally overshadowed by dense vegetation where not readily browsed by animals. My only encounter with a wild *H. parviflora* was in West Texas. I was sitting in the bed of a pickup watching the plants zoom by, when I caught a glimpse of a flower stalk peeking out of some roadside vegetation.

DESCRIPTION: This stemless, clumping plant grows to 2½–3 feet tall and spreads to 3–4 feet across. Dark green, arching leaves are deeply channeled, with thin white threads along the edges. A 3–7-foot-tall flower spike hosts the incredible display of red-, pink-, coral-, or yellow-colored, tubular flowers from late spring until fall. Woody pods follow the flowers.

CULTURE/MAINTENANCE: The common, red-flowered form is easy to grow. The plant will do best in full or even reflected sun and a soil with decent drainage. The red form will survive on less than 11 inches of annual rainfall once established. Twice-monthly supplemental water during the summer will speed growth and boost flowering. It is cold-hardy to at least 0° F. Take down the flower stalk after it has bloomed

out, and you've finished your annual maintenance.

IDENTIFICATION: *H. parviflora* is easily distinguished from all other species of *Hesperaloe* by its red to yellow flowers.

LANDSCAPE APPLICATION: Red hesperaloe works as a stand-alone accent plant in a cactus and succulent garden. It makes an outstanding display as a mixture of the color forms, especially when the yellow form is splashed in with the reds. Try grouping with drought-tolerant ground covers, perennials, shrubs, and small trees. Some great companion plants would be *Ageratum corymbosum, Calliandra eriophylla, Dalea capitata, Eysenhardtia orthocarpa, Leucaena retusa, Leucophyllum candidum, Penstemon baccharifolius,* and *Salvia greggii.* It also blends well with tall *Yucca* species such as *Y. elata, Y. grandiflora, Y. rigida,* and *Y. rostrata.*

PRECAUTIONS: Protect red hesperaloe from voracious rabbits and javelinas that will eat the leaves; sometimes javelinas will uproot the whole plant to get at the succulent roots.

Heuchera sanguinea | Coral Bells

FLOWERING PERENNIAL	
SIZE (height x width)	6–8 inches (12–24 inches with flower stalks) x 12–15 inches
FLOWER COLOR	Bright red to coral pink, occasionally white
FLOWER SEASON	Late spring–fall
EXPOSURE	Full or partial shade, or full sun in mild climates
WATER	Moderate–ample
GROWTH RATE	Fast
PRUNING	Minimal
HARDINESS	Hardy to at least 10° F
NATURAL ELEVATION RANGE	4,000–8,500 feet
SUITABLE CITIES	All cities in all zones; needs afternoon shade in hot, interior low-elevation zone cities and in mid-elevation-zone cities

FIELD NOTES: *Heuchera sanguinea* grows in moist, shaded areas in southern Arizona and northern Mexico from 4,000 to 8,500 feet elevation. Look around your shady rest stop on a summertime canyon hike, and odds are good you'll spot this plant.

DESCRIPTION: This pretty perennial forms a mound of dark green foliage to 6–8 inches tall and 12–15 inches across, up to 24 inches tall with the flower stalks. Dark green, rounded leaves, with long petioles and toothed margins, all arise from the base, giving coral bells a tufted look. Clusters of bright red to coral pink, ½-inch-wide, bell-shaped flowers on 1–2-foot-long stalks top the plant from late spring through fall and will bring in the occasional hummingbird.

CULTURE/MAINTENANCE: *H. sanguinea* is hardy to at least 10° F and probably lower. Plants require moderate to ample supplemental water from late spring until fall depending on the planting location. They will tolerate full sun in cooler summer climates but require kinder, filtered sun or afternoon shade and cool soil in hot, desert climates. Mulch the soil with some compost or organic matter to help keep it cooler in summer. They grow fast and require little maintenance beyond dividing the clumps every 3–4 years.

IDENTIFICATION: Clusters of bright red to coral-pink, bell-shaped flowers on a little stalk easily identify *H. sanguinea.*

LANDSCAPE APPLICATION: In a hot, desert climate, coral bells is best planted in part to full shade in the mini-oasis. In a cooler climate, use it in a rock garden with bulbs and other summer-flowering perennials. Mix it with other flowering beauties of modest size like *Aquilegia chrysantha, Justicia spicigera, Salvia greggii,* and *Tagetes lemmonii.*

PRECAUTIONS: Young, newly planted coral bells are likely to be eaten by rabbits. Minimize this problem by installing them in the mini-oasis, where human activity intimidates rabbits, or in an enclosed space. Mealybugs can be a problem in mild climates.

Hibiscus coulteri | Desert Mallow

FLOWERING PERENNIAL

SIZE (height x width)	1–2 feet x 1–2 feet
FLOWER COLOR	Light to medium yellow with a red spot at the base of the petals

FLOWER SEASON	Late spring–fall
EXPOSURE	Full or filtered sun
WATER	Low
GROWTH RATE	Moderately fast
HARDINESS	Hardy perennial
PRUNING	Cut to ground level in late winter
NATURAL ELEVATION RANGE	1,500–4,500 feet
SUITABLE CITIES	All low- and mid-elevation-zone cities

FIELD NOTES: *Hibiscus coulteri* is at home in canyons, on rocky slopes, and occasionally along roadsides in central and southern Arizona east through New Mexico, into western Texas and south into Mexico from 1,500 to 4,500 feet elevation. This plant is all about the flower. Try taking an early morning hike in April or May, and you should be able to see these plants, if they are in bloom, in Saguaro National Park on the west side of the Tucson Mountains.

DESCRIPTION: This nifty little perennial gets 1–2 feet tall by 1–2 feet across, depending on where it is growing. It virtually disappears from sight when not in bloom. Rich green, 2-inch-long, deeply 3-lobed leaves with long, sticky hairs look a bit out of place on such a tough plant. Soft yellow, 2-inch-wide flowers appear from late spring into summer and fall on the new growth of each stem. Cup-shaped fruits with small, hairy seeds follow the flowers.

CULTURE/MAINTENANCE: Plants are root-hardy to at least 10° F, although the tops might die back. Place them in full sun for most compact growth, or under the dappled light of a wispy tree. This smart plant is moderately fast-growing and low-water-using, surviving on 10–12 inches of annual rainfall. Provide supplemental water once every 7–14 days from late spring through summer and you will be rewarded with more growth and a much longer flowering season. Plants can be cut back to nearly

ground level in the late winter and once or twice during the growing season to create a thicker, fuller form.

IDENTIFICATION: The yellow flowers readily distinguish *H. coulteri* from other native or near native *Hibiscus* species.

LANDSCAPE APPLICATION: This plant is best used as supplemental color around the base of accents such as *Agave, Dasylirion,* or tall *Yucca* species. Mix it with *Echinocactus grusonii, Ferocactus* species, or even *Opuntia violacea* var. *santa rita* in a cactus and succulent garden, to provide a dash of color during the hot time of year. Toss it in with other perennials or small shrubs like *Ageratum corymbosum, Conoclinium dissectum, Penstemon* species, *Poliomintha maderensis, Salvia greggii, Scutellaria suffrutescens,* or *Zinnia acerosa.*

PRECAUTIONS: Rabbits might munch on the stems if there is nothing else around for them to feast on.

Hibiscus denudatus | Rock Rose Mallow

SMALL SHRUB

SIZE (height x width)	1–2 feet x 1–2 feet
FLOWER COLOR	Pinkish-lavender
FLOWER SEASON	Late winter–fall
EXPOSURE	Full sun
WATER	Low
GROWTH RATE	Moderately fast
PRUNING	Cut to ground level in late winter
HARDINESS	Hardy perennial
NATURAL ELEVATION RANGE	Near sea level–4,500 feet
SUITABLE CITIES	All low- and mid-elevation-zone cities

FIELD NOTES: *Hibiscus denudatus* loves the dry, rocky soils of the desert Southwest and is generally found in washes and along roadsides from western Texas across to southern California and south into northern Mexico and Baja California from near sea level to 4,500 feet elevation. This plant is all about the flower, which can appear just about anytime from late winter until late fall. I love being surprised by the pinkish-lavender flowers dotting the plants while on early morning bicycle rides through Saguaro National Park on the west side of the Tucson Mountains.

DESCRIPTION: This nifty little perennial gets 1–2 feet tall by 1–2 feet across, depending on where it is growing. The dusky, yellowish foliage blends into the surrounding desert vegetation, leaving a nondescript plant until it breaks out its vibrant, pinkish-lavender, 2-inch-wide, cup-shaped flowers. Cup-shaped fruits with small, hairy seeds follow the flowers.

CULTURE/MAINTENANCE: Plants are root-hardy to at least 10° F, although the tops might die back. Place *H. denudatus* in full sun for most compact growth, or under the dappled light of a wispy tree. This moderately fast-growing, low-water-using, tough desert native will survive on 10–12 inches of annual rainfall once established. Give it supplemental water every 7–14 days from late spring through summer and you will be rewarded with more growth and a much longer flowering season. Cut plants back to nearly ground level in the late winter and once or twice during the growing season to create a thicker, fuller plant.

IDENTIFICATION: The pinkish-lavender, 2-inch-wide, cup-shaped flowers readily distinguish *H. denudatus* from other native or near native *Hibiscus* species.

LANDSCAPE APPLICATION: This plant is best used as supplemental color around the base of accents such as *Agave, Dasylirion,* or tall *Yucca* species. Mix it with *Echinocactus grusonii, Ferocactus* species, or even *Opuntia violacea* var. *santa rita* in a cactus and succulent garden, to provide a dash of color during the hot time of year. Toss it in with other perennials or small shrubs like *Ageratum corymbosum, Conoclinium dissectum, Penstemon* species, *Poliomintha maderensis, Salvia greggii, Scutellaria suffrutescens,* or *Zinnia acerosa* to add color and flower shape variety.

PRECAUTIONS: Rabbits might munch on the stems if there is nothing else around for them to feast on.

Hibiscus martianus | Synonym: *H. cardiophyllus* | Heart Leaf Hibiscus

SMALL SHRUB

SIZE (height x width)	1–2 feet x 1–2 feet
FLOWER COLOR	Bright crimson red
FLOWER SEASON	Mostly summer–fall
EXPOSURE	Full or filtered sun
WATER	Low–moderate
GROWTH RATE	Moderately fast
PRUNING	Cut to ground level in late winter
HARDINESS	Hardy perennial
NATURAL ELEVATION RANGE	700–5,000 feet
SUITABLE CITIES	All low- and mid-elevation-zone cities

FIELD NOTES: It is always a pleasant surprise to be bumping along a dirt track or scouring the canyons in northeastern Mexico and spot the brilliant red flowers of *Hibiscus martianus* peeking out through the low shrubs along the roadside. This little shrub can be found in western Texas, south into the states of Coahuila, Nuevo León, Tamaulipas, and San Luis Potosí in Mexico from 700 to 5,000 feet elevation. As with other *Hibiscus* species, it is all about the flower, which usually shows up in summer and fall but can appear just about any time of the year as long as the conditions are right.

DESCRIPTION: This perennial grows to 1–2 feet tall by 1–2 feet across, depending on where it lives. Dark green leaves provide a dramatic backdrop for the electric, bright crimson-red, 2½-inch-wide, cup-shaped flowers. Dried, tan capsules with small, black seeds follow the flowers.

CULTURE/MAINTENANCE: Plants are root-hardy to at least 10° F, although the tops might die back. Place *H. martianus* in full sun for most compact growth, or under the dappled light of a wispy tree. This moderately fast-growing, low-water-using, desert native will survive on 10–12 inches of annual rainfall but will look better and flower more if given supplemental water once every 7–14 days from late spring through summer. Cut back to nearly ground level in the late winter and once or twice during the growing season to create a thicker, fuller plant.

IDENTIFICATION: Bright, crimson-red, 2½-inch-wide, cup-shaped flowers readily distinguish *H. martianus* from other native or near-native *Hibiscus* species. The name *H. martianus*, derived from Mars, the Roman god of war, and probably referring to the red flowers, was published before the name *H. cardiophyllus,* which refers to the heart-shaped leaves. The rules of nomenclature tell us to follow the first name published even though the second name is better known in horticulture.

LANDSCAPE APPLICATION: This plant is best used as supplemental color around the base of accents such as *Agave, Dasylirion, Hesperaloe funifera,* or tall *Yucca* species. Mix *H. martianus* with *Echinocactus grusonii, Ferocactus* species, or even *Opuntia* species in a cactus and succulent garden, to provide a dash of color during the hot time of year. The Martian flowers will zing up collections of perennials or small shrubs like *Ageratum corymbosum, Conoclinium dissectum, Penstemon* species, *Poliomintha maderensis, Scutellaria suffrutescens,* or *Zinnia acerosa.*

PRECAUTIONS: Rabbits might munch on the stems if there is nothing else around for them to feast on.

Justicia californica | Chuparosa

MEDIUM–LARGE SHRUB	
SIZE (height x width)	3–6 feet x 4–6 feet
FLOWER COLOR	Red, rarely yellow
FLOWER SEASON	Spring–fall
EXPOSURE	Full or reflected sun
WATER	Drought-tolerant–moderate
GROWTH RATE	Moderately fast
PRUNING	Remove frozen growth in late winter
HARDINESS	Half-hardy (when young or new growth damaged at mid-20s F) to hardy (established plants)
NATURAL ELEVATION RANGE	Near sea level–2,500 feet
SUITABLE CITIES	All low-elevation-zone cities; Tucson in mid-elevation zone

FIELD NOTES: *Justicia californica* prefers dry, gravelly, or sandy soil and rocky slopes in southern California, southern Arizona, Baja California, and Sonora from near sea level to about 2,500 feet elevation. Hiking in dry, earth-tone habitats in the Tucson Mountains, it is always a pleasure to come across this shrub in full flower.

DESCRIPTION: This shrub normally grows to 3 feet tall and 3–4 feet wide. Under ideal conditions it can grow to 5–6 feet tall and 5–6 feet wide. It is a host plant for the checkerspot butterfly. Medium green leaves are semisucculent and measure about 1

inch long and 1 inch wide. Thin, tubular, 1½-inch-long, red or rarely yellow flowers are most abundant in spring but can appear almost any time of the year if the conditions are right. Hummingbirds love the abundant flowers, which provide an important source of energy. Small, slightly woody fruits pop open when ripe.

CULTURE/MAINTENANCE: Chuparosa is hardy to the mid-20s F but incurs some tip damage if subjected to those temperatures for any length of time. It may freeze to the ground when winter lows hit the high teens for an extended period. Place it in full sun or reflected sun to keep it dense and compact. Remember that chuparosa is native to washes and other areas with fast-draining soil. Plants are drought-tolerant once established and can grow on 10 inches or less of annual rainfall. The growth rate is moderate to fast, and the foliage is sparse; however, you can give both a boost by thoroughly soaking the root every 7–10 days from spring until fall. Prune out frozen stems in late winter or early spring and cut back hard once every 3–5 years to increase density.

IDENTIFICATION: *J. californica* is readily separated from the other species of *Justicia* by its small leaves and thin, red flowers without a large lower lip. *J. candicans* has larger, less succulent leaves and red flowers with a larger lower lip. *J. spicigera* has bright orange flowers.

LANDSCAPE APPLICATION: For a natural look, install one or more plants in a simulated wash or rocky outcrop. Because *J. californica* requires little water or maintenance, it fits in well with desert tough guys. It softens the effect of *Dasylirion, Nolina,* and various *Yucca* species, and combines artistically with desert trees like *Acacia constricta, Eysenhardtia orthocarpa, Leucaena retusa,* and *Parkinsonia* species. The red blossoms constrast nicely with the yellow of plants like *Encelia farinosa, Psilostrophe cooperi,* and *Tetraneuris acaulis.*

PRECAUTIONS: New plants may be susceptible to rabbit damage. However, once a plant is established and grown hard (not overwatered or overfertilized) it is less likely to be eaten. Aside from watching for rabbits and trimming back frost damage, you can neglect mature plants.

Justicia candicans | Red Justicia

SMALL–MEDIUM SHRUB	
SIZE (height x width)	1½–3 feet x 1½–3 feet
FLOWER COLOR	Red
FLOWER SEASON	Spring–fall
EXPOSURE	Full, filtered, or reflected sun
WATER	Low–moderate
GROWTH RATE	Moderately fast
PRUNING	Prune frozen stems in late winter
HARDINESS	Hardy to at least 20° F
NATURAL ELEVATION RANGE	1,500–3,500 feet
SUITABLE CITIES	All low-elevation-zone cities; warm microclimates in Tucson

FIELD NOTES: *Justicia candicans* hides in dry, rocky ravines and canyons in the mountains of southern Arizona south into Sonora, western Chihuahua, and northern Sinaloa. Plants are not common, but I've spotted them in canyons with plants of more tropical origin between 1,500 and 3,500 feet elevation.

DESCRIPTION: This small shrub scatters eye-catching, bright red flowers among soft, evergreen leaves along upright stems. It typically grows to about 1½ –2 feet tall and 1½–2 feet wide but can eventually reach a size of 3 feet tall by 3 feet wide. Small, bright green leaves can stay on the plant through the winter. They measure about 1–1 ½ inch long by 1 inch wide and are slightly hairy and velvety to the touch. *J. candicans* is normally shrubby with woody stems; however, the stems may freeze to ground level in severe cold. Bright red, tubular flowers appear along the stem from spring through summer and on into fall and are irresistible to hummingbirds. Plants may even flower in the winter if the temperatures are mild enough.

CULTURE/MAINTENANCE: Plants are hardy to about 20° F and possibly lower in a protected area. They are drought-tolerant but will grow faster and flower more enthusiastically if given weekly watering during the warmer months. This plant is slow to establish, but after the first year or two in the ground, it is moderately fast-growing. It grows best in soil that has good drainage yet does not dry out too quickly. It handles full sun or light shade, although flowering is diminished on shaded plants. The only maintenance required is pruning back any frozen stems in late winter or early spring.

IDENTIFICATION: Red justicia is easily distinguished from the other *Justicia* species by its red flowers with a larger, flared lower lip. *J. spicigera* has thin, tubular, orange flowers.

LANDSCAPE APPLICATION: Red justicia can fit neatly into many situations. Its hummingbird-attracting flowers make a fine addition to bird gardens. Use it as a perennial flowering plant or small shrub in full sun, reflected sun, or light shade. The lush foliage and attractive flowers are particularly useful in patio settings and near entryways, but the arching stems can also soften boulders, larger accent plants, or the margins

of simulated washes. Nearly litter-free, red justicia is equally at home in more formal settings, near pools, or in raised planters or color beds as soft background. It mixes well with spiky characters such as *Agave* species, *Dasylirion* species, and *Nolina matapensis*. It also gets along with small trees such as *Acacia willardiana*, *Bauhinia lunarioides*, *Leucaena retusa*, and *Sophora secundiflora*.

PRECAUTIONS: Screen young plants to minimize rabbit damage. They do not seem to be susceptible to any insect damage and are tolerant of most soils as long as watering is adjusted accordingly.

Justicia spicigera | Mexican Honeysuckle, Firecracker Bush

SMALL–MEDIUM SHRUB	
SIZE (height x width)	2–4 feet x 3–5 feet
FLOWER COLOR	Orange
FLOWER SEASON	Any time of the year
EXPOSURE	Full or filtered sun, or partial shade
WATER	Low–moderate
GROWTH RATE	Moderately fast
PRUNING	Shear in spring if frozen
HARDINESS	Half-hardy to hardy, stem damage at mid to high 20s F, frozen to ground at low 20s F
NATURAL ELEVATION RANGE	30–3,000 feet
SUITABLE CITIES	All low-elevation-zone cities; Tucson in mid-elevation zone

FIELD NOTES: *Justicia spicigera* grows in forested areas in eastern Mexico and Central America between about 30 and 3,000 feet. Frequent traveling partner Ron Gass and I stopped for a much-needed lunch in a deeply shaded, subtropical area of Nuevo León, Mexico. We were fortunate to spot a couple of these hard-to-find plants on the slopes under the trees.

DESCRIPTION: Narrowly tubular, bright orange flowers set against large, velvety, rich green leaves provide a popular hangout for hummingbirds. This small to medium shrub grows to 2–4 feet tall and spreads to 3–5 feet wide depending on its planting location. Soft leaves are about 2–3 inches long and 1–2 inches wide and provide a sub-tropical look. Clusters of the 1½-inch-long orange blossoms can appear almost any time of the year. The flowering schedule seems to depend on the planting location and winter temperature. When given summer shade and winter sun *J. spicigera* blooms more in winter. When planted in full sun, it blooms more in spring, summer, and fall.

Not surprisingly, if killed back by frost, flowering is delayed.

CULTURE/MAINTENANCE: Plants are hardy to about the low 20s F, freezing to the ground in open, exposed locations but recovering quickly in the spring and summer. Plants grown in a protected location will tolerate lower temperatures than those in an open, exposed area. This is a low- to moderate-water-user but looks better when given a thorough soaking once every 7–10 days. Place it in part shade, filtered sun, or full sun and adjust watering accordingly. It has a moderate to fast growth rate, varying with watering, and is not particularly fussy about type of soil as long as the drainage is adequate. Cut back any frozen growth in late winter or early spring as new growth emerges.

IDENTIFICATION: *J. spicigera* is easily separated from all other *Justicia* species by its bright orange, narrowly tubular flowers.

LANDSCAPE APPLICATION: Use this colorful shrub as a magnet for hummingbirds and occasionally butterflies. Plant it under the shade of *Acacia* species, *Eysenhardtia orthocarpa*, *Parkinsonia* species, or *Prosopis velutina*. The bright orange flowers mix well with white or purple flowers of plants such as *Cordia* species, *Lantana montevidensis*, *Leucophyllum langmaniae*, and *Ruellia peninsularis*. Group plants at the base of large accent plants such as *Agave*, *Dasylirion*, or *Yucca* species.

PRECAUTIONS: *J. spicigera* is frost-sensitive and should be grown in a sheltered location. It is ideal for the mini-oasis and areas protected from wildlife. It does not seem susceptible to insects or fungal diseases.

Lantana montevidensis | Trailing Lantana

GROUND COVER, FLOWERING PERENNIAL	
SIZE (height x width)	1–2 feet x 3–6 feet
FLOWER COLOR	Lavender, rosy lilac, white
FLOWER SEASON	Spring–fall
EXPOSURE	Full or reflected sun
WATER	Moderate

GROWTH RATE	Fast
PRUNING	Frost-damaged plants can be cut back in spring; undamaged plants can be cut back every couple of years
HARDINESS	Hardy to the mid to low 20s F
NATURAL ELEVATION RANGE	150–3,000 feet
SUITABLE CITIES	All low- and mid-elevation-zone cities; marginal in high-elevation-zone cities

FIELD NOTES: *Lantana montevidensis* is native to tropical South America and lives at 150–3,000 feet elevation.

DESCRIPTION: This spreading plant has stems that grow up 1–2 feet and out 3–6 feet. Fragrant, small, medium to dark green, oval leaves have crenately scalloped edges, are simple and opposite, and measure about 1 inch long by ¾ inch wide. Terminal clusters of lavender to rosy lilac flowers will appear from late spring through fall and draw in the butterflies. 'White Lightning' is a white-flowered form, and 'Lavender Swirl' has clusters of all white, all purple, and mixed white and purple flowers.

CULTURE/MAINTENANCE: Trailing lantana grows and flowers best when placed in full sun or even the reflected heat of a wall or building. Plants are hardy to the mid to low 20s F, recovering in one spring season from any frost damage sustained in the winter. They perform best if watered thoroughly once every 7–10 days from spring through fall but will need to be cut back frequently. If kept slightly drier and grown more slowly, they can go 3–4 years before being cut back, either selectively or sheared nearly to the ground.

IDENTIFICATION: *L. montevidensis* is readily distinguished from the *L. camara* cultivars by the low, spreading habit and lavender, rosy lilac, or white flowers, and from *Lantana* x 'New Gold' by the flower color.

LANDSCAPE APPLICATION: Place this plant in full sun and use it as a ground cover that attracts butterflies. Try it around pools or water features and blend with other butterfly favorites like *Ageratum corymbosum, Buddleja marrubiifolia, Chrysactinia mexicana, Conoclinium dissectum, Dalea frutescens, Ericameria laricifolia,* and *Lantana* x

'New Gold.' Surround large accent plants like *Dasylirion acrotrichum, Dasylirion wheeleri, Nolina nelsonii, Yucca rigida,* and *Yucca rostrata* with this spreading greenery.

PRECAUTIONS: Trailing lantana needs to be planted in a soil containing some organic matter and adequate drainage to reduce iron chlorosis. If the soil pH is too alkaline, try supplementing with some compost and ammonium sulfate. Water the plant or spray the foliage with an iron chelate as a temporary fix. Unripe berries are toxic, and pets have become ill after eating foliage.

Lantana x 'New Gold' | New Gold Lantana

GROUND COVER, FLOWERING PERENNIAL	
SIZE (height x width)	18–24 inches x 3–4 feet
FLOWER COLOR	Golden yellow
FLOWER SEASON	Spring–early fall
EXPOSURE	Full or reflected sun
WATER	Low–moderate
GROWTH RATE	Fast
PRUNING	Prune off frost damaged parts in early spring
HARDINESS	Foliage hardy to mid 20s, roots hardy to at least 10° F
SUITABLE CITIES	All low- and mid-elevation-zone cities; marginal in high-elevation-zone cities except Albuquerque

FIELD NOTES: *Lantana* x 'New Gold' is a hybrid developed at Texas A&M.

DESCRIPTION: This woody ground cover is grown primarily for its brilliant warm season flower display. 'New Gold' has bright green, 1½–2-inch-long leaves and 1½–2-inch-wide clusters of bright golden yellow flowers produced at the tips of new growth from spring through fall, that are beloved by butterflies. Unlike other species of *Lan-*

tana, 'New Gold' does not produce seed after flowering, so it is a cleaner plant with a longer bloom season.

CULTURE/MAINTENANCE: 'New Gold' shows foliage damage at the mid 20s F and is killed to ground level at the low 20s F. The roots are hardy to 10° F, so the plant will sprout back even in the coldest winters in the mid-elevation deserts. It is low-water-using, although it will produce more flowers and bloom longer with extra water from spring until fall. It has a fast growth rate and even if killed to the ground, it bounces back to mature size in one season. Plant it in full sun or reflected heat. This ground cover was selected as superior to the many other cultivars tested by Texas A & M because of its seedless nature, long and profuse bloom, compact growth form, and relative cold-hardiness. The primary maintenance is cutting out the dead growth in late winter or early spring.

IDENTIFICATION: Lack of seed production is the best way to distinguish 'New Gold' from other mounding plants with yellow or gold flowers.

LANDSCAPE APPLICATION: This plant is a great choice for medians, streetscapes, and parking lots. It provides long-lived and intense summer color, and many landscapers are using it in place of annual color. Mass plant with bold accents such as *Dasylirion*, *Nolina*, and *Yucca* species. It makes a colorful sidekick for evergreen large shrubs or small trees that lack showy flowers or are in flower very briefly, like *Acacia salicina, Diospyros texana, Dodonaea viscosa, Fraxinus greggii, Rhus choriophylla, Simmondsia chinensis,* and *Vauquelinia californica.*

PRECAUTIONS: Whiteflies love 'New Gold' and other *Lantana* species. Prune back frost-damaged plants in early spring. Rabbits leave this plant alone.

Larrea divaricata | Creosote

MEDIUM–LARGE SHRUB	
SIZE (height x width)	2–10 feet x 2–10 feet
FLOWER COLOR	Yellow
FLOWER SEASON	Anytime following sufficient rainfall
EXPOSURE	Full or reflected sun
WATER	Drought-tolerant–low
GROWTH RATE	Slow
PRUNING	None
HARDINESS	Hardy to at least 0° F
NATURAL ELEVATION RANGE	Below sea level to 4,600 feet
SUITABLE CITIES	All cities in all zones

FIELD NOTES: *Larrea divaricata* is found growing from below sea level in Death Valley to about 4,600 feet elevation. This ubiquitous, variable shrub is found in all three North American deserts. Plants can be found on the sandy dunes near Yuma, Arizona, on valley bottoms and plains in sandy or gravelly soil, and frequently in soil with a

prominent caliche layer. The wonderful fragrance in the desert after a summer rainstorm comes from this plant.

DESCRIPTION: Plants can be small, dense, and uniform or large, open, and rangy. The size will vary from about 2 feet tall by 2 feet wide to 6–10 feet tall by 6–10 feet wide. Small, leathery leaves are divided into 2 sticky, sickle-shaped leaflets. Small, bright yellow, 5-petalled flowers appear almost anytime of the year following sufficient rain. Small, fuzzy, white fruits follow the flowers and can be nearly as attractive.

CULTURE/MAINTENANCE: Plants are hardy to at least 0° F. Creosote is a champion of drought tolerance, surviving on less than 10 inches of annual rainfall. The growth rate is slow, and supplemental water should be applied judiciously. Place it in soil that has good drainage. Plants require very little maintenance and do not need to be pruned.

IDENTIFICATION: The plant shape, leathery leaves, yellow flowers, and fuzzy fruits help identify *L. divaricata*.

LANDSCAPE APPLICATION: Place creosote in full sun in the outer zone of a xeriscape. It becomes too leggy if planted in any shade. Creosote does quite well in harsh situations like parking lots and street medians without requiring a lot of maintenance. Give it tough companions like *Carnegiea gigantea, Opuntia violacea* var. *santa rita*, and species of *Agave, Dasylirion, Hesperaloe, Nolina*, and *Yucca.* Its color, size, and form mix nicely with flowering shrubs such as *Bauhinia lunarioides, Buddleja marrubiifolia, Calliandra eriophylla, Dalea frutescens, Leucophyllum* species, and *Salvia greggii.*

PRECAUTIONS: Creosote produces compounds that deter animals from eating them. Planting in soil with good drainage will minimize root rot due to standing water in the root zone.

Leucaena retusa | Golden Ball Lead Tree

SMALL TREE	
SIZE (height x width)	15 feet x 10 feet
FLOWER COLOR	Golden yellow
FLOWER SEASON	Spring–summer

EXPOSURE	Full or reflected sun
WATER	Low–moderate
GROWTH RATE	Moderately slow
PRUNING	Only to shape
HARDINESS	Hardy to at least 5° F
NATURAL ELEVATION RANGE	1,200–5,000 feet
SUITABLE CITIES	All cities in all zones except Albuquerque

FIELD NOTES: *Leucaena retusa* can't decide whether it's a tree or a shrub—I've spotted both along Texas State Highway 285 from Ft. Stockton south to Del Rio. It prefers limestone or igneous soil in canyons, arroyos, and roadsides in western Texas and adjacent northern Mexico from about 1,200 to 5,500 feet elevation. Keep your eyes open for lush specimens between Langtry and the Pecos River, in Big Bend National Park, and in the Guadalupe Mountains.

DESCRIPTION: This small, deciduous tree tops out around 15 feet and spreads to 10 feet across. It displays one or more main, upright trunks then branches to form a rounded to slightly flat crown. Leaves are bipinnately compound with small, bright green leaflets with rounded tips that darken with maturity. The leaflet tips are rounded, a characteristic used for the species name, as *retus* is Latin for "blunt." Bright, golden yellow puffballs are quite showy in the late winter on an otherwise bare tree, causing a buzz of bee activity. The 1-inch-diameter flower clusters keep up the show after leaves return. Thin, woody, 6-inch-long dehiscent pods mature during the late spring, summer, and fall.

CULTURE/MAINTENANCE: *L. retusa* is hardy to at least 5° F. It tolerates a wide range of soils, as long as drainage is adequate, and is low-water-using once established, growing on 11 inches of annual rainfall. It responds to a thorough soaking of the root zone 2–3 times a month during the hottest, driest part of the year. Slow-growing *L. retusa* can also be speeded some by supplemental water during the growing season. Plant it in full or reflected sun for best performance. It is somewhat messy, constantly shedding leaves, flowers, and pods.

IDENTIFICATION: A big *L. retusa* is easy to recognize. Small plants may look a little like *Caesalpinia mexicana* or *C. pulcherrima,* but the *Leucaena* will have brown, woody bark, while the *Caesalpinia* species will not.

LANDSCAPE APPLICATION: Place *L. retusa* in the sun in a desert landscape or where it will cast summer shade and welcome winter sun on the west side of a building. It works as an overstory tree providing light shade for plants underneath, and nicely sets off flowering shrubs including *Anisacanthus quadrifidus* var. *wrightii, Dalea capitata, Dalea frutescens, Gaura lindheimeri, Justicia candicans, Leucophyllum candidum, Salvia greggii,* and *Wedelia acapulcensis* var. *hispida.*

PRECAUTIONS: I know of no insect pests or diseases. Screen young plants to prevent rabbit damage, but as the trunk thickens, the screening can be removed.

Leucophyllum candidum | Violet Silverleaf

MEDIUM SHRUB

SIZE (height x width)	3–5 feet x 3–5 feet
FLOWER COLOR	Dark violet
FLOWER SEASON	Summer–fall
EXPOSURE	Full or reflected sun
WATER	Drought-tolerant–low
GROWTH RATE	Slow
PRUNING	Shear in late spring
HARDINESS	Hardy to at least 10° F
NATURAL ELEVATION RANGE	3,000–4,300 feet
SUITABLE CITIES	All cities in all zones except Albuquerque

FIELD NOTES: *Leucophyllum candidum* is native to rocky or gravelly hills and flat brushlands in the Big Bend area of west Texas and adjacent northern Mexico primarily between 3,000 and 4,300 feet elevation. Shrubs should be easy to spot in Big Bend National Park when in full flower during the summer rainy season.

DESCRIPTION: This dense, compact evergreen shrub has small, silvery white leaves that are spoon-shaped and measure about ¾ inch across. Deep purple, ¾-inch flowers appear in summer and fall when the humidity is up and create a dynamite look against the foliage. Two cultivars are on the market. 'Silver Cloud' is the larger of the two, reaching 4–5 feet by 4–5 feet, while 'Thunder Cloud' is smaller, 3–4 feet by 3–4 feet, with more tightly packed, deeper purple flowers.

CULTURE/MAINTENANCE: Plants are hardy to around 5° and maybe lower if they are not watered and fertilized in late fall and winter. Violet silverleaf is low-water-

using, surviving on 10–12 inches of annual rainfall. It grows slowly but will speed up a little and may manufacture more flowers if watered once every week or two, depending on the soil type, in late spring and summer. Place it in full or reflected sun and in soil with good drainage to minimize root rot from excess water. It requires very little maintenance and should be pruned once in early spring, if at all.

IDENTIFICATION: *L. candidum* is easily distinguished from other *Leucophyllum* species by the size of the plant and the color of the leaves and flowers. Young plants could be confused with small *L. pruinosum,* but *L. candidum* has smaller leaves, a stiffer, more rigid appearance, and darker purple blossoms.

LANDSCAPE APPLICATION: Because of its size, violet silverleaf can sneak into tight spaces, such as parking lot and street medians, without requiring a lot of care. Its drought tolerance lets it mix well with a variety of succulents and semisucculents. Try that silver foliage against bold *Agave, Dasylirion, Hesperaloe, Nolina,* and *Yucca* species. Or put it together with an eclectic selection of desert favorites: *Bauhinia lunarioides, Buddleja marrubiifolia, Calliandra eriophylla, Dalea capitata, Dalea frutescens,* other *Leucophyllum* species, *Muhlenbergia* species, and *Salvia greggii.*

PRECAUTIONS: Tender young plants are susceptible to rabbit damage, while older, tough guys who have kicked the irrigation habit are not. Be sure to plant the shrubs in a soil with good drainage to minimize root rot due to standing water in the root zone.

Leucophyllum frutescens | Texas Ranger, Texas Rain Sage, Cenizo

LARGE SHRUB	
SIZE (height x width)	5–8 feet x 5–6 feet
FLOWER COLOR	Rose-purple, white
FLOWER SEASON	Summer–fall
EXPOSURE	Full or reflected sun
WATER	Drought-tolerant–moderate
GROWTH RATE	Fast
PRUNING	Once or twice in spring or early summer

HARDINESS	Hardy to 5° F
NATURAL ELEVATION RANGE	800–5,000 feet
SUITABLE CITIES	All cities in all zones except Albuquerque

FIELD NOTES: *Leucophyllum frutescens* grows on rocky limestone hills, bluffs, arroyos, and roadsides in western and southern Texas and adjacent northeastern Mexico from 800 to 5,000 feet elevation. If you happen to cruise through Big Bend National Park about 10–12 days after a good summer rainstorm you should catch some nice specimens in full flower.

L. frutescens 'Green Cloud' (left) with *L. laevigatum*

DESCRIPTION: This large spreading shrub can fill out to 6–8 feet tall and 6 feet across. Gray-green leaves measure nearly 1 inch long and stick with the plant through most winters in low deserts. During colder winters, or in mid-elevation desert locations, the plant will shed about half its foliage. The 1-inch-long, rose-purple flowers appear from June through October, seemingly triggered by periods of high humidity. The cultivar 'Green Cloud' features dark rose-purple flowers and bicolored foliage that is green above and light gray-green below. 'White Cloud' has gray foliage and large white flowers. 'Compactum' has pink flowers and short spaces between the leaves that keep the plant at about 5 feet tall by 5 feet wide.

CULTURE/MAINTENANCE: Plants are hardy to 5° F if they are allowed to go dormant in fall and winter. They are low-water-using to drought-tolerant, but they will fill in and flower with supplemental water in the summer. The plant can achieve a fairly large size in one or two growing seasons. The growth rate will vary a little depending on watering during the growing season. Place it in full or reflected sun and give it plenty of room for development. Prune back ruthlessly in the spring to increase density then leave it at the mercy of nature throughout the summer and fall blooming seasons.

IDENTIFICATION: Distinguish *L. frutescens* by its combination of gray-green foliage and large, rose-purple flowers.

LANDSCAPE APPLICATION: Plant it singly, group it loosely, or use it as an informal hedge in full or reflected sun in a desert landscape. It proudly serves along highways, or in large, open expanses. Its culture and appearance are compatible with other desert rats like *Dasylirion acrotrichum, Dasylirion quadrangulatum, Diospyros texana, Eysenhardtia orthocarpa, Leucaena retusa,* other *Leucophyllum* species, *Nolina matapensis, Nolina nelsonii,* and *Yucca* species. It also looks great in combination with summer

Variety 'White Cloud'

bloomers such as *Caesalpinia pulcherrima, Lantana* species, and *Tecoma stans.*

PRECAUTIONS: As with other species and cultivars of the genus, *L. frutescens* is susceptible to root rot in poorly drained soils. Rabbits and deer might eat young plants, but older, more established plants or those that are grown hard (not watered and fertilized heavily) are less attractive to nibblers. Prune in the spring and not summer or fall to avoid trimming off potential flowers.

Leucophyllum laevigatum | Chihuahuan Rain Sage

MEDIUM–LARGE SHRUB

SIZE (height x width)	4–6 feet x 5–7 feet
FLOWER COLOR	Lavender
FLOWER SEASON	Summer–fall
EXPOSURE	Full or reflected sun
WATER	Drought-tolerant–low
GROWTH RATE	Moderately fast
PRUNING	Once in spring
HARDINESS	Hardy to at least 10° F
NATURAL ELEVATION RANGE	3,600–6,700 feet
SUITABLE CITIES	All low- and mid-elevation-zone cities; Sierra Vista in high-elevation zone

FIELD NOTES: *Leucophyllum laevigatum* is found on limestone and caliche hills and alluvial fans in northeastern Mexico from 3,600 to 6,700 feet elevation. You might catch this plant at Carneros Pass, about 23 miles south of Saltillo along Mexico Highway 54. I traveled through northern Mexico in July of 2008. Good rains a week or two before our arrival must have triggered the full, glorious flowering of all the *Leucophyllum* species we encountered. One of the most incredible sights was driving through the mountains of Coahuila and Durango where hundreds, if not thousands, of *L. laevigatum* were the showiest plants around.

DESCRIPTION: This medium to large shrub grows 4–6 feet tall by 5–7 feet across, depending on amount and frequency of supplemental water. Small, dark green leaves sit close together on stiff, erect to spreading branches. Also, the unique, angular growth habit blends well in a "native" landscape. This is one of the most desirable species of *Leucophyllum* because of its ability to bloom profusely nearly every 7–10 days. The dark green leaves provide an excellent background for the out-of-control, ¾-inch-long lavender flowers. The best displays tend to occur as the weather gets stickier in late summer, although other *Leucophyllum* species are more dependent on that increased humidity.

CULTURE/MAINTENANCE: Chihuahuan rain sage is hardy to at least 10° F and can survive lower temperatures if "hardened off" by reducing supplemental water in early fall. This smart plant grows well in most any soil as long as drainage is adequate or amount of supplemental water is adjusted accordingly. It is quite drought-tolerant and will survive on about 12 inches of annual rainfall, although plants will perk up with summer watering or until the summer rains begin. Plants have a moderately fast growth rate; prune heavily in the spring, then allow the plant to grow naturally. Late-season pruning may reduce flower production.

IDENTIFICATION: Nurseries carry three species of *Leucophyllum* that have green leaves. *L. laevigatum* can be distinguished from *L. langmaniae* and *L. frutescens* 'Green Cloud' by its smaller leaves, stiff and angular form, and lighter lavender flower color.

LANDSCAPE APPLICATION: This medium-size shrub slides right into full sun and reflected heat spots in low- and mid-elevation-zone cities, and even Sierra Vista of the high-elevation zone. Mass as an informal hedge, or intersperse with small to large shrubs, small trees, or bold accent plants. Companion suggestions are a wild mixture of shapes, sizes, and flower color: *Buddleja marrubiifolia, Calliandra eriophylla, Chrys-actinia mexicana, Dalea capitata, Dalea frutescens, Dasylirion acrotrichum, Dasylirion quadrangulatum, Hesperaloe funifera, Nolina matapensis, Nolina nelsonii, Penstemon baccharifolius, Yucca grandiflora, Y. rigida,* and *Y. rostrata.*

PRECAUTIONS: Overwatering can get you into trouble with root rot. Plants work well on gentle slopes or in rocky soils that allow water to move away from roots.

Leucophyllum langmaniae | Monterrey Rain Sage

MEDIUM SHRUB	
SIZE (Height x Width)	5 feet x 5 feet
FLOWER COLOR	Lavender-blue
FLOWER SEASON	Summer–fall

EXPOSURE	Full or reflected sun
WATER	Low–moderate
GROWTH RATE	Moderately fast
PRUNING	Shear in spring
HARDINESS	Hardy to at least 10° F
NATURAL ELEVATION RANGE	3,400–3,500 feet
SUITABLE CITIES	All low- and mid-elevation-zone cities

FIELD NOTES: *Leucophyllum langmaniae* is known only from limestone areas in the mountains between Monterrey and Saltillo in northeastern Mexico, at 3,400–3,500 feet elevation. I have had the good fortune of seeing this gem in habitat and in bloom and even surviving the trek into Hausteca Canyon, a place described by words like narrow, sheer, and vertical.

DESCRIPTION: *L. langmaniae* fills out as a rounded form, 5 feet tall by 5 feet across. Leaves are as large as 1 inch long and ½ inch wide. Lavender-blue flowers are about 1 inch across and create a spectacular display on the upper parts of the stems from late May or early June on into November or until frost. The best flowering comes 5–10 days after a good rainstorm.

CULTURE/MAINTENANCE: Plants are hardy to about 10° F, provided they are allowed to harden off in the fall. Give this plant full or reflected sun and a soil that drains well to reduce the chance of root rot from excess moisture. It has a moderately fast growth rate, is moderately drought-tolerant once established, but appreciates water during the hottest and driest months. Prune it according to the *Leucophyllum* formula, before major late summer flowering. Like its relatives, it will grow fine without any supplemental fertilizing.

IDENTIFICATION: *L. langmaniae* resembles *L. laevigatum* but has a more lush appearance. The leaves are larger and the plant has a softer, more rounded look than the stiff, spiky *L. laevigatum*. The cultivar names for this plant are somewhat confusing. First, there are two names being applied to one clone, which is a horticultural no-no. There is a form that originated in Texas that has been given the cultivar name 'Lynn's Everblooming,' which is being grown in Arizona under the name 'Lynn's Legacy.' This form is nearly the same as 'Rio Bravo' except it is slower-growing and blooms more frequently.

LANDSCAPE APPLICATION: *L. langmaniae* works as a decent screen, masses comfortably for a spectacular flower display, or artistically sets off accents like *Agave, Dasylirion, Nolina,* or *Yucca* species. It needs full sun and combines easily with desert landscape plants. Mix it with low-water-use pros such as *Buddleja marrubiifolia, Chrysactinia mexicana, Encelia farinosa,* other *Leucophyllum* species, *Poliomintha maderensis,* and *Salvia greggii,* in all low- and mid-elevation-zone cities, and even in warm microclimates of high-elevation-zone cities.

PRECAUTIONS: Rabbits are fond of young plants and new shoots, so be sure to screen them for the first year or two.

Leucophyllum pruinosum | Grape-scented Rain Sage

MEDIUM–LARGE SHRUB

SIZE (height x width)	4–6 feet x 4–6 feet
FLOWER COLOR	Blue-violet
FLOWER SEASON	Summer–fall
EXPOSURE	Full or reflected sun
WATER	Low–moderate
GROWTH RATE	Moderately fast
PRUNING	Shear in late winter and/or early spring
HARDINESS	Hardy to at least 10° F
NATURAL ELEVATION RANGE	3,000–5,200 feet
SUITABLE CITIES	All low- and mid-elevation-zone cities

FIELD NOTES: *Leucophyllum pruinosum* prefers rocky, limestone slopes and alluvial outwash fans in mixed desert scrub and short-tree forest in southern Nuevo León, southwestern Tamaulipas, and eastern San Luis Potosí. Ron Gass and I happened upon a population near the town of Miquihuana in southern Tamaulipas while searching for new plant material to test out. Shrubs are found growing between 3,000 and 5,200 feet elevation with desert favorites *Acacia, Ferocactus, Larrea,* and *Yucca* species.

DESCRIPTION: This rounded shrub has soft, velvety, silver-gray leaves about ½ inch in diameter. It grows to 4–6 feet tall and 4–6 feet wide and has a loose, fluffy appearance. Iridescent blue-violet flowers broadcast a fragrance reminiscent of grape Kool Aid®. Flowering can begin in June and continue through November. A batch of several seedlings was grown and given the sniffer test. This resulted in the selection of the cultivar 'Sierra Bouquet,' which was named for its strong fragrance.

CULTURE/MAINTENANCE: *L. pruinosum* is hardy to about 10° F. It has a moderately fast growth rate and will survive on only 12 inches of annual rainfall. Extra water in the spring and summer will boost growth and flowering. Place it in full or reflected sun and in a soil with good drainage. Prune during spring or early summer to avoid trimming off future flowers.

IDENTIFICATION: *L. pruinosum* could be confused only with *L. candidum,* but not if you study. *L. pruinosum* has larger leaves that are not as densely hairy, its flowers are broader and more translucent, and the plant is larger and not as stiff-looking.

LANDSCAPE APPLICATION: Plant it singly or mass in a desert landscape, and mix with other low-water-users in all low- and mid-elevation-zone cities. It blends attractively with plants that have bold foliage or a strong vertical form. The silvery gray contrasts nicely with green-leaved shrubs and small trees, such as *Agave colorata, Agave parryi var. truncata, Carnegiea gigantea, Dasylirion acrotrichum, Dasylirion quadrangulatum, Fouquieria splendens, Nolina matapensis, Nolina nelsonii,* and *Yucca grandiflora.* Try combining with small trees like *Diospyros texana, Eysenhardtia orthocarpa, Leucaena retusa,* and *Sophora secundiflora.*

PRECAUTIONS: Go easy on the watering to prevent root rot. Heavily watered or fertilized plants look open and leggy and also draw in rabbits to feed on their succulent stems.

Leucophyllum zygophyllum | Blue Ranger

MEDIUM SHRUB

SIZE (height x width)	3 feet x 3 feet
FLOWER COLOR	Deep bluish-purple
FLOWER SEASON	Summer–fall
EXPOSURE	Full or reflected sun
WATER	Low–moderate
GROWTH RATE	Slow–moderate
PRUNING	None
HARDINESS	Hardy to at least 10° F
NATURAL ELEVATION RANGE	3,900–7,000 feet
SUITABLE CITIES	All low- and mid-elevation-zone cities

FIELD NOTES: *Leucophyllum zygophyllum* is found growing on rocky limestone and caliche soil with mesquite, chaparral, and oak-pine forest in southern Nuevo León, southwestern Tamaulipas, and north-central San Luis Potosí from 3,900 to 7,000 feet elevation. You can spot wild plants near the town of Miquihuana in Tamaulipas or between Galeana and Linares on Mexico Highway 31 in Nuevo León.

DESCRIPTION: Yellowish, gray-green leaves are ½ inch long by ½ inch wide and shaped like little spoons. This is an attractive, compact shrub. The dense form and interesting leaf color make an ideal background for the deep, bluish-purple flowers. Individual blossoms measure about ½ inch long and ½ inch wide and densely pack together along the stem. Flowering season can begin as early as June and continue as late as November. The cultivar 'Cimarron' can bloom in several flushes throughout the summer monsoon season.

CULTURE/MAINTENANCE: This versatile, small to medium shrub thrives in full or reflected sun and is hardy to at least 10° F. It will perform well in desert soil without any supplemental organic matter as long as the soil has superb drainage and is kept dry. It is extremely drought-tolerant and will survive on 11 inches of annual rainfall after plants have become established. If your area receives less than that, try a little supplemental water through the hottest part of the year. Little or no pruning is required to maintain the naturally dense, rounded form.

IDENTIFICATION: This is the only *Leucophyllum* with leaves opposite or nearly opposite on the stem. Leaves of the other species are arranged alternately on the stem.

LANDSCAPE APPLICATION: *L. zygophyllum* is just right for the transition and outer zones of a xeriscape in all low- and mid-elevation-zone cities as long as the drainage is excellent. This tough little shrub can even be used in street medians, parking lots, and other areas where abuse is a possibility. Plant it with drought-tolerant shrubs, trees, and accent plants. In the tree department, try *Bauhinia lunarioides,* and *Leucaena retusa, Parkinsonia praecox,* and *Parkinsonia* x 'Desert Museum.' Some pretty companion shrubs include *Anisacanthus quadrifidus* var. *wrightii, Dalea frutescens, Salvia greggii,* and *Wedelia acapulcensis* var. *hispida. Agave, Dasylirion,* and *Yucca* species are dramatic accents that set off *L. zygophyllum.*

PRECAUTIONS: Provide a very well-drained soil that will allow excess water to move away from the roots. For this reason, plants work well on gentle slopes or in rocky soils.

Lonicera sempervirens | Coral Honeysuckle, Trumpet Honeysuckle

VINE	
SIZE (height x width)	8–20 feet x 4–8 feet
FLOWER COLOR	Red, orange-red, yellow on the inside
FLOWER SEASON	Spring–summer
EXPOSURE	Full or reflected sun, or part shade
WATER	Low–ample
GROWTH RATE	Slow to establish, fast once established
PRUNING	None
HARDINESS	Hardy to 10° F and maybe 0° F
NATURAL ELEVATION RANGE	50–800 feet
SUITABLE CITIES	All low- and mid-elevation-zone cities

FIELD NOTES: *Lonicera sempervirens* is found in open woodlands, along roadsides, and on the edges of clearings throughout much of the eastern half of the United States.

DESCRIPTION: This beautiful vine is evergreen (the species name means evergreen) to partly deciduous. Brilliant red or orange-red flowers, butterfly and hummingbird magnets, make it a knockout in spring. With its long stems tied to a support, this shrubby plant can easily cover an 8-foot-tall trellis and stretch to 20 feet. Leaves are opposite on the stem, dull green, broadly ovate to elliptic, and measure about 2 inches long by 1½ inches wide. The leaves just below the inflorescence are quite intriguing, being fused around the stem giving the appearance of being skewered. The terminal inflorescence is short and congested with about 18–24 tubular, 2-inch-long flowers. Flowering usually starts in the spring and continues through the summer.

CULTURE/MAINTENANCE: This vine is hardy to at least single digits and probably as low as 0° F, although the leaves will be deciduous when the plant is exposed to prolonged cold temperatures. Once established, it is fast-growing and drought-tolerant, but it grows faster and flowers more enthusiastically if you regularly soak the roots through the growing season. It will grow in nearly any soil type with sufficient water. Place plants in full sun, half-day of full sun, or reflected sun and allow them to twine on a support structure.

IDENTIFICATION: There are several cultivars of *L. sempervirens*. 'Cedar Lane' is a vigorous grower with deeper red flowers. 'Sulfurea' has yellow flowers. 'Dropmore Scarlet' is a selection of *Lonicera* x *brownii*, a hybrid of *L. sempervirens* and *L. hirsute*.

LANDSCAPE APPLICATION: Use this vine on a support for its showy flower display. Turn it loose to cover an arbor, embankment, or chain-link fence. Place it against the south, east, or west side of a blank wall or building. Try using it as a background plant for *Aloe, Agave, Dasylirion, Nolina,* or *Yucca* species. Use colorful low-growing shrubs or perennials in the foreground to overdo the color throughout the year, such as *Baileya multiradiata, Calylophus hartwegii, Tetraneuris acaulis, Penstemon* species, *Salvia* species, *Tagetes lemmonii,* and *Zauschneria californica.*

PRECAUTIONS: Watch for powdery mildew and treat as necessary. Bacterial crown gall results in warty growths on the stems near the ground. Remove and destroy infected plants. Watch for iron chlorosis in alkaline soil. Using a high nitrogen fertilizer will result in more foliage but reduce flowering.

Lophocereus schottii | Senita

CACTUS/SUCCULENT

SIZE (height x width)	6–10 feet x 3–4 feet
FLOWER COLOR	Pale pink
FLOWER SEASON	Late spring–summer
EXPOSURE	Full or reflected sun
WATER	Drought-tolerant–low
GROWTH RATE	Slow
PRUNING	None
HARDINESS	Hardy to about mid 20s F
NATURAL ELEVATION RANGE	1,000–2,000 feet
SUITABLE CITIES	All low-elevation-zone cities; warm microclimates in Tucson

FIELD NOTES: *Lophocereus schottii* is found on rocky hillsides and desert plains from 1,000 to 2,000 feet in extreme southern Arizona, and in Sonora and Baja California, Mexico. Watch for these columnar beauties in Organ Pipe National Monument in southern Arizona and across the border on the way to Puerto Peñasco.

DESCRIPTION: Senita makes a bold statement in any landscape with its upright, thick, gray-green stems that grow to 6–10 feet tall. In cultivation expect this cactus to

attain a size of about 6 feet tall by 3–4 feet across. As it ages, it begins to develop bristly "hairs" near the top of the stem. In fact, the genus name *Lophocereus* reflects this interesting characteristic, as *lopho* is Greek for "tuft," referring to the tuft of bristly spines. Small, pale pink, night-blooming flowers appear in the "hairy" section from April to August. Small, red, tasty fruit mature in the summer.

CULTURE/MAINTENANCE: *L. schottii* is hardy to about the mid-20s F and should have the tips covered when temperatures are going to drop that low in the winter. This slow-growing plant takes several years to reach a substantial size. Water use is low to drought-tolerant, but established plants will grow a bit faster with monthly irrigation from late spring through summer. Potted plants will need more frequent irrigation, usually once or twice weekly in summer. Place plants out in relentless, blazing sun, even in the interior parts of the low-elevation zone. The soil should be rocky and have good drainage. No pruning is needed unless you put it too close to a walk. Please don't do that—just give it ample room to develop.

IDENTIFICATION: *L. schottii* is easily identified by its form. *Stenocereus thurberi* has narrower stems that are covered with dark spines.

LANDSCAPE APPLICATION: Use senita as a focal point in a cactus and succulent garden. Mix flowering shrubs and perennials around the base for beautiful color, such as *Anisacanthus quadrifidus, Berlandiera lyrata, Buddleja marrubiifolia, Chrysactinia mexicana, Hibiscus martianus,* any *Penstemon* species, *Salvia greggii, Thymophylla pentachaeta,* or *Zinnia grandiflora.* Also mingle with small trees such as *Acacia willardiana, Eysenhardtia orthocarpa, Havardia pallens,* and *Sophora secundiflora.*

PRECAUTIONS: Protect young plants from damage by rabbits and javelina, and cover tips when freezing temperatures are expected.

Lysiloma watsonii ssp. *thornberi* | Feather Tree

LARGE SHRUB,
SMALL–MEDIUM TREE

SIZE (height x width)   15–20 (25) feet x 18–20 (25) feet

FLOWER COLOR   Creamy white

FLOWER SEASON	Late spring–early summer
EXPOSURE	Full or reflected sun, warm microclimate, or partial shade
WATER	Low–moderate
GROWTH RATE	Moderate
PRUNING	Shape as a tree; remove frozen stems and seedpods
HARDINESS	Half-hardy; damage at the low 20s
NATURAL ELEVATION RANGE	2,500–3,500 feet
SUITABLE CITIES	All low-elevation-zone cities; warm microclimates in Tucson

FIELD NOTES: In Arizona, *Lysiloma watsonii* ssp. *thornberi* is found only in south-facing canyons of the Rincon Mountains at about 3,500 feet elevation. Hikers in these mountains east of Tucson can easily spot the big shrubs because of their rich green, feathery leaves. It is more common in the thorn scrub of Sonora, Chihuahua, Sinaloa, and Durango, Mexico, but can be found between 2,500 and 3,500 feet in the Sonoran Desert along low-lying areas where there is extra moisture.

DESCRIPTION: A dense, spreading canopy of rich green, fernlike foliage provides a tropical appearance. Dark brown bark and profuse flower display are features that add to the beauty of the tree. Depending on the climate, it turns into either a large shrub or a small tree. Typically, most trees will not grow much larger than about 15–20 feet tall and 15–20 feet across; however, in frost-free areas the exceptional specimen can reach 25 feet tall with a canopy 25 feet across. During mild winters or in warm microclimates, the foliage will remain on the plant through the winter, dropping off just before new leaves appear. During cold winters or in cold spots, the plants are deciduous, can suffer freeze damage, and will remain shrubby. Creamy white puffball-like flower clusters appear in late spring or early summer. Brown, papery pods follow the flowers.

CULTURE/MAINTENANCE: This tree is generally hardy to temperatures in the mid to low 20s. Young plants, twigs, and smaller branches suffer damage around 22–25° F, and it's definitely not pretty when temperatures drop into the mid or high teens. Where temperatures dip regularly below the low 20s, place it in a warm microclimate. In colder areas, it will most likely decide to be a large shrub. It has a moderate growth rate and will tolerate most soil types, but it seems to grow best with good soil drainage. It is low-water-using once established but will grow faster if the root zone is thoroughly soaked 3 or 4 times a month during the late spring and summer. Overwatering does it no favors, especially in a heavy or poorly drained soil. Pruning to grow as a tree, removal of frozen stems, and pod cleanup are the primary maintenance requirements.

IDENTIFICATION: *L. watsonii* ssp. *thornberi* looks a little like *Acacia berlandieri*, but the lack of thorns on the *Lysiloma* clears up that confusion.

LANDSCAPE APPLICATION: Place this tree in full sun or reflected heat in the mini-oasis. It gives a lush atmosphere to a front entry or nicely shades a building on the south, west, or east side. In mild winter areas where a warm microclimate is not needed, it provides that tropical vacation feel to pools and patios. It can provide welcome relief for plants that like some shade, such as *Agave bovicornuta, Ageratum corymbosum, Aquilegia chrysantha, Cycas revoluta, Dioon edule, Gaura lindheimeri, Heuchera sanguinea, Justicia spicigera, Poliomintha maderensis,* and *Tagetes lemmonii.*

PRECAUTIONS: Young trees freeze at temperatures below the low 20s. Seedpod production increases as the plant gets larger, but pods can be trimmed off or swept easily away.

Melampodium leucanthum | Blackfoot Daisy

FLOWERING PERENNIAL

SIZE (height x width)	8–12 inches x 15–24 inches
FLOWER COLOR	White
FLOWER SEASON	Spring–fall
EXPOSURE	Full or filtered sun
WATER	Low–moderate
GROWTH RATE	Fast
PRUNING	Shear severely in late fall
HARDINESS	Hardy to the mid-teens F
NATURAL ELEVATION RANGE	2,000–5,000 feet
SUITABLE CITIES	All cities in all zones

FIELD NOTES: *Melampodium leucanthum* grows in Kansas, Oklahoma, Colorado, south through Texas, Arizona, and into Chihuahua and Coahuila, Mexico. Arizona plants live on dry, rocky slopes and mesas, frequently on limestone from 2,000 to 5,000 feet elevation.

DESCRIPTION: The incredible spring flower display of this low-growing, spreading perennial cheers up any landscape. Herbaceous stems sprout from a woody base,

and shrublets quickly reach 8–12 inches tall by 15–24 inches across. Narrow, dark green leaves are nearly 2 inches long by ¼ inch wide. Flowering season can extend from March to November with peak bloom in spring and fall. During peak bloom, white, daisy-like flowers completely cover this little charmer.

CULTURE/MAINTENANCE: *M. leucanthum* is hardy to at least the mid-teens F. It has a fast growth rate, reaching full size in just a couple of years. It uses low to moderate amounts of water and requires a soil with very good drainage. Plants will bloom best if given a little extra water in spring and summer, but they are not fond of soggy roots. They will tolerate light shade, but they stay dense and compact and flower more enthusiastically when placed in full sun. Rejuvenate older plants by cutting back severely in late fall. This short-lived plant can reseed in your wildflower gardens.

IDENTIFICATION: White daisy-like flowers and horseshoe-shaped seeds easily identify *M. leucanthum.*

LANDSCAPE APPLICATION: Use blackfoot daisy as a spring- and fall-flowering perennial in any type of landscape. It fits neatly into raised planting beds, along walkways, in parking lot medians, or anyplace where space is tight. Mass plant for a great display of the lightly fragrant, butterfly-attracting flowers. Plant it with drought-tolerant, limestone-loving plants in cactus and succulent beds. Place with bold accents like *Agave, Dasylirion, Ferocactus, Hesperaloe,* and *Yucca* species. You can give it perennial playmates closer to its own size like *Berlandiera lyrata, Calylophus hartwegii, Psilostrophe cooperi, Verbena gooddingii,* and *Zinnia grandiflora.*

PRECAUTIONS: Allow the soil to dry out between water applications. This short-lived plant will need periodic replacement.

Menodora longiflora | Long-flowered Twin Berry

FLOWERING PERENNIAL,
SMALL SHRUB

SIZE (height x width)	18–24 inches x 18–24 inches
FLOWER COLOR	Yellow
FLOWER SEASON	Late spring–fall

EXPOSURE	Full or filtered sun
WATER	Low–moderate
GROWTH RATE	Fast
PRUNING	Prune off developing fruits, cut severely in late winter
HARDINESS	Hardy to at least 15° F
NATURAL ELEVATION RANGE	1,500–4,600 feet
SUITABLE CITIES	Low- and mid-elevation-zone cities

FIELD NOTES: *Menodora longiflora* can be spotted growing in rocky soil on ledges and in canyons in western Texas and southern New Mexico, south to central Mexico from 1,500 to 4,600 feet elevation. Because the flowers open late in the day and wilt the following morning, an early morning hike is best for photographs.

DESCRIPTION: From late spring through fall, this sturdy little plant pumps out a brilliant display of tubular, 2-inch-long, bright lemon-yellow flowers. Herbaceous stems arise from a woody crown and can reach 18–24 inches tall by 18–24 inches across. Bright green, narrow leaves are about 1 inch long. Small, rounded, ball-like fruits top the plant after flowering.

CULTURE/MAINTENANCE: This shrub-like plant is hardy to at least 15° F and probably much lower. It is low- to moderate-water-using with a moderate growth rate; it will bloom more profusely and growth will be faster with regular water from spring through summer. It is not particular about soil, as long as the drainage is adequate. Although it puts up with light shade, it will be fuller and flower more vigorously in full sun. Prune off the developing fruits to encourage more flowers. You can grow it as a small shrub, but it can also be treated like a seasonal perennial and be cut back radically in the late winter to increase density.

IDENTIFICATION: *M. longiflora* is separated from *M. scabra* by its longer flowers.

LANDSCAPE APPLICATION: Use *M. longiflora* as a show-stopping small perennial with big, bold accent plants or mixed with other desert perennials and small shrubs.

Mass plant them for a showy display of flowers in entryways or even along street medians. They hold their own with the tall *Nolina matapensis* and *N. nelsonii, Yucca rigida,* and *Y. rostrata,* medium-size *Agave parryi* var. *truncata,* and *Hesperaloe funifera.*

PRECAUTIONS: There are no known insect pests or diseases.

Muhlenbergia capillaris | Pink Muhly

GRASS	
SIZE (height x width)	3 feet x 3 feet (4 feet x 4 feet with spikes)
FLOWER COLOR	Pinkish-red
FLOWER SEASON	Fall
EXPOSURE	Full, reflected, or filtered sun
WATER	Moderate
GROWTH RATE	Moderately fast
PRUNING	Shear in late winter
HARDINESS	Hardy to at least 0° F
NATURAL ELEVATION RANGE	100–6,000 feet
SUITABLE CITIES	All cities in all zones

FIELD NOTES: *Muhlenbergia capillaris* inhabits sandy prairies and open areas in pine forests throughout much of the eastern and southeastern United States and eastern Mexico. The elevation ranges from about 100 feet in coastal regions to 5,000–6,000 feet elevation in southern Mexico. Plants grown in the southwestern U.S. are from the lower end of the range in eastern Texas.

DESCRIPTION: This clumping grass grows to 3 feet tall and 3 feet across. Flowering clusters add about 1 foot to each dimension, with narrow leaf **blades** that reach 1½ feet long. Flower spikes are a deep pinkish-red, with a loose, open, feathery look. In the hot, low-elevation interior plants start blooming in late September and continue until November with a peak in October. In the mid-elevation region, plants start blooming a little earlier. The cultivar 'Regal Mist' was selected for its deeper red-pink flower color.

CULTURE/MAINTENANCE: Plants are hardy to 0° F. They survive extended periods with minimal supplemental water once established. However, they look more robust and flower more reliably if watered regularly from spring through fall. They have a moderate–fast growth rate, flowering even in one-gallon containers. They grow naturally in very sandy soils but will tolerate other decently draining soils in the garden. Place them in reflected, full, or lightly filtered sun. Shear clumps by mid-February every year or two so the rich green new growth comes out unencumbered by the old stalks. Although *M. capillaris* is not sterile, I haven't witnessed reseeding in drip-irrigated landscapes.

IDENTIFICATION: Currently there are five species of *Muhlenbergia* in cultivation. *M. capillaris* is readily distinguished from the others by its smaller size and its feathery plume of pinkish-red flowers.

LANDSCAPE APPLICATION: Use pink muhly for fall color—flower color, that is. You'll find that the early morning or late afternoon sun beautifully backlights the delicate pink flowering stalk. Group several plants together for a meadow effect. They are especially attractive when grouped in large, wide-open spaces and they spruce up street medians and roadsides. Pink muhly makes a handsome understory for a grove of *Prosopis velutina* or *Chilopsis linearis*.

PRECAUTIONS: You may have to chase off rabbits targeting new leaves.

Muhlenbergia dumosa | Bamboo Muhly

GRASS	
SIZE (height x width)	4–6 feet x 4–6 feet
FLOWER COLOR	Insignificant
FLOWER SEASON	Summer
EXPOSURE	Full or filtered sun, or partial shade
WATER	Moderate–ample
GROWTH RATE	Moderately fast
PRUNING	Plants can be cut back once every 3–5 years
HARDINESS	Hardy to at least 10° F
NATURAL ELEVATION RANGE	2,800–8,200 feet
SUITABLE CITIES	All low- and mid-elevation-zone cities

FIELD NOTES: Loose, flowing *Muhlenbergia dumosa* inhabits rocky canyon slopes and valleys in southern Arizona and northwestern Mexico south to southern Mexico. I've seen its full subtropical potential in a little palm canyon tucked away on a curve on Mexico Highway 16. In southern Arizona, these beauties are found at lower elevations and have been documented at 2,800–3,000 feet, while further south in central and southern Mexico, plants have been collected at elevations ranging from 4,300 to 8,200 feet.

DESCRIPTION: Upright to arching stems reach 4–6 feet tall while the plant grows 4–6 feet across. This grass resembles clumps of bamboo but has a softer, fluffier appearance and fine texture. Inconspicuous, wispy clusters of tiny flowers appear in fall to winter.

CULTURE/MAINTE-NANCE: Plants are hardy to at least 10° F. They survive extended periods with minimal supplemental water once established but will look fuller and lusher if given water from spring through fall. Plants have a moderate–fast growth rate that can be sped up some with consistent irrigation when the weather is hot. *M. dumosa* will clump out by means of rhizomes to 4–6 feet across. If kept slightly dry and grown in less of a hurry, it can go 3–4 years before needing a major trim. Subject it either to selective cutting or shearing nearly to the ground.

IDENTIFICATION: Currently there are five species of *Muhlenbergia* in cultivation. *M. dumosa* is readily distinguished from the others by its bamboo-like appearance.

LANDSCAPE APPLICATION: Use bamboo muhly for its subtropical ambiance in filtered sun or partial shade. It looks glamorous as a silhouette against a blank wall and especially striking around pools or water features. Try planting it among a grove of *Lysiloma watsonii* ssp. *thornberi* or *Prosopis velutina*. Mix it with other rich green companions to play up the tropical mood: *Agave bovicornuta, Aquilegia chrysantha, Cordia boissieri, Cycas revoluta, Dioon edule,* and *Sophora secundiflora*.

PRECAUTIONS: *M. dumosa* needs a fast-draining soil. Rabbits will eat new leaves.

Muhlenbergia emersleyi | Bull Muhly

GRASS

SIZE (height x width)	2–3 feet x 2–3 feet (5 feet x 5 feet with inflorescences)
FLOWER COLOR	Reddish-purple
FLOWER SEASON	Fall
EXPOSURE	Full sun in the middle or high desert zones, afternoon shade or filtered sun in low desert
WATER	Moderate
GROWTH RATE	Fast
PRUNING	Shear off dead growth in late winter
HARDINESS	Hardy to minus 10° F

NATURAL ELEVATION RANGE   3,600–8,000 feet
SUITABLE CITIES   All cities in all zones

FIELD NOTES: *Muhlenbergia emersleyi* grows on rocky slopes from central and southern Arizona east to west Texas, and south throughout Mexico into Guatemala. Seeds for the plants under cultivation regionally were originally collected in southeastern Arizona and selected for showy reddish-purple panicles.

DESCRIPTION: This tufted clumping grass grows 2–3 feet tall and 2–3 feet wide without the flower stalks. Flowering plants reach 4–5 feet tall and 4 feet across. Blue-green, folded leaves are sharply keeled on the back like the bottom of a boat and can get 1–2 feet long and ¼ inch wide. This muhly has a coarser texture than its relatives. Loosely spreading flower clusters appear from late summer to fall and have a reddish-purple cast when young, turning a deep straw color with age. Stalks will persist through winter and can be cut in late winter or early spring as new growth begins to appear.

CULTURE/MAINTENANCE: Bull muhly is root-hardy to minus 10° F. Of the *Muhlenbergias* in cultivation, this species is the most water-thrifty and can withstand short periods without supplemental water. If it looks too stressed, apply water on a regular basis from spring through summer. It grows fast, reaching 3 feet by 3 feet in a few years, and will grow in just about any soil but seems to favor good drainage. It can be grown in full sun, filtered sun, or partial shade, and will even tolerate reflected heat if watered regularly through the summer. Put it where its gorgeous flower display will be backlit by the late afternoon or early evening sun. Shade-grown plants tend to disappoint in the flower department. Shear in early spring to encourage summer growth.

IDENTIFICATION: Loose, pyramidal reddish-purple flower clusters, and upright growth are the distinguishing features.

LANDSCAPE APPLICATION: *M. emersleyi* holds its own singly as a specimen or mass planted for a meadow effect. It takes to parking lots, street medians, roadsides, and retention basins. It forms an attractive silhouette against walls and is a handsome accessory to water features. It mixes well with a variety of plants, looking equally at home with *Quercus* species as well as more drought-tolerant plants such as *Acacia schaffneri, Agave* species, *Bauhinia lunarioides, Dasylirion* species, *Eysenhardtia orthocarpa, Larrea divaricata, Lysiloma watsonii* ssp. *thornberi, Poliomintha maderensis,* and *Salvia greggii.*

PRECAUTIONS: Plants do best with a lot of sun, but they'll need some water to stay unstressed.

Muhlenbergia lindheimeri | Lindheimer's Muhly

GRASS

SIZE (height x width)	3 feet x 3 feet (4–5 feet x 4–5 feet with inflorescences)
FLOWER COLOR	Silvery white to tan when mature
FLOWER SEASON	September–October
EXPOSURE	Full sun in the middle or high desert zones, afternoon shade in low desert
WATER	Moderately low
GROWTH RATE	Fast
PRUNING	Shear off dead growth in late winter
HARDINESS	Hardy to minus 10° F
NATURAL ELEVATION RANGE	3,000–7,000 feet
SUITABLE CITIES	All cities in all zones

FIELD NOTES: *Muhlenbergia lindheimeri* is native to the limestone uplands in west-central Texas, and plants are usually found near small streams. The elevation range varies from 3,000 to 7,000 feet.

DESCRIPTION: Grass clumps will grow to 3 feet tall and 3 feet wide and balloon to 4–5 feet tall by 4–5 feet wide with the flower spikes. Sharply folded leaves grow to 1½ feet long. Thick flower clusters are 1½–2 feet long and first appear in September with peak bloom in October. Fresh flower stalks are whitish with a hint of silver, and with age they fade to a brilliant straw color then finally a deep, rich tan. The cultivar 'Autumn Glow' has light yellow flowers.

CULTURE/MAINTENANCE: This big grass is hardy to minus 10° F. It can withstand short periods without supplemental water but tends to look stressed. The usual recommendation is watering on a regular basis from spring through summer. Plants hit 3 feet by 3 feet in a couple of years. They will grow in just about any soil but prefer good drainage. Install plants in full sun or filtered light for best appearance. They will tolerate a few hours of daily shade at a cost of subprime flowering. Shear the plants in late winter or at least by mid-February to achieve the best growth that summer.

IDENTIFICATION: *M. lindheimeri*, *M. rigida*, and *M. rigens* all have dense, spike-like flower stalks. *M. rigida* flower stalks have a purplish cast to them, while the flower stalks of *M. lindheimeri* and *M. rigens* are tan to yellowish-tan when mature.

LANDSCAPE APPLICATION: Use this grass as a substitute for the widespread but invasive *Pennisetum setaceum* (fountain grass), which is similar in form and size. This one works singly as an attention-grabbing specimen or mass planted for a meadow effect mixed with just about any *Quercus* species. Mix it with desert favorites such as *Acacia schaffneri*, *Agave* species, *Bauhinia lunarioides*, *Dasylirion* species, *Eysenhardtia orthocarpa*, *Larrea divaricata*, *Lysiloma watsonii* ssp. *thornberi*, *Poliomintha maderensis*, and *Salvia greggii*.

PRECAUTIONS: Although moderately drought-tolerant, plants will become stressed if not watered regularly in the spring and summer.

Muhlenbergia rigens | Deer Grass

GRASS

SIZE (height x width)	3–4 feet x 3–4 feet (5–6 feet x 5–6 feet with inflorescences)
FLOWER COLOR	Tan
FLOWER SEASON	Fall
EXPOSURE	Full sun in the middle or high desert zone, afternoon shade or filtered sun in low desert
WATER	Moderate
GROWTH RATE	Fast
PRUNING	Shear off dead growth in late winter or early spring
HARDINESS	Hardy to minus 10° F
NATURAL ELEVATION RANGE	200–8,000 feet
SUITABLE CITIES	All cities in all zones

FIELD NOTES: *Muhlenbergia rigens* grows on loamy flats and near small streams from west Texas across to California and south into northern Mexico. This grass is known

from 200 feet elevation in California to 8,000 feet in the highland region of north-central Mexico in the state of Durango.

DESCRIPTION: This coarse, clumping perennial grass gets about 3–4 feet tall and 3–4 feet wide. With the flower stalks, it fills a space up to 5–6 feet tall by 5–6 feet diameter. The very narrow, dark greenish-gray leaves are about 2 feet long and have a finer texture than the leaves of other *Muhlenbergia* species. Tight, dense, slender, tan flower spikes reach about 2 feet long and only ½ inch thick. Stalks appear from late summer to fall and create a dazzling contrast to the dark greenish-gray mound of foliage. They will persist through winter and can be cut in late winter or early spring as new growth begins to appear.

CULTURE/MAINTENANCE: Deer grass is root-hardy to minus 10° F. It prefers a loose, loamy soil with good drainage and consistent irrigation. It withstands short periods of drought, but the foliage will turn brown if stressed too much. When regular watering resumes, it will recover and put on a fresh crop of leaves. It can be grown in full sun, filtered sun, or partial shade, and will even tolerate reflected heat if watered regularly through the summer. It grows to 3 feet by 3 feet in a couple of years. Shear it in early spring to achieve the best growth that summer.

IDENTIFICATION: Dense, slender, tan flower spikes and spreading leaves are the distinguishing features.

LANDSCAPE APPLICATION: *M. rigens* is a dependable and versatile workhorse plant. It softens the hard forms of boulders and water features, slows water in retention basins, and greens up parking lots, street medians, and roadsides. Mass it for a meadow effect or use it for erosion control. It mixes well with *Prosopis velutina* and *Quercus* species, and green-leaved desert plants like *Larrea divaricata* and *Salvia greggii*, as well as gray-leaved drought tolerators such as *Buddleja marrubiifolia*, *Encelia farinosa*, and *Leucophyllum candidum*. Try it with large cacti and succulents such as *Aloe ferox*, *Aloe marlothii*, *Lophocereus schottii*, *Stenocereus thurberi*, *Yucca* species *faxoniana*, *rigida*, and *rostrata*.

PRECAUTIONS: Although moderately drought-tolerant, plants will become stressed if not watered regularly in the spring and summer.

Muhlenbergia rigida | Purple Muhly

GRASS	
SIZE (height x width)	1½ feet x 2 feet (2–3 feet x 3–4 feet with inflorescences)
FLOWER COLOR	Purplish-tan
FLOWER SEASON	Late summer–fall
EXPOSURE	Full sun in the middle or high desert zones, afternoon shade or filtered sun in low desert
WATER	Moderate
GROWTH RATE	Fast
PRUNING	Shear off dead growth in late winter or early spring
HARDINESS	Hardy to 0° F
NATURAL ELEVATION RANGE	5,000–7,500 feet (up to 10,000 feet in Peru)
SUITABLE CITIES	All cities in all zones

FIELD NOTES: *Muhlenbergia rigida* is found on sunny, rocky slopes in west Texas, New Mexico, and Arizona south to southern Mexico and northern South America. In the United States, this grass is usually seen at 5,000–7,500 feet elevation. Farther south in central Mexico and South America, it grows at an elevation as high as 10,000 feet.

DESCRIPTION: This small, tufted, fine-textured, perennial grass grows about 1½ feet tall and 2 feet across when not in bloom. When the flower stalks appear in the summer and fall, the overall size can be 2–3 feet tall and 3–4 feet wide. The very narrow, fine-textured, light green foliage is about 1 foot long and goes dormant in the winter. Purplish-tan, 1½ -foot-long flower spikes emerge from late summer to fall and provide a gorgeous contrast to the light green foliage. The stalks will turn the color of wheat and persist through winter. They should be cut in late winter or early spring as new growth begins to appear.

CULTURE/MAINTENANCE: *M. rigida* is root-hardy to 0° F with the tops going brown for the winter. It requires moderate amounts of water to look its best, going dormant unless given supplemental water on a regular basis from spring through summer. Plants grow quickly, and established plants reach their full size every year after a severe pruning. The plant prefers a loose, loamy soil with good drainage. It can be grown in full sun, filtered sun, or partial shade and will even put up with reflected heat if watered 2–3 times a week from spring through summer. Shear it in early spring to make room for a fresh crop of leaves.

IDENTIFICATION: The combination of its smaller size and narrow yet loose purplish-tan flower stalks set *M. rigida* apart from other *Muhlenbergias* currently cultivated.

LANDSCAPE APPLICATION: Though small and fine-textured, this grass likes to be put to work—mass planted for erosion control or installed in commercial land-scapes, parking lots, along street medians and roadsides, around water features, and in retention basins. It adds a soft touch next to *Prosopis velutina* and *Quercus* species. Combine it with green-leaved desert plants like *Larrea divaricata* and *Salvia greggii* as well as gray-leaved drought-tolerant plants such as *Buddleja marrubiifolia*, *Encelia farinosa*, and *Leucophyllum candidum*. It is comfortable next to large cacti and other succulents such as *Aloe ferox*, *Aloe marlothii*, *Lophocereus schottii*, and *Yucca* species *faxoniana*, *rigida*, and *rostrata*.

PRECAUTIONS: If you let them, rabbits will feast on *M. rigida*.

Nolina matapensis | Sonoran Tree Beargrass

CACTUS/SUCCULENT	
SIZE (height x width)	8–15 feet x 6 feet
FLOWER COLOR	Tan
FLOWER SEASON	Unknown in cultivation
EXPOSURE	Full or reflected sun
WATER	Drought-tolerant–low
GROWTH RATE	Slow
HARDINESS	Hardy to high teens F
PRUNING	Remove dead leaves if desired
NATURAL ELEVATION	3,000–5,500 feet
SUITABLE CITIES	All low-elevation-zone cities except Austin and San Antonio; Tucson in mid-elevation zone

FIELD NOTES: I've encountered some large specimens of *Nolina matapensis* towering above the surrounding shrubs on rocky slopes in east-central Sonora on the way from Hermosillo to the town of Matape for which this plant was named. The vegetation was so thick and the slope so steep, it was nearly impossible to get to the plant and check out the trunk. Plants are found in short-tree forest, oak, and pine-oak vegetation in

central and southern Sonora from 3,000 to 5,500 feet elevation.

DESCRIPTION: A large, full-grown *N. matapensis* is an unforgettable sight. In habitat, it is a tall, treelike plant with a trunk to 10–20 feet tall. Trunks develop at about 2–4 inches per year and may realistically reach about 6–10 feet tall in urban landscapes. Plants will branch with age and can have 3 or more branches. Dark green leaves are 3–5 feet long and about 1 inch wide. New leaves emerge from the center of the plant and resemble water spraying out of a fountain, growing up, spreading out and then draping down over the trunk. Razor-sharp edges can inflict "paper" cuts. The inflorescence is a branched panicle about 4 feet long. Seeds are inside a papery fruit.

CULTURE/MAINTENANCE: This plant develops best in full sun. Give it soil with good drainage, but expect it to take 20–30 years to reach 6–10 feet tall. Plants are cold-hardy to at least 15° F if they are kept on the dry side during winter, which limits their use in Austin and San Antonio in the low-elevation zone. Also, protect plants if they are subjected to extreme cold for several nights without sufficient warming during the day. Plants are drought-tolerant once established, surviving on 11 inches of annual rainfall. Dead leaves will persist on the trunk, but they do not need to be removed unless you object to the shaggy appearance.

IDENTIFICATION: *N. matapensis* is easily distinguished from *N. nelsonii* by its greener, more flexible leaves. When young, it could be confused with *N. longifolia* at first glance. However, its leaf serration cannot be seen without a magnifying lens, while the serrated edges on *N. longifolia* can be seen with the naked eye. Also, *N. longifolia* tends to have brighter green leaves that droop even more.

LANDSCAPE APPLICATION: Use this plant as an accent or focal point in the landscape. Plants can be massed for a spectacular grouping, planted singly with sub-tropical plants for a lush look, mixed with drought-tolerant shrubs and perennials to re-create desert, or even grown in an extra-large decorative pot. A variety of good companions includes *Agave* species, *Brahea armata*, *Chrysactinia mexicana*, *Dalea capitata*, *Dalea frutescens*, *Ericameria laricifolia*, *Larrea divaricata*, *Leucophyllum* species, *Penstemon* species, and *Salvia greggii*.

PRECAUTIONS: This tough plant could be killed by too much care.

Nolina microcarpa | Sacahuista, Bear Grass

CACTUS/SUCCULENT	
SIZE (height x width)	3–5 feet x 4–8 feet
FLOWER COLOR	Tan
FLOWER SEASON	Summer
EXPOSURE	Full or reflected sun
WATER	Low–moderate
GROWTH RATE	Slow–moderate
PRUNING	None
HARDINESS	Hardy at least -10° F
NATURAL ELEVATION RANGE	3,000–6,500 feet
SUITABLE CITIES	All cities in all zones

FIELD NOTES: *Nolina microcarpa* is relatively common on open slopes throughout much of Arizona, New Mexico, west Texas, and adjacent Mexico from 3,000 to 6,500 feet elevation. If you want to find it in habitat, get off the interstate, hit the back roads that take you through oak-dotted hills, and look for the large clumps of grass-like leaves with curly ends.

DESCRIPTION: Decorative leaf tips add visual interest to this robust accent. The 3-foot-long, narrow, glossy green leaves have curly, frayed tips and very fine teeth along the edge that can inflict "paper" cuts if you're not careful. The 3–6-foot-tall flowering stalk appears in early summer and is loosely covered with clusters of small, yellowish-green flowers.

CULTURE/MAINTENANCE: *N. microcarpa* is hardy to -10° F. It puts its best form forward in full or reflected sun; it is guaranteed to look sparse and pitiful when planted in any shade. It grows moderately slowly on little water but will speed up and look healthier if the root zone is thoroughly soaked 2–3 times a month in the summer.

It needs a soil with good drainage. Unless you want to remove the old flowering stalks, no pruning is required.

IDENTIFICATION: The clumping habit sets *N. microcarpa* apart from *N. matapensis* and *N. nelsonii*. *N. texana* is another stemless, clumping species being cultivated, but its

¼-inch-wide leaves are about half the width of *N. microcarpa* leaves. Just to make sure, the *N. microcarpa* flowering stalk is 3–6 feet long, while that of *N. texana* is about 2 feet long.

LANDSCAPE APPLICATION: Use sacahuista as an accent or focal point in a desert landscape or to supplement grasses and oak trees in a woodsy landscape. Solo plants make a bold statement, or try massing and mixing with small shrubs and perennials. It blends equally well with drier- and wetter-look plants. For companions try *Agave* species, *Brahea armata*, *Chrysactinia mexicana*, *Dalea capitata*, *Dalea frutescens*, *Dasylirion acrotrichum*, *Larrea divaricata*, *Leucophyllum* species, *Penstemon* species, *Salvia greggii*, and *Wedelia acapulcensis* var. *hispida*.

PRECAUTIONS: There are no insect pests or diseases that affect *N. microcarpa*. Keep it away from your house in a fire-prone area; the stuff burns incredibly hot.

Nolina nelsonii | Blue Leaf Nolina

CACTUS/SUCCULENT	
SIZE (height x width)	12 feet x 4 feet
FLOWER COLOR	Tan
FLOWER SEASON	Summer
EXPOSURE	Full sun
WATER	Drought-tolerant–low
GROWTH RATE	Slow–moderate
PRUNING	None
HARDINESS	Hardy to at least 17° F
NATURAL ELEVATION RANGE	5,200–9,000 feet
SUITABLE CITIES	All low- and mid-elevation-zone cities; all high-elevation-zone cities except Albuquerque

FIELD NOTES: Frequent traveling partner Ron Gass and I encountered *Nolina nelsonii* in southern Tamaulipas on the road from Palmillas to the town of Doctor Arroyo. We thought these majestic, blue-leaved beauties were some amazing kind of *Yucca*. We finally spotted one with a flowering stalk and knew right away it was a *Nolina*. In order to get seeds, I climbed onto Ron's shoulders and clipped some of the massive stalk. The plants were not common but could be found growing on the flat areas and the lower slopes of large, rounded hills thickly covered with a mix of desert and subtropical vegetation. Records exist for this plant from the Mexican states of Nuevo León and Tamaulipas between 5,200 and 9,000 feet elevation.

DESCRIPTION: This tall, unbranched, trunk-forming plant can grow to 12 feet or more. Juvenile leaves are green or gray-green and flexible, while the mature leaves are powder blue and somewhat rigid. Four-footers in the wild had the powder-blue, slightly rigid leaves. Individual leaves are 2–3 feet long and about 1 inch wide. The edges are razor sharp and freely slash handlers—no kidding, always wear gloves when working with these plants. The inflorescence is a 6–9-foot-tall panicle of small, tan-colored flowers and appears in the summer.

CULTURE/MAINTENANCE: Blue leaf nolina develops best when planted in full sun. It is drought-tolerant once established, surviving on 11 inches of annual rainfall. Grow it in a soil that has good drainage, and be careful not to water too much. The moderate growth rate can be increased by occasional, thorough, summer-only watering. Plants are cold-hardy to at least 17° if they are kept on the dry side during the winter. Protect plants that are subjected to extreme cold for several nights without sufficient warming during the day. Dead leaves persist on the trunk, but they do not need to be removed unless you object to the shaggy appearance.

IDENTIFICATION: Young plants can be distinguished from other cultivated *Nolina* species by their stiffer leaves. Confusion between mature *N. nelsonii* and *Yucca rigida* is cleared up by the *Yucca's* thin yellow stripe along the margin of the leaf.

LANDSCAPE APPLICATION: Powder-blue leaves, combined with the plant size and striking inflorescence, make for an outstanding accent plant. This combination has made *N. nelsonii* a favorite of mine for any xeriscape. Mass for a spectacular grouping, or plant singly in among other desert shrubs and perennials. Good companions are *Agave* species, *Brahea armata, Chrysactinia mexicana, Dalea capitata, Dalea frutescens, Dasylirion acrotrichum, Larrea divaricata, Leucophyllum* species, *Penstemon* species, *Salvia greggii,* and *Wedelia acapulcensis* var. *hispida.*

PRECAUTIONS: There have been no reports of any insect pests, diseases, or wildlife damage.

Oenothera caespitosa | White-tufted Evening Primrose

GROUND COVER,
FLOWERING PERENNIAL

SIZE (height x width)   1 foot x 2 feet

FLOWER COLOR	White
FLOWER SEASON	Spring–summer, occasionally fall
EXPOSURE	Full or filtered sun
WATER	Moderate in the summer
GROWTH RATE	Fast
PRUNING	Trim dead leaves and seed pods
HARDINESS	Hardy to at least 0° F
NATURAL ELEVATION RANGE	Below 7,500 feet
SUITABLE CITIES	Best in coastal low-, mid, and high-elevation-zone cities; needs some shade in the hot, interior, low-elevation zones

FIELD NOTES: *Oenothera caespitosa* ranges widely from Washington to California, Utah, Arizona, New Mexico, and western Texas below 7,500 feet elevation.

DESCRIPTION: Short-lived *O. caespitosa* forms mounds of foliage up to 1 foot tall by 2 feet across. Leaves are dark grayish-green, softly pubescent, and 4–5 inches long. In bloom the plant is topped by dozens of spectacular, 3-inch-wide, pure white flowers that open in the evening during spring, summer, and occasionally fall. Flowers are pollinated by hawk moths at night, resulting in the production of woody, 2-inch-long pods near the center of the plant.

CULTURE/MAINTENANCE: This plant tolerates winter lows of at least 0° F. Place it in full sun or filtered sun and in a soil with excellent drainage. When preparing the soil, dig a large hole, and add enough clean, sharp sand to account for ¼ to ½ of the backfill soil. The plants have a fast growth rate and need replacement when they begin to decline or die out. Supplemental water applied from spring through late summer or early fall will spruce up plants and encourage flowering. Occasional trimming of dead leaves and seedpod removal will keep the plants looking clean.

IDENTIFICATION: *O. caespitosa* develops clumps of leaf rosettes, while *O. stubbei* develops long runners and has yellow flowers.

LANDSCAPE APPLICATION: The mounding form and unusual texture create visual interest in entryways, patios, and other small spaces. This plant complements medium-size (2–4 feet) *Agave* species or the ever-primeval *Cycas revoluta* and *Dioon edule*. It can be used in a cactus and succulent garden or in a bed with perennials if provided with separate irrigation. It has also been used effectively on gentle slopes that allow excess water to drain quickly from the base of the plant.

PRECAUTIONS: *O. caespitosa* is suspectible to flea beetles, which can be controlled with a contact insecticide. It needs a fast-draining soil and good sunlight in order to look its best.

Oenothera stubbei | Trailing Yellow Primrose

GROUND COVER	
SIZE (height x width)	6–12 inches x 4–6 feet
FLOWER COLOR	Lemon yellow
FLOWER SEASON	Spring–fall
EXPOSURE	Full or filtered sun
WATER	Moderate
GROWTH RATE	Fast
PRUNING	None
HARDINESS	Hardy to at least 10° F
NATURAL ELEVATION RANGE	6,900–7,200
SUITABLE CITIES	All cities in all zones, needs some afternoon shade in hot, interior, low- and mid-elevation-zone cities

FIELD NOTES: In 1978, University of Arizona Professor Warren Jones and traveling partner Bill Kinnison took a collecting trip to northeastern Mexico, and one of the gems they found was *Oenothera stubbei*. They were traveling on Nuevo León Highway 2 from Galeana to Doctor Arroyo when they came upon this yellow-flowered, trailing plant growing alongside the road. It prefers the shade of trees or north slopes in this area at about 6,900–7,200 feet elevation.

DESCRIPTION: This prostrate, spreading ground cover has dark green leaves and large, showy, bright yellow flowers. It stays low, reaching about 6–12 inches tall, and sends out aboveground runners to a 4–6-foot diameter. Narrow, dark green leaves are about 4 inches long, and the beautiful dark mat of foliage provides an excellent backdrop for the 3-inch-wide, lemon-yellow, night-blooming flowers. The flowering season begins in the spring and continues through summer and fall.

CULTURE/MAINTENANCE: *O. stubbei* has withstood temperatures as low as 10° F in El Paso. This fast-growing plant can expand to a 4-foot diameter in two growing seasons. It prefers some afternoon shade in the hot, interior, low- and mid-elevation desert areas, otherwise withstanding full sun in the coastal regions and high-elevation zones. It grows well in native, unamended soil but will require supplemental irrigation in summer.

IDENTIFICATION: Dark green leaves and 3-inch, lemon-yellow flowers readily identify *O. stubbei*. It has mistakenly been called "Baja primrose" because it was thought to have originated in Baja California.

LANDSCAPE APPLICATION: Trailing yellow primrose grows best in filtered sun and looks good in the mini-oasis zone of a xeriscape and in patio areas, courtyards, and around pools. It produces a nice flower display under tree canopies but can manage in full sun, if there are few other options. Slip it underneath a deciduous tree such as *Bauhinia lunarioides, Eysenhardtia orthocarpa,* or *Prosopis velutina.* Also use it for erosion control.

PRECAUTIONS: Whiteflies can be a problem in a greenhouse (not as much in a landscape), and they can be treated with Margosan, a product of the neem tree. Flea beetles are especially troublesome, chewing on the leaves and making the plant look shabby. With a heavy infestation, you might need to unlock something more potent to control these beetles.

Olneya tesota | Ironwood

SMALL–MEDIUM TREE

SIZE (height x width)	15–30 feet x 15 feet
FLOWER COLOR	Pinkish-lavender
FLOWER SEASON	Late spring (May–June)
EXPOSURE	Full or reflected sun
WATER	Drought-tolerant–low
GROWTH RATE	Slow
PRUNING	Shape to desired tree form
HARDINESS	Hardy to at least 20° F
NATURAL ELEVATION RANGE	Below 2,500 feet
SUITABLE CITIES	All hot, interior low-elevation-zone cities; Tucson in mid-elevation zone

FIELD NOTES: Stately ironwood can be found along washes and on low hills in gravelly, sandy, or silty soil in western and southern Arizona south into southern Sonora,

also Baja California. It grows at elevations below 2,500 feet. I've seen inspirational June blooms on the stately trees in the washes near my house while on early morning walks with my wife, Carol, and Nikki, our ever-vigilant, rabbit-chasing, four-legged bundle of joy.

DESCRIPTION: Whether young or mature, ironwood has a beautiful shape and flair as a single-specimen tree. The flowering display may be short, but it is quite spectacular when covering the whole tree. This medium-size tree can grow to 15–30 feet tall with a dense, broad, spreading crown that can reach 15–30 feet across. The small, gray-green leaves are about 2 inches long and are divided into ½-inch-long, oval leaflets. The leaves persist through the winter and then drop as the new leaves emerge in the spring. Trees are armed with paired, ½-inch-long spines. Pinkish-lavender, pealike flowers, a favorite of bees and the occasional hummingbird, appear in May and June. In good years, trees in bloom look like pinkish or lavender clouds. Pods are tan and about 2 inches long.

CULTURE/MAINTENANCE: In general, the species is hardy to about 20° F, although some populations are hardy to lower temperatures. Young plants will grow faster when supplemental water is applied through the summer, but you just can't speed up mature ones. Typically, ironwood has multiple trunks that give it a shrubby appearance when young; however, with age it can be pruned as a tree. It is adapted to soils with good drainage, and older plants are extremely drought-tolerant. Maintenance is a bit of pod and leaf cleanup throughout the year if you care about that sort of thing.

IDENTIFICATION: Because it is evergreen and has distinctive gray-green foliage, *O. tesota* is readily recognizable at all times of the year. Its classic pealike flowers are a helpful identifier.

LANDSCAPE APPLICATION: A large ironwood can shade a patio, although the thorns might be a drawback until the branches are up above head height. Or let one pose as a specimen tree in any xeriscape. Left unpruned, it works as a screening or barrier plant. It gets along with every desert plant I know, so I'll suggest some favorites: *Larrea divaricata, Simmondsia chinensis,* and *Dalea, Dasylirion, Leucophyllum,* and *Yucca* species.

PRECAUTIONS: Choose the planting location carefully since spiny branches can be troublesome. You'll want to do some pruning if the tree is in a high-traffic area. A native fungus (*Ganaderma* sp.) has been killing mature specimens. It is not clear whether the fungus has recently become more virulent or if prolonged drought or even Texas root rot are factors causing mortality.

Opuntia basilaris | Beavertail Cactus

CACTUS/SUCCULENT

SIZE (height x width)	2–3 feet x 4–6
FLOWER COLOR	Pink, magenta
FLOWER SEASON	Late spring
EXPOSURE	Full sun
WATER	Drought-tolerant
GROWTH RATE	Slow
PRUNING	Treat for cochineal scale
HARDINESS	Hardy to at least 0° F
NATURAL ELEVATION	0–4,000 feet (one form 5,000–9,000 feet)
SUITABLE CITIES	All low- and mid-elevation-zone cities

FIELD NOTES: This distinctive species is common in the desert regions of southern California, southern Nevada, southwestern Utah, western Arizona, and adjacent Mexico from sea level to 4,000 feet elevation. Occasionally plants sneak up to 5,000–9,000 feet, growing in piñon-juniper woodland or rarely in the coniferous forest. You should be able to spot some of these plants at Cattail Cove State Park near Lake Havasu City in northwestern Arizona.

DESCRIPTION: This low-growing species sprawls to about 2–3 feet tall by 4–6 feet across. Blue-green pads turn purplish with cold weather, are devoid of large spines,

and come loaded with nasty, nearly invisible glochids. The pads are narrow at the base and broadest near the end, and they get 4–6 inches long by 3–5 inches across. Three-inch-wide, pink to magenta flowers open in late spring, covering the edges of the pads and creating a knockout display. Fleshy, tan, 2-inch-long fruits follow in the summer.

CULTURE/MAINTENANCE: *O. basilaris* is cold-hardy, tolerating winter lows of at least 0° F. This tough native relishes full sun but is in no hurry to reach full size. After it gets settled, it can survive on rainfall, and too much water makes it unhappy. It will tolerate most soil types with good drainage. No pruning is required, which is fortunate, given the glochid situation.

IDENTIFICATION: *O. basilaris* is easily identified by its spineless, beavertail-shaped pads and pink or magenta flowers.

LANDSCAPE APPLICATION: Use this cactus as a focal point in a xeriscape or natural landscape where the wintertime purplish pads can attract attention. It blends well with other cacti, low shrubs, and small trees. Plant it alongside *Bauhinia lunarioides*, *Carnegiea gigantea*, *Eysenhardtia orthocarpa*, *Ferocactus* species, other *Opuntia* species, *Parkinsonia microphylla*, *Salvia greggii*, and *Simmondsia chinensis*. Toss in several spring wildflowers such as *Baileya multiradiata*, *Penstemon* species, and *Verbena gooddingii*, or combine with bold accent plants such as *Agave*, *Dasylirion*, *Hesperaloe*, and *Yucca* species.

PRECAUTIONS: As with other prickly pear species, check for cochineal scale and treat as necessary. Wash with a hard stream of water for a light infestation, or, for heavier infestations, spray with soapy water or even prune.

Opuntia phaeacantha | Prickly Pear

CACTUS/SUCCULENT

SIZE (height x width)	3–5 feet x 4–6 (rarely 8) feet
FLOWER COLOR	Lemon yellow
FLOWER SEASON	Late spring
EXPOSURE	Full sun
WATER	Drought-tolerant
GROWTH RATE	Slow–moderate (with supplemental water)
PRUNING	None
HARDINESS	Hardy to at least 10° F
NATURAL ELEVATION RANGE	2,000–7,000 feet
SUITABLE CITIES	All cities in all zones

FIELD NOTES: This character is probably one of the most common and variable *Opuntia* species seen throughout much of the desert Southwest. Plants are scattered from southern California to Arizona, New Mexico, Colorado, and west-central Texas from 2,000 to 7,000 feet elevation.

On my early morning walks in the desert on the west side of Tucson, I especially like to watch the fruits turn from green to deep reddish-purple as the summer progresses.

DESCRIPTION: This sprawling to upright, bushy plant grows to 3–5 feet tall by 4–6 (rarely 8) feet across. Large, blue-green pads are narrow at the base and broadest near the end, growing to 6–10 inches long by 5–8 inches across. Long white spines are easily avoided; it's the nasty, nearly invisible glochids that will wreak havoc on skin if you are not careful. Bright lemon-yellow flowers appear in late spring and cover the ends of the pads, creating an impressive display. Fleshy, purple, 1–3-inch-long fruits follow in the summer and promote an outstanding, edible ornamental appeal even after the flowers are gone. These fruits can be harvested when ripe and turned into a delicious alcoholic beverage similar to the mead so readily imbibed by the warriors of King Arthur's time in England.

CULTURE/MAINTENANCE: This cold-hardy cactus tolerates winter lows of at least 10° F, and some forms are able to withstand below 0° F. It takes several years to achieve its full size and should be placed only in full sun. Mature plants can survive on 12–15 inches of annual rainfall, although they will grow a little faster if watered every 2 weeks in spring and summer. The plant will tolerate most soil types with good drainage. No pruning is required except to kidnap pads for starting new plants.

IDENTIFICATION: It's tricky; *Opuntia phaeacantha* is highly variable, yet widely grown in the nursery industry.

LANDSCAPE APPLICATION: Use prickly pear as a focal point in a xeriscape or natural landscape, allowing space for negotiating around the prickles. It blends well with other cacti, low shrubs, and small trees, such as *Bauhinia lunarioides, Diospyros texana, Eysenhardtia orthocarpa, Parkinsonia microphylla, Salvia greggii, Simmondsia chinensis, Vauquelinia californica,* and *Verbena gooddingii.* Bold accents such as *Agave, Dasylirion, Hesperaloe,* and *Yucca* species mix dramatically with prickly pear.

PRECAUTIONS: Check this and other prickly pear species for cochineal scale and treat as necessary. Remedies include washing off with a hard stream of water for a light infestation, treating heavy infestations with soapy water, or pruning.

Opuntia violacea var. *santa rita* | Purple Prickly Pear

CACTUS/SUCCULENT

SIZE (height x width)	4–6 feet x 4–6 feet
FLOWER COLOR	Lemon yellow
FLOWER SEASON	Spring
EXPOSURE	Full sun
WATER	Drought-tolerant
GROWTH RATE	Slow–moderate (with supplemental water)
PRUNING	None
HARDINESS	Hardy to at least 15° F
NATURAL ELEVATION RANGE	2,000–5,000 feet
SUITABLE CITIES	All cities in all zones

FIELD NOTES: *Opuntia violacea* var. *santa rita* undergoes one of those fairy tale transformations when its pads turn an intense purplish-red in the winter. Plants can be found in southeastern Arizona between 2,000 and 5,000 feet elevation.

DESCRIPTION: This upright to spreading, bushy plant grows to 4–6 feet tall by 4–6 feet across. Rounded, 5-inch pads turn purplish-red when stressed by drought and cold and are topped by a layer of new, bluish-green pads in the summer. Each pad has one long, reddish-brown to black spine surrounded by numerous small, nasty, golden yellow glochids. This prickly pear breaks all the color combination rules when 3-inch, lemon-yellow flowers top those purple pads in spring. Fleshy, purple, 1-inch-long fruits follow flowers in the summer.

CULTURE/MAINTENANCE: This cold-hardy cactus tolerates winter lows of at least 15° F. One layer of new, bluish-green pads is added annually, so it takes several years to achieve its full size. Use it only in full sun for the gaudiest pad coloration. After establishment, it can survive on 12–15 inches of annual rainfall, although it will grow a little faster if given supplemental water once every 2 weeks in spring and summer. It will

tolerate most soil types with good drainage. No pruning is required.

IDENTIFICATION: This cactus is not easily confused with any other *Opuntia* species. *O. macrocentra* has bluish-green or purplish pads but is easily distinguished by the smaller size and 3-inch-long black spines on the upper parts of the pads.

LANDSCAPE APPLICATION: Use purple prickly pear as a focal point in a xeriscape or natural landscape. It blends well with other cacti, low shrubs, and small trees, such as *Diospyros texana, Opuntia engelmannii, Parkinsonia microphylla, Salvia greggii, Simmondsia chinensis,* and *Verbena gooddingii.* It even perks up bold *Agave, Dasylirion, Hesperaloe,* and *Yucca* species.

PRECAUTIONS: Check for white, powdery cochineal scale and treat as necessary. Remedies include washing off a light infestation with a hard stream of water, treating heavy infestations with soapy water, or pruning.

Pachycereus marginatus | Fence Post

CACTUS/SUCCULENT	
SIZE (height x width)	5–6 feet x 3–4 feet
FLOWER COLOR	Pinkish–greenish
FLOWER SEASON	Spring
EXPOSURE	Full, reflected, or filtered sun
WATER	Drought-tolerant–moderate
GROWTH RATE	Slow
PRUNING	None
HARDINESS	Hardy to about mid-20s F
NATURAL ELEVATION RANGE	Near sea level–7,800 feet
SUITABLE CITIES	All low-elevation-zone cities; protected areas in Tucson

FIELD NOTES: *Pachycereus marginatus* is a frequently cultivated native from central Mexico, and south to the Isthmus of Tehuantepec of Oaxaca in southern Mexico. Stems cut and stuck in the ground make a fine fence or barrier. Wander through most any small town in Hidalgo, Querétaro, or Guanajuato and you'll see the plant pressed into service to keep animals corralled. Plants are found from near sea level to as high as 7,800 feet in the warmer parts of Mexico.

DESCRIPTION: This columnar cactus with narrow, upright stems is a marvelous addition to any desert landscape. Plan for it to expand to 5–6 feet tall (occasionally up to 10–12 feet) by 3–4

feet across in your landscape. Nonspectacular flowers are small, pink to greenish, and appear in the spring. Spiny, yellowish to reddish fruits follow the flowers in summer.

CULTURE/MAINTENANCE: *P. marginatus* is hardy to about the mid-20s F and appreciates having tips covered when temperatures are going to drop that low in the winter. Plants are slow-growing, taking several years to reach a substantial size. This cactus doesn't need a lot of water, but established plants will grow a bit faster with monthly irrigation from late spring through summer. Potted plants will need more frequent irrigation, usually once or twice weekly in summer. It can tolerate full or reflected sun or filtered light and prefers rocky soil with good drainage. No pruning is needed unless you put it too close to a walk, which I really don't recommend.

IDENTIFICATION: Narrow stems with very small spines on five ramrod-straight ribs easily distinguish *P. marginatus* from other upright, columnar types of cacti.

LANDSCAPE APPLICATION: Use fence post as a focal point in a cactus and succulent garden, mixing it among *Agave, Dasylirion, Ferocactus,* and *Yucca* species. Weave in some flowering shrubs and perennials to break up all the juicy greenness. For colorful companions, try *Anisacanthus quadrifidus* var. *wrightii, Berlandiera lyrata, Buddleja marrubiifolia, Chrysactinia mexicana, Hibiscus martianus,* any *Penstemon* species, *Salvia greggii, Thymophylla pentachaeta,* or *Zinnia grandiflora.* Also mix this cactus with small trees such as *Acacia willardiana, Eysenhardtia orthocarpa, Havardia pallens,* and *Sophora secundiflora.* Just remember to give it lots of space.

PRECAUTIONS: Protect young plants from damage by rabbits and javelinas.

Parkinsonia florida | Synonym: *Cercidium floridum* | Blue Palo Verde

SMALL–MEDIUM TREE

SIZE (height x width)	15–30 feet x 15–30 feet
FLOWER COLOR	Yellow
FLOWER SEASON	Mid–late spring
EXPOSURE	Full or reflected sun
WATER	Drought-tolerant–low
GROWTH RATE	Moderate
PRUNING	Prune to tree form
HARDINESS	Hardy to 10° F
NATURAL ELEVATION RANGE	Below 4,000 feet
SUITABLE CITIES	All low- and mid-elevation-zone cities except Austin and San Antonio

FIELD NOTES: *Parkinsonia florida* is found on sandy plains and in dry washes in southeastern California, southern Arizona, Sonora, extreme northern Sinaloa, and Baja California below 4,000 feet elevation. This tree is a great source of shade out in the desert and in tamer landscapes. There are many times when this tree has provided me wonderful relief from the blazing sun during a hike in the desert on a warm spring day.

DESCRIPTION: Blue palo verde is highly valued for its fantastic mid-spring flower display, picturesque blue-green bark, and multiple trunks. It can grow to 15–30 feet tall with a spread of 15–30 feet. Its tiny leaves are cold- and drought-deciduous, but because of the bark color, this tree always looks "evergreen" from a distance.

CULTURE/MAINTENANCE: Plants are reliably hardy to 10° F. Although they are drought-tolerant when established and grow with less than 10 inches of annual rainfall, young, nursery-grown plants are a little spoiled and will beg for supplemental water. The growth rate is moderate to slow depending on the amount of water applied. This tree should be planted in full or reflected sun and in a soil with good drainage. Young plants require vigilant pruning to sculpt into "walk-under" trees.

IDENTIFICATION: *P. florida* is easily distinguished from the other species of *Parkinsonia* by its bluish bark.

LANDSCAPE APPLICATION: Flowering blue palo verde becomes a spring focal point in landscapes, parking lots, and street medians. More can be better—mass plant to create a grove. In high-traffic areas, the trees will need to be pruned up to keep the small spines and sharp tips from vaccinating passersby. This tree casts moderately dense shade and can be used to cool a patio or front entry, or to shade the south or west sides of buildings.

PRECAUTIONS: Young trees will need to be protected from damage by rabbits and other wildlife. Watch out for the palo verde root borer, which destroys the roots. Some people recommend treating with a systemic insecticide in the spring and summer. A healthy tree is usually less susceptible. Mistletoe can infect and weaken or even kill the tree, so this should be pruned out whenever it appears. Also, a mite causes distorted growths called witches-broom, and you'll need to cut these patches out as well.

Parkinsonia microphylla | Synonym: *Cercidium microphyllum* |
Little Leaf Palo Verde, Foothills Palo Verde

SMALL TREE

SIZE (height x width)	12–20 (25) feet x 15–20 (25) feet
FLOWER COLOR	Pale yellow
FLOWER SEASON	Spring

EXPOSURE	Full or reflected sun
WATER	Drought-tolerant–low
GROWTH RATE	Slow
PRUNING	None
HARDINESS	Hardy to at least mid-teens F
NATURAL ELEVATION RANGE	Below 4,000 feet
SUITABLE CITIES	All low- and mid-elevation-zone cities except Austin and San Antonio

FIELD NOTES: *Parkinsonia microphylla* is found on sandy plains, mesas, and rocky hillsides throughout southern and western Arizona, southeastern California, Sonora, and Baja California below 4,000 feet elevation. I usually set my calendar by the flowering season, as blooms are reliable in late April in the desert near my house on the western fringe of Tucson. One of the methods I teach my students for distinguishing this one from *P. florida* is the different terrain the two inhabit. *P. microphylla* is almost always on the rocky terrain above the wash, while *P. florida* is the one in the sandy washes.

DESCRIPTION: This venerable icon turns a generic low-water-use landscape into the Sonoran Desert. In habitat, it grows as a low-branching, multiple-stemmed shrublike tree. The typical tree usually grows about 12–20 feet tall by 15–20 feet across; however, an exceptional specimen can reach 25 feet tall by 25 feet across. Stout, gnarly trunks provide interest and a bonsai effect. Small yellowish-green leaves are composed of 4–6 pairs of tiny leaflets and measure about 1 inch long. A mature tree in full flower is a sight to behold! Small, pale yellow flowers transform the tree for about two weeks in late April or early May. Small, tan seedpods follow the flowers.

CULTURE/MAINTENANCE: The best way to grow this palo verde is to respect any natives that happen to be growing on your property. This tough plant is hardy to at least the mid-teens F, withstands heat, and demands full sun. It prefers soil types with excellent drainage in the root zone, and an established tree will survive on 10–12 inches of annual rainfall. It refuses to be rushed—irrigate a young plant from spring until fall, and it will grow only slightly faster. This tree is rarely grown from seed in containers, and most nursery specimens are salvaged from the desert. Prune only young container-grown plants to coax them into a desired shape, and even then it'll take some time to see their inner gnarliness. On older trees prune only growth that becomes infested with mistletoe or stems that die. Respect the mature natives in your landscape by foregoing pruning and irrigation. Any change in culture leads to a decline in health.

IDENTIFICATION: *P. microphylla* is distinguished from *P. florida* and *P. praecox* by its stout, gnarly trunks and pale yellow flowers.

LANDSCAPE APPLICATION: In nature, this tree is usually large, multiple-trunked, and shrub-like. When planted in landscapes, use it as a spring-flowering specimen. It is not a great shade tree for people, but other plants enjoy its filtered shade. Bring in other tough desert companions for a beautiful, truly drought-tolerant effect: *Agave* species, *Baileya multiradiata, Carnegiea gigantea, Dasylirion* species, *Encelia farinosa, Hesperaloe* species, *Opuntia violacea* var. *santa rita, Penstemon* species, *Verbena gooddingii,* and *Yucca* species. Twiggy ends of branches are pretty sharp, so route traffic accordingly.

PRECAUTIONS: Occasionally, the palo verde root borer attacks. Mistletoe and witches' broom are two infestations that can be pruned out if caught early. The plant might shed twigs and even larger branches during extended drought periods.

Parkinsonia praecox | Synonym: *Cercidium praecox* | Palo Brea

MEDIUM TREE

SIZE (height x width)	20–25 feet x 20–25 feet
FLOWER COLOR	Yellow
FLOWER SEASON	Late spring to early summer
EXPOSURE	Full or reflected sun
WATER	Drought-tolerant–moderate
GROWTH RATE	Moderate
PRUNING	Only to select main trunks
HARDINESS	Hardy to the low 20s F
NATURAL ELEVATION RANGE	Sea level–5,900 feet
SUITABLE CITIES	All low-elevation-zone cities; warm microclimates in Tucson

FIELD NOTES: My first encounter with the very striking *Parkinsonia praecox* in habitat was in northeastern Sonora where it was growing as a low, spreading tree with twisting branches and distinctive powder-green bark. Plants generally live on slopes and plains in Sonora southward into South America. They are at home in desert scrub, thorn scrub, desert grassland, and tropical deciduous forest vegetation from near sea level to about 5,900 feet elevation.

DESCRIPTION: Beautiful, smooth, lime-green bark, intriguing, angular branching, and an attractive spring flower display make a very eye-catching tree that is superb in any desert landscape. It generally has one main trunk with multiple, trunk-like branches that start a short distance up from the ground, creating a wide-spreading umbrella-like canopy. Small, bluish-green leaflets are evergreen except in extreme cold spells when the tree may go completely deciduous. On the stems and branches there are 1–2 spines at each **node**, which sometimes makes pruning a difficult job. Bright yellow flowers appear from March through May if conditions are favorable, followed by tan, 2-inch-long pods.

CULTURE/MAINTENANCE: Palo brea is hardy to the low 20s F, at which point there may be some twig dieback. More dieback occurs if the cold is prolonged or if there are several successive nights of low temperatures without much daytime warming. It is drought-tolerant once established, growing well with a thorough soaking once a month in the spring and summer, and minimal supplemental water in the fall and winter. The moderate growth rate warrants starting with a larger-size plant. The naturally high branching pattern reduces the need for pruning; however, you may want to select 2–3 branches as main trunks.

IDENTIFICATION: *P. praecox* is easily distinguished from its cousins, *P. florida* and *P. microphylla,* by the lime-green bark, darker green leaves, denser crown, and angular growth pattern.

LANDSCAPE APPLICATION: This excellent medium-size tree can be used singly as a focal point or massed for a nice shady-grove effect. The seasonal color produced by the flower display is an added bonus. Because it can be grown with a high canopy, this is an excellent choice for parking lots, streets, and medians. Its makes a good overstory plant for many cacti and other succulents, such as agaves, aloes, and many decorative cacti. Try to stay away from large shrubs or vines that would hide the attractive bark. Smaller shrubs and ground covers with bold flowers like *Ageratum corymbosum, Dalea capitata, Salvia darcyi, Salvia greggii,* and *Zauschneria californica* are flattering companions.

PRECAUTIONS: The branches are adorned with sharp thorns that can rip skin and clothing, so it is best to keep the tree away from high-traffic areas. Be sure to wear heavy gloves when pruning to avoid ripping your hands on the thorns. There have not been any reports of *P. praecox* dying due to the palo verde beetle, but preventive treatments in the spring wouldn't hurt.

Parkinsonia x 'Desert Museum' | Synonym: *Cercidium* x 'Desert Museum' | Desert Museum Palo Verde

MEDIUM TREE

SIZE (height x width)	20–25 (30) feet x 20–25 (30) feet
FLOWER COLOR	Bright yellow
FLOWER SEASON	Late spring–summer
EXPOSURE	Full or reflected sun
WATER	Drought-tolerant–moderate
GROWTH RATE	Fast
PRUNING	Thinning and shaping
HARDINESS	Hardy to at least mid-teens F
ELEVATION RANGE	Two of three parent species are found below 4,000 feet
SUITABLE CITIES	All low- and mid-elevation-zone cities

FIELD NOTES: The Desert Museum palo verde is a hybrid developed by Mark Dimmitt at the Arizona-Sonora Desert Museum on the outskirts of Tucson. The plant is a cross between *Parkinsonia florida* and the offspring of *P. microphylla* and *P. aculeata*. The concoction of species yielded about one hundred seedlings that were tested and sorted. This particular form stood head and shoulders above the rest.

DESCRIPTION: This medium-size tree grows to 20–25 feet tall and 20–25 feet across (rarely 30 feet by 30 feet), with pretty, smooth, light green bark. Its desirable features include an upright growth habit that allows tall people to walk underneath with some pruning, the nearly unrivaled mass of flowers produced in late spring, and sporadic flowering throughout the summer when given supplemental water.

CULTURE/MAINTENANCE: This tree is hardy to at least 15° F and possibly lower. Once established, it is quite drought-tolerant, surviving on 11 inches of annual rainfall, but it grows faster and flowers more profusely if given supplemental water in spring and summer. It grows best in loosened, well-drained native soil and doesn't care about organic matter. It will need to be shaped or thinned because of the tendency to produce many branches down low and in the crown. The abundance of yellow flowers can carpet your brick or flagstone patio and if you find this habit annoying, keep your broom handy.

IDENTIFICATION: The combination of large (for a palo verde) flowers, no thorns, and leaf structure set Desert Museum palo verde apart from all the others.

LANDSCAPE APPLICATION: Place this palo verde in full or reflected sun and use it as a fast-growing shade tree in any part of your landscape. Its light shade makes it an ideal nurse plant for cacti and other succulents. However, the propensity to produce a lot of branches may force you to sharpen your pruning saw and loppers every year. Because Mark Dimmitt selected for no thorns or spines, the trees are ideal for use in parking lots and street medians. Use this tree for seasonal color produced by the brilliant display of flowers in spring and summer.

PRECAUTIONS: Because of the very fast growth rate, overwatering can lead to top-heaviness and disaster after a windy storm. Protect young trees from rabbits, javelinas, and deer. They love to eat bark and young branches, which can deform and sometimes kill whole plants. Butterfly or moth larvae can defoliate other species of *Parkinsonia* in the spring and summer. According to Dr. Dimmitt, the hybrid resists this defoliation. However, do check plants.

Pedilanthus macrocarpus | Slipper Flower

CACTI/SUCCULENT,
SMALL–MEDIUM SHRUB

SIZE (height x width)	3–5 feet x 3–4 feet
FLOWER COLOR	Red
FLOWER SEASON	Spring–fall
EXPOSURE	Full, filtered, or reflected sun
WATER	Drought-tolerant–low
GROWTH RATE	Fast for stems, slow to fill in
PRUNING	None
HARDINESS	Hardy to the mid-20s F, new growth damaged at high to mid-20s F while mature growth damaged at low 20s F
NATURAL ELEVATION RANGE	Near sea level on the western coast of Mexico to 2,300 feet in Baja California
SUITABLE CITIES	All low-elevation-zone cities; protected areas in Tucson

FIELD NOTES: The gray-stemmed form of *Pedilanthus macrocarpus* is found along arroyos in Baja California from 1,000 to 2,300 feet elevation. The green-stemmed form shows itself along the coast of Sonora, Mexico, on the way to vacation hot spots like Kino Bay and San Carlos. It grows as far south as Colima in southwestern Mexico.

DESCRIPTION: The odd, candle-like look produced by numerous upright, semisucculent stems make *P. macrocarpus* an attraction whether planted in the ground or a decorative container. The many erect, succulent stems grow to roughly 3–5 feet tall and form clumps to 3–4 feet across. Red, slipper-shaped, 1-inch flowers appear from late spring into summer and occasionally fall, and draw in hummingbirds.

CULTURE/MAINTENANCE: New growth will suffer frost damage when temperatures drop to the high to mid-20s F. Mature growth is more frost-resistant, withstanding temperatures into the low 20s F and getting nipped when temperatures reach the low 20s F. Place slipper flower in filtered, full, or reflected sun and in a soil that drains quickly. The stems grow quickly once the weather heats up, but clusters will take several years to fill out. Slipper flower is quite drought-tolerant, but the growth rate will speed up some if it is watered twice a month from late spring until early fall. Allowing it to go dormant in the fall will increase its frost tolerance.

IDENTIFICATION: Currently there are no other species of *Pedilanthus* in cultivation. *Euphorbia antisyphilitica* has a similar form, but the stems are much thinner.

LANDSCAPE APPLICATION: In the low desert, use slipper flower as a specimen plant or desert accent and mix with low-growing perennials, ground covers, or small shrubs. Surround it with *Berlandiera lyrata, Calylophus hartwegii, Salvia farinacea,* and *Zinnia grandiflora.* In the mid-elevation desert regions, use this beauty as a container plant that can be put on a covered patio or protected some other way when nights get frigid.

PRECAUTIONS: When wounded, *P. macrocarpus* oozes milky latex that should be washed off exposed skin.

Penstemon baccharifolius | Rock Penstemon

SMALL SHRUB	
SIZE (height x width)	1–3 feet x 1–2 feet
FLOWER COLOR	Scarlet red
FLOWER SEASON	Summer–fall
EXPOSURE	Full or filtered sun
WATER	Low–moderate
GROWTH RATE	Moderately fast

PRUNING	Late winter and after flowering
HARDINESS	Hardy to at least mid-teens F, probably much lower
NATURAL ELEVATION RANGE	1,300–4,700 feet
SUITABLE CITIES	All low- and mid-elevation-zone cities; Sierra Vista in high-elevation zone

FIELD NOTES: Pretty little *Penstemon baccharifolius* adorns limestone bluffs in western Texas and adjacent northern Mexico from 1,300 to 4,700 feet elevation. Take a drive to Langtry, Texas, the home of Hangin' Judge Roy Bean, in summer and you're likely to encounter some nice specimens along the roadside and on the bluffs near town.

DESCRIPTION: This small evergreen shrub grows to 1–2 feet (2–3 feet with flower stalk) tall and spreads to 2 feet across. Thick, ¾-inch-long leaves are closely set on round, reddish stems. Scarlet-red, 1-inch-long flowers open on 8–12-inch-long stalks that rise above the foliage. This bloom, set against the dark green foliage, lasts all summer for a knockout effect.

CULTURE/MAINTENANCE: This shrub is hardy to at least the mid-teens F, and judging by where it comes from, it is probably hardy to 0° F. It is low-water-using once established, surviving on 11 inches of annual rainfall, but it looks fuller and flowers more profusely when thoroughly watered once a week. It has a moderate-fast growth rate, taking only one or two years to achieve a respectable size. It grows best when planted in full or filtered sun. In nature, it grows in rocky soils, and under cultivation it should be placed in a soil with good drainage and very little or no organic amendments. Prune off old flower stalks in midsummer to encourage more flowers. Come late winter, shear back to develop bushiness.

IDENTIFICATION: *P. baccharifolius* is easily distinguished from all other *Penstemon* species because it refuses to die back after flowering, the summer flowering season is unusual, and the small leaves are of uniform size from the base of the plant to the flower spike.

LANDSCAPE APPLICATION: Because of its small size, this is an excellent plant to use in tight spaces such as planters, narrow entries, street medians, and parking lots. In the hot, interior, low desert, be kind to this plant and give it half-day or filtered sun, and not full or reflected sun. In the low-elevation, coastal region, and the intermediate desert, it can be placed in full sun. The flowers do attract hummingbirds, so plant it in a patio or bird-attracting garden. In the transition and outer zones of a xeriscape, plant it at the base of a tall accent such as *Yucca elata, Y. rigida,* or *Y. rostrata.* Its small size works well with smaller *Agave* and *Dasylirion* species. It mixes easily with other low-water-use shrubs and trees such as *Ageratum corymbosum, Bauhinia lunarioides, Chrysactinia mexicana, Eysenhardtia orthocarpa, Poliomintha maderensis, Sophora secundiflora,* and *Tetraneuris acaulis.*

PRECAUTIONS: *P. baccharifolius* is probably susceptible to rabbit damage and should be protected for the first year or two.

Penstemon eatonii | Firecracker Penstemon

FLOWERING PERENNIAL	
SIZE (height x width)	2–3 feet x 3–4 feet
FLOWER COLOR	Scarlet red
FLOWER SEASON	Late winter–spring
EXPOSURE	Full sun
WATER	Low
GROWTH RATE	Fast
PRUNING	Cut seed stalks in the summer
HARDINESS	Hardy to at least 10° F
NATURAL ELEVATION RANGE	2,000–8,000 feet
SUITABLE CITIES	All cities in all zones

FIELD NOTES: Find *Penstemon eatonii* on mesas and roadsides from southwestern Colorado to central Arizona and California from 2,000 to 8,000 feet elevation. You can spot the occasional plant while driving through the forests near Flagstaff, Arizona, and even on dry, gravelly slopes in the piñon-juniper woodland in the San Bernardino Mountains in southern California.

DESCRIPTION: This low-growing, shrubby, evergreen perennial has rich, dark green foliage and fiery scarlet-red flowers that appear in late winter and early spring. It makes a small mound of dark green leaves, about 1 foot high and 2 feet across, with flower spikes adding another 1–2 feet to the height. Hummingbirds quickly zero in on the 1-inch-long flowers densely clustered along the stalk.

CULTURE/MAINTENANCE: This plant is hardy to at least 10° F and probably lower. Plants are low- to moderate-water-using, surviving on 12–15 inches of annual rainfall. A little extra irrigation in the fall and spring will yield faster plant growth and more prolific flowering. These fast-growing plants reach mature size after a couple of

growing seasons, but full sun and a soil with good drainage are essential for them to flourish. Harvest the flowering spikes after the seeds have ripened to scatter seeds and add more of these beauties to your garden.

IDENTIFICATION: *P. eatonii* is easily recognized by its shape, dark green, lance-shaped leaves, and thick clusters of scarlet-red flowers that often hang to one side of the inflorescence.

LANDSCAPE APPLICATION: Place this plant in full sun in the transition or outer zones of a xeriscape where it will add a splash of color during late winter and spring when many desert plants are still dormant. Hummingbirds will seek it out as a rare early-season nectar source. Try it among a grove of tall *Yucca* species such as *Y. elata, Y. rigida,* or *Y. rostrata.* Group it with spring-flowering perennials such as *Baileya multiradiata, Calylophus hartwegii, Encelia farinosa, Sphaeralcea ambigua,* and *Verbena gooddingii.* Mass plant for the seasonal blast of scarlet to spruce up streets, medians, and retention basins.

PRECAUTIONS: This relatively carefree plant thrives when provided with good light, good air circulation, and a soil with good drainage. Aphid and mealybug problems on new growth and flower stalks can be washed off by hose spray and insecticidal soap solution. It can show its age after a few years, so collect and scatter the seeds to encourage a succession of new plants. Protect the flowering stalks from hungry rabbits.

Penstemon parryi | Parry's Penstemon

FLOWERING PERENNIAL	
SIZE (height x width)	3–4 feet x 1–2 feet
FLOWER COLOR	Pink, sometimes white
FLOWER SEASON	Late winter–spring
EXPOSURE	Full sun
WATER	Low
GROWTH RATE	Fast
PRUNING	Cut seed stalks and scatter the seeds
HARDINESS	Hardy to 15° F
NATURAL ELEVATION RANGE	1,500–5,000 feet
SUITABLE CITIES	All low- and mid-elevation-zone cities; warm spots in high elevation cities

FIELD NOTES: *Penstemon parryi* will surely be one of the most prevalent wildflowers you encounter hiking in the southern Arizona desert on a spring day, especially after a rainy winter. Plants appear on hillsides, slopes, washes, and canyons in the Sonoran Desert from 1,500 to 5,000 feet elevation. This perky plant now also appears deliberately planted along roadsides by enlightened transportation departments.

DESCRIPTION: This spring-flowering perennial has light to dark pink or sometimes white flowers. It starts as a low rosette of leaves that usually rises less than 10 inches. Flower stalks shoot up to 4 feet tall, and with sufficient water, the whole plant fills up a space about 2 feet in diameter. Dark gray-green leaves are wider at the tip than at the base and measure up to 4 inches long. Flower stalks appear as early as February and continue emerging through March or April. Individual flowers are nearly 1 inch long, packed in loose clusters along the stalk. *P. parryi* delivers a veritable feast for hummingbirds and an unbeatable spring flower display. It dies back after seed formation and returns with more stems the following fall.

CULTURE/MAINTENANCE: Plants are hardy to at least 15° and probably lower. Because they escape the summer heat by going dormant, they require very little water in the summer and can survive on less than 12 inches of annual rainfall. For maximum flower production, however, water them periodically in the fall, winter, and spring. *P. parryi* sometimes grows fast enough to flower the first year from seed sown the previous fall. It requires very little maintenance when grown as a wildflower. Allow the flower spikes to mature with ripe seeds then cut the stalks and scatter the seeds around your landscape.

IDENTIFICATION: Pink, narrowly tubular flowers and bluish-green leaves easily distinguish *P. parryi*. There are two similar species: *P. superbus* displays distinctive coral-colored flowers and the pink-flowered *P. wrightii* has thick, fleshy, gray-green, ovate leaves.

LANDSCAPE APPLICATION: Treat this plant like a star for coming through with its incredible spring greeting every year. The soft rose-pink flowers mix well with summer- and fall-blooming plants to insure a continuous floral display through the growing season. Create a field of hummingbird-attracting color by mass planting in open spaces, or group plants at the base of accents such as *Agave, Dasylirion,* and *Yucca* species, and *Nolina nelsonii.* For a riot of spring color, combine with *Baileya multiradiata, Calliandra eriophylla, Sphaeralcea ambigua, Verbena gooddingii,* and any other *Pen-*

stemon species. Its flowers may be pink, but Parry's penstemon is tough enough to dress up streets and medians.

PRECAUTIONS: This short-lived perennial can naturalize and persist in the right area. Protect container-grown plants until they can survive without supplemental water. Rabbits will eat emerging flower shoots and cut into the flower display.

Penstemon superbus | Coral Penstemon

FLOWERING PERENNIAL

SIZE (height x width)	3–5 feet x 1–2 feet
FLOWER COLOR	Coral red
FLOWER SEASON	Late winter–spring
EXPOSURE	Full, reflected, or filtered sun
WATER	Low–moderate
GROWTH RATE	Fast
PRUNING	Cut seed stalks in late summer
HARDINESS	Hardy to 10° F
NATURAL ELEVATION RANGE	3,500–5,500 feet
SUITABLE CITIES	All cities in all zones

FIELD NOTES: I can count on spotting *Penstemon superbus* in bloom when exploring southeastern Arizona's mountains in the late spring and summer. It inhabits rocky canyons and washes on sandy or gravelly soil. Plants are native to southeastern Arizona, New Mexico, and Chihuahua, Mexico, from 3,500 to 5,500 feet elevation.

DESCRIPTION: This short-lived perennial has tall spikes of attractive dark coral-red, tubular flowers. Each spring several 3–5-foot-tall stalks emerge from the overwintering basal rosette of leaves to display the vivid, show-stopping flowers well above the plant. At the peak of flowering, a mass planting, often alive with swooping hummingbirds, is quite spectacular. Glaucous, gray-green leaves can be 4 inches long, narrow at the base and broad near the tip. After flowering, seeds develop in small, hard, oval capsules on the long, flowering stems that will die back after the seeds ripen.

CULTURE/MAINTENANCE: This heat-tolerant plant is hardy to at least 10° F, preferring full or reflected sun, and is low- to moderate-water-using when actively growing. It will tolerate filtered light, but the price is a little legginess. It avoids the summer heat by going dormant and dying back to a low cluster of leaves or even just the rootstock. Place it in a well-drained soil and, for finest flowering, supply periodic irrigation from fall until spring flowers fade. The fast-growing plant can flower the first

year from seed. Mature plants keep getting bigger and will produce more flowering stems each season. Remove dried flowering stems after the seeds ripen, then collect and scatter seeds in September to naturalize new seedlings in the landscape.

IDENTIFICATION: *P. superbus* can be distinguished from *P. parryi* by its darker, coral-red flowers.

LANDSCAPE APPLICATION: Plant coral penstemon for its spectacular spring bloom that attracts hummingbirds. Plant from containers or scatter seeds in late summer to get plants established in a wildflower garden for a superb spring flower show. Use it also to soften the base of semisucculent accents such as *Agave, Dasylirion,* or *Yucca* species. Mix with other spring-flowering plants such as *Baileya multiradiata, Calliandra eriophylla, Sphaeralcea ambigua, Tetraneuris acaulis,* and *Verbena gooddingii.* Mass plant this wildflower for a blast of color in your garden or along streets, in medians, and in retention basins.

PRECAUTIONS: This short-lived perennial's life span is shortened even more by overwatering. It reseeds readily and will perpetuate itself under the right conditions if seeds are allowed to mature and scatter when ripe. Protect container-grown plants until they can grow without supplemental water. Rabbits will eat emerging flower shoots. Remember that late summer or fall is the best time to plant.

Penstemon triflorus | Hill Country Penstemon

FLOWERING PERENNIAL	
SIZE (height x width)	1½–2 feet x 1–2 feet
FLOWER COLOR	Dark pinkish-red
FLOWER SEASON	Spring
EXPOSURE	Full sun
WATER	Low–moderate
GROWTH RATE	Fast
PRUNING	Cut seed stalks in late summer
HARDINESS	Hardy to at least 10° F
NATURAL ELEVATION RANGE	500–2,000 feet

SUITABLE CITIES	All low- and mid-elevation-zone cities, Sierra Vista in high-elevation zone

FIELD NOTES: *Penstemon triflorus* is found only in the Edwards Plateau of central Texas from about 500 to 2,000 feet elevation.

DESCRIPTION: This utterly eye-popping late winter–early spring perennial produces 10–15-inch-diameter rosettes of 4-inch-long, dark, glossy green leaves. The 1½–2-foot-tall spikes of 1-inch-long, brilliant dark pinkish-red flowers first appear in February or March and keep blooming through April. After flowering, seeds develop in small, hard, oval capsules on the long flowering stems that will die back after the seeds ripen.

CULTURE/MAINTENANCE: This heat-tolerant plant is hardy to at least 10° F, and it grows and flowers best in full sun. Give it moderate amounts of water when actively growing but less while dormant in summer. Place it in a soil with good drainage and, for best flowering, irrigate regularly from fall until summer. This fast-growing plant can flower the first year from seed, but mature plants will get larger and produce more flowering stems each season. Virtually no maintenance is required other than removal of dried flowering stems after the seeds ripen. Collect and scatter seeds in September to naturalize a colony of new seedlings in the landscape.

IDENTIFICATION: The foliage and flowers easily distinguish *P. triflorus*.

LANDSCAPE APPLICATION: This plant is best used mixed among other spring wildflowers, or in combination with semisucculent accents such as *Agave, Dasylirion,* or *Yucca* species. Mass plant for seasonal color and to attract hordes of hummingbirds. Mix with contrasting spring flowering plants such as *Baileya multiradiata, Calliandra eriophylla, Sphaeralcea ambigua, Tetraneuris acaulis,* and *Verbena gooddingii.* Use this *Penstemon* for temporary color along streets, in medians, or in retention basins.

PRECAUTIONS: This short-lived perennial should be protected from rabbits. Though it blooms in the spring, fall is the best time to plant.

Poliomintha maderensis | Mexican Oregano

SMALL–MEDIUM SHRUB

SIZE (height x width)	3 feet x 3 feet
FLOWER COLOR	Lavender purple
FLOWER SEASON	Spring–fall
EXPOSURE	Full sun or light shade
WATER	Low–moderate

GROWTH RATE	Moderate–fast
PRUNING	Shear in late winter
HARDINESS	Hardy to 10° F
NATURAL ELEVATION RANGE	8,000 feet
SUITABLE CITIES	All cities in all zones; needs some shade in hot, interior low-elevation-zone cities

FIELD NOTES: *Poliomintha maderensis* is known only from the crest of the Sierra de la Madera in Coahuila, where it is tucked in with pine and oak trees at an elevation of about 8,000 feet. It's going to take some expert hiking and exploring to find this elusive creature in habitat.

DESCRIPTION: This rounded shrub puts out a few flowers in late spring or early summer then cranks up flower production. By about late summer or early fall, it is awash with white and light-to-dark lavender, hummingbird-attracting flowers. It stays at a small to medium size for some time, then one day it'll be 3 feet tall and 3 feet wide. Small (about ½ inch long), bright green leaves give off the delicious fragrance of oregano. Purple, tubular, 1-inch-long flowers are densely clustered together at the stem tips. The extremely long flowering season is a nice bonus for this beautiful shrub that spices up any low-water-use landscape and can be used to draw in hummingbirds.

CULTURE/MAINTENANCE: This hardy shrub tolerates lows of at least 10° F. Although low-water-using, plants bloom more profusely when the root zone is thoroughly soaked every 7–10 days from late spring until early fall. Young plants grow fast but slow to a moderate rate as they age. Growth rate will vary with the amount and frequency of supplemental watering. This shrub is forgiving about soil types, growing well in a native soil without organic amendments. Place it in full sun or at the edge of a tree that gives light shade. Cut back severely once every couple of years to increase density and sturdiness.

IDENTIFICATION: When in bloom, *P. maderensis* is not easily confused with any other plant. When not flowering, it might be confused with *Salvia greggii* but is easily distinguished by its fragrance.

LANDSCAPE APPLICATION: Use this plant as an evergreen shrub in full sun or very light shade in all zones of a xeriscape. The flower color looks good next to shrubs and perennials that have white, blue, blue-purple, or reddish-purple flowers such as *Ageratum corymbosum, Asclepias linaria, Conoclinium dissectum, Eysenhardtia ortho-carpa, Gaura lindheimeri,* and *Sophora secundiflora.* The size is perfect for nestling against large accent plants: *Dasylirion acrotrichum, Dasylirion quadrangulatum,* and *Hesperaloe funifera.* Try it as a singleton among other shrubs or massed for a spectacular display of flowers from spring through fall.

PRECAUTIONS: No insect pests or diseases bother this plant.

Prosopis glandulosa var. *torreyana* | Western Honey Mesquite

MEDIUM–LARGE TREE

SIZE (height x width)	20–30 feet x 20–30 feet
FLOWER COLOR	Light yellowish-green
FLOWER SEASON	Late spring–early summer
EXPOSURE	Full or reflected sun
WATER	Low–moderate
GROWTH RATE	Moderate
PRUNING	Shape to desired form
HARDINESS	Hardy to 0°
NATURAL ELEVATION RANGE	Sea level–5,000 feet
SUITABLE CITIES	All cities in all zones, although it remains more shrub-like in Albuquerque

FIELD NOTES: *Prosopis glandulosa* var. *torreyana* grows near major river drainages in western Arizona and along washes and sandy flats throughout much of southeastern California and the southern tip of Nevada. Isolated populations pop up in southeastern Arizona and along the Rio Grande in southern New Mexico and western Texas. Look for sizeable specimens along the Colorado River in the Grand Canyon region and along the Gila River from west of Phoenix to where it meets the Colorado River near Yuma.

DESCRIPTION: This multiple-stemmed, deciduous tree grows to 20–30 feet tall with a spread of 20–30 feet. Twisted, crooked trunks with shallowly fissured, rough bark, make this an intriguing specimen in any xeriscape. Twice pinnate, softly pubescent, gray-green leaves drop in the fall and come out in spring. Stout thorns are prevalent on young growth but disappear as they get absorbed into older, larger stems. Three-inch-long spikes of yellowish-green flowers appear in late spring and summer. In late summer, 4–9-inch-long, straight to curved, shiny brown seedpods cover the tree until they fall.

CULTURE/MAINTE-NANCE: This tree is hardy to about 0° F. In general, it is drought-tolerant once established, but it responds to supplemental water applied during the growing season. Thoroughly soak the root zone, which usually extends beyond the diameter of the canopy and to a depth of at least 3 feet, once every 3–4 weeks in summer. This tree grows in most soil types as long as the watering is adjusted accordingly. The growth rate is moderate, so give it plenty of time to achieve maximum size. Prune from the start in order to create a shape you can walk under.

IDENTIFICATION: The leaf structure and growth form easily identify *P. glandulosa.*

LANDSCAPE APPLICATION: Use this tree for that one-two punch of summer shade and winter sun. It makes a perfect oasis centerpiece and offers shade for plants such as *Ageratum corymbosum, Aquilegia chrysantha, Heuchera sanguinea,* and *Stachys coccinea.* This is an excellent tree in all regions of the desert Southwest, although in Albuquerque it tends to remain more shrub-like.

PRECAUTIONS: Avoid pruning large branches because it encourages suckering growth. The trees produce an abundance of seedpods that can make cleanup annoying.

Prosopis Hybrid | Hybrid Mesquite, South American Mesquite, Thornless Chilean Mesquite

MEDIUM–LARGE TREE

SIZE (height x width)	20–30 feet x 20–40 feet
FLOWER COLOR	Golden yellow
FLOWER SEASON	Late spring
EXPOSURE	Full sun
WATER	Low–ample
GROWTH RATE	Fast
PRUNING	To shape and thin crown
HARDINESS	Hardy to 10°–15° F
SUITABLE CITIES	All low- and mid-elevation-zone cities; Sierra Vista in high-elevation zone

FIELD NOTES: The prevailing theory is that this mesquite is a cross between the North American native *Prosopis velutina* and the South American *Prosopis alba.*

DESCRIPTION: This medium-size tree has a broad, spreading crown. Mature trees can reach 20–30 feet tall with a canopy 20–40 feet wide. The dense shade and lush, semitropical appearance have won over gardeners. It's ideal for the hot, low- and mid-elevation desert regions of the Southwest. Typically the dark green leaves will hang on through the winter and fall just before, or right when, the new leaves show up in spring. Spikes of cream-colored flowers appear in late spring, followed by a heavy crop of pods in the summer.

CULTURE/MAINTENANCE: The forms in cultivation are generally hardy to 10–15° F. They use little water once established but have no shame and will also make use of any water that comes their way. Water young plants thoroughly to encourage an extensive root system that will help anchor them as they get larger. The fast-growing plants can grow as much as 8–10 feet in one year and need to be properly staked and thinned. Regular thinning will reduce crown density, allow the wind to pass through the canopy, and reduce the potential for toppling in high winds. The abundance of seedpod production can make cleanup a regular chore through the heat of summer.

IDENTIFICATION: *Prosopis* identification has gotten harder, now that North American species are hybridizing with South American species. However, the hybrids tend to keep their old leaves until the new leaves come out in spring. Hybrid leaves are brighter green and the flowers are a more golden yellow.

LANDSCAPE APPLICATION: This is an ideal shade tree for patios, parking lots and street medians. The dense shade is useful in helping reduce energy costs around houses and office buildings. Install on the east, south and west sides to provide sun relief for exposed buildings. Because it is one of the fastest-growing shade trees for the desert Southwest, it has been overused in some landscapes.

PRECAUTIONS: Rabbits see young trees as opportunities to lop off young shoots, strip the bark, and even girdle the trunk. Screen until the main trunk is at least 2 inches in diameter.

Prosopis velutina | Velvet Mesquite

MEDIUM TREE

SIZE (height x width)	20–30 feet x 20–30 feet
FLOWER COLOR	Light yellow
FLOWER SEASON	Late spring–early summer
EXPOSURE	Full or reflected sun
WATER	Thoroughly soak every 3–4 weeks in summer, none when leafless
GROWTH RATE	Moderate
PRUNING	Shape to desired form
HARDINESS	Hardy to 5° F
NATURAL ELEVATION RANGE	1,000–4,500 feet
SUITABLE CITIES	All low- and mid-elevation-zone cities; Sierra Vista in high-elevation zone

FIELD NOTES: Velvet mesquite, as interpreted here, grows along dry washes, valleys, and flood plains from 1,000 to 4,500 feet elevation in southern Arizona and Sonora, Mexico. A mesquite bosque (forest) provides magical habitat for a host of wildlife. The shade of these low-branching, wide-spreading trees is a welcome relief when you're out hiking. One of the best places to find a true bosque is not far from the Santa Cruz River near Tumacácori in southern Arizona.

DESCRIPTION: This native can usually be found growing as a large, multiple-stemmed, shrub-like deciduous tree reaching 20–25 feet tall with a spread of 25–30 feet. Under ideal conditions, it can reach 30 feet tall with a canopy spread of nearly 40 feet. Gnarly trunks and soft, velvety, gray-green leaves are signature features. Please prune respectfully—find something else to turn into a single-trunked lollipop. Leaves fall in the winter. Three-inch-long spikes of yellow flowers appear in late spring and early summer and are followed by tan seedpods.

CULTURE/MAINTENANCE: Velvet mesquite tolerates 5° F. In general, the trees have a moderately slow growth rate and are drought-tolerant once established but respond to supplemental water applied during the growing

season. Supplemental water should be applied to the root zone, which usually extends 2 or 3 times the diameter of the canopy, and to a depth of at least 3–5 feet. It grows in most soil types as long as the watering is adjusted accordingly. The growth rate is moderate, and the tree takes many years to hit maximum size. When in flower, it can be quite showy and is used for its seasonal color. Careful pruning in the early years is required in order to create a walk-under tree, and periodic leaf and seedpod cleanup is necessary to pass inspection in groomed or public landscapes.

IDENTIFICATION: *P. velutina* is distinguished from other species by the velvety pubescent leaves.

LANDSCAPE APPLICATION: One of the best uses for velvet mesquite is as a deciduous shade tree; just make sure to allow ample room for full development. Stick it anywhere you want summer shade and winter sun, such as the east, south, and west sides of a house. It makes a great oasis centerpiece and nicely shades sun-sensitive plants like *Agave bovicornuta, Cycas revoluta,* and *Dioon edule*; as well as flower producers such as *Ageratum corymbosum, Aquilegia chrysantha, Heuchera sanguinea, Poliomintha maderensis,* and *Stachys coccinea.* It survives street medians and parking lots if the main trunks are coaxed into growing upright and the lower branches are pruned above head height.

PRECAUTIONS: Avoid pruning large branches, which encourages suckering growth. Desert mistletoe is guaranteed to find your mesquite, so make it a habit to remove infected branches.

Psilostrophe cooperi | Paper Flower

FLOWERING PERENNIAL	
SIZE (height x width)	12–20 inches x 12–20 inches
FLOWER COLOR	Bright yellow
FLOWER SEASON	Spring, frequently early summer and fall
EXPOSURE	Full sun
WATER	Drought-tolerant–low (survives on < 12 inches of annual rainfall)
GROWTH RATE	Fast
PRUNING	Prune off old flower heads
HARDINESS	Hardy to at least 15° F
NATURAL ELEVATION RANGE	2,000–5,000 feet
SUITABLE CITIES	All cities in all zones

FIELD NOTES: *Psilostrophe cooperi* is found along roadsides and on slopes, mesas, and plains in Arizona, southern California, Utah, New Mexico, and northwestern Mexico

from 2,000 to 5,000 feet elevation. This cheerful plant is readily spotted along roadsides when driving around the desert just outside of Tucson, or in washes on early morning springtime walks in the Tucson Mountain and Catalina foothills.

DESCRIPTION: This semi-woody perennial forms a hemispherical mound 12–20 inches tall and 12–20 inches across. Yellow, 1-inch, daisy-like flowers cover the shrub after rains from March through September. Long, narrow, silvery gray-green leaves provide a perfect background for the bright yellow flowers. At peak bloom the leaves are nearly hidden by the mass of flowers. As the flowers pass their peak, the petals turn a papery brown and persist on the plant, hence the common name.

CULTURE/MAINTENANCE: Paper flower is hardy, tolerating winter lows of 15° F or lower. It accepts drought but will keep flowering if given a little water in the summer. However, too much water spurs vegetative growth at the expense of flower production. It grows quickly and prefers full sun; any shade causes weak, spindly growth. Plant it in a soil with good drainage, and prune off old flower heads to encourage new growth and more flowers.

IDENTIFICATION: *P. cooperi* is distinguished from its near relative *P. tagetina* by its larger, shrubbier habit and more pubescent stems.

LANDSCAPE APPLICATION: The spectacular flower display could be a focal point in any xeriscape throughout all zones in the desert Southwest. Overdo it and try a mass planting amongst a mass of *Agaves* or *Yuccas* for a stunning display when everything comes into full bloom. Combine with the complementary flower colors of *Ageratum corymbosum*, *Conoclinium dissectum*, and *Salvia farinacea* to create a party atmosphere in a xeriscape.

PRECAUTIONS: To avoid leggy growth, place *P. cooperi* in full sun only and do not overwater.

Quercus buckleyi | Synonym: *Quercus texana* | Texas Red Oak

MEDIUM–LARGE TREE

SIZE (height x width)	25–30 feet x 25–30 feet
FLOWER COLOR	Insignificant

FLOWER SEASON	Insignificant
EXPOSURE	Full sun or half-day of full sun
WATER	Moderate–ample
GROWTH RATE	Slow
PRUNING	None
HARDINESS	Hardy to at least 0° F
NATURAL ELEVATION RANGE	1,200 feet
SUITABLE CITIES	All mid- and high-elevation-zone cities; low-elevation-zone cities with sufficient water

FIELD NOTES: *Quercus buckleyi* (sometimes sold as *Q. texana*) is found on rocky lime-stone slopes in central Texas. Watch for plants west of the White Rock Escarpment, which is just west of Dallas near Interstate 35. In habitat, these trees will hybridize with *Q. shumardii*. Seed for cultivated *Q. buckleyi* was collected from a pure stand. Another nice stand of these stately trees can be seen in Pedernales Falls State Park, located in the hill country of east central Texas at an elevation of about 1,200 feet.

DESCRIPTION: In its native territory, this slow-growing, medium-size, deciduous shade tree will grow to 30–50 feet tall and wide. However, in the desert Southwest it grows to about 25–30 feet tall and 25–30 feet wide. The leaves are ovate to nearly round in outline, with 2–4 lobes on each side. The shiny, dark green foliage turns a stunning scarlet in the fall. The bark is either black and furrowed or gray and smooth.

CULTURE/MAINTENANCE: *Q. buckleyi* is cold-hardy to at least 0° F. It requires at least a half-day of full sun and ample room for full development, both above and below ground. Although moderately drought-tolerant, it will grow best when planted in a deep, fast-draining soil and given ample water. Plants are slow-growing and will take many years to achieve full size. Although not particular about soil pH, they do not like to have wet feet, so good drainage is a must.

IDENTIFICATION: Dark bark and evergreen leaves distinguish *Q. buckleyi*.

LANDSCAPE APPLICATION: Use *Q. buckleyi* for its woodsy feel in large, open, nonresidential expanses. It grows well in lawn situations, which makes it perfect for parks or fancy corporate head-quarters. It performs fine in the mid-elevation desert climates but is probably best used in higher-elevation regions where summer temperatures rarely go above 100° F. Foliage will complain in the summer in hot exposures in the low desert regions of the Southwest, but the plants will survive.

PRECAUTIONS: Leaves will burn in the hot, interior, low desert.

Quercus emoryi | Emory Oak

SMALL–MEDIUM TREE

SIZE (height x width)	15–30 (50) feet x 15–35 (60) feet
FLOWER COLOR	Insignificant
FLOWER SEASON	Insignificant
EXPOSURE	Full sun or half-day of full sun
WATER	Moderate–ample
GROWTH RATE	Slow
PRUNING	None
HARDINESS	Hardy to at least 0° F
NATURAL ELEVATION RANGE	3,000–8,000 feet
SUITABLE CITIES	All mid- and high-elevation-zone cities; low-elevation-zone cities with sufficient water

FIELD NOTES: *Quercus emoryi* livens up dry hills and moist canyons from western Texas to Arizona and south into adjacent Mexico from 3,000 to 8,000 feet. Cruise down Arizona Highway 83 from I-10 towards the town of Sonoita, and look for the spreading trees dotting the rolling hills and as you descend from the crest.

DESCRIPTION: This stalwart Southwestern native is a slow-growing medium-size shade tree with roughly furrowed, black bark and leaves that persist through the win-ter. In nutrient-poor or shallow desert soil, the trees remain somewhat stunted, in time, reaching about 15–20 feet tall and 15–20 feet wide. However, in deep, acidic soil or in the high-elevation zone above the desert floor, the trees can attain a size of 15–30 (rarely 50) feet tall by 15–35 (rarely 50–60) feet wide. Thick, leathery, semi-

evergreen leaves vary between 1 and 3 inches long and are generally about 1 inch wide with smooth, toothed, or lobed margins.

CULTURE/MAINTENANCE: *Q. emoryi* is cold-hardy to at least 0° F and will hold most of its leaves through the winter. The tree needs full sun and plenty of space to spread. It struggles in the alkaline soil of low desert, preferring a slightly acidic soil with some humus. This is a perfect tree for the high-elevation zones throughout the Southwest. If you are in a city outside the high-elevation zone, spread mulch or compost underneath the tree to increase the organic matter and provide sufficient water for good health.

IDENTIFICATION: The dark bark and semievergreen leaves distinguish *Q. emoryi*.

LANDSCAPE APPLICATION: Emory oak can unleash its full grandeur in large, open expanses like parks and commercial landscapes. Mix with other mid- to higher-elevation plants to recreate a woodsy feel. Suitable companions could be *Agave parryi*, *Aloysia gratissima*, *Berlandiera lyrata*, *Calylophus hartwegii*, *Chrysactinia mexicana*, *Hesperaloe parviflora*, *Muhlenbergia* species, *Penstemon triflorus*, *Rhus choriophylla*, *Vauquelinia californica*, and *Zinnia grandiflora*. This is arguably the best oak tree for landscape use in the mid-elevation-zone cities of Tucson and Las Vegas and well worth seeking out if you are considering a native oak for your landscape.

PRECAUTIONS: Growth rate is slow, so start with a large specimen and provide ample water to give it a kick-start.

Quercus hypoleucoides | Silverleaf Oak

MEDIUM TREE

SIZE (height x width)	20–25 (30) feet x 20–25 (30) feet
FLOWER COLOR	Insignificant
FLOWER SEASON	Insignificant
EXPOSURE	Full sun or half-day of full sun
WATER	Low–ample
GROWTH RATE	Fast
PRUNING	None
HARDINESS	Hardy to at least 0° F
NATURAL ELEVATION RANGE	4,000–7,500 feet
SUITABLE CITIES	All mid- and high-elevation-zone cities

FIELD NOTES: The wonderfully apt name (*hypo* means below and *leuco* means white) perfectly describes the distinctive leaves of this Southwestern native. This widespread

species can be found growing on slopes and in canyons from western Texas to Arizona, south into northern Mexico from 4,000 to 7,500 feet. Take a trip to Chiricahua National Monument near Willcox, Arizona, or Ramsey Canyon near Sierra Vista, Arizona, and check this oak off your life list.

DESCRIPTION: With the undersides of its leaves shimmering white, this regal, single-trunked tree makes a fine specimen in higher-elevation landscapes. In the right spot, it can quickly reach a reasonable size of 20–25 feet tall and 20–25 feet wide and might even reach 30 feet by 30 feet. Thick, leathery, persistent leaves are up to 4 inches long and about 1 inch wide with smooth or lightly toothed margins. My good friend and oak fanatic, Petey Mesquitey, tells me the new growth is a gorgeous pinkish-red that is quite striking and eye-catching.

CULTURE/MAINTENANCE: Silverleaf oak is cold-hardy to at least 0° F and will hold on to most of its leaves through the winter. Give it at least a half-day of full sun and plenty of space. It loves a slightly cooler climate and prefers a neutral or slightly acidic soil with adequate drainage. The growth rate is quite fast for an oak, and Petey Mesquitey has one that grew 20 feet tall in just 8 years. If you are outside the high-elevation zone and are considering this oak, spread a generous amount of mulch or compost underneath the canopy and provide sufficient water for best results. The natural, single-trunked form does not require any pruning.

IDENTIFICATION: The bicolored leaves distinguish *Q. hypoleucoides*.

LANDSCAPE APPLICATION: Use this oak for its fast growth, dense shade, and spectacular display of glistening white leaves. Mix with other mid- to higher-elevation plants, like *Agave parryi, Aloysia gratissima, Berlandiera lyrata, Calylophus hartwegii, Chrysactinia mexicana, Hesperaloe parviflora, Muhlenbergia* species, *Penstemon triflorus, Rhus choriophylla, Vauquelinia californica,* and *Zinnia grandiflora*. Although this tree will put up with conditions in the mid-elevation-zone cities of Tucson and Las Vegas, it'll take ample water to keep it looking sharp.

PRECAUTIONS: There are no known insect pests or diseases.

Quercus virginiana | Southern Live Oak

MEDIUM–LARGE TREE	
SIZE (height x width)	20–30 (60) feet x 20–30 (100) feet
FLOWER COLOR	Insignificant
FLOWER SEASON	Insignificant
EXPOSURE	Full sun or half-day of full sun
WATER	Moderate–ample
GROWTH RATE	Moderately slow
PRUNING	None
HARDINESS	Hardy to at least 0° F
NATURAL ELEVATION RANGE	100 feet
SUITABLE CITIES	All cities in all zones

FIELD NOTES: *Quercus virginiana* grows on clay loam or gravelly clay loam soil in eastern and southern Texas, east to the Atlantic and up the coast to Virginia. Some fine stands of these magnificent trees can be seen east of the Brazos River in southeast Texas at an elevation of about 100 feet. Keep your pets on a leash and watch for the alligators that patrol the waters of the area.

DESCRIPTION: *Q. virginiana* is a moderately slow-growing, medium to large, evergreen or semievergreen shade tree. In nutrient-poor or shallow desert soil, it usually grows to about 20–30 feet tall and 20–30 feet wide. However, in deep rich soil or in zones above the desert floor and with enough water, it eventually tops out at 60 feet tall by 60–100 feet wide. The leaves are dark, shiny green above and white pubescent below, 2–3 inches long, and about 1 inch wide with smooth, toothed, or lobed margins. The bark is dark brown to black and deeply furrowed. This is a beautiful shade tree for wide open spaces.

CULTURE/MAINTENANCE: This oak is cold-hardy to at least 0° F and will hold on to its leaves until temperatures drop that low. It needs at least a half-day of full sun and plenty of space. Roots will need plenty of room to spread, as well. It will grow best in a deep soil with ample water. Although it is considered the fastest-growing oak, it loses any race with an *Acacia* or *Prosopis*.

IDENTIFICATION: The dark bark and evergreen leaves distinguish *Q. virginiana.*

LANDSCAPE APPLICATION: Use this oak for its woodsy feel in large, open expanses like parks and commercial landscapes. It grows well in lawns, which makes it perfect for park settings, but it's probably too big for a backyard. It is the best oak for the lower-elevation desert climates but is happier in higher-elevation regions where summer temperatures rarely go above 100° F.

PRECAUTIONS: *Q. virginiana* is susceptible to oak wilt fungus.

Rhus choriophylla | Evergreen Sumac

LARGE SHRUB	
SIZE (height x width)	5–8 feet x 8–12 feet
FLOWER COLOR	White
FLOWER SEASON	Late summer–fall
EXPOSURE	Full sun
WATER	Low–moderate
GROWTH RATE	Moderate–moderately fast
PRUNING	None
HARDINESS	Hardy to at least 0° F
NATURAL ELEVATION RANGE	2,100–5,000 feet
SUITABLE CITIES	All low- and mid-elevation-zone cities; Sierra Vista in high-elevation zone

FIELD NOTES: *Rhus choriophylla* is found in open areas in southern Arizona and northern Sonora, Mexico, from 2,100 to 5,000 feet elevation. I first came across some very nice specimens in 1981 while looking for *Sophora arizonica* in the Whetstone Mountains in southern Arizona. In 1993, Ron Gass and I ventured back to the Whetstones and spotted more beautiful, spreading sumacs.

DESCRIPTION: This large, evergreen shrub grows to 5–8 feet tall and 8–12 feet wide. The shiny, thick, leathery leaves are composed of 3–5 leaflets, each measuring 1–2 inches long. Large clusters of flowers appear on the branch tips in late summer and fall. Queen butterflies seek out the tiny, white blossoms.

CULTURE/MAINTENANCE: This shrub is hardy to at least 0° F and remains evergreen even during the coldest winters. It uses little water but will accept supplemental water while actively growing. The moderate growth rate can be accelerated some if the root zone is soaked 2–3 times a month in late spring and summer. Plants are not fussy about soil type; they will grow well in a rocky, fast-draining soil or in a somewhat poorly drained soil, as long as you adjust the amount of supplemental water accordingly. Grow this plant only in full sun to maintain the best form.

IDENTIFICATION: Thick, dark green, shiny leaves and clusters of white flowers easily identify *R. choriophylla.*

LANDSCAPE APPLICATION: Use evergreen sumac as a large shrub or screen. It is tolerant of a wide range of conditions and can be used in the transition or outer zones of a xeriscape or in a butterfly garden. Its size is perfect for use with large accent plants and trees, such as *Prosopis velutina.* In nature it grows in the oak zone, and that combination also looks great in landscapes using the commercially available *Quercus* species. Other suitable companions include *Agave parryi, Fouquieria splendens, Sophora secundiflora,* and *Wedelia acapulcensis* var. *hispida.*

PRECAUTIONS: *R. choriophylla* is very drought-tolerant once established, although it may look a little stressed in the heat of summer. Rabbits and javelinas do not eat stems of larger plants, although one-gallon-size plants should be screened as a precaution.

Ruellia peninsularis | Rama Parda

MEDIUM–LARGE SHRUB	
SIZE (height x width)	3–4 feet x 4–6 feet
FLOWER COLOR	Purple
FLOWER SEASON	Year-round (mostly spring)
EXPOSURE	Full or reflected sun, or partial shade
WATER	Low–moderate
GROWTH RATE	Moderately fast
PRUNING	After frost
HARDINESS	Half-hardy to 25° F
NATURAL ELEVATION RANGE	Near sea level–3,000 feet
SUITABLE CITIES	All low-elevation-zone cities; Tucson in mid-elevation zone

FIELD NOTES: *Ruellia peninsularis* is found on dry gravelly soil and rocky slopes from west-central Baja California to the Cape region and across the gulf near Guaymas, Sonora, from near sea level to about 3,000 feet. On a 1981 excursion through Baja

California, we saw it mixed in with *Bursera* and a treelike *Fouquieria*. We ferried from Loreto to Guaymas and then headed north to Nacapule Canyon near San Carlos, along the coast. This canyon is a botanical wonderland where tough, water-hating plants meet figs and palms. Scattered among the statuesque, treelike drought-tolerators were fine, rich green specimens of *R. peninsularis.*

DESCRIPTION: This medium-size shrub can grow to 3–4 feet tall and spread to 4–6 feet across. It has many white or gray-white branches, small, bright green, oval leaves, and contrasting purple flowers. The 2-inch-long by 1½-inch-wide, funnel-shaped flowers occur singly in the leaf **axils** sporadically throughout the year, but mostly in spring and fall. Small, dry capsules spring open when ripe.

CULTURE/MAINTENANCE: Rama parda is hardy to about the mid-20s F with tip damage occurring at those temperatures. Nighttime temperatures in the mid-teens F bring on total leaf kill and stem dieback. It revives quickly in spring. It is extremely drought-tolerant once established, surviving on annual rainfall of about 11 inches. It will produce more flowers if given extra water in summer. It hits a mature size in two or three years, and grows best in a rocky or sandy soil with good drainage. Prune out any frost-damaged growth in early spring.

IDENTIFICATION: *R. peninsularis* is readily identified by its small green leaves, white bark, and rich purple, funnel-shaped flowers.

LANDSCAPE APPLICATION: The rich green color and lush appearance fits into a tropical scheme for the mini-oasis or near pools and patios. This shrub can also be used in the transition or outer zones of a xeriscape. Because of its cold sensitivity, it works well under overhangs and tree canopies. It is versatile enough to be planted in full or reflected sun, or even on the north side of a building where it will get summer sun and winter shade. It makes a scene at the base of shade trees such as *Bauhinia lunarioides, Eysenhardtia orthocarpa, Leucaena retusa, Parkinsonia florida, Parkinsonia* x 'Desert Museum,' and *Prosopis velutina* or large accents like *Nolina matapensis, N. nel-*

sonii, and various *Yucca* species. Try it as a backdrop for smaller, flowering shrubs and ground covers such as *Conoclinium dissectum, Dalea capitata,* and *Penstemon baccharifolius.* From time to time, hummingbirds may visit.

PRECAUTIONS: Rama parda shows damage in the mid-20s F and leaf blackening and stem dieback in the low 20s F.

Sabal uresana | Sonoran Palmetto

PALM/CYCAD

SIZE (height x width)	10–15 (40) feet tall with a crown spread of 8–10 (15) feet
FLOWER COLOR	Creamy yellow
FLOWER SEASON	Spring–early summer
EXPOSURE	Full sun or half-day of shade, or full shade
WATER	Moderate–ample
GROWTH RATE	Slow
PRUNING	None
HARDINESS	Hardy to mid-20s F
NATURAL ELEVATION RANGE	Sea level–3,700 feet
SUITABLE CITIES	All low- and mid-elevation-zone cities

FIELD NOTES: *Sabal uresana* is part of the mix in Sonoran desert scrub, thorn scrub, or tropical deciduous forest in west-central and eastern Sonora, from near sea level to about 3,700 feet. Look for a stand about 13 miles east of the Rio Yaqui as you travel on Mexico Highway 16 from Hermosillo to Yecora in Sonora. This stand hosts several very tall, mature plants and some very small, young plants with no intermediates in sight.

DESCRIPTION: *S. uresana* eventually grows to 30–40 feet tall. Crowns spread to about 10–15 feet, and trunks end up a slender 12–14 inches in diameter. It grows extremely slowly, and a realistic size for garden planning purposes is closer to 10–15 feet tall with a leaf spread of 8–10 feet. Silver-blue to blue-gray leaves measure 12–13 feet long with the petiole making up a little over half the length and the blade just under half. The petiole extends well into the blade, giving the appearance of a blade that is in between a fan type and a feather type. This graceful, backward curving, silvery blue foliage makes a beautiful statement in Southwestern landscapes. The inflorescence can be 3–7 feet long, is spreading to arching but not drooping, and is generally shorter than the leaves.

CULTURE/MAINTENANCE: This medium-size palm is cold-hardy to about the mid-20s F. It may grow slowly, but it actually grows faster than the popular *Brahea armata.* It grows best in full sun, although it can forgive a half-day of shade or even full shade in the hot, interior desert region and prefers a soil with good drainage. Water needs vary depending on soil type, but the deep roots of established plants should be thoroughly soaked 4 or 5 times a month from spring until fall, and then reduced to 1 or 2 times a month in the winter.

IDENTIFICATION: *S. uresana* is easily recognized by the backward curving midrib (petiole extension) of the leaf blade.

LANDSCAPE APPLICATION: Use this palm on the north side of a building with winter shade and summer sun. It makes a great specimen plant and can be used in a variety of residential or commercial projects. Mix it with other plants that build a semi-tropical mood such as *Agave bovicornuta, Aquilegia chrysantha, Cycas revoluta, Dioon edule, Havardia mexicana, Heuchera sanguinea,* and *Lysiloma watsonii* ssp. *thornberi.*

PRECAUTIONS: Bruchid beetles will eat the seeds, but there are no other known insect pests or diseases. Plants are difficult to transplant bare-root, so plant from containers.

Salvia chamaedryoides | Blue Sage

FLOWERING PERENNIAL, SMALL SHRUB	
SIZE (height x width)	1½–2 feet x 2–3 feet
FLOWER COLOR	Cobalt blue
FLOWER SEASON	Spring–fall
EXPOSURE	Full sun
WATER	Low
GROWTH RATE	Fast
PRUNING	Shear in late winter and/or midsummer
HARDINESS	Hardy to at least 10° F
NATURAL ELEVATION RANGE	4,000–9,000 feet
SUITABLE CITIES	All cities in all zones

FIELD NOTES: I've gotten pretty good at identifying *Salvia chamaedryoides* while negotiating the byways of Zacatecas, Nuevo León, Hidalgo, and San Luis Potosí of central Mexico at 4,000–9,000 feet elevation.

DESCRIPTION: This low-growing subshrub has herbaceous stems that are woody near the base and produce an orderly mound of grayish-green leaves. Six-inch-long spikes of ¾-inch-long cobalt-blue flowers top this sage spring through fall.

CULTURE/MAINTENANCE: This plant is hardy to about 10º F and grows best in full sun in a soil with good drainage to reduce the possibility of root rot. It is sensitive

to excess water, so let the soil dry out between waterings. It lives fast and dies young, filling out rather quickly during the growing season and lasting only a few years. Shear mature plants seasonally to encourage rejuvenated growth. Trim old flower spikes to encourage more flowering, and cut back hard.

IDENTIFICATION: The diminutive stature, grayish-green leaves, and small cobalt-blue flowers easily distinguish *S. chamaedryoides* from other *Salvia* species. Pat McNeal of Austin, Texas, introduced a green-leaved cultivar called 'Desert Green' in 1990.

LANDSCAPE APPLICATION: Put blue sage in full sun in the low-water-use zones. Mass plant for a ground cover effect, or install handfuls around large accents such as *Agave* and *Yucca* species. The grayish-green foliage contrasts nicely with "regular" greens. The blue flowers set off the yellow blooms of plants such as *Baileya multiradiata, Dalea capitata,* and *Encelia farinosa.* Blue sage looks and flowers best during the cooler spring and fall months. Mix with plants that peak during summer or winter.

PRECAUTIONS: Overwatering really can lead to death by root rot. Black aphids may congregate on the new growth and flowering stalks. Wash these little friends off with a spray of soapy water or an insecticidal soap solution.

Salvia clevelandii | Chaparral Sage

MEDIUM SHRUB	
SIZE (height x width)	4 (6) feet x 4 (6) feet
FLOWER COLOR	Blue-violet
FLOWER SEASON	Spring–early summer
EXPOSURE	Full sun
WATER	Low–moderate
GROWTH RATE	Fast
PRUNING	Prune after blooming or prior to new growth in the fall
HARDINESS	Hardy to at least 10° F
NATURAL ELEVATION RANGE	< 3,000 feet
SUITABLE CITIES	All low- and mid-elevation-zone cities; Sierra Vista in high-elevation zone

FIELD NOTES: In the springtime, flowering *Salvia clevelandii* dots the dry slopes below 3,000 feet elevation in chaparral and coastal sage scrub in San Diego County and northern Baja California.

DESCRIPTION: This aromatic, 4-foot-tall by 4-foot-wide (rarely 6 feet by 6 feet) shrub puts up an impressive flower display in spring and summer. The gray-green leaves are potently fragrant, make a good tea, and can stand in for *S. officinalis* (garden sage) in cooking. Clusters of deep blue-violet flowers, stacked 2–4 high, appear at the ends of branches in spring and early summer.

CULTURE/MAINTENANCE: This shrub is hardy to at least 10° F. Because it comes from an area dominated by winter rainfall, it grows during the cooler weather and goes dormant in summer. It is a fast-growing plant, reaching full size in just a couple of years and using low to moderate amounts of water. It tends to die out after a few years, possibly because it's supposed to or because of root rot caused by overwatering. Planting in full sun and a soil with excellent drainage might squeeze out a few more years. Prune in the fall just prior to its growing season.

IDENTIFICATION: There are several California *Salvias* that have stacks of **whorled** flowers and are difficult to distinguish from *S. clevelandii*. However, only *S. clevelandii* has a combination of ashy gray leaves with crenate (rounded) leaf margins, long **exserted** stamens, and deep blue-violet flowers. *S. leucophylla* is most similar, but the flower color is more pinkish. The hybrid *Salvia* 'Allen Chickering' is difficult to distinguish. There are two named cultivars, *S. clevelandii* 'Aromas' which is shorter and more compact and *S. clevelandii* 'Winifred Gilman' which has larger, more intense violet-blue flowers.

LANDSCAPE APPLICATION: Use chaparral sage for its spring and early summer color, combining it with longer-lived plants and yellow-flowered shrubs that bloom at the same time such as *Encelia farinosa*. Mix it with larger *Agave, Dasylirion,* and tall *Yucca* species or Australian *Sennas* such as *S. artemisioides* and *S. phyllodinea*. It will attract both butterflies and hummingbirds, and it puts up with life along streets, in medians, and around pools.

PRECAUTIONS: Plants may be short-lived, especially if grown fast, and the root rot threat is a real consequence of overwatering. Occasionally aphids will attack the flowers and flowering stalks.

Salvia darcyi | Lipstick-red Salvia

FLOWERING PERENNIAL, MEDIUM SHRUB	
SIZE (height x width)	4–5 feet x 5–7 feet
FLOWER COLOR	Bright scarlet red
FLOWER SEASON	Spring–fall
EXPOSURE	Full sun or partial shade
WATER	Moderate–ample
GROWTH RATE	Fast
PRUNING	Shear in late winter
HARDINESS	Root-hardy
NATURAL ELEVATION RANGE	9,000 feet
SUITABLE CITIES	All cities in all zones; treat as a perennial in mid- and high-elevation-zone cities

FIELD NOTES: *Salvia darcyi* is a treasure hidden in pine-forest vegetation in the state of Nuevo León in northeastern Mexico. Find it near the town of Galeana at about 9,000 feet elevation.

DESCRIPTION: From spring through fall *S. darcyi* maintains 18–24-inch-long flower stalks covered with striking scarlet-red, 1½-inch-long, hummingbird-attracting flowers. Herbaceous stems with sticky leaves will reach about 3 feet tall before flowering, and then the shrub fills up a space 5 feet tall and 5 feet wide with the flower stalks. Flowering explodes in late spring, slows down in the heat of summer in the hot, interior desert, resumes in late summer, and returns to full glory in the fall. Where winter lows drop below freezing, plants die to the ground, and even in more mild climates they are best treated as perennials. They can eventually form large colonies.

CULTURE/MAINTENANCE: Although *S. darcyi* will freeze to the ground in most winters, it is root-hardy and will regrow quickly as the weather warms up in the spring. Because of its fast growth rate, this plant will reach its full size each year. In mid-elevation regions, it can tolerate full sun but will need consistent watering in the summer. In the hot, interior, low desert, it requires a little shade and ample water to make it through the summer. It's not finicky about desert soils as long as there is sufficient moisture. It's a good idea to mulch around the roots with a thick layer of organic material to keep the soil and roots cool in summer. *S. darcyi* is best treated as a perennial and cut to ground level in late winter.

IDENTIFICATION: *S. darcyi* is easily identified by the combination of large, red flowers, the sticky leaves, and the production of **stolons** that generate colonies.

LANDSCAPE APPLICATION: Put this plant in the xeriscape oasis for its beautiful flower display in all elevation zone cities. The large, scarlet-red flowers are extremely showy during the spring and fall and easily attract hummingbirds. This perennial dies back, so it enjoys small trees and large accents as companions, such as *Diospyros texana, Eysenhardtia orthocarpa, Leucaena retusa, Dasylirion acrotrichum, Dasylirion quadrangulatum, Nolina matapensis, Nolina nelsonii, Yucca rigida,* and *Yucca rostrata.* Also, try mixing it with other somewhat thirsty plants such as *Conoclinium dissectum, Gaura lindheimeri,* and *Tecoma* x 'Orange Jubilee.'

PRECAUTIONS: Glandular, sticky leaves hold dirt or small pieces of debris and latch onto adjacent plants.

Salvia farinacea | Mealy Cup Sage

FLOWERING PERENNIAL	
SIZE (height x width)	1–3 feet x 1–2 feet
FLOWER COLOR	Violet-blue
FLOWER SEASON	Spring–fall
EXPOSURE	Full or filtered sun
WATER	Low–moderate
GROWTH RATE	Fast
PRUNING	Shear in winter, trim off old flower spikes as they fade
HARDINESS	Perennial, root-hardy to at least 10° F
NATURAL ELEVATION RANGE	750–4,900 feet
SUITABLE CITIES	All cities in all zones

FIELD NOTES: My only run-in with *Salvia farinacea* in habitat was in 1991, coming back from northeastern Mexico with Ron Gass and Dave Palzkill. We were driving

through a wide, dry wash just north of Del Rio, Texas, and stopped to snag a few cuttings. We were able to get them to root and have been growing it off and on since. *S. farinacea* is found in sandy washes, prairies, meadows, hillsides, and floodplains in central and western Texas and New Mexico.

DESCRIPTION: This perennial shrub grows to 1–2 feet tall and 1–2 feet wide. With the 8–12-inch-long spikes of rich violet-blue flowers, the overall height approaches 3 feet. Herbaceous stems die back each winter and sprout anew in the spring. Long, narrow, bright green leaves measure 2–4 inches long and about ½ inch wide. The spikes put out tight, dense clusters of blue to violet-blue flowers, from early spring to early fall. Individual flowers are about ¾ inch long and stick out a broad, flaring, showy lower lip. The **calyx** is covered with soft, white hairs, is tinged with purple at the tip, and nicely sets off the flowers.

CULTURE/MAINTENANCE: *S. farinacea* dies to the ground in winter and recovers from the hardy roots quickly in the spring. Stems are very fast-growing, reaching 1–2 feet tall by mid to late spring. Plants do not require a lot of supplemental water once established. However, regular hot-season watering produces speedier growth and more flowers. Gauge supplemental watering by soil type and planting exposure. This plant is not particular about soil type, growing well in both sandy and heavy clay soils. Remove spent flower spikes, and cut the stems to ground level in winter. Bedding plant forms are not covered here.

IDENTIFICATION: The looser, wilder appearance separates *S. farinacea* from the bedding plant forms.

LANDSCAPE APPLICATION: The relaxed growth habit blends well with desert plants in the transition or outer zones, yet the plant is lush enough to work in the mini-oasis. Mix it for striking effect with white-, blue-, or purple-flowering plants such as *Ageratum corymbosum, Asclepias linaria, Conoclinium dissectum, Cordia parvifolia, Gaura lindheimeri, Ruellia peninsularis,* and *Sophora secundiflora.* Because it is a perennial that dies back, you might try planting it with always-there-for-you *Agave, Dasylirion, Hesperaloe,* and *Yucca* species. It handles the shade of small trees like *Bauhinia lunarioides, Eysenhardtia orthocarpa,* and *Fraxinus greggii.*

PRECAUTIONS: Expect *S. farinacea* to die to the ground in cold places.

Salvia greggii | Autumn Sage

SMALL SHRUB	
SIZE (height x width)	2–3 feet x 2–3 feet
FLOWER COLOR	Pink, red, white, purple, orange, yellow
FLOWER SEASON	Spring–fall
EXPOSURE	Full sun or partial shade
WATER	Low–moderate
GROWTH RATE	Fast
PRUNING	Shear in late winter and midsummer
HARDINESS	Hardy to at least 5° F
NATURAL ELEVATION RANGE	4,000–10,000 feet
SUITABLE CITIES	All cities in all zones

FIELD NOTES: If you drive on the back roads through the mountains in central and western Texas, look for the distinctive flowers of *Salvia greggii* on rocky slopes and hillsides. I've seen some impressive stands while winding through the canyons and open rolling hills around Monterrey and Saltillo in northern Mexico. And I see it planted all over the Southwest and never get tired of it. This wide-ranging species occurs from western Texas south throughout much of north-central Mexico from 4,000 to 10,000 feet.

DESCRIPTION: *S. greggii* comes alive with 1-inch-long, pinkish-red flowers on 6–10-inch-long spikes in the cooler weather of spring and fall. This small shrub has dark green leaves and grows 2–3 feet tall and 2–3 feet wide. While there are forms with flower colors of purple, orange, yellow, or white, the toughest ones have pinkish-red flowers. Hummingbirds love these flowers, and butterflies also have been known to sip the tasty nectar.

CULTURE/MAINTENANCE: *S. greggii* is hardy to at least 5° F and maybe even lower. It is moderate to low-water-using, surviving but not thriving on 10–12 inches

of annual rainfall. It looks perkier in summer with supplemental water every week. It is fast-growing, attaining a mature size in two growing seasons. It grows best when placed in full sun (in mid- and high elevation desert areas) or light shade (in low-elevation desert areas), and in a soil that has good drainage. It benefits from a pruning makeover in midsummer and late winter. Every 4–5 years whack the plants back to about 6–8 inches above the ground to invigorate and rejuvenate them.

IDENTIFICATION: The flowers and foliage make *S. greggii* easy to recognize. Several flower colors are making their way into the landscape trade.

LANDSCAPE APPLICATION: This tidy plant fits nicely in entryways, in planters, and around pools. When massed, the spectacular flower display can attract mobs of hummingbirds. It blends well with succulent accents like *Agave parryi* var. *truncata, Dasylirion acrotrichum, Dasylirion quadrangulatum, Yucca rigida,* and *Y. rostrata;* small trees *Acacia willardiana, Bauhinia lunarioides, Diospyros texana,* and Eysenhardtia orthocarpa; and herbaceous perennials *Ageratum corymbosum, Conoclinium dissectum, Penstemon* species, and *Zinnia grandiflora.*

PRECAUTIONS: Use flower color variations judiciously. The toughest form is the pink one sometimes offered as the cultivar 'Sierra Linda.' Various shades of red flowers are in second place for toughness, followed by white, then purple, orange, and yellow. The plant may get infested with spittlebug—you'll know it when you see it, a white, gooey blob near the tips of the stems. Just prune off those parts. New growth may attract black aphids which can be washed off with mild soapy water.

Salvia leucantha | Mexican Bush Sage

FLOWERING PERENNIAL, SMALL–MEDIUM SHRUB	
SIZE (height x width)	3–5 feet x 3–5 feet
FLOWER COLOR	Purple or white
FLOWER SEASON	Summer–fall
EXPOSURE	Full or filtered sun, or partial shade
WATER	Moderate
GROWTH RATE	Fast
PRUNING	Cut out any frozen stems in late winter or early spring
HARDINESS	Root-hardy to at least 17° F
NATURAL ELEVATION RANGE	2,600–8,000 feet
SUITABLE CITIES	Treat as a perennial in all cities in all zones

FIELD NOTES: *Salvia leucantha* is reported to be from tropical and subtropical coniferous forest in east-central Mexico, south into Central America and even northern South America from 2,600 to 8,000 feet elevation. I would love to see this one in habitat but

have not been able to track it down. The first record that I could find of this being in cultivation was in *The Illustrated Dictionary of Gardening* by Nicholson from 1887.

DESCRIPTION: Mexican bush sage, a medium-size perennial, has a woody crown and herbaceous stems. In the mid-elevation regions, it fills out at about 3 feet tall by 3 feet wide, while in the coastal climate of southern California, it routinely gets 4–5 feet tall by 4–5 feet wide. Densely white pubescent stems will sprout in the dead of winter and die back with frost, but resprout quickly in the spring. The leaves are lance-shaped, about 4 inches long and ¾ inch wide. Small, densely pubescent, white or purple flowers occur on 6–10-inch-long flower spikes at the end of each stem from summer through fall. The white stems and olive-green leaves are attractive features, but the reward to the gardener is the spectacular late summer and fall flower display.

CULTURE/MAINTENANCE: This perennial plant is root-hardy to at least 17° F. The stems will die back when temperatures hit the low 20s F, but the roots and crown will tolerate much lower temperatures. It is somewhat drought-tolerant, but giving it supplemental water during the growing season and planting it in some shade will allow for faster growth and better flower production. Once established, this fast grower will reinflate to 4 feet by 4 feet each year after frosting back to the crown. It handles native, rocky soil as well as enriched garden soil. Snipping off the frozen stems in the winter cleans up the appearance and facilitates new stem growth. Plants are best treated as a perennial in all elevation zones.

IDENTIFICATION: *S. leucantha* is easily distinguished from all other species by its very pubescent flowers and overall appearance.

LANDSCAPE APPLICATION: Use *S. leucantha* in a little shade, as a summer- and fall-flowering specimen. It will perform singly or put on a truly stunning flower display when mass planted. Try mixing it with cacti and other succulents that can carry on through the winter when it is frozen back. The flowers attract hummingbirds and are a showy addition to any bird garden.

PRECAUTIONS: When deciding where to plant, keep in mind that the stems will freeze back.

Scutellaria suffrutescens | Cherry-pink Skullcap

GROUND COVER, FLOWERING PERENNIAL, SMALL SHRUB	
SIZE (height x width)	18–24 inches x 24–36 inches
FLOWER COLOR	Cherry pink, red
FLOWER SEASON	Spring–fall
EXPOSURE	Full or filtered sun
WATER	Low–moderate
GROWTH RATE	Fast
PRUNING	Cut back to nearly ground level once every 3–5 years to rejuvenate the plant
HARDINESS	Hardy to at least 15° F
NATURAL ELEVATION RANGE	5,000–6,600 feet
SUITABLE CITIES	All cities in all zones; needs shade in hot, interior, low-elevation-zone cities

FIELD NOTES: *Scutellaria suffrutescens* is native to the mountains of northeastern Mexico and resides between about 5,000 and 6,600 feet elevation. Specimens have been collected from the very steep limestone mountains around the city of Monterrey in Nuevo León.

DESCRIPTION: This tidy, dense, evergreen subshrub sends out numerous herbaceous stems from a woody base and grows to about 12–18 inches tall, spreading to 24–36 inches across. Small, medium green, oval leaves are opposite each other on the stem and measure about ½ inch across. In late spring and summer, and even in fall, this plant is covered with deep cherry-pink to red, 1-inch-long flowers that attract hummingbirds.

CULTURE/MAINTENANCE: Plants are hardy to at least 15° F and can probably tolerate lower temperatures without being killed. This low- to moderate-water-user grows a bit faster and flowers more profusely if given extra water from spring through fall. It will fill out a 2-foot diameter area in 2–3 years. Thoroughly soaking the root zone once every 7–10 days in the spring and summer will encourage more flowering. Cut back to nearly ground level once every 3–5 years to rejuvenate the plant.

IDENTIFICATION: The combination of leaves, size, and flowers readily identify *S. suffrutescens*.

LANDSCAPE APPLICATION: This tough little plant is a good companion for succulent and semisucculent plants such as *Agave, Aloe, Dasylirion, Ferocactus, Hesperaloe, Nolina,* and *Yucca* species, and small trees such as *Acacia willardiana, Bauhinia lunarioides, Diospyros texana, Eysenhardtia orthocarpa, Havardia pallens,* and *Leucaena retusa.* The rich green color and mounding, sprawling shape are ideal to soften the hard edges of those sculptural accents, or the edges of planters and walkways. Take advantage of its cherry-pink or red flowers as seasonal color that brings in hummingbirds. It needs a bit of dappled shade in the hot, interior, low-elevation cities; otherwise they can take full sun in the mid- and high-elevation zones.

PRECAUTIONS: Spider mites can cause stippling of the leaves in late spring and summer.

Senna artemisioides | Feathery Cassia

MEDIUM–LARGE SHRUB

SIZE (height x width)	5–6 feet x 5–6 feet
FLOWER COLOR	Yellow
FLOWER SEASON	Late winter–early spring
EXPOSURE	Full or reflected sun
WATER	Drought-tolerant–low
GROWTH RATE	Fast
PRUNING	Shear as pods develop
HARDINESS	Hardy (high teens to low 20s F)
NATURAL ELEVATION RANGE	Unknown
SUITABLE CITIES	All low- and mid-elevation-zone cities

FIELD NOTES: *Senna artemisioides* lives in dry areas across the entire Australian mainland except in the state of Victoria.

DESCRIPTION: Silvery gray foliage provides a nice backdrop for the spectacular display of late winter color. This rounded, evergreen, medium-size shrub grows 5–6 feet tall and 5–6 feet wide. Leaves are composed of 1-inch-long, narrow, almost needlelike leaflets that shimmer in the early morning sunlight. Flowers cover the shrubs with yellow in late winter and sring, then turn into 3-inch-long seedpods.

CULTURE/MAINTENANCE: This shrub is hardy to temperatures in the high teens to low 20s F. It is a low- to moderate-water-user, requiring some supplemental water in the heat of summer in low and middle elevation desert areas. It can reach full size quickly with adequate water and grows best in full sun and a soil with good

drainage. To maintain a smaller, more compact shrub, shear as seedpods develop in late spring or summer.

IDENTIFICATION: *S. artemisioides* is part of a complex group of plants from Australia. It is easily distinguished from *S. nemophila* by its silvery gray leaves and smaller size.

LANDSCAPE APPLICATION: Mass plant feathery cassia for its spectacular late winter–early spring color. It makes a beautiful hedge, space definer, or informal screen and is a pretty workhorse for streets and medians. It fits right in with other Australians like *Acacia* species, *Eremophila maculata,* and *Eucalyptus* species. Stretch the color season by mixing with plants that give summer and fall color such as *Caesalpinia pulcherrima, Dalea frutescens,* and *Leucophyllum* species. Use it to soften large accent plants like *Nolina nelsonii* and *Yucca* species.

PRECAUTIONS: Rabbits or deer might eat young plants, but the appeal wanes as plants get bigger and tougher.

Senna nemophila | Australian Desert Senna

LARGE SHRUB

SIZE (height x width)	6–9 feet x 6–9 feet
FLOWER COLOR	Yellow
FLOWER SEASON	Late winter–early spring
EXPOSURE	Full or reflected sun
WATER	Low–moderate
GROWTH RATE	Fast
PRUNING	Shear as pods develop
HARDINESS	Hardy to at least high teens F
NATURAL ELEVATION RANGE	Unknown
SUITABLE CITIES	All low- and mid-elevation-zone cities

FIELD NOTES: *Senna nemophila* is a variable shrub that is widespread throughout the southern half of Australia.

DESCRIPTION: Bright green foliage and the spectacular display of color from late winter to spring will brighten any large area. This large, rounded shrub grows 6–9 feet tall and 6–9 feet wide. Green leaves are composed of narrow, almost needlelike leaflets and provide a nice backdrop for the yellow flowers. Brown, 3-inch-long seedpods follow the flowers. Although there are several forms of *S. nemophila,* nobody has thought up clever names for them. The smaller form is tighter and more compact even in nursery containers.

CULTURE/MAINTENANCE: *S. nemophila* is hardy to at least the high teens F, with some variation across the different selections. Some forms show damage at temperatures in the low 20s F while others have toughed it out in Las Vegas and El Paso until temperatures dropped below 15° F. It is low- to moderate-water-using once established, surviving on 10–15 inches of annual rainfall. It can get large rather quickly, especially in full sun and a soil with good drainage. To maintain a smaller, more compact shrub, shear as the seedpods develop in late spring or summer.

IDENTIFICATION: *S. nemophila* is part of a complex bunch of plants from Australia. Some botanists consider it to be a variety of *S. artemisioides.* However, it is well known in the trade as *S. nemophila* and to keep the peace, I leave it as such. It is easily distinguished from *S. artemisioides* by its greener leaves and massive size.

LANDSCAPE APPLICATION: Mass plant this shrub for its spring color in wide-open spaces such as street medians and along highways. It makes a beautiful hedge, space definer, or informal screen and is often mixed with other Australian plants such as *Acacia* and *Eucalyptus* species. It also looks great with shrubs that give summer and fall color such as *Caesalpinia pulcherrima, Dalea frutescens,* and *Leucophyllum* species.

PRECAUTIONS: Remember this shrub gets big, so give it a wide berth. Rabbits or deer might eat it until it gets big and tough.

Senna phyllodinea | Silvery Cassia

MEDIUM–LARGE SHRUB

SIZE (height x width)	5–7 feet x 5–7 feet
FLOWER COLOR	Yellow

FLOWER SEASON	Late winter–early spring
EXPOSURE	Full or reflected sun
WATER	Drought-tolerant–low
GROWTH RATE	Moderately fast
PRUNING	Shear as pods develop
HARDINESS	Hardy to low 20s F
NATURAL ELEVATION RANGE	Unknown
SUITABLE CITIES	All low- and mid-elevation-zone cities

FIELD NOTES: *Senna phyllodinea* grows in a variety of soil types in Victoria and New South Wales in southern Australia.

DESCRIPTION: Come late winter to spring, this shrub will be covered with yellow, lightly fragrant flowers. Its rounded form will easily reach 5–7 feet tall and 5–7 feet wide. The 3-inch-long, sickle-shaped leaves are actually modified petioles called "phyllodes." Silvery foliage shimmers in the early morning or late afternoon sun and provides a great backdrop for the yellow flowers that occur in clusters of 2–5 near the ends of the branches. Brown, 3-inch-long seedpods follow the flowers.

CULTURE/MAINTENANCE: While *S. phyllodinea* is hardy to the low 20s F, new growth bites the dust in extreme cold and recovers quickly in the spring. It survives on 12–15 inches of annual rainfall and will appreciate supplemental water 2–3 times a month in the summer in areas receiving less annual rainfall. It grows moderately fast and prefers full or reflected sun and a soil with good drainage. Give it plenty of room to spread out. To eliminate the need for pod cleanup and to maintain a smaller, more compact shrub, shear the plants as the seedpods develop in late spring or summer.

IDENTIFICATION: *S. phyllodinea* is easily distinguished from the other Australian *Sennas* by its sickle-shaped phyllodes.

LANDSCAPE APPLICATION: Use *S. phyllodinea* for its year-round silvery color and seasonal flower display. Mass plant it to use as a hedge, space definer, or informal screen, or to adorn streets and highways. It fits right in with a variety of Australian plants like *Acacia* species, *Eremophila maculata,* and *Eucalyptus* species, and complements plants that give summer and fall color such as *Caesalpinia pulcherrima, Dalea frutescens,* and *Leucophyllum* species. Combine it with large accent plants like *Nolina nelsonii,* and *Yucca* species.

PRECAUTIONS: Rabbits and deer chew on young plants but are less interested in larger, tougher ones.

Simmondsia chinensis | Jojoba

MEDIUM–LARGE SHRUB	
SIZE (height x width)	Up to 4–6 feet x 6–10 feet
FLOWER COLOR	Yellowish
FLOWER SEASON	Winter–spring
EXPOSURE	Full sun
WATER	Low
GROWTH RATE	Slow
PRUNING	None
HARDINESS	Hardy to low 20s F; young plants, new growth, and flower buds damaged in the mid-20s
NATURAL ELEVATION RANGE	Sea level–5,000 feet
SUITABLE CITIES	All low- and mid-elevation-zone cities

FIELD NOTES: *Simmondsia chinensis* does not occur in China but is actually native to the Sonoran Desert—one of those "oops" moments in botany. The first official specimen got mixed into a batch of plants from China, and voila, the name *chinensis*. Plants grow in southern Arizona, southern California, and Baja California and Sonora, Mexico, on open desert and canyon slopes from sea level to about 5,000 feet elevation. This plant reassures me as I spot it in the nearby Tucson Mountains because it looks handsome and unchanging no matter what season.

DESCRIPTION: This dense, evergreen shrub can tolerate neglect. It grows slowly to an eventual size of 4–6 feet high and 6–10 feet across, although it is usually smaller. The 1-inch-long, oval, gray-green leaves are thick and fleshy, allowing the plant to survive extended periods of drought. It blooms in the winter or spring with small, yellowish flowers. Male and female flowers appear on separate shrubs. Male flowers occur in small clusters and are visible although not showy. Female flowers are solitary and develop into the brown seeds that are loaded with oil valued for use in cosmetics and lubricants.

CULTURE/MAINTENANCE: Cold-hardiness varies with age and growth stage. Mature plants without new growth in the fall are hardy to about the low 20s F while

young plants, new growth, and flower buds may be damaged in the mid-20s F. Jojoba survives on 12 inches or less of annual rainfall. It is native to rocky slopes and grows best in a soil with good drainage or where water will not pond up around the roots. It takes a number of years to achieve a respectable size. It requires no maintenance but tolerates pruning.

IDENTIFICATION: Leathery leaves make *S. chinensis* easy to recognize.

LANDSCAPE APPLICATION: Densely packed jojoba can be used as an informal screen or even a clipped hedge. It stands alone bravely or fits right in with trees, shrubs, and tall accents like *Acacia constricta, Carnegiea gigantea, Encelia farinosa, Fouquieria splendens, Nolina nelsonii, Parkinsonia microphylla,* and *Yucca rigida.* It begs for full sun in the transition or outer zones of a xeriscape. Use plants in roadside and highway plantings because they think nothing of harsh conditions. If you need a tough, dependable, drought-tolerant shrub in the low and mid-elevation desert Southwest, consider this wonderful native.

PRECAUTIONS: Insects will attack various parts of the plants, but these visitors have been observed only in large fields where the plants were being grown for seed production.

Sophora secundiflora | Texas Mountain Laurel

LARGE SHRUB, SMALL TREE	
SIZE (height x width)	10–15 feet x 6–10 feet
FLOWER COLOR	Violet-purple
FLOWER SEASON	Spring
EXPOSURE	Full, filtered, or reflected sun, or partial shade
WATER	Drought-tolerant–moderate
GROWTH RATE	Slow
PRUNING	Shape to tree form; too much removes next year's flower buds
HARDINESS	Hardy to at least 10° F
NATURAL ELEVATION RANGE	1,000–5,000 feet
SUITABLE CITIES	All low- and mid-elevation-zone cities; Sierra Vista in high-elevation zone

FIELD NOTES: *Sophora secundiflora* stands out on limestone soil along bluffs, slopes, and in canyons from southern New Mexico across to western and west central Texas, south into northern Mexico between 1,000 and 5,000 feet elevation. I've found them when driving or hiking in the Guadalupe Mountains in Texas and New Mexico, and they are fairly common around Carlsbad Caverns.

DESCRIPTION: Large clusters of purple flowers radiate the fragrance of grape Kool-Aid® and announce the arrival of spring. Normally this large, multi-trunked, evergreen shrub can be pruned into a small tree when young. It grows slowly, eventually reaching 10–15 feet tall by 6–10 feet across. Glossy, green, compound leaves have 7–11 1-inch-long leaflets. Flowers are followed by tan, woody pods containing bright red, yikes-I'm-poisonous seeds. The cultivar 'Silver Peso' sports striking leaves covered with silvery hairs.

CULTURE/MAINTENANCE: This plant is hardy to at least 10° F. It is low- to moderate-water-using and even drought-tolerant, although it will not get very big unless watered in the spring and summer. The growth rate is slow; it takes a quite a few years to produce a tree. Supplemental water in warm weather will nudge it along a little. This plant is native to rocky outcrops, but it will tolerate heavy soil if not overwatered. The caterpillars of a small moth *(Uresiphita reversalis)* will skeletonize the leaves, feasting selectively on the new growth in late spring and early summer. Pick these critters off or treat with *Bacillus thurengensis,* an effective biological control. Prune to train as a tree, but wait until after the plant has finished flowering and before it sets the buds for the next year's flowers.

IDENTIFICATION: *S. secundiflora* is easily recognized by its glossy, evergreen leaves, fragrant purple flowers, or distinctive seedpods. 'Silver Peso' has silvery gray leaves.

LANDSCAPE APPLICATION: This plant will get along with part shade, full sun, filtered sun, or reflected sun. Display it for its fragrant flowers and seasonal color. As a tree, it can be used near entryways, pool areas, and patios to give a lush, mildly tropical feel. Try it in the mini-oasis with *Dalea capitata, Lantana* x 'New Gold,' *Poliomintha maderensis, Salvia farinacea, Salvia greggii, Tecoma* x 'Orange Jubilee,' and *Tecoma stans.* It also mixes well with bold xeric forms such as *Fouquieria splendens, Dasylirion, Nolina,* and *Yucca* species, and with gray- or white-leaved plants like *Buddleja marrubiifolia* and all *Leucophyllum* species. It can be mass planted, and it toughs out life along streets and in medians.

PRECAUTIONS: The seed interior contains a toxic compound, but it is extremely difficult to chew due to the rock-hard seed coat. Because of the slow growth rate, start with at least a 5- or 15-gallon plant. Prune sparingly to preserve the flower buds for the following year that form at the end of the current year's growth. Dose with *Bacillus thurengensis* when the caterpillars show up in spring and summer.

Sphaeralcea ambigua | Globe Mallow

FLOWERING PERENNIAL, SMALL SHRUB	
SIZE (height x width)	3 feet x 3 feet
FLOWER COLOR	Orange, white, pink, lavender, red
FLOWER SEASON	Spring
EXPOSURE	Full sun
WATER	Drought-tolerant–low
GROWTH RATE	Fast
PRUNING	Remove dead stems or shear after flowering
HARDINESS	Hardy to at least 15° F
NATURAL ELEVATION RANGE	< 3,500 feet
SUITABLE CITIES	All low- and mid-elevation-zone cities; Sierra Vista in high -elevation zone

FIELD NOTES: In the spring following plentiful winter rains in southern Arizona, highway 79 between Tucson and Florence will be awash with colorful *Sphaeralcea ambigua.* The plants are common throughout the southwestern United States on dry rocky slopes, washes, and roadsides below 3,500 feet elevation.

DESCRIPTION: This perennial has a dozen or two herbaceous stems shooting up from a woody base. New stems emerge in late fall and winter, and they grow to as much as 3 feet tall and 3 feet across. Grayish-green, three-lobed leaves measure about 1½ inches long. In spring, a profusion of 1-inch-wide, cup-shaped flowers adorns the stems. Flowers come in white, pink, lavender, red, or the default orange. Two cultivars currently available are diluting the orange pool: 'Louis Hamilton' with watermelon-red flowers and 'Papago Pink' with large, light pink flowers.

CULTURE/MAINTENANCE: Plants are cold-hardy to at least 15° F and probably lower. They are extremely drought-tolerant once established, growing and flowering with annual rainfall of 11 inches or less. Plants will be lusher and reward you with more flowers with extra rations of water in late winter and spring. They grow fast and can reach that cubic-yard size in one season. Older stems start showing their age; either remove weary material annually or cut the whole plant to about 6 inches above ground level in late summer or early fall to renew the plant and promote vigorous new growth.

IDENTIFICATION: Although it is often difficult to distinguish among *Sphaeralcea* species, few have the regular, bushy, multistemmed growth habit of *S. ambigua*.

LANDSCAPE APPLICATION: Use this short-lived perennial for its mass of spring color. Plant with other spring perennials such as *Baileya multiradiata* and *Penstemon* species, and you'll have an instant wildflower display. Its size, form, and abundant flowers combine beautifully with large accent plants such as *Nolina matapensis, Nolina nelsonii, Yucca rigida,* and *Yucca rostrata.* Tough globe mallow can be used in full sun in the transition and outer zones of a xeriscape, along streets, and in medians.

PRECAUTIONS: A plant that is grown hard will not flower as profusely as one that is given supplemental water, but it will be less likely to be eaten by rabbits. Some people may have an allergic reaction to the hairs on the leaves, so push it back from high-traffic areas.

Stachys coccinea | Betony

FLOWERING PERENNIAL, SMALL SHRUB	
SIZE (height x width)	12–18 inches x 18–24 inches
FLOWER COLOR	Red, coral-red, scarlet, pink, white
FLOWER SEASON	Spring–fall
EXPOSURE	Full sun, light shade, or afternoon shade
WATER	Moderate, once every 7–10 days
GROWTH RATE	Fast

PRUNING	Cut back after frost and to keep from getting leggy
HARDINESS	Hardy to mid-teens F
NATURAL ELEVATION RANGE	1,500–8,000 feet
SUITABLE CITIES	All mid- and high-elevation-zone cities; cooler parts of the low-elevation zone

FIELD NOTES: *Stachys coccinea* grows in canyons and on slopes from southern Arizona across to west Texas and into northern Mexico from 1,500 to 8,000 feet elevation. I have come across plants in a couple of small canyons in Sonora, Mexico, and on Kitt Peak in the Baboquivari Mountains in southern Arizona.

DESCRIPTION: A profusion of red, coral-red, scarlet, pink or white flowers that hummingbirds love is the outstanding feature of betony. This herbaceous perennial grows to about 12–18 inches tall and 18–24 inches across. Oval, medium green leaves are about 1–1½ inch long by ¾–1 inch wide. They sit oppositely arranged on the distinctly square stems. One-inch-long blossoms appear in clusters on 6–10-inch-long stalks from January through September or October. The cultivar 'Hot Spot Coral' has coral-red flowers.

CULTURE/MAINTENANCE: This hardy perennial tolerates temperatures to at least the mid-teens F. Plants should receive sun for most of the day at higher elevations; however, they benefit from late afternoon shade in the summer. They require consistent supplemental water during the summer and a soil that has been enriched with some organic matter. Periodic pruning should refresh growth and spur flowering throughout the growing season.

IDENTIFICATION: Superficially, *S. coccinea* may resemble some members of the genus *Salvia*, but one look at the flowers should distinguish it.

LANDSCAPE APPLICATION: This is an ideal plant for shaded areas and confined spaces such as narrow planters and walkways. Use it with other herbaceous flowering favorites that need summer watering like *Aquilegia chrysantha, Chrysactinia mexicana, Dalea frutescens, Poliomintha maderensis, Tetraneuris acaulis,* and *Zauschneria californica.* In the mid-elevation cities of Las Vegas and Tucson, *Stachys coccinea* thrives in the light shade of small trees such as *Acacia willardiana, Eysenhardtia orthocarpa, Havardia pallens,* and *Leucaena retusa.* It does great in full sun in the higher-elevation-zone cities and the cooler, coastal low-elevation cities. Plant to attract both butterflies and hummingbirds.

PRECAUTIONS: Pay attention to watering, especially if plants have little relief from the sun.

Stenocereus thurberi | Organ Pipe

CACTUS/SUCCULENT

SIZE (height x width)	6–8 feet x 3–4 feet
FLOWER COLOR	Reddish-purple
FLOWER SEASON	Spring–summer
EXPOSURE	Full or reflected sun
WATER	Drought-tolerant–low
GROWTH RATE	Slow
PRUNING	None
HARDINESS	Hardy to about mid-20s F
NATURAL ELEVATION RANGE	Near sea level–4,000 feet
SUITABLE CITIES	All low- and mid-elevation-zone cities; try in Austin and San Antonio, taking care to provide soil with good drainage

FIELD NOTES: *Stenocereus thurberi* is found on rocky hillsides and desert plains in extreme southwestern Arizona, throughout much of Sonora, and in Baja California, Mexico, from near sea level to 4,000 feet elevation. Organ Pipe Cactus National Monument in southern Arizona is an inspiring landscape that shows off this beauty and a multitude of other desert botanical icons.

DESCRIPTION: Ancient plants can achieve a height of 20 feet or more, clustering 10–12 feet across. In cultivation expect 6–8 feet tall by 3–4 feet across over a reasonable amount of time. Multiple stems can grow to 8 inches in diameter. The 3–4-inch-long reddish-purple, night-blooming flowers appear near the stem tips from April to July. Spiny, green fruits with bright red pulp inside follow the flowers in summer to fall.

CULTURE/MAINTENANCE: *S. thurberi* is hardy to about the mid-20s F; make sure to cover the tips when winter lows that cold are expected. It takes many years to attain a substantial size. Water use is low to drought-tolerant, but established plants will grow a bit faster with monthly irrigation from late spring through summer. Potted plants will need more frequent irrigation, usually once or twice weekly in summer. Plants grow best in full or reflected sun. The soil should be rocky and have good drainage. No pruning is needed unless you inherited one too close to a walk.

IDENTIFICATION: *S. thurberi* is a distinctive, multistemmed columnar cactus with reddish spines.

LANDSCAPE APPLICATION: Multi-stemmed organ pipe will be a star in a cactus and succulent garden in all low- and mid-elevation cities except possibly Austin and San Antonio where the summer rainfall might be too much. However, it is worth trying in a raised bed with other succulents. Mix it with other robust succulents such as *Agave, Dasylirion, Ferocactus,* and *Yucca* species. Add color and soften with flowering shrubs and perennials such as *Anisacanthus quadrifidus, Berlandiera lyrata, Buddleja marrubiifolia, Chrysactinia mexicana, Hibiscus martianus,* any *Penstemon* species, *Salvia greggii, Thymophylla pentachaeta,* or *Zinnia grandiflora.* Also plant it next to small trees such as *Acacia willardiana, Eysenhardtia orthocarpa, Havardia pallens,* and *Sophora secundiflora.*

PRECAUTIONS: Protect young plants from damage by rabbits and javelinas.

Tagetes lemmonii | Mountain Marigold

FLOWERING PERENNIAL, SMALL SHRUB	
SIZE (height x width)	2–3 feet x 2–3 feet
FLOWER COLOR	Golden yellow
FLOWER SEASON	Fall–spring
EXPOSURE	Full or filtered sun, or partial shade
WATER	Moderate
GROWTH RATE	Fast
PRUNING	Shear after flowering
HARDINESS	Half-hardy (root-hardy to the mid- or high-teens F)
NATURAL ELEVATION RANGE	2,600–8,000 feet
SUITABLE CITIES	All low- and mid-elevation-zone cities; should be tested in Sierra Vista and El Paso

FIELD NOTES: *Tagetes lemmonii* grows in rich soil in canyons and on slopes in Sonora, Chihuahua, and Sinaloa in Mexico and southeastern Arizona. It grows in oak and pine forests from 2,600 to 8,000 feet elevation. Plants I have spotted in the Santa Catalina Mountains near Tucson have been single-stemmed, while the cultivated ones are many-branched and much more robust.

DESCRIPTION: This aromatic perennial reaches a size of 3 feet tall by 3 feet across in one growing season. Severe pruning after flowering keeps it a more compact 2 by 2. The dark green leaves are divided into 7–9 thin leaflets that are pinnately arranged and tipped with oil glands. Stunning, yellow-gold, daisy-like flowers appear at the ends of stems in winter, spring, and fall.

CULTURE/MAINTENANCE: *T. lemmonii* is root-hardy to at least the high teens F. In the mid- and high-elevation desert areas the tops may freeze, but if the roots are mulched, the plant should regrow in the spring. Even if frozen back in the winter, it can still recover and produce a beautiful flower display in late spring. For best growth it should be placed in full or filtered sun and in a soil that has been amended with some organic matter. The soil does not have to be "vegetable garden" quality, but extra organic matter will increase water holding capacity. This perennial has a fast growth rate and can be sheared severely after the winter, spring, and fall flower displays wrap up.

IDENTIFICATION: Distinctive gland-tipped leaves and yellow daisy-like flowers readily identify mountain marigold.

LANDSCAPE APPLICATION: This versatile flowering perennial grows fine in full sun exposures of street medians and parking lot islands in the mid-elevation deserts. However, these exposures are bad news in the hot, interior, low-elevation deserts of Phoenix and Palm Desert. The flower display is spectacular when plants are massed together. It combines beautifully with large accents such as *Agave montana, Dasylirion acrotrichum,* or *Yucca rostrata.* Try planting it under the shade of *Eysenhardtia orthocarpa Havardia pallens,* or *Parkinsonia microphylla.*

PRECAUTIONS: Take care not to plant *T. lemmonii* in high-traffic areas or where skin might brush against the oil glands and foliage. On the other hand, bunnies leave this plant alone, possibly because of those irritating glands.

Tecoma stans | Yellow Bells

MEDIUM–LARGE SHRUB	
SIZE (height x width)	4–15 feet x 3–10 feet
FLOWER COLOR	Yellow
FLOWER SEASON	Late spring–fall, early winter in mild winter areas
EXPOSURE	Full or reflected sun
WATER	Low–moderate
GROWTH RATE	Fast
PRUNING	Prune out frozen stems in late winter or early spring
HARDINESS	Hardy to half-hardy, with damage occurring at high 20s F
NATURAL ELEVATION RANGE	Around 3,000 feet for cultivated stock
SUITABLE CITIES	All low- and mid-elevation-zone cities

FIELD NOTES: *Tecoma stans* is found on hillsides, sandy valleys, arroyos, and outwash slopes throughout much of Mexico south to tropical South America, and the West Indies. Nice examples can be seen nearly throughout Mexico, and I've seen particularly handsome plants in the mountains of Guanajuato and Querétaro in central Mexico. I've also seen fine specimens in the Tucson Mountains and in west Texas on the way to Big Bend. Plants grow near sea level in Baja California and as high as 9,500 feet in Bolivia. Typically, nursery stock is derived from plants growing closer to 3,000 feet in the United States.

DESCRIPTION: This evergreen shrub picks its size depending on where it lives. Typically it is taller (4–15 feet) than it is wide (3–10 feet). In Tucson, where it freezes quite a few times each winter, this plant may grow to 5–8 feet, while in Phoenix it might grow to 12–15 feet. Rich green leaves are pinnately divided into 5–13 leaflets, each about 1½–4 inches long and ¾–2 inches wide. Bright yellow, trumpet-shaped flowers are about 2 inches long and 2 inches wide. These blossoms form large clusters up to 6–8 inches long beginning as early as April and continuing through summer, fall, and into winter in mild areas. Frost will shorten the season from both ends. When it's all over, 6-inch-long, tan pods house small, papery winged seeds.

CULTURE/MAINTENANCE: Yellow bells suffers some minor frost damage when the temperatures drop into the high 20s F. Temperatures in the low 20s F inflict major damage and can even kill plants that aren't well established. Some frost damage can be beneficial, as new growth sprouts quickly in the spring, providing increased flower production. A plant that is hardened off in the fall will be hardier than one grown soft through the fall. Yellow bells has a fast growth rate and is moderately drought-tolerant once established. For best results, plant it in full or reflected sun, and in a soil with good drainage. Prune out the frost damage in late winter or early spring.

IDENTIFICATION: *Tecoma stans* var. *stans* comes from subtropical and tropical regions of the Americas, while *Tecoma stans* var. *angustata* is native to southern Arizona, Texas, and northern Mexico. Both are in cultivation. The variety *stans* has larger, lusher leaves and is less hardy than the narrower-leaved *angustata*. Both varieties are easily distinguished from *Tecoma garrocha, Tecoma arequipensis,* and *Tecoma* x 'Orange Jubilee' by the yellow flower color.

LANDSCAPE APPLICATION: The subtropical appearance created by the lush foliage and showy flowers makes yellow bells a natural for patio or poolside. It works alone as a colorful accent, or massed for a knockout flower display. Because the flowers attract hummingbirds, yellow bells makes a great addition to a bird garden. Use it with large accent plants such as *Dasylirion, Nolina,* and *Yucca* species that will carry an area through the winter if yellow bells is frozen back.

PRECAUTIONS: *T. stans* is not susceptible to any insect pests or fungal diseases. It is frost-sensitive and may be browsed by wildlife, but it is generally regarded as a low-maintenance species.

Tecoma x 'Orange Jubilee' | Orange Jubilee Tecoma

LARGE SHRUB, SMALL TREE	
SIZE (height x width)	12 feet x 8 feet
FLOWER COLOR	Orange-red
FLOWER SEASON	Spring–fall
EXPOSURE	Full or reflected sun
WATER	Moderate
GROWTH RATE	Fast
PRUNING	Cut back in late winter or early spring
HARDINESS	Hardy to half-hardy, with damage occurring at mid to high 20s F
SUITABLE CITIES	All low- and mid-elevation-zone cities

FIELD NOTES: *Tecoma* x 'Orange Jubilee' is thought to be a hybrid of *Tecoma stans* and an unknown *Tecoma* species.

DESCRIPTION: This upright shrub grows to 12 feet tall and 8 feet across if not frozen back for a couple of winters. Full, rich, green foliage gives this plant a subtropical appearance. Pinnately compound leaves are about 6 inches by 4 inches wide and form 9–11 leaflets, with each leaflet about 1½–2 inches long. Clusters of 2½-inch-long, orange-red, trumpet-shaped flowers appear at the tips of the stems from spring through fall and even through the winter if it is mild enough. The lobes are large and showy but folded back over the tube, darker red-orange near the base, and more orange near the mouth. The yellowish flower interior comes with orange guidelines to direct pollinators, especially hummingbirds, to the nectar. This clone also seems to produce very few seedpods.

CULTURE/MAINTENANCE: This shrub is hardy in the low-elevation zone but is considered half-hardy in the mid-elevation zone. It may lose some foliage when the temperatures drop into the mid-20s F or go completely deciduous and even freeze back with low 20s F. No worry—it bounces back to 5–7 feet in a season. It survives on minimal supplemental water during the summer. However, it will thank you in flowers when watered somewhat regularly from spring until fall. It prefers full or reflected sun and can be grown in a variety of soil types. A plant in rocky, native soil tends to be more tolerant of inconsistent watering than one in a rich, highly amended soil. Cut back frost-damaged plants in the late winter or early spring.

IDENTIFICATION: The flowers easily identify *Tecoma* x 'Orange Jubilee.' Currently there are four other species of *Tecoma* in cultivation. *T. stans* has large yellow flowers, and *T. garrocha* has salmon or orangish flowers but is distinguished by its leaves, which are longer and narrower. *T. arequipensis* is another species with orangish flowers, but it has much smaller leaves and reddish stems. *T.* (*Tecomaria*) *capensis* has orange-red flowers that are similar to the flowers of 'Orange Jubilee,' but it has a more sprawling form and small, dark green leaves.

LANDSCAPE APPLICATION: Place 'Orange Jubilee' against a large blank wall either singly or grouped to show off its rich green foliage and brilliant flower display. Mix with colorful ground covers and shrubs such as *Encelia farinosa*, *Lantana montevidensis* and *Lantana* x 'New Gold' for near year-round garden activity. Nestle it against large accent plants like *Yucca* species. Use in wide street medians or entryways to shopping malls or parking lots. The lush, tropical appearance fits in with a variety of landscape themes.

PRECAUTIONS: Rabbits may find their way to young plants but usually leave older, less tender plants alone. The dreaded tomato hornworm caterpillars will eat the leaves, and I've seen them nearly defoliate a young plant.

Tetraneuris acaulis | Synonym: *Hymenoxys acaulis* | Angelita Daisy

FLOWERING PERENNIAL, SMALL SHRUB	
SIZE (height x width)	4–6 inches (10–14 inches with flowers x 8–12 inches
FLOWER COLOR	Golden yellow
FLOWER SEASON	Nearly all year, heaviest bloom in spring
EXPOSURE	Full sun
WATER	Low–moderate
GROWTH RATE	Fast
PRUNING	Deadhead old flowers
HARDINESS	Hardy to at least 5° F
NATURAL ELEVATION RANGE	4,000–7,000 feet
SUITABLE CITIES	All cities in all zones

FIELD NOTES: Home for *Tetraneuris acaulis* is limestone soil on bluffs, slopes, and roadsides all over the West from Canada to Texas. In Arizona, plants are found between 4,000 and 7,000 feet elevation.

DESCRIPTION: This perennial can also be considered a small shrub, with a basal cluster of leaves. It stays short, about 4–6 inches tall, and spreads to 8–12 inches across. Flowers perch on 6–8-inch-tall, leafless stems. The bright green foliage is very narrow and about 1½–2 inches long. Golden yellow flowers open at the ends of the naked stems and are a 1-inch-diameter version of the typical daisy. Plants will bloom primarily in spring, frequently attracting butterflies.

CULTURE/MAINTENANCE: *T. acaulis* is hardy to at least 5° F and probably lower. While the species is widespread throughout the Southwest and grows at elevations as high as 7,000 feet, the plants being offered by Mountain States Wholesale Nursery were collected in western Texas and selected for their tolerance of blazing heat. This species handles most desert soils as long as drainage is adequate. These fast-growing plants grow best in full sun. They use low to moderate amounts of water but

will perk up with some supplemental water during the spring and summer months. Deadhead the old, tired flowers to encourage repeated and prolonged flowering.

IDENTIFICATION: The form is reminiscent of *Baileya multiradiata* but is easily distinguished by its brighter green foliage and more golden flower color.

LANDSCAPE APPLICATION: This is a perfect little specimen for full sun in any desert landscape in all elevation zone cities. Place it in open spaces with ample sunlight. It is small enough to fit in narrow spaces and does nicely in raised planters. Mass plant for a fantastic flower display, or try it as a border for larger shrubs such as *Dalea frutescens, Leucophyllum* species, and *Ruellia peninsularis.* Plant it at the base of large accent plants such as *Agave, Dasylirion, Hesperaloe,* or *Yucca* species or mix with smaller cacti and succulents.

PRECAUTIONS: No insect pests are known for this perennial, but bunnies love the tasty plants.

Thymophylla pentachaeta | Synonym: *Dyssodia pentachaeta*
Golden Dogweed

FLOWERING PERENNIAL

SIZE (height x width)	8–12 inches x 10–24 inches
FLOWER COLOR	Yellow
FLOWER SEASON	Spring–fall
EXPOSURE	Sun
WATER	Low–moderate
GROWTH RATE	Fast
PRUNING	None or shear in late winter or early spring every 2–3 years
HARDINESS	Hardy to at least 15° F
NATURAL ELEVATION RANGE	2,100–5,000 feet
SUITABLE CITIES	All cities in all zones

FIELD NOTES: You can spot cheerful *Thymophylla pentachaeta* along back roads in Texas west to southern Nevada and southern California, south through Arizona and into northern Mexico. When not hanging out along highways, it inhabits dry slopes and mesas from 2,100–5,000 feet.

DESCRIPTION: This short-lived perennial splashes color around any low-water-use landscape. It forms a mound, 8–12 inches tall by 10–24 inches across, of small dark green to dusty green leaves. Needlelike leaflets give the plant a very fine texture. Yellow flowers with ½-inch-diameter heads top plants from spring through fall and attract butterflies.

CULTURE/MAINTENANCE: This plant withstands overnight lows down into the teens F without damage. In order to get the maximum flower production and to keep the plants dense, grow it in full sun. Plants are low- to moderate-water-using and will tolerate a variety of soil types as long as the supplemental watering is adjusted accordingly. Encourage more flowers by deadheading the spent blooms, and cut back severely once a year to increase density. Short-lived *T. pentachaeta* will probably need to be replaced in your garden unless it reseeds on its own.

IDENTIFICATION: Small leaves with needlelike leaflets readily distinguish *T. pentachaeta* from other yellow-flowered perennials.

LANDSCAPE APPLICATION: Massed in the landscape, this makes a great little filler plant or informal ground cover in all elevation zones. It provides exceptional seasonal color in a young, low-water-use landscape. Plant it among more permanent accents like *Agave, Dasylirion, Hesperaloe, Nolina,* and *Yucca* species. Try using it around small trees like *Acacia willardiana, Bauhinia lunarioides, Eysenhardtia orthocarpa, Leucaena retusa,* and *Sophora secundiflora* for its incredible seasonal color.

PRECAUTIONS: There are no known insect pests or disease problems.

Vauquelinia californica | Arizona Rosewood

LARGE SHRUB, SMALL TREE

SIZE (height x width)	10–20 feet x 8–16 feet
FLOWER COLOR	White
FLOWER SEASON	Late spring–early summer
EXPOSURE	Full or reflected sun, north side of a building or wall

WATER	Low–moderate (deep watering 1–2 times a month in winter and 2–4 times a month in summer)
GROWTH RATE	Moderately slow
PRUNING	None or train as a tree
HARDINESS	Hardy to -10° F
NATURAL ELEVATION RANGE	2,500–7,000 feet
SUITABLE CITIES	All cities in all zones

FIELD NOTES: *Vauquelinia californica* inhabits canyons and rocky slopes at elevations between 2,500 and 5,000 feet in Arizona and up to 7,000 feet further south in Durango, Mexico. It can be found growing with mesquite, oak, juniper, and even pine trees in southern Arizona, southwestern New Mexico, Baja California, and northern Mexico. This distinctive, evergreen shrub is easily spotted near Molino Basin on the drive up Mt. Lemmon in the Santa Catalina Mountains near Tucson.

DESCRIPTION: This large, evergreen shrub typically reaches 10–20 feet tall by 8–16 feet across. Dark green, stiff, leathery leaves are 2–3 inches long, about ½ inch wide, and edged with small, closely set teeth like those on a saw blade. Showy, 3-inch-wide clusters of small, white flowers appear at the ends of the stems in late spring and early summer and draw in the butterflies. Brown or reddish-brown, woody fruit capsules hang on the plant well into winter. The common name comes from the red to deep brown color of the heartwood.

CULTURE/MAINTENANCE: Though an established plant is hardy to -10° F, Arizona rosewood appreciates a warm spot in the coldest parts of the Southwest. Water use is low to moderate, with the plants responding to a thorough soaking once every 7–14

days during the summer. The moderately slow growth rate means it will take several years to stretch to 10 feet. Give it full sun, soil with good drainage, and plenty of room. It is generally grown as a large shrub, but some gardeners out there make it their mission to train it as an upright tree with an ovoid crown. When the plant is young, select one or more upright shoots to serve as the trunk. Keep some lower side shoots that capture energy to feed the trunk. When the trunk is sturdy enough to support the top, trim those side shoots off.

IDENTIFICATION: Leathery, dark green leaves with coarsely serrated edges easily identify *V. californica*. Occasionally *Vauquelinia corymbosa* var. *angustifolia* and *Vauquelinia corymbosa* var. *heterodon* are grown in the trade. Both of these can be distinguished from *V. californica* by their more sharply serrated leaf edges.

LANDSCAPE APPLICATION: When grown as a large shrub, this plant can be grouped as a tall, unclipped hedge or screen, a space divider, wind or dust block, or noise barrier. Place it only in full or reflected sun. Either as a shrub or small tree, it makes a wonderful evergreen specimen that fits well in most any Southwestern landscape. Being evergreen and not messy, it is an easy choice for pool areas. It is compatible with all forms of desert-adapted plants including *Acacia* species, *Bauhinia lunarioides*, *Chrysactinia mexicana*, *Dodonaea viscosa*, *Poliomintha maderensis*, *Prosopis velutina*, *Quercus* species, *Rhus choriophylla*, *Simmondsia chinensis*, and various *Yucca* species. When planning the placement, make sure there is ample room for development because, in time, the plant can get up to 16 feet across.

PRECAUTIONS: Red spider mites and aphids can attack. They can be controlled with an insecticidal soap if the infestation is not too bad. If the situation is more dire, any chemical that controls mites or aphids will work.

Verbena gooddingii | Desert Verbena

FLOWERING PERENNIAL	
SIZE (height x width)	1 foot x 2 feet
FLOWER COLOR	Lavender-blue
FLOWER SEASON	Spring–fall
EXPOSURE	Full sun
WATER	Low
GROWTH RATE	Fast
HARDINESS	Hardy to at least 5° F
PRUNING	Occasional shearing
NATURAL ELEVATION RANGE	1,000–6,100
SUITABLE CITIES	All cities in all zones

FIELD NOTES: *Verbena gooddingii* is a reassuring sight on springtime hikes in the Sonoran Desert, because it will bloom even with a mediocre winter rainy season.

Plants pop up in sandy washes, on dry rocky slopes, and along roadsides throughout much of the southwestern United States from 1,000 to 6,100 feet. The two d's are not a typo—Leslie Goodding was a botanist with the U.S. Conservation Service in Arizona from 1918 to 1944.

DESCRIPTION: In spring, an abundance of lavender-blue, butterfly-attracting flowers carpet the dull green vegetation of this low-growing perennial. It forms a compact, hemispherical mound 18–24 inches tall by 24–30 inches across. The blossoms are dearly loved by butterflies; they appear in spring, early summer, and sometimes fall if given supplemental water. The deeply lobed, sometimes three-parted leaves measure 1–2 inches long by 1 inch wide.

CULTURE/MAINTENANCE: Desert verbena is a winter-hardy species, tolerating temperature as low as 5° F. It is programmed to dodge the summer heat by going dormant. However, it will continue to grow and flower through the summer with periodic supplemental water. It behaves well in full sun and a fast-draining soil, and it can zoom to full size in a year. A plant that you water may ask for occasional pruning to generate new growth while a plant grown on rainfall alone should be sheared hard just prior to resumption of new growth. The best planting time is in the fall.

IDENTIFICATION: *V. gooddingii* is identifiable by its lavender-blue flowers and semishrubby habit. Drab, lightly fuzzy leaves and paler flowers distinguish it from non-natives in the landscaping trade.

LANDSCAPE APPLICATION: This reliable perennial works well in the transition and outer zones of a xeriscape. Its color scheme nicely offsets other perennial wildflowers such as *Baileya multiradiata*, *Melampodium leucanthum*, *Penstemon* species, and *Thymophylla pentachaeta*. It also brings perfect colors and texture to the mix when combined with accent plants such as *Agave parryi* var. *truncata*, *Agave vilmoriniana*, *Carnegiea gigantea*, *Dasylirion quadrangulatum*, *Dasylirion wheeleri*, *Ferocactus* species, *Yucca rigida*, and *Y. rostrata*. It dresses up large shrubs such as *Larrea divaricata* and *Simmondsia chinensis*.

PRECAUTIONS: Expect recent plantees to be susceptible to damage by rabbits, but as they become established and even naturalized, they lose their culinary appeal. Desert verbena tends to be short-lived but is in the habit of reseeding. Overwatering can rot roots.

Wedelia acapulcensis var. *hispida* | Synonyms: *Wedelia hispida,* *Zexmenia hispida* | Rough Zexmenia

FLOWERING PERENNIAL, SMALL SHRUB

SIZE (height x width)	2–3 feet x 2–3 feet
FLOWER COLOR	Orange-yellow
FLOWER SEASON	Spring–fall
EXPOSURE	Full or reflected sun
WATER	Low–ample
GROWTH RATE	Fast
PRUNING	Late winter or early spring, midsummer
HARDINESS	Half-hardy (low 20s F); root-hardy to at least 10° F
NATURAL ELEVATION RANGE	1,400–1,500 feet
SUITABLE CITIES	All low- and mid-elevation-zone cities; Sierra Vista in high-elevation zone

FIELD NOTES: *Wedelia acapulcensis* var. *hispida* grows throughout much of central and west-central Texas and northeastern Mexico at around 1,400–1,500 feet elevation.

DESCRIPTION: *W. acapulcensis* var. *hispida* (sometimes sold as *Wedelia hispida* or *Zexmenia hispida,* an argument that has been going on since the late 1880s) is a half-hardy, compact, shrubby plant. It is best treated like a perennial and cut to nearly ground level in late winter. Dark green leaves are about 2 inches long and ¾ inch wide and roughly pubescent, and they feel like sandpaper. Orange-yellow, 2-inch-diameter, daisy-like flowers appear from spring through fall on long, naked stalks that rise above the plant. Watch for butterflies flitting about the blossoms.

CULTURE/MAINTENANCE: The foliage takes a hit when temperatures fall to the low 20s F, but the plant grows back rapidly as soon as the weather warms up. It is root-hardy, having recovered from a low of 8° F in El Paso. Even in the hot low deserts, it can look scruffy in the winter, so severe pruning in early spring is recommended. Plant it in full sun and thoroughly soak the root zone once every 7–10 days in the mid and low-elevation, interior regions to keep it blooming from spring through fall. A little less water is needed in areas with cooler summers, and this plant has actually survived 10 days midsummer without watering after having been in the ground only 3 months. If planted in shade, it tends to sprawl out and flower less profusely. It grows to 3 feet tall and 3 feet wide in only one season, and it will tolerate all soil types. In addition to spring pruning, snip periodically during the growing season to boost flower production.

IDENTIFICATION: Dark green, sandpapery leaves and orange-yellow "daisy-like" flowers make this species easily recognizable. Its form somewhat resembles *Viguiera deltoidea,* but its leaves are a deeper green. Also, its blossoms are more orange than the light yellow flowers of *V. deltoidea.*

LANDSCAPE APPLICATION: Add color to any desert garden with rough zexmenia. Try mass planting in open spaces, or clustering it at the base of tall accent plants such as *Nolina nelsonii* or *Yucca* species. Hide the scruffy winter appearance behind evergreen shrubs and cut plants to nearly ground level to rejuvenate and clean them

up. Plants tolerate hot, exposed locations and work well in streetscapes if cut back once a year in late winter.

PRECAUTIONS: In spite of its rough foliage, rough zexmenia is susceptible to rabbit damage. Fertilizing it will cause unusually fast and weak growth.

Yucca elata | Soaptree Yucca

CACTUS/SUCCULENT	
SIZE (height x width)	8–15 feet x 5–10 feet
FLOWER COLOR	White
FLOWER SEASON	Summer
EXPOSURE	Full sun
WATER	Low
GROWTH RATE	Slow
PRUNING	None
HARDINESS	Hardy to 0° F
NATURAL ELEVATION RANGE	1,500–6,000 feet
SUITABLE CITIES	All cities in all zones

FIELD NOTES: *Yucca elata* can be found in southern Utah, Arizona, New Mexico, western Texas, and adjacent Mexico between 1,500 and 6,000 feet elevation. It is widespread and abundant in grassland vegetation on flats, plains, and hills. In my travels around the Southwest, I see soaptree yucca as a sure sign I'm not in the Sonoran Desert proper anymore. A particularly robust stand occurs along Interstate 10 in southern New Mexico between Deming and Lordsburg.

DESCRIPTION: The bold, striking form adds drama to any low-water-use landscape. The 10–15-foot-tall, showy flower stalk is an added visual treat in the summer and will serve as a perch for all kinds of birds. A specimen that grows a trunk 8–15 feet tall with 2–5 branches occupies a big, 5–10-foot diameter footprint. Dense clusters of narrow leaves shoot out from the branches and form a nearly spherical outline. Pale green leaves are usually about 1–2 feet long (rarely 3 feet) and about ½ inch wide with a white margin that peels off into thin, curly fibers. White, waxy 2-inch-long flowers briefly decorate the upper ⅓ of the stalk.

CULTURE/MAINTENANCE: These genuine tough guys are hardy to at least 0° F. They are very drought-tolerant once established and look great after two months or more in summer without supplemental water. They grow best in full sun or reflected sun and in native soil. This slow-growing plant should be purchased in a 5-gallon container at the smallest. Growth rate will increase a little with supplemental water. Plants are virtually maintenance-free unless you live where they are native and have to discourage new ones popping up in the wrong places. Bare-root specimens are difficult to reestablish and should be avoided.

IDENTIFICATION: *Y. elata* is easily identified by the very narrow leaves with many fine threads along the edges.

LANDSCAPE APPLICATION: *Y. elata* is an excellent accent plant for the transition and outer zones of a xeriscape. Try mixing it with other bold accents such as *Agave, Dasylirion,* and other *Yucca* species. Some great partner trees and shrubs include *Acacia constricta, Aloysia gratissima, Anisacanthus thurberi, Dalea frutescens* 'Sierra Negra,' *Leucophyllum* species, *Simmondsia chinensis,* and *Vauquelinia californica.*

PRECAUTIONS: Leave the skirt of old leaves that protect the trunk from sunburn and cold. Keep the sharp leaf tips away from high-traffic areas.

Yucca faxoniana | Including *Y. carnerosana* | Spanish Bayonet

CACTUS/SUCCULENT	
SIZE (height x width)	>10 feet x 4–5 feet
FLOWER COLOR	White
FLOWER SEASON	Summer
EXPOSURE	Full sun
WATER	Low
GROWTH RATE	Slow
PRUNING	None or remove lower leaves
HARDINESS	Hardy to at least 10° F
NATURAL ELEVATION RANGE	1,650–7,200 feet
SUITABLE CITIES	All cities in all zones

FIELD NOTES: *Yucca faxoniana,* with its stout, unforgiving leaves, is one of the most lethal plants you can run into while out hiking on rocky slopes, ridges, and bajadas in west central to western Texas or northeastern Mexico. No wonder "bayonet" is part of its common name. But the dominating form of a mature *Y. faxoniana* is a remarkable sight. It is generally associated with Chihuahuan Desert scrub, grassland, and oak-pinyon-juniper vegetation from 1,650 to 7,200 feet elevation. There is a spot as you are driving south on Mexico Highway 57 between Saltillo and Matehuala where you crest a low rise, and as you come down the other side, a large, broad valley opens up where there are thousands of *Yuccas* standing watch over the terrain like soldiers protecting their homeland.

DESCRIPTION: This impressive arborescent species grows to 10–15 feet tall with a leaf crown about 4–5 feet across. It has huge, stout leaves and generally a single thick trunk, but very rarely there might be as many as eight trunks forming a dense clump up to 10 feet in diameter. The heads are packed with 2-foot-long, 2–3-inch-wide leaves and measure up to 4 or 5 feet in diameter. A 4-foot-long panicle of white, 3–4-inch-long flowers will appear in spring and early summer. Most of the panicle rises visibly above the leaf crown and produces a spectacular flower display.

CULTURE/MAINTENANCE: *Y. faxoniana* can tolerate temperature extremes from winter lows of at least 10° F to summer highs of over 115° F. It is drought-tolerant, surviving on about 11 inches of annual rainfall. It will grow a little faster if given supplemental water from late spring until late summer. Water it about every 14–21 days—any more frequently than that could cause rot. The growth rate is slow, and large container specimens are best for their initial impact. Place this species in full sun for best appearance and health. It is virtually maintenance-free but make sure you give it a lot of space.

IDENTIFICATION: Large, stout leaves readily identify *Y. faxoniana*.

LANDSCAPE APPLICATION: Use massive *Y. faxoniana* as a bold focal point of a desert landscape. It is probably a poor choice for a small-scale patio garden. Use plants with a variety of shapes and flower colors as companions, such as *Buddleja marrubiifolia, Cordia parvifolia, Dasylirion wheeleri, Ferocactus pilosus, Leucophyllum* species*, Opuntia phaeacantha, Rhus choriophylla, Salvia greggii,* and *Sophora secundiflora.*

PRECAUTIONS: Do not plant *Y. faxoniana* in any shade. Also, water infrequently and from below the leaf crown. Shade and overhead water can combine to rot the leaf crown, thereby killing the plant.

Yucca filifera | Palma China

CACTUS/SUCCULENT	
SIZE (height x width)	15 (rarely 20–40) feet x 8 feet
FLOWER COLOR	White
FLOWER SEASON	Summer
EXPOSURE	Full sun
WATER	Drought-tolerant–low
GROWTH RATE	Slow–moderate
PRUNING	Trim the leaf terminal spine if near a high-traffic area
HARDINESS	Hardy to at least 15° F
NATURAL ELEVATION RANGE	1,450–7,900 feet
SUITABLE CITIES	All cities in all zones

FIELD NOTES: The monstrous, arborescent *Yucca filifera* is a dominant plant on flat, open plains from north-central to south-central Mexico. It inhabits Chihuahuan Desert scrub, grassland, thorn scrub, and pinyon-oak-juniper vegetation between 1,450 and 7,900 feet elevation. Annual rainfall varies from 12–25 inches in these areas. Massive specimens are easily spotted in Mexico on the drive from Saltillo south to San Luis Potosí.

DESCRIPTION: Young or old, these yuccas are attractive. Sturdy young plants display densely packed, dark green leaves. It may take your lifetime for the plant to tower above the rest of your landscape, but it will eventually grow to about 40 feet tall with the crown spreading to about 25 feet in diameter, so allow ample room for full development even if you won't be there to see it. It is satisfied with a single thick trunk and puts out dozens of branches to form a large "tree," perhaps 15–20 feet of height with a few branches to form a small crown. The massive trunk can reach 6 feet across and is covered with rough bark. Leaves are nearly 2 feet long and about 2 inches wide with a wicked tip. The species name *filifera* is derived from the white threads along the edges. Flower stalks grow to about 5 feet long, and the fruit clusters hang down.

CULTURE/MAINTENANCE: This species is hardy to at least 15° F and probably lower. It is drought-tolerant but will grow faster as a young plant if given consistent supplemental water throughout the summer. It should be planted in full sun and in a soil with good drainage. In really well-drained soil, you might run the hose as often as once a week in the summer growing season. The plant is virtually maintenance-free, although from experience I won't be shy about recommending you trim the sharp leaf tips off until the plant is above head height.

IDENTIFICATION: *Y. filifera* is easily distinguished from several other species by its stiff, green leaves with marginal threads. Both *Y. filifera* and *Y. decipiens* develop into huge, 30–40-foot-tall, treelike specimens distinguished only by *Y. filifera*'s drooping inflorescence.

LANDSCAPE APPLICATION: Press *Y. filifera* into service as a bold, dramatic focal point in any landscape. Consider using it as a solitary specimen or grouped to create a small forest. Provide ample room if you go for the convention effect. This yucca can be used as the backbone for many perennials, ground covers, shrubs, and even small trees, such as *Ageratum corymbosum, Anisacanthus quadrifidus* var. *wrightii, Bauhinia lunarioides, Buddleja marrubiifolia, Dalea capitata, D. frutescens, Dasylirion acrotriche, D. quadrangulatum, Eysenhardtia orthocarpa, Fraxinus greggii, Larrea divaricata, Leucaena retusa,* all *Leucophyllum* species, *Rhus choriophylla,* and *Wedelia acapulcensis* var. *hispida.*

PRECAUTIONS: There are no known insect pests or diseases. Remember the very sharp leaf tips can be lethal, so ample room is necessary to eliminate potential accidents.

Yucca pallida | Pale Leaf Yucca

CACTUS/SUCCULENT

SIZE (height x width)	1–3 feet x 2–3 feet
FLOWER COLOR	White
FLOWER SEASON	Summer
EXPOSURE	Full or reflected sun, or light shade
WATER	Drought-tolerant–moderate
GROWTH RATE	Moderately slow
PRUNING	None or remove spent flower stalks
HARDINESS	Hardy to at least -10° F
NATURAL ELEVATION RANGE	600–1,000 feet
SUITABLE CITIES	All cities in all zones

FIELD NOTES: *Yucca pallida* is found only in the blackland prairies of northern and central Texas. This plant is easily overlooked, even when in flower. The surrounding vegetation usually overshadows it, but if you are traveling the back roads from Dallas south to Waco, Texas, during late spring or early summer, and look at the right time, you should be able to spot the flower stalks poking out.

DESCRIPTION: This stemless yucca will develop up to 30 heads and form a cluster to about 1–3 feet tall and 2–3 feet across. The flexible, strikingly beautiful powder blue leaves are 8–12 inches long by 1–2 inches wide with a thin yellow margin and fine striations. In late spring and summer, a 3–7-foot-tall inflorescence covered with white, 2-inch-long-flowers rises above the leaves.

CULTURE/MAINTENANCE: Pale leaf yucca makes it through

winter lows down to -10° F without damage. The plant is low-water-using with a moderately slow growth rate; however, it will grow faster when given consistent, thorough watering through the summer months. It prefers soil with good drainage and full sun or, in the low desert, very light shade. It takes patience to watch it reach its full size.

IDENTIFICATION: The combination of the stemless habit and powder blue leaves readily distinguish *Y. pallida* from other *Yucca* species.

LANDSCAPE APPLICATION: *Y. pallida* makes a great potted patio plant. Mix it in with small shrubs and perennials and use the spiky form as a contrast to softer, more rounded forms. Mass plant for an incredible summer flower display while using smaller perennials in a supporting role. Tuck plants around small trees for the contrasting forms and textures. Some plants that work well with this yucca include: *Ageratum corymbosum, Baileya multiradiata, Conoclinium dissectum, Dalea capitata, Eysenhardtia orthocarpa, Penstemon* species, *Salvia greggii, Sophora secundiflora,* and *Wedelia acapulcensis* var. *hispida.*

PRECAUTIONS: There are no reported problems.

Yucca rigida | Blue Yucca

CACTUS/SUCCULENT

SIZE (height x width)	12 feet x 8 feet
FLOWER COLOR	Creamy white
FLOWER SEASON	Spring
EXPOSURE	Full or reflected sun
WATER	Drought-tolerant–low
GROWTH RATE	Moderate
PRUNING	None
HARDINESS	Hardy to at least 5° F
NATURAL ELEVATION RANGE	3,900–5,900 feet
SUITABLE CITIES	All cities in all zones

FIELD NOTES: I first encountered the striking powder blue leaves of *Yucca rigida* in 1986 while with plant-explorer buddy Ron Gass. Between Torreón and the famous Cuatrocienegas region of central Coahuila we found it on rocky, gravelly soil on the slopes and hills, poking its head above the thick stands of *Larrea divaricata.* This *Yucca* grows in much of the central part of the Chihuahuan Desert region in the states of Chihuahua, Coahuila, and Durango in Mexico around 3,900–5,900 feet elevation.

DESCRIPTION: This trunk-forming species grows to 12 feet tall and can have a spread of 8 feet. These attractive plants will branch after flowering and usually develop at least 3–5 branches. One-inch-wide leaves have a narrow yellow margin and very sharp tips, and their blue hue stands out against more traditional green neighboring plants. Rigid leaves stretch to 3 feet long and should be given a wide berth in the garden. Showy panicles of white flowers appear above the leaves during summer but not necessarily every year. Dead leaves refuse to drop off the trunk and give the plant a "shaggy" look that actually blends in nicely with a desert landscape.

CULTURE/MAINTENANCE: Blue yucca is cold-hardy down to at least 5° F. It is low-water-using and quite drought-tolerant once established. It is best grown in full or reflected sun. In habitat, it grows in rocky, desert soils; plant it where drainage is decent. The moderate growth rate can be increased by supplying supplemental water from spring through summer. However, the plant behaves badly if you overwater, especially during the winter.

IDENTIFICATION: *Y. rigida* is not easily confused with any other yucca except *Y. rostrata*. At maturity, *Y. rigida* has longer, wider, and stiffer leaves than *Y. rostrata*.

LANDSCAPE APPLICATION: Use this yucca as a focal point in the landscape. Try it either singly with smaller shrubs and ground covers or massed for an absolutely striking effect. Some good companions include *Ageratum corymbosum, Anisacanthus quadrifidus* var. *wrightii, Baileya multiradiata, Conoclinium dissectum, Dalea capitata, D. frutescens, D. greggii, Larrea divaricata, Leucophyllum* species, *Penstemon* species, *Salvia greggii, Sophora secundiflora,* and *Wedelia acapulcensis* var. *hispida*.

PRECAUTIONS: Choose the planting location carefully. Allow ample room for the leaf crown to develop where it won't attack pedestrians in high-traffic areas. As with other *Yucca* species, roots may be eaten by beetle larvae, so pretreatment is an option.

Yucca rostrata | Beaked Yucca

CACTUS/SUCCULENT	
SIZE (height x width)	> 10 feet x 3 feet
FLOWER COLOR	Creamy white
FLOWER SEASON	Late spring–summer
EXPOSURE	Full sun or very light shade
WATER	Drought-tolerant
GROWTH RATE	Moderate
PRUNING	None
HARDINESS	Hardy to at least 5° F
NATURAL ELEVATION RANGE	1,000–4,500 feet
SUITABLE CITIES	All cities in all zones

FIELD NOTES: *Yucca rostrata* is easily spotted standing tall among the shrubs on dry rocky hills and slopes in Chihuahua and Coahuila in northern Mexico. The most beautiful specimens I've seen were on the road between Laredo, Texas, and Monterrey, Mexico. The flexible, powder blue leaves and oversize stalks of white flowers were a sight to behold! This plant grows in west Texas, south into northeastern Mexico from about 1,000 to 4,500 feet elevation.

DESCRIPTION: The trunk gets 10–12 feet tall while the leaves spread 2–4 feet. The plant is unbranched when young, and an older plant may have 2–5 branches near its top. The plant, at least in the wild, tends to have a tall, narrow form without much bulk. Powder blue leaves and a long, lean figure provide sculptural qualities that spice up any landscape. Leaves grow to 2 feet long and ½ inch wide with a thin yellow edge. The spectacular flower display is an added bonus when the plants get older. The 3–5-foot-tall, branched stalk sprouts in late spring and summer, rises up above the crown of leaves, and sports clusters of pure white, 2-inch-long flowers. The common name is derived from the beak-like extension found on the seed capsules. These plants do not set seed in cultivation, so you could travel to Big Bend National Park in Texas to witness that characteristic.

CULTURE/MAINTENANCE: This easygoing plant is hardy to at least 5° F and possibly lower. It will tolerate very light shade but attains its best form in full or reflected sun. It handles most desert soils but seems to do a little better in a rocky, well-drained soil without supplemental organic matter. The moderate growth rate will speed up slightly with extra water from spring through early fall. No maintenance is required except to treat 2–3 times a year for grubs that may attack the roots.

IDENTIFICATION: *Y. rostrata* is similar to *Y. rigida* but is distinguished by its shorter, more flexible, narrow leaves. At maturity, *Y. rostrata* is taller and narrower with less bulk relative to its height. *Y. rigida* is shorter, with a broader, bulkier crown.

LANDSCAPE APPLICATION: Use *Y. rostrata* to draw attention to the transition or outer zones of a xeriscape. It gets along nicely with desert perennials and small to medium-size shrubs. It can be used either singly or mass planted depending on the amount of space available. Smart companions include *Ageratum corymbosum, Anisacanthus quadrifidus* var. *wrightii, Baileya multiradiata, Cordia parvifolia, Dalea capitata, D. frutescens, D. greggii, Gaura lindheimeri, Larrea divaricata, Leucophyllum* species, *Penstemon* species, *Salvia greggii, Vauquelinia californica, Verbena gooddingii, Wedelia acapulcensis* var. *hispida,* and *Zephyranthes* species.

PRECAUTIONS: As with other *Yucca* species, the grub of a desert beetle may find roots delicious, and preventive maintenance is a good idea. Watch for leaf tip dieback that affects growth and overall health. The cause is still not known, but the problem may be due to overwatering or excessive summer heat.

Yucca rupicola | Twisted Leaf Yucca

CACTUS/SUCCULENT	
SIZE (height x width)	2 feet x 2–3 feet
FLOWER COLOR	White
FLOWER SEASON	Late spring–summer
EXPOSURE	Full or reflected sun, or light shade
WATER	Drought-tolerant–low
GROWTH RATE	Slow
PRUNING	None or remove spent flower stalks
HARDINESS	Hardy to at least -10° F
NATURAL ELEVATION RANGE	600–3,000 feet
HARDY IN THESE CITIES	All cities in all zones

FIELD NOTES: *Yucca rupicola* is found only on rocky limestone ledges, grass-covered plains, and open woodlands in west-central Texas, from 600 to 3,000 feet elevation. In fact, the species name *rupicola* means "dweller of rocky places." I recall stopping along Interstate 10 between Fredericksburg and Ozona, Texas, and checking out

some of these plants on the return trip from northeastern Mexico in 1989. However, my most vivid memory of that place is of spotting a rattlesnake curled up on a low ledge while we moseyed over to an area that appeared to hold some interesting plants.

DESCRIPTION: This diminutive, stemless yucca is great for small areas. Plants will produce offsets and form clusters of 10–15 rosettes, with the whole cluster reaching 1–2 feet tall and 2–3 feet across. Undulating or twisting leaves have a thin, reddish-brown or yellow margin and, on mature plants, can get 12–24 inches long by nearly 1½ inches wide. In late spring and summer, the 5-foot-tall, branched inflorescence emerges and is covered with bell-shaped, 2–3-inch-long flowers. With its bright green leaves and short stalks of creamy white flowers, this little beauty makes a statement planted among boulders and spring perennials or even sitting in a large container.

CULTURE/MAINTENANCE: *Y. rupicola* is blasé about cold and survives winter lows down to -10° F without damage. It is low- to moderate-water-using and slow-growing. However, it will perk up noticeably when thoroughly watered every 1–2 weeks through the summer months. It develops its best form in a soil with good drainage in full sun or, in the less forgiving low desert, part shade or very light shade. The growth rate is moderately slow, and *Y. rupicola* will take several years to reach its full size.

IDENTIFICATION: The combination of the stemless habit and wavy, twisting leaves readily distinguish *Y. rupicola* from other yucca species.

LANDSCAPE APPLICATION: The small stature of *Y. rupicola* qualifies it for small spaces or as a potted patio plant. Mass plant for an incredible summer flower display while sprinkling in the smaller perennials for added interest. Mix it in with small shrubs and perennials to play its spikiness off softer, rounder forms, or tuck it around small trees for the contrasting forms and textures. Some good companions include *Ageratum corymbosum, Baileya multiradiata, Conoclinium dissectum, Dalea capitata, Eysenhardtia orthocarpa, Penstemon* species, *Salvia greggii, Sophora secundiflora,* and *Wedelia acapulcensis* var. *hispida.*

PRECAUTIONS: Although there are no reports of any insect pests or diseases, this species, along with other *Yucca* species, may have roots eaten by beetle larvae, and pre-treatment should be considered.

Yucca thompsoniana | Thompson's Yucca

CACTUS/SUCCULENT	
SIZE (height x width)	5–8 feet x 6 feet
FLOWER COLOR	White
FLOWER SEASON	Late spring–summer
EXPOSURE	Full or reflected sun, or light shade
WATER	Drought-tolerant–low
GROWTH RATE	Slow
PRUNING	None or remove spent flower stalks
HARDINESS	Hardy to at least 0° F
NATURAL ELEVATION RANGE	700–5,000 feet
SUITABLE CITIES	All cities in all zones

FIELD NOTES: *Yucca thompsoniana* is abundant on exposed, rocky slopes and hills in western Texas and easily spotted when driving around Fort Stockton and Big Bend country. Plants are native to western Texas and adjacent northern Mexico, frequently on rocky limestone slopes and ridges from 700 to 5,000 feet elevation.

DESCRIPTION: This highly branched *Yucca* with tight, dense leaf clusters adds atmosphere to any desert landscape. Stiff, narrowly linear blue leaves have a thin, yellow margin and measure 6–12 inches long by about ½ inch wide. In late spring and early summer, the 5-foot-tall flower stalk rises above the leaf heads and is covered with white, bell-shaped, 3-inch-long flowers.

CULTURE/MAINTENANCE: *Y. thompsoniana* has survived winter lows to -20° F without damage. It grows slowly but it won't use much water. It will grow marginally faster when thoroughly watered every 2–3 weeks through the summer months. It develops its best form in a soil with good drainage and in full sun or, in the low desert, very light shade. Because of its slow growth rate, you might want to start with one big enough to need your neighbor's help to wrestle into the garden.

IDENTIFICATION: Botanists with nothing better to do have declared that *Y. thompsoniana* is the same as *Y. rostrata*. If you actually cultivate them, you'll find that *Y. thompsoniana* grows multiple heads and *Y. rostrata* produces an unbranched, single trunk.

LANDSCAPE APPLICATION: Use this yucca as an accent or centerpiece in a desert landscape and mix with many native or near-native (green-carded) desert shrubs and perennials. This spiky plant complements the softer forms of small trees, small shrubs and perennials such as *Ageratum corymbosum, Baileya multiradiata, Chrysactinia mexicana, Conoclinium dissectum, Dalea capitata, Eysenhardtia orthocarpa, Leucophyllum candidum, Penstemon* species, *Poliomintha maderensis, Salvia greggii, Sophora secundiflora,* and *Zinnia grandiflora.*

PRECAUTIONS: Provide room for full development. This plant, along with other *Yucca* species, may appeal to root-eating beetle larvae, so consider pretreating.

Zauschneria californica | Hummingbird Trumpet Bush

FLOWERING PERENNIAL, GROUND COVER	
SIZE (height x width)	2–3 feet x 2–4 feet
FLOWER COLOR	Scarlet red
FLOWER SEASON	Summer–fall
EXPOSURE	Full or filtered sun
WATER	Moderate
GROWTH RATE	Fast
PRUNING	Winter, spring
HARDINESS	Root-hardy to at least 0° F
NATURAL ELEVATION RANGE	1,000–9,000 feet
SUITABLE CITIES	All cities in all zones

FIELD NOTES: *Zauschneria californica* occurs in moist areas on dry slopes, ridges, and canyons and can be found between 2,500 and 7,000 feet elevation in southern Arizona, southwestern New Mexico, and northern Sonora. In southern California it gets even higher at 9,000 feet. Scour the canyons, and you just might spot this hummingbird magnet in the San Gabriel Mountains and the Little San Bernardino Mountains in southern California.

DESCRIPTION: This herbaceous perennial grows to nearly 2–3 feet tall, spreads underground by rhizomes, and can expand to 2–4 feet in diameter. Brittle stems have an outer layer that peels off, and the effect is artistic, not annoying. Leaves are light green and softly pubescent; they measure about 2 inches long by ¼ inch wide. Older leaves die, turn brown, and hang on the stems, leaving the plant with a bare look near the base. Bright scarlet-red, nearly 2-inch-long flowers emerge in the summer and fall and bring in the hummingbirds and even butterflies.

CULTURE/MAINTENANCE: The stems routinely die to the ground in the winter, but the roots are hardy and plants sprout every spring from the roots. No need to water in the winter, but once it starts growing in the spring, water on a weekly basis. The plant springs back more quickly and flowers more profusely if irrigated regularly. Once established, it is a fast-growing plant that will reach its mature height every year. In the low desert regions, it should be planted in filtered sun. In the mid-elevation deserts, it tolerates either full or filtered sun. Soil type doesn't matter much; just water according to the speed of drainage. Because the lower leaves die off and turn brown, the plant can be sheared a few times early in the growing season. However, skip the pruning when the plants are flowering. Mow to the ground in late winter to remove the dead stems and foliage.

IDENTIFICATION: Abundant, brilliant scarlet-red flowers readily identify *Z. californica.*

LANDSCAPE APPLICATION: Put this plant in a perennial garden, a cactus and succulent garden, or in a bird garden as a splashy color accent in any city in the desert Southwest. It beautifully softens *Agave, Dasylirion, Nolina,* and *Yucca* species. Its scarlet-

red flowers could challenge your color creativity, but try mixing with plants that have yellow or purple flowers, such as *Ageratum corymbosum, Conoclinium dissectum, Salvia farinacea,* and *Tetraneuris acaulis. Penstemon* species make good companion plants since they bloom earlier in the year, stretching out the flower availability for hummingbirds.

PRECAUTIONS: Pruning too late in the season will put the brakes on flower production at the branch tips.

Zephyranthes candida | White Rain Lily

BULB	
SIZE (height x width)	12 inches x 12 inches
FLOWER COLOR	White
FLOWER SEASON	Summer–fall
EXPOSURE	Full or filtered sun
WATER	Moderate
GROWTH RATE	Moderately fast
PRUNING	None
HARDINESS	Hardy to at least 0° F
NATURAL ELEVATION RANGE	Unknown
SUITABLE CITIES	All cities in all zones

FIELD NOTES: *Zephyranthes candida* comes from the Rio de la Plata region in Argentina and was first brought into European horticulture by the Spaniards in 1515.

DESCRIPTION: This delightful little evergreen, summer-growing bulb multiplies rapidly and can form a clump of rich green foliage about 10–12 inches tall by 10–12 inches across. Leaves are narrowly linear and measure about 8–12 inches long by 1/10 inch wide. White, star-shaped, 1½-inch-wide flowers bloom repeatedly through the summer and fall.

CULTURE/MAINTE-NANCE: *Z. candida* will hold onto its green leaves through the winter and

tolerate temperatures as low as 0° F unscathed. It flourishes when placed in full sun but will also tolerate very light shade in the hottest desert areas. Water use will vary with climate and the time of year. In the winter, plants require very little water, possibly once every 2–4 weeks. In the summer, give plants water about once a week. Give them a short period of drought after flowering to encourage multiple bloom cycles. Flower production plummets if plants get too much shade, water, and fertilizer. Bulbs grow best in a soil that has good drainage. As with other bulbs, no pruning is required.

IDENTIFICATION: White star-shaped flowers and skinny leaves readily distinguish *Z. candida.*

LANDSCAPE APPLICATION: White rain lily is an excellent choice for rock gardens or as a change of texture in a cactus and succulent garden. Tuck it in among *Agave, Astrophytum,* and *Ferocactus* species, and other smaller cacti. Mass plant several bulbs together for a spectacular flush of flowers during the summer. These lilies add flowering interest when planted with succulents in decorative pots.

PRECAUTIONS: Foliage is likely to be eaten by rabbits and rodents.

Zephyranthes citrina | Gold Cup Rain Lily

BULB	
SIZE (height x width)	8–12 inches x 12 inches
FLOWER COLOR	Lemon yellow–yellow-gold
FLOWER SEASON	Summer
EXPOSURE	Full or filtered sun
WATER	Moderate
GROWTH RATE	Moderately fast
PRUNING	None
HARDINESS	Hardy to about 10° F
NATURAL ELEVATION RANGE	Below 3,000 feet
SUITABLE CITIES	All cities in all zones

FIELD NOTES: *Zephyranthes citrina* has been cited rather haphazardly as being native to the Yucatan Peninsula, the West Indies, Cuba, Trinidad, Tobago, Panama, Honduras, and the Guianas in northern South America. In Panama, plants are found below 3,000 feet elevation.

DESCRIPTION: This summer-growing bulb has narrow, bright green leaves that measure roughly 6–12 inches long by ⅛ inch wide. It will grow to about 12 inches tall by 12 inches across. Lemon-yellow to yellow-gold, 1½-inch-wide, cup-shaped flowers

decorate this lily repeatedly throughout summer and fall.

CULTURE/MAINTE-NANCE: *Z. citrina* is cold-hardy to about 10° F. Plant bulbs in full sun or very light shade. In the winter, they require very little water; once every 2 weeks should be sufficient. In the summer, water once a week. Place the bulbs in a soil amended with some organic matter. The next step is to neglect this plant—too much shade, water, and fertilizer will reduce flower production, and pruning is unnecessary.

IDENTIFICATION: *Z. citrina* is easily recognized by the bright lemon-yellow, cup-shaped flowers.

LANDSCAPE APPLICATION: *Z. citrina* is an excellent choice for use in a rock garden or a cactus and succulent garden. Scatter these lilies among *Agave, Astrophytum,* and *Ferocactus* species, and other smaller succulents. Mass plant several bulbs together for a spectacular flush of flowers during the summer. Try planting with succulents in decorative pots for a flowering bonus.

PRECAUTIONS: Foliage is likely to be eaten by rabbits and rodents.

Zephyranthes grandiflora | Pink Rain Lily

BULB

SIZE (height x width)	12 inches x 12 inches
FLOWER COLOR	Light pink–deep pink
FLOWER SEASON	Summer
EXPOSURE	Full or filtered sun
WATER	Moderate
GROWTH RATE	Moderately fast
PRUNING	None
HARDINESS	Hardy to about 10° F
NATURAL ELEVATION RANGE	4,000–6,000 feet
SUITABLE CITIES	All cities in all zones

FIELD NOTES: *Zephyranthes grandiflora* is native to northern and central Mexico, Costa Rica, Honduras, and Guatemala at about 4,000–6,000 feet elevation. Since the flowers respond to rain and don't last very long, you have to be in the right place at the right time to catch the flowers in habitat. I have not yet had the good fortune to catch this lily in bloom in the wild, but plants are known from southern Nuevo León near an area that I have visited a couple of times. Maybe some day, while hiking in those mountains, I'll take a break in the right spot at the right time.

DESCRIPTION: This summer bulb has narrow, bright green leaves that measure about 6–12 inches long by ⅛ inch wide. It will fill in at roughly 12 inches tall by 12 inches across. Large, pink, funnel-shaped-flowers measure 3 inches wide and offer a pleasant surprise throughout warm summer and fall months.

CULTURE/MAINTENANCE: True *Z. grandiflora* is cold-hardy to about 10° F. Place it in full sun or very light shade. Water once every 2 weeks in the winter and once every 7–10 days in the summer. Too much shade, water, and fertilizer will reduce flower production. Place the bulbs in a soil amended with some organic matter. No pruning is required.

IDENTIFICATION: There are probably 6 species of *Zephyranthes* with pink flowers. Both *Z. grandiflora* and *Z. rosea* are common in cultivation. *Z. grandiflora* flowers are about 3 inches long by 3 inches wide versus the 1-inch-long by 1-inch-wide flowers of *Z. rosea.*

LANDSCAPE APPLICATION: Pink rain lily is an excellent addition to rock gardens or cactus and succulent gardens. Try it among *Agave, Astrophytum,* and *Ferocactus* species, and other smaller cacti. Mass plant several bulbs together or plant with succulents in decorative pots to highlight the gorgeous blossoms.

PRECAUTIONS: Rabbits and rodents will most likely eat the foliage.

Zinnia acerosa | Desert Zinnia

FLOWERING PERENNIAL, SMALL SHRUB	
SIZE (height x width)	6–10 inches x 12–18 inches
FLOWER COLOR	White
FLOWER SEASON	April–October
EXPOSURE	Full sun
WATER	Low
GROWTH RATE	Moderately fast
HARDINESS	Hardy to at least 10° F
PRUNING	Remove old flower heads
NATURAL ELEVATION RANGE	2,500–7,500 feet
SUITABLE CITIES	All cities in all zones

FIELD NOTES: *Zinnia acerosa* grows in Arizona with Sonoran Desert vegetation, along washes and on dry slopes and mesas from 2,500 to 5,000 feet elevation. It is also widespread in deserts and desert grasslands in New Mexico and western Texas and south throughout much of northern Mexico from 3,500 feet all the way up to 7,500 feet elevation. This diminutive subshrub is a favorite of mine on desert hikes in the Tucson Mountains, but it is always a happy surprise any time I see it on trips to Mexico. I've encountered it growing near the town of Doctor Arroyo in Nuevo León and on the road to Guadalcázar in San Luis Potosí.

DESCRIPTION: This small shrubby plant has stems that are woody at the base and herbaceous above. It forms a neat, hemispherical mound about 6–10 inches high and 12–18 inches wide. Narrowly linear gray-green leaves measure about 1 inch long and ⅟₁₆ inch wide. Daisy-like (but with 4–6 petals), 1-inch-wide flower heads top slender stalks from April through October. Blossoms turn tan and persist on the plant as the seeds ripen.

CULTURE/MAINTENANCE: Plants are hardy to at least 10° F, going dormant during a dry or cold winter. If the winter is unusually warm and moist, plants can remain active. Desert zinnia is very drought-tolerant, but when given a good drink of water during hot weather, this little gem will reward you with a nice flower display. It is fast-growing and recovers from drought or cold rapidly once established. Trim the old flowers to rejuvenate the plants and encourage more flower production.

IDENTIFICATION: *Z. acerosa* is readily distinguished from its close relatives *Z. grandiflora* and *Z. juniperifolia* by its white flowers.

LANDSCAPE APPLICATION: Desert zinnia is an asset to most desert landscapes with its long blooming season and compact size. Use in full sun in most any dry garden landscape, although it is a bit fussy in Albuquerque. Mass the plants by themselves for a ground cover, add them to a cactus and succulent garden for some seasonal color, or throw them in with big accent plants. Desert zinnia fits in nicely at the base of *Agave, Dasylirion, Hesperaloe,* and *Yucca* species. It also blends seamlessly with other small shrubs and low-water-use perennials such as *Ageratum corymbosum, Dalea capitata, Justicia candicans, Melampodium leucanthum, Penstemon* species, *Poliomintha maderensis, Salvia greggii, Scutellaria suffrutescens,* and *Verbena gooddingii.* I love the mix of this zinnia and *Psilostrophe cooperi*—happy little same-size mounds with white and yellow flowers.

PRECAUTIONS: Rabbits might eat young plants and fresh new growth, but established plants are generally unaffected.

Zinnia grandiflora | Prairie Zinnia

GROUND COVER, FLOWERING PERENNIAL	
SIZE (height x width)	6–8 inches x 10–12 inches
FLOWER COLOR	Golden yellow
FLOWER SEASON	Spring–fall
EXPOSURE	Full sun
WATER	Low–moderate
GROWTH RATE	Moderately fast
PRUNING	Remove old flower heads
HARDINESS	Hardy to at least 0° F
NATURAL ELEVATION RANGE	2,600–6,600 feet
SUITABLE CITIES	All cities in all zones

FIELD NOTES: *Zinnia grandiflora* is native to grasslands from 2,600 to 6,600 feet elevation in Arizona, New Mexico, Colorado, Texas, Kansas, and adjacent Mexico. Although it is a wide-ranging species, it is hard to spot from the car unless plants are in flower. Then, when you find a population in bloom, you can't believe you missed it before. It happened to my longtime traveling buddy, Ron Gass, and me as we were speeding through the grasslands of southeastern Arizona on our way back from Mexico. We knew we had to be in prairie zinnia country, then all of a sudden, bingo! We saw one patch after another after another, blessing the roadside with splashes of golden color for miles.

DESCRIPTION: This sprawling, perennial subshrub forms a low mound about 6–8 inches tall by 10–12 inches across. Stems are woody near the base and herbaceous above. Plants spread by rhizomes and in time will form small colonies. Thin, linear, needlelike leaves are about 1 inch long and $\frac{1}{10}$ inch wide; foliage is easily trimmed back when dormant in winter. Golden yellow, daisy-like, 1-inch flowers top the plant from April or May until October or November and cheer up any low-water-use garden. Flowers dry up, and the papery seeds will persist for months.

CULTURE/MAINTENANCE: *Z. grandiflora* is hardy to 0° F. It completely disappears during the cold then sprouts once the weather warms enough in the spring. It needs little water, but it responds to supplemental water applied every 7–14 days from spring until fall. Plants grow moderately fast, slowly spread by rhizomes, and eventually form small colonies. Plants flower best when planted in full sun, but very light shade works, too. Pruning old flower heads will encourage bushiness and repeated flowering.

IDENTIFICATION: Bright golden yellow flowers distinguish *Z. grandiflora* from *Z. acerosa*.

LANDSCAPE APPLICATION: Prairie zinnia can be used in any desert zone to add color to a rock garden, along a walkway, or in a raised planter. Tuck it into borders or tight spaces with cool-season perennials, other warm-season perennials, and small shrubs with striking flowers such as *Justicia candicans, Penstemon* species, *Poliomintha maderensis, Salvia greggii, Scutellaria suffrutescens,* and *Verbena gooddingii.* It provides seasonal

color and looks fabulous next to bold and spiny succulents like *Echinocactus grusonii* and any *Agave, Aloe, Dasylirion, Echinocereus, Ferocactus, Hesperaloe,* or *Yucca* species.

PRECAUTIONS: Rabbits may eat young plants and new growth, but established plants seem to get by just fine.

GLOSSARY

Alluvial outwash fan: The deposit of a stream or river.

Alternate: Leaves are attached singly at a node and alternate as they go along the stem.

Angiosperm: (*angion* = a vessel, *sperma* = seed) The group of plants that have seeds enclosed in a fruit. Also known as "flowering plants." Some common examples are roses, citrus, orchids, and oak trees. Angiosperms and Gymnosperms are the two groups called "seed plants" (*See also* **gymnosperm**)

Areole: The bumps on cactus from which the spines originate.

Aril: An extra, outer covering on a seed.

Axil: The junction of leaf and stem from which new stems can grow.

Basal: At the base of a plant.

Bipinnate: A leaf that is twice pinnate with the primary leaflets (pinnae) divided into secondary leaflets. Both the pinnae and leaflets are arranged along both sides of a rachis. *See illustration on p. 320.*

Blade: The expanded part of the leaf; it may or may not be attached to the stem with a petiole.

Bract: Modified leaf below the flower or flower cluster.

Bulb: An underground bud and small stem with modified leaves attached. The thickened leaf bases store food to enable the bulb to survive periods of unfavorable conditions. An onion is an example of a bulb.

Bulbil: A small plant growing on the inflorescence after flowering.

Calcareous: Soil that is high in calcium.

Caliche: Hardened layer of calcium carbonate similar to cement that is impervious to water and roots. It occurs worldwide in arid and semiarid regions.

Calyx: The sepals or the outermost series of flower parts.

Capitate: Dense cluster of flowers.

Cation exchange capacity: The ability of a soil to hold positively charged nutrients, called cations, and exchange them into the soil solution so they become available to plants.

Chlorosis: Yellowing of leaf tissue.

Clasping: The leaf blade partially surrounds the stem.

Clay: The smallest particles in the soil measuring less than 0.002 mm. Individual particles can be seen with an electron microscope. Clay is formed by chemical weathering or hydrothermal (hot water circulation) activity. A clay soil has poor drainage, a high water-holding capacity, and a high cation exchange capacity.

Claypan: An accumulation of silt or clay particles below the topsoil that bind together to create a layer that is nearly impervious to water and roots. This accumulation is accentuated in arid climates because of the lack of rainfall. When wet, claypan becomes a soft, plastic mass.

Compound Leaf: A leaf that is divided into leaflets.

Cones: The reproductive structure of Cycads, the equivalent of a flower.

Cotyledons: The embryonic leaves within the seed of Angiosperms and Gymnosperms.

Crenate: A leaf edge that is scalloped.

Decumbent: A stem that grows flat on the ground and rises at the tip.

Decurrent: The leaf blade partially surrounds the stem.

Decussate: Pairs of leaves are rotated 90° to each other along the stem.

Dehiscent: Split open.

Dicotyledons: The group of plants whose seeds have two cotyledons or embryonic leaves. Also referred to as "dicots." (*See also* **monocotyledon**)

Dioecious: A plant species that has male and female flowers on separate plants.

Distichous: Two vertical rows along the stem, usually referring to leaf arrangement.

Exserted: Stamens protruding beyond the edge of the petals.

Flower: The reproductive structure of an Angiosperm or flowering plant.

Flower shapes: *See illustrations on p. 320.*

Fruit: A mature ovary that encloses seeds.

Glaucous: Covered with a whitish or bluish powder.

Gymnosperm: (*gymnos* = naked, *sperma* = seed) Group of plants that bears seed not enclosed in a fruit or ovary. Conifers like pine trees and fir trees are common examples of gymnosperms.

Hardpan: Layer of soil, usually clay, that prevents water and root movement.

Imbricate: Overlapping evenly.

Inflorescence: Grouping of flowers. There are several different types. (*See also* **spike, raceme, panicle**)

Internode: Stem between the nodes.

Iron chlorosis: Yellowing between the veins while the veins remain green.

Keeled: A ridge along the outside of a fold, like the keel of a boat.

Leaflet: The ultimate division of a compound leaf.

Leaf shapes: *See illustrations on p. 320.*

Midrib: The central vein on a leaf.

Monocotyledon: Group of plants whose seeds contain one cotyledon. Also referred to as "monocots." Many economically important plants are monocots. The grains (rice, wheat, corn), grasses, agaves, and yuccas. (*See also* **dicotyledons**)

Monocultures: A stand of one type of plant.

Node: The place on the stem where the leaf or leaves are attached.

Offset: Baby plants attached to the main plant.

Opposite: Leaves are arranged in pairs at a node.

Overstory: The canopy of a tree.

Ovoid: Egg shaped.

Panicle: A compound inflorescence in which the main axis is branched and the side branches are composed of loose flower clusters.

Paniculate: Branched inflorescence on an *Agave*.

Pedicel: A stem that attaches single flowers to the main stem of an inflorescence.

Petiolate: A leaf that has a petiole.

Petiole: The stalk that attaches the leaf blade to the stem.

Phyllode: An expanded, modified petiole that functions like the leaf blade.

Pinna: The first division of a bipinnate leaf, consisting of few to many leaflets.

Pinnate: A compound leaf with leaflets arranged along a central axis, like a bird's feather.

Pinnately compound: Leaves are divided into leaflets that are arranged along a central rachis.

Pubescent: Covered with soft, downy hairs.

Raceme: An inflorescence where the flowers are attached to the main axis with a **pedicel**.

Ray flower: The "petals" of a daisy or daisy-like flower.

Rhizome: An underground, horizontal stem that is able to produce a new plant.

Rosette: The leaves are arranged in a circular or spiral pattern and all appear to radiate from a common point.

Sand: These are chemically inert particles that are relatively large. They measure 0.05-2.0 mm, and can be seen with the naked eye. Sand can be used to improve drainage in heavy, clay soils.

Sessile: A leaf that has the blade attached directly to the stem without a petiole.

Silt: Granular particles derived from soil or rock and produced by mechanical weathering. The particles are medium size, measuring 0.002-0.05 mm, and can be seen with the help of a microscope.

Soil: The part of the earth's surface that is composed of disintegrated rock, organic matter (humus), air, water, and organisms.

Spike: An inflorescence where the flowers are sessile, that is, attached directly to the main axis without a pedicel.

Stamen: The male or pollen-producing part of a flower.

Stolon: A horizontal, aboveground stem that grows along the ground and might form roots. Two examples are the runners produced by Bermuda grass and strawberry plants.

Subcapitate: A slightly elongated cluster of flowers.

Trifoliate: A pinnate leaf with three leaflets.

Tuber: The thickened end of a stolon or rhizome composed primarily of storage cells containing starch.

Tuberous: Tuber-like in appearance.

Understory: Plants growing underneath the canopy of a tree.

Whorled: Referring to a group of leaves or flowers at one node. A whorled inflorescence refers to the group of flowers at a node.

Xerophytic: Low-water using.

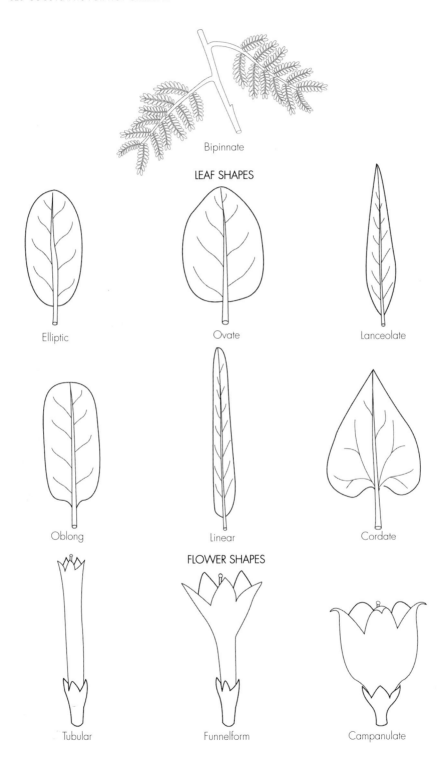

Bipinnate

LEAF SHAPES

Elliptic

Ovate

Lanceolate

Oblong

Linear

Cordate

FLOWER SHAPES

Tubular

Funnelform

Campanulate

ACKNOWLEDGMENTS

First and foremost, I would like to thank my wife Carol for her patience and tolerance of my hobby gone wild, all the while helping with the nursery and encouraging my interest in plants. Many thanks to my mom, Patti, who helped me grow my very first plant, a Creeping Charlie that just struggled to survive my black thumb of death. I would also like to thank Warren Jones and Lemoyne Hogan for teaching me and other students about plant materials. Many thanks to Ron Gass of Mountain States Wholesale Nursery for sharing travels, plant knowledge, and his incredible insights and thoughtful answers to my many questions. Thanks to Russ Buhrow for acting as a sounding board and sharing his enthusiasm for native and drought-tolerant plants. I would also like to thank Scott Calhoun for putting the bug in my ear to put my compiled information into book form. Thanks to Janet Rademacher, George Hull, and Bart Worthington at Mountain States Wholesale Nursery for their continued support, encouragement, and words of wisdom throughout the years. Yes, your tidbits of information do sometimes stick in my head. Thank you to Paul Connolly at Sonoran Gardens Landscape for his expert suggestions. Many thanks to Brooke Gebow for her brilliant way with words and for helping me to see this from a different perspective and keep it from being boring. Finally, I would like to say thank you very much to my son Brian for his drive and infectious enthusiasm for this book as well as his fresh outlook, perspective, and insight with editing tasks. He says, "It's fun."

INDEX OF PLANTS BY COMMON NAMES

NOTE: Plants are also listed by categories at the end of this alphabetical list; see bottom of page 323 to end of book.